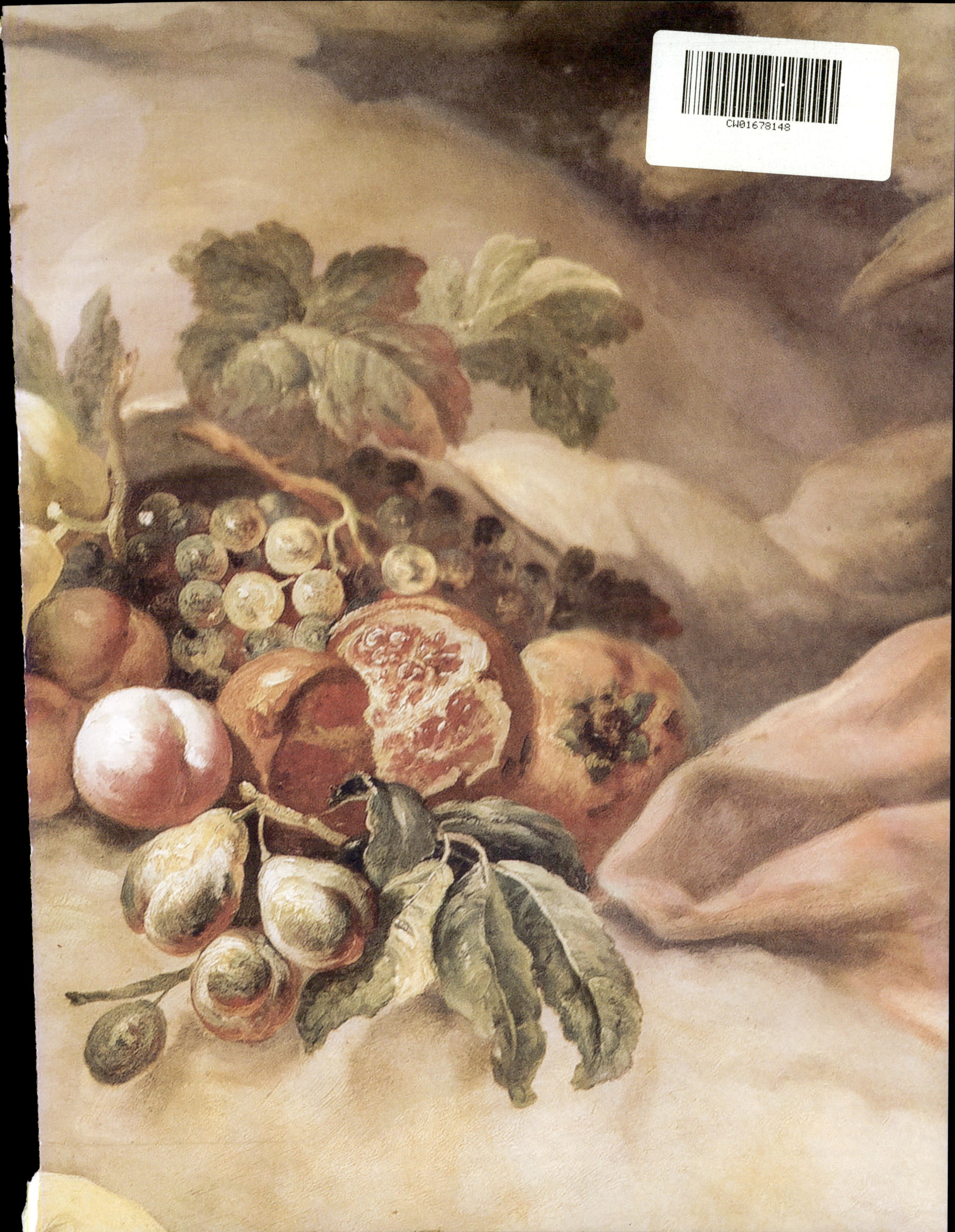

The Painted Hall

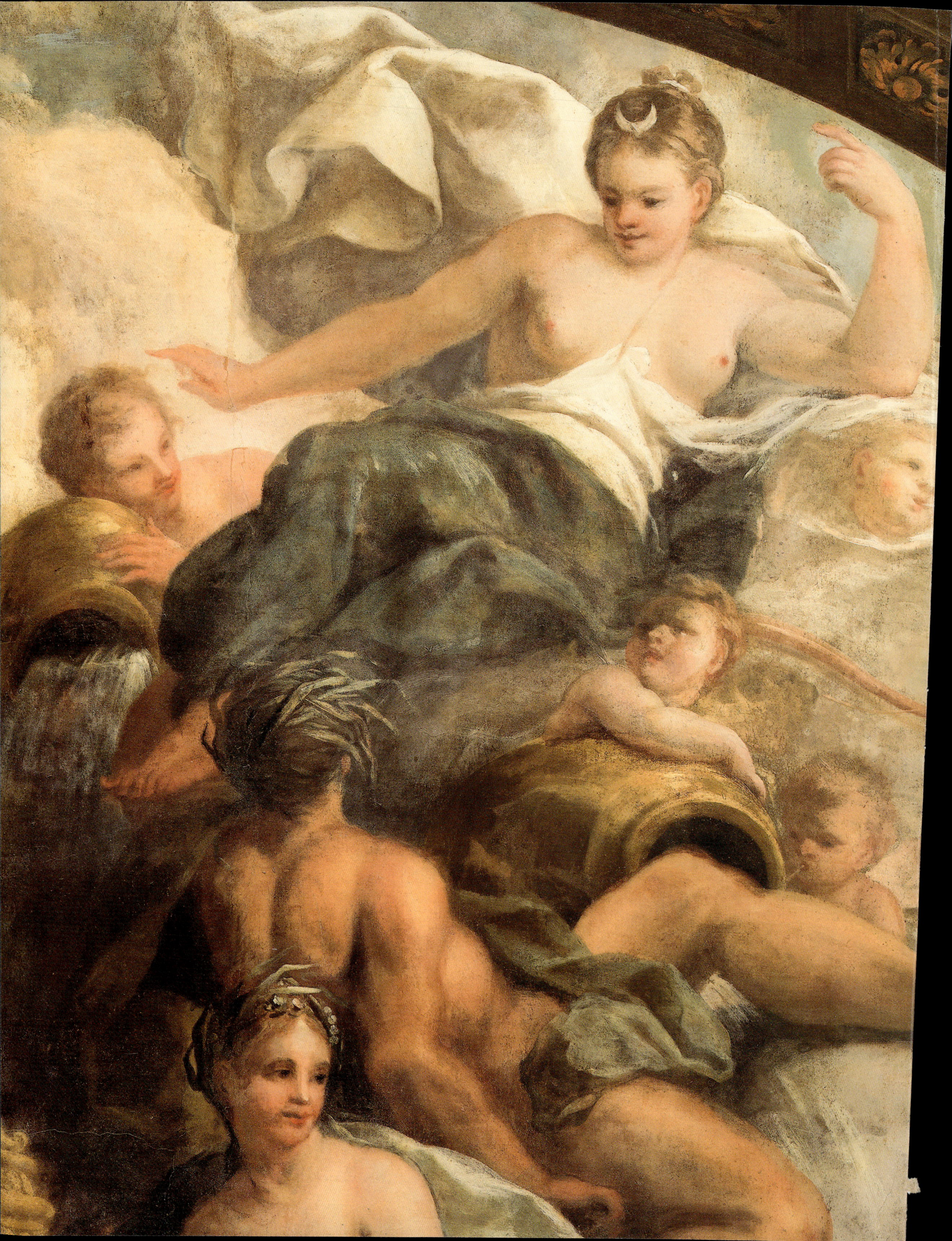

The Painted Hall

Sir James Thornhill's Masterpiece at Greenwich

ANYA LUCAS
RICHARD JOHNS
SOPHIE STEWART & STEPHEN PAINE

Preface by
WILLIAM PALIN

MERRELL
LONDON • NEW YORK

OLD ROYAL NAVAL COLLEGE GREENWICH

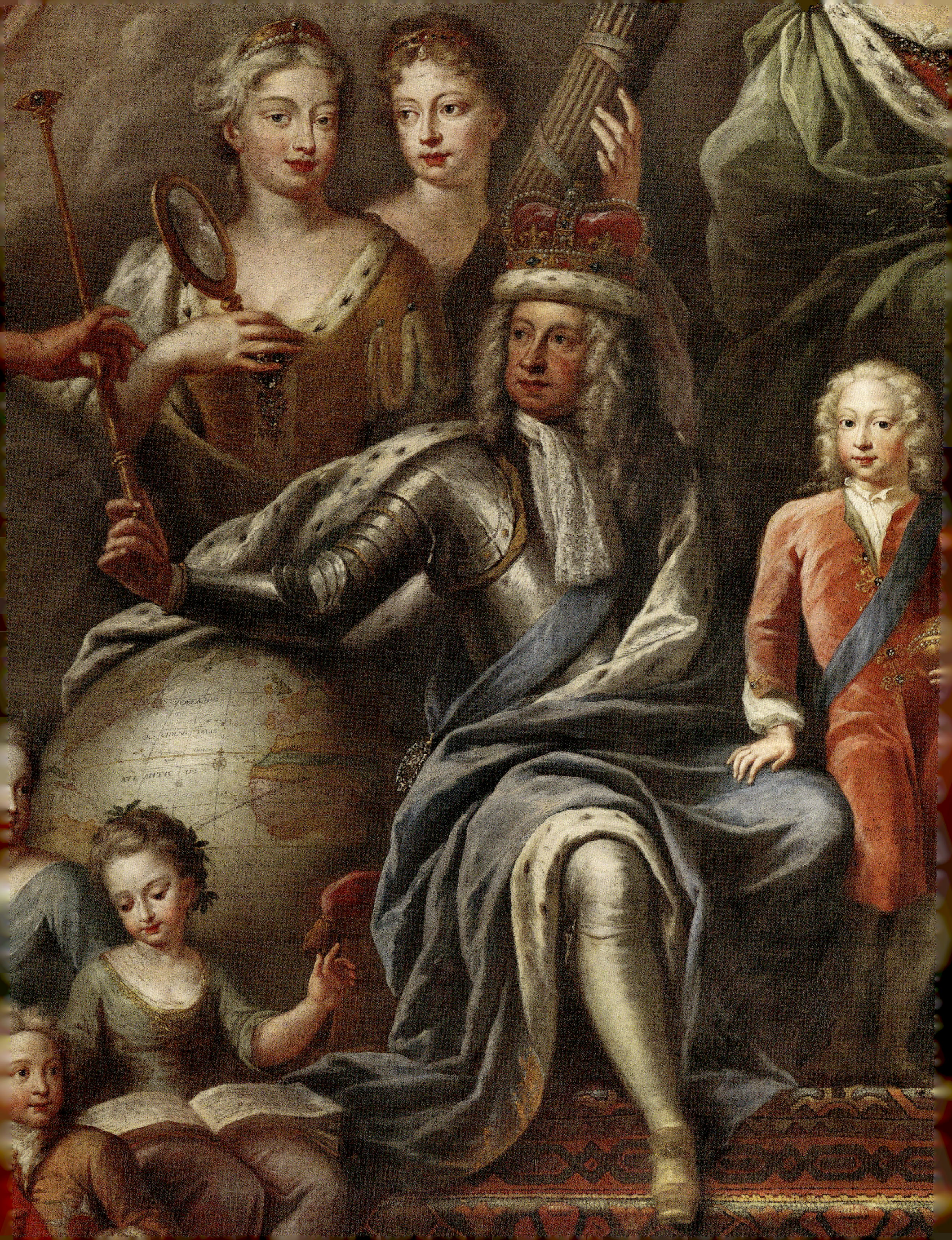

CONTENTS

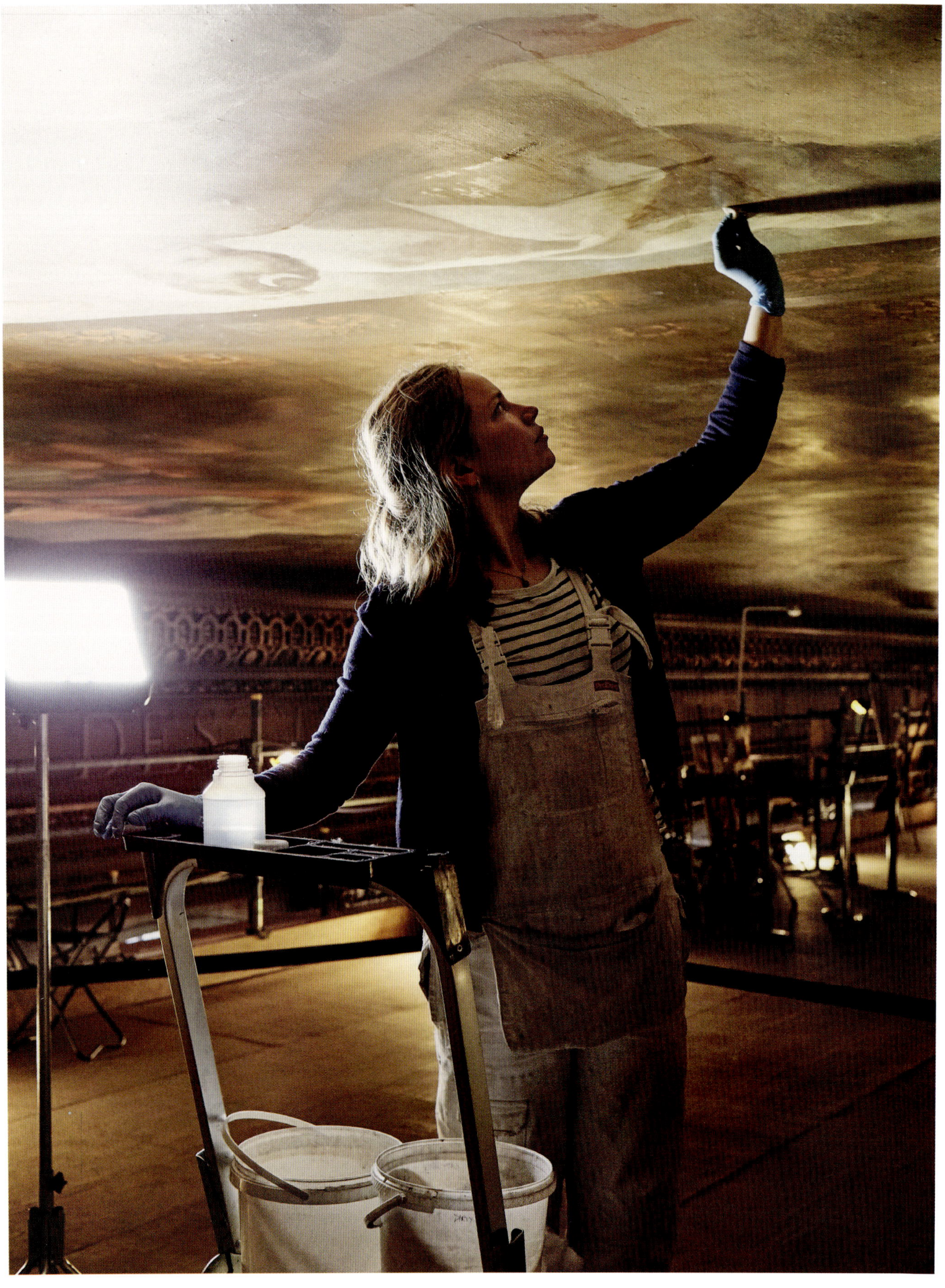

The conservator Eliza Doherty applies treatment to the drapery of Diana, goddess of the Moon, on the Lower Hall ceiling in 2018.

Preface

The project to decorate the Painted Hall at Greenwich was of a scale and ambition matched only by the building project of which it was part. The Royal Hospital for Seamen was conceived and initiated by England's Protestant rulers William III and Mary II as the nation's grandest charitable institution. Ostensibly it was for the benefit of those men, now injured or infirm, who had served in the Royal Navy, but its primary purpose was as an architectural and artistic showpiece to promote and celebrate England's naval power and burgeoning cultural confidence within Europe and the world. Sir Christopher Wren was appointed Surveyor in 1696, and the foundation stone was laid in the same year.

As the ceremonial and public heart of the new Hospital, the Painted Hall (or 'Refectory Grenvicani', as the Clerk of the Works, Nicholas Hawksmoor, rather grandly called it on his early drawings) required a decorative scheme like no other. The commission was awarded to a native artist, James Thornhill, who enjoyed the support and patronage of a number of key Hospital directors, including the Duke of Devonshire. The early intention appears to have been to restrict the painting to the great ceiling of the Lower Hall (which was prepared immaculately for the purpose, and at great expense, by Wren's master plasterer, Henry Doogood), but Thornhill had grander ambitions, and the brief was expanded to include the walls and ceilings of the Vestibule and Upper Hall, eventually covering about 45,200 square feet (4200 sq. m) of plaster, stone and timber, leaving barely a square inch untouched by the artist's brush.

The Painted Hall was the commission that defined Thornhill's career. In 1707, when he submitted his first designs for Greenwich, he was only in his early thirties. The vicissitudes of the project meant that he was still working there nineteen years later, having in the meantime completed the decoration of the dome of St Paul's Cathedral. As work progressed, Thornhill's reputation increased (together with his wealth and status) until, with his knighthood in 1720, it had exceeded that of any British artist before him.

When the Greenwich Foundation took over the stewardship of the former Royal Hospital buildings after the departure of the Navy in 1998, it inherited a substantial backlog of repairs. Extensive conservation

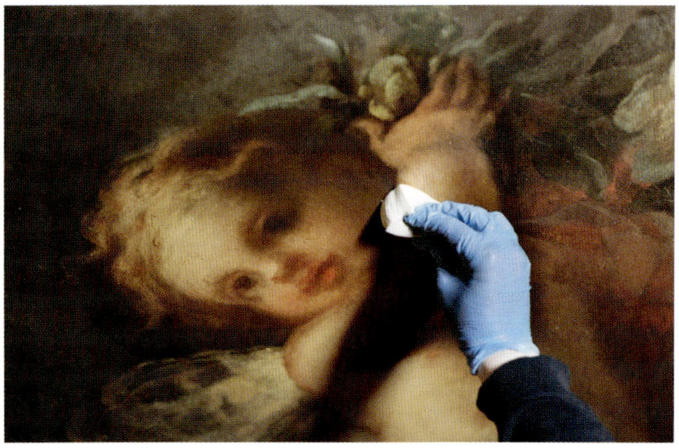

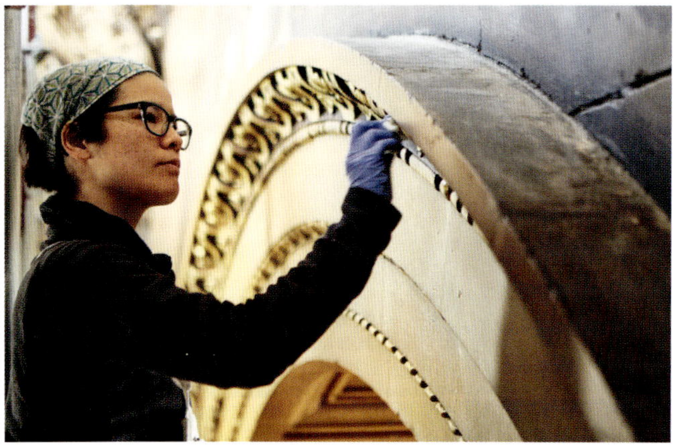

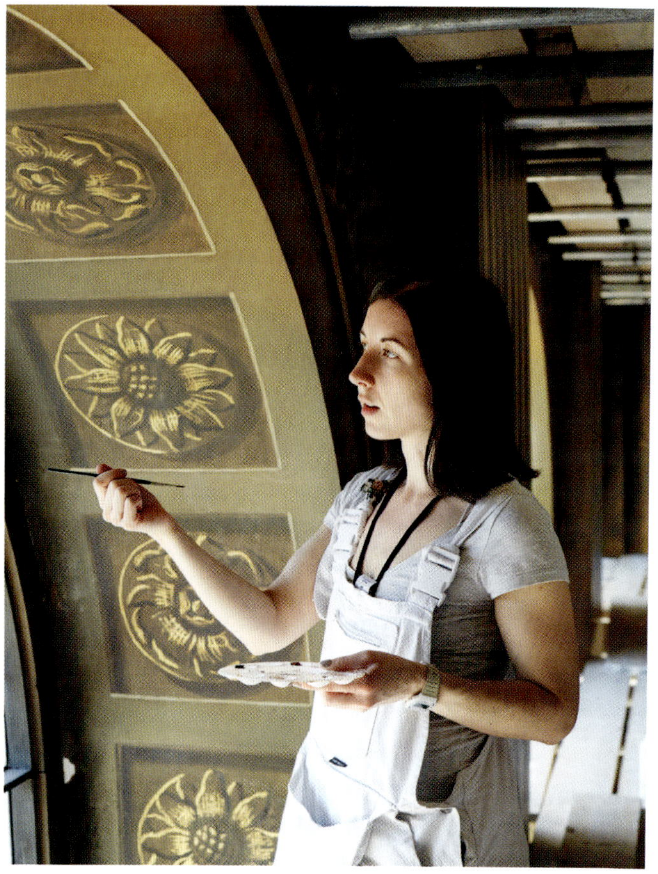

The 2016–19 conservation project involved the cleaning and treatment of some 40,000 sq. ft (3700 sq. m) of painted surface. The work was carried out by a small team led by Stephen Paine and Sophie Stewart, including Denise Invamoto (left) and Lucy Odlin (right).

works to the built fabric were undertaken during the ensuing decade. In 2012–13 a pilot project, supported by what was then the Heritage Lottery Fund, addressed the cleaning of the west wall and Upper Hall ceiling of the Painted Hall. The results were impressive, with a dramatic improvement in the colour and clarity of the paintings.

This success gave the Greenwich Foundation the confidence to face the huge task of addressing the remaining 40,000 square feet (3700 sq. m) of painting. The west wall work had been fairly straightforward, with a surface clean producing an excellent result. But environmental conditions in other parts of the Hall were harsher and had resulted in more dramatic deterioration – most obviously blanching, or whitening of the surface of the paintings, caused by the formation of microscopic cracks in the varnish layer. The Vestibule (under the dome) was in particularly poor condition, having suffered historically from water ingress and condensation.

Importantly, what the 2012–13 clean had not tackled were the underlying environmental issues that were causing the deterioration of the paintings. It was clear that any future campaign should seek to stabilize (as far as possible) the relative humidity inside the Hall through a number of high- and low-tech interventions, including a bespoke heating system and solar shading. All had to be detailed and installed in a way that would not damage the fabric of this Grade I-listed building and Scheduled Monument.

In September 2016, after four years in the planning, and thanks to a £3.1 million grant from the National Lottery Heritage Fund (towards a total budget of £8.5 million), work commenced on the Painted Hall conservation project.

The Foundation took care to weave public engagement into the project from the earliest planning stage, and this approach shaped the ambitious plan to allow the public access to scaffolding in order to witness the conservation work in progress. The scaffolding in the

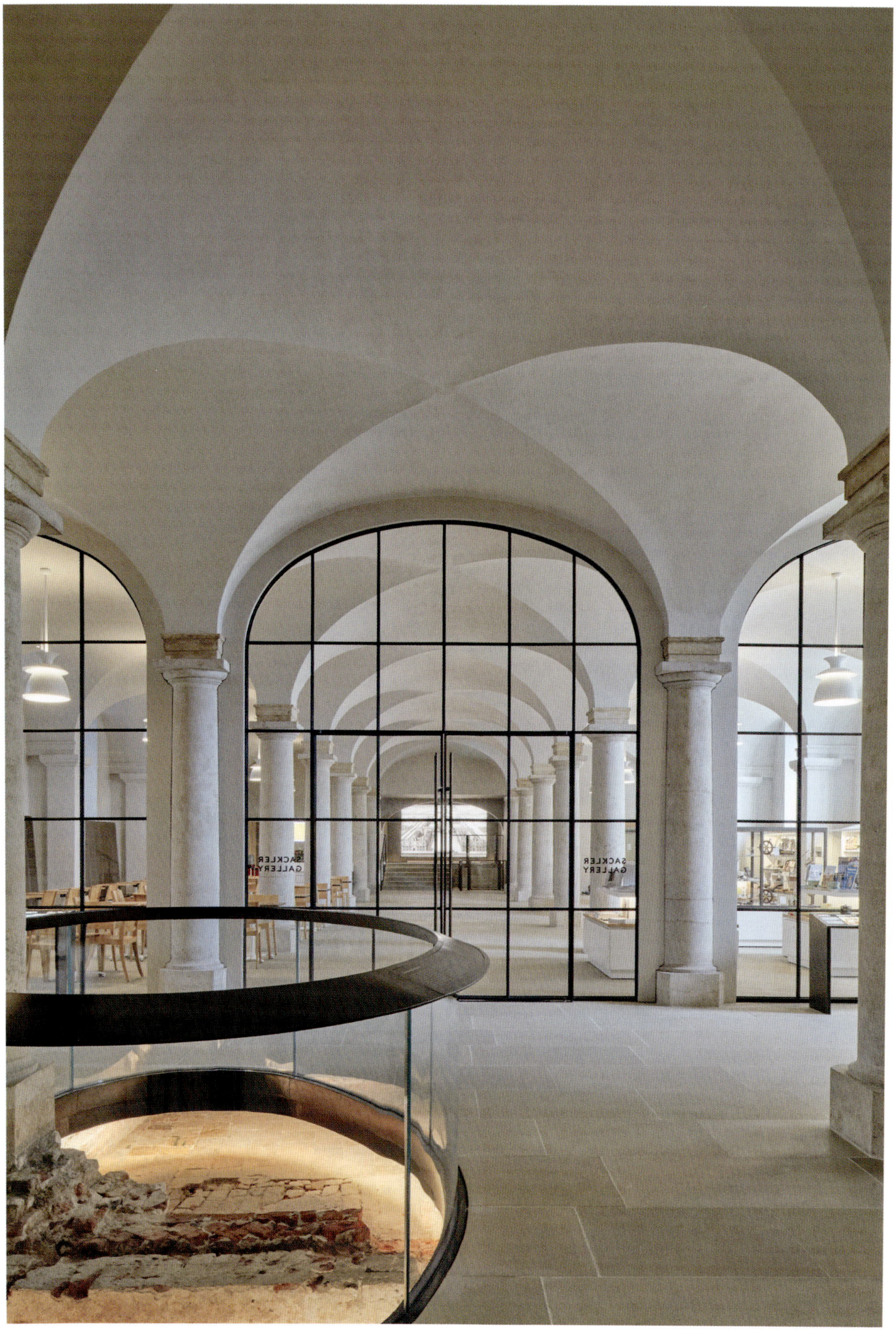

The King William Undercroft, beneath the Painted Hall, after its restoration.
Fragments of the Tudor Greenwich Palace uncovered during works were preserved as part of a permanent display.

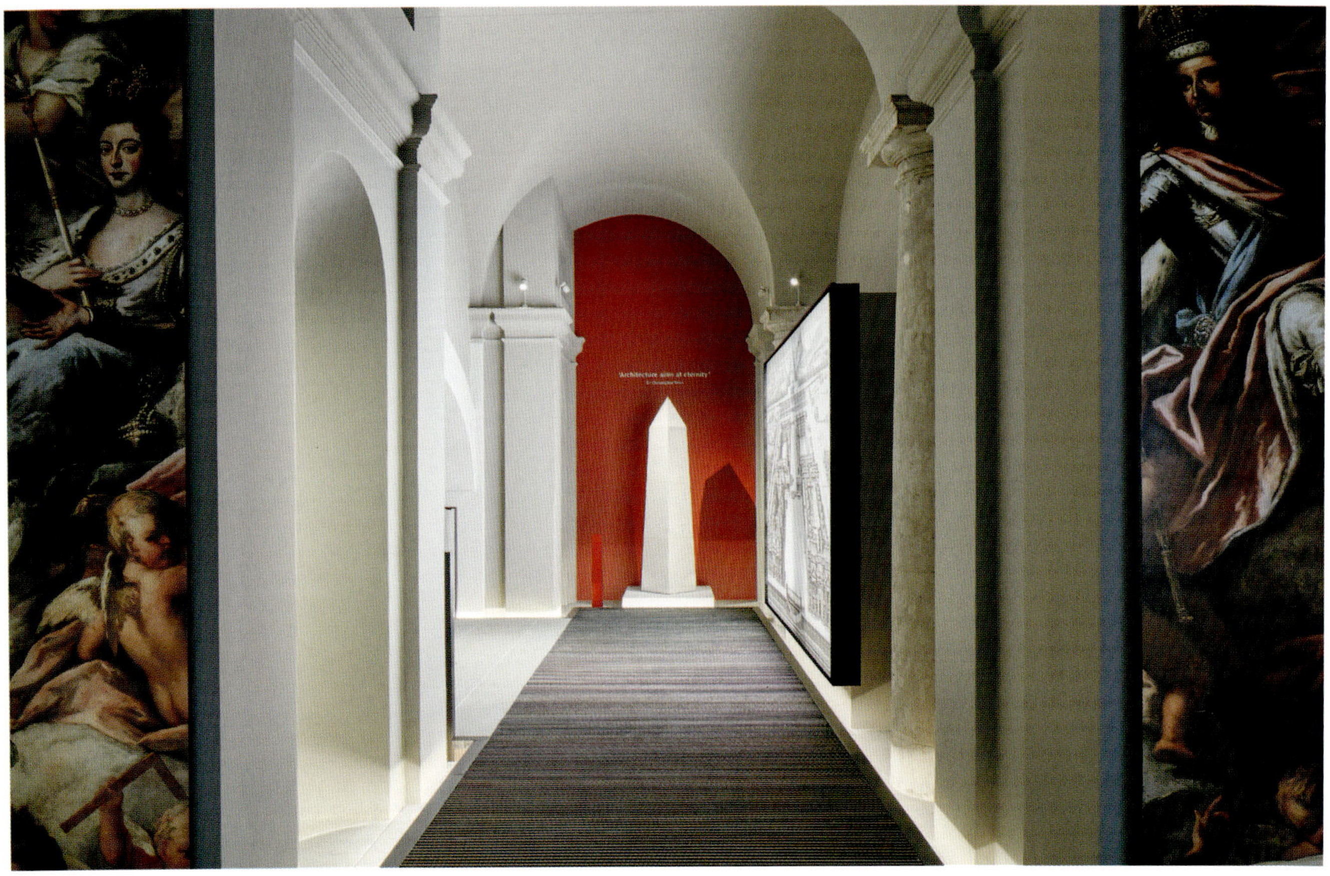

In order to better control the environment in the Painted Hall, the visitor journey begins in the King William Undercroft, which originally served as a dining hall for the naval pensioners. Today it houses a visitor centre and interpretation gallery.

Lower Hall was designed to function both as a working platform for the conservators and other team members and as a viewing platform for the public. Allowance was made for two generous staircases and a lift to bring people safely and comfortably to the deck, some 40 feet (12 m) above the floor.

The scaffolding – often likened to a cathedral, with a 'nave' of tubular steel rising dramatically to the underside of the viewing platform – permitted visitors to enjoy a close encounter with Thornhill's masterpiece over the duration of the project, delivering them to within touching distance of a huge, swirling mass of mythical, allegorical and historical figures.

The Painted Hall reopened to the public in March 2019, meticulously conserved and resplendent under the natural and (when necessary) subtly enhanced lighting. A conservation project that would ordinarily have seen the space shut off from public gaze for two and a half years instead amazed and beguiled nearly 100,000 visitors.

Meanwhile, the King William Undercroft below the Hall was undergoing a separate transformation. This sublime vaulted space had been compromised by alterations in the 1930s, and the task was to open it out to its original extent and thereby restore its special atmosphere and character. Stone paving replaced a modern concrete floor, and a delicate bronze glazed screen was added as an environmental buffer at the east end, marking the entrance to an interpretation gallery. The Undercroft now serves as a new visitor area with shop and cafe, providing a magnificent prelude to the Painted Hall itself. And there is a surprise, too: a remnant of Henry VIII's lost Greenwich Palace, uncovered during building works, has been preserved and displayed *in situ*, allowing visitors a glimpse of the earlier, royal history of this important site.

The ambitious and groundbreaking conservation project provided an unprecedented opportunity to gain a more sophisticated understanding of how Thornhill

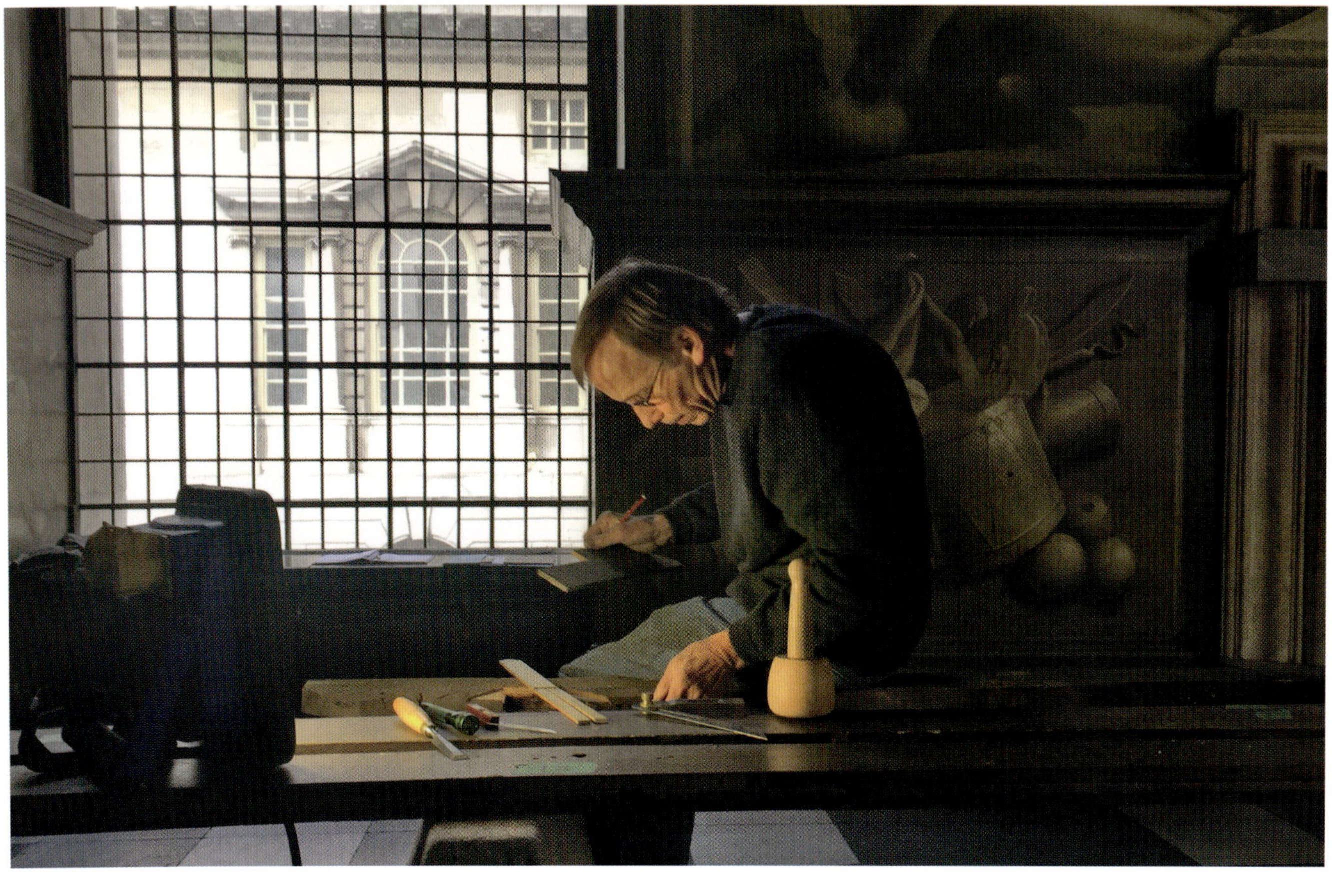

The specialist joiner Jim Quenby at work in the Upper Hall in 2016, repairing historic woodwork.

conceived, developed and executed his vast scheme. In the following pages, Anya Lucas and Richard Johns recount the story of the conception and genesis of this monumental commission, exploring both the evolution of the building project and the development and execution of Thornhill's design, as he sought a coherent aesthetic response to political power shifts and practical challenges. Thornhill emerges from this fascinating study as an artist of supreme skill and confidence, one who successfully negotiated the twists and turns of a commission spanning two decades and the reigns of several monarchs.

The final section of this book is concerned with the conservation work itself, as Sophie Stewart and Stephen Paine take us through the meticulous cleaning, treatment and repair of the painted surfaces undertaken between 2016 and 2019.

Today Thornhill's name is not widely known, and his work at the Painted Hall is often overlooked. This is an injustice, and something this new publication aims to both explain and redress. However, the cloud has a silver lining: Thornhill's underexposure ensures that the artist and his work at Greenwich retain a certain freshness, providing readers of this book with a wealth of new discoveries.

William Palin
Conservation Director, The Greenwich Foundation

Overleaf The buildings of the former Greenwich Hospital (built 1696–1751) – today known as the Old Royal Naval College – seen from the north bank of the Thames. The Queen's House (1616) completes the central visual axis to the south. The King's House of the 1660s is subsumed in the Hospital's western riverside block (right).

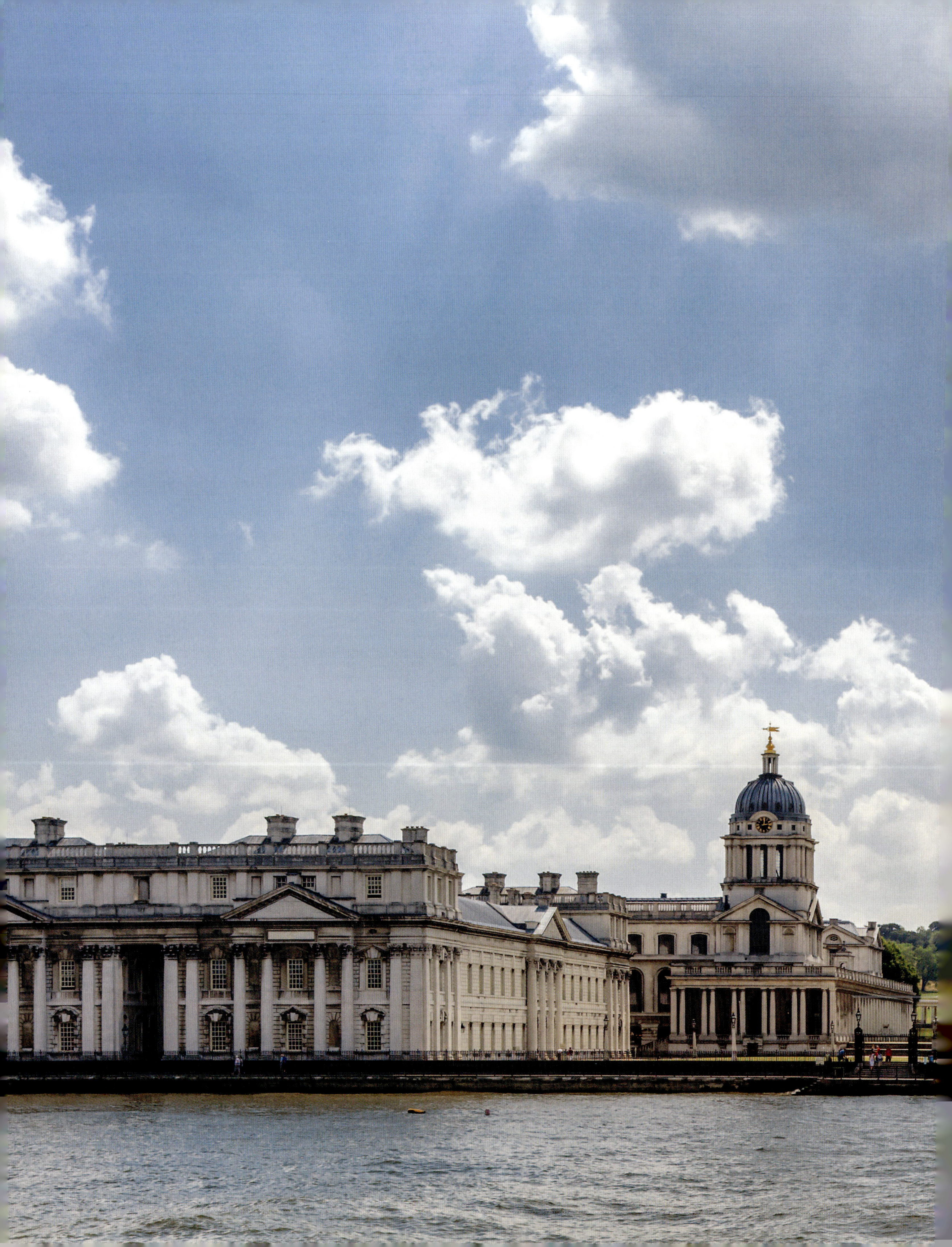

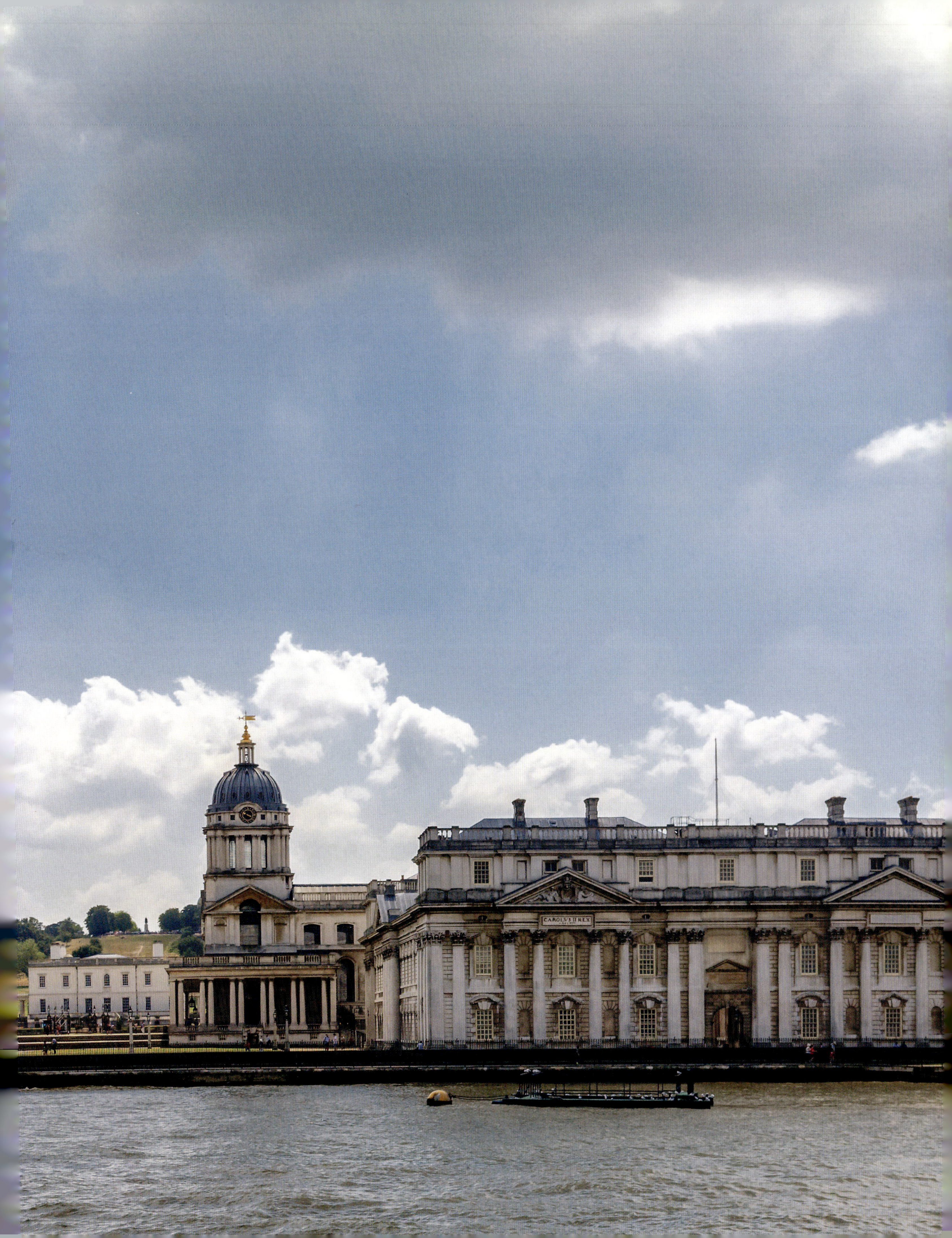
CAROLVS II REX

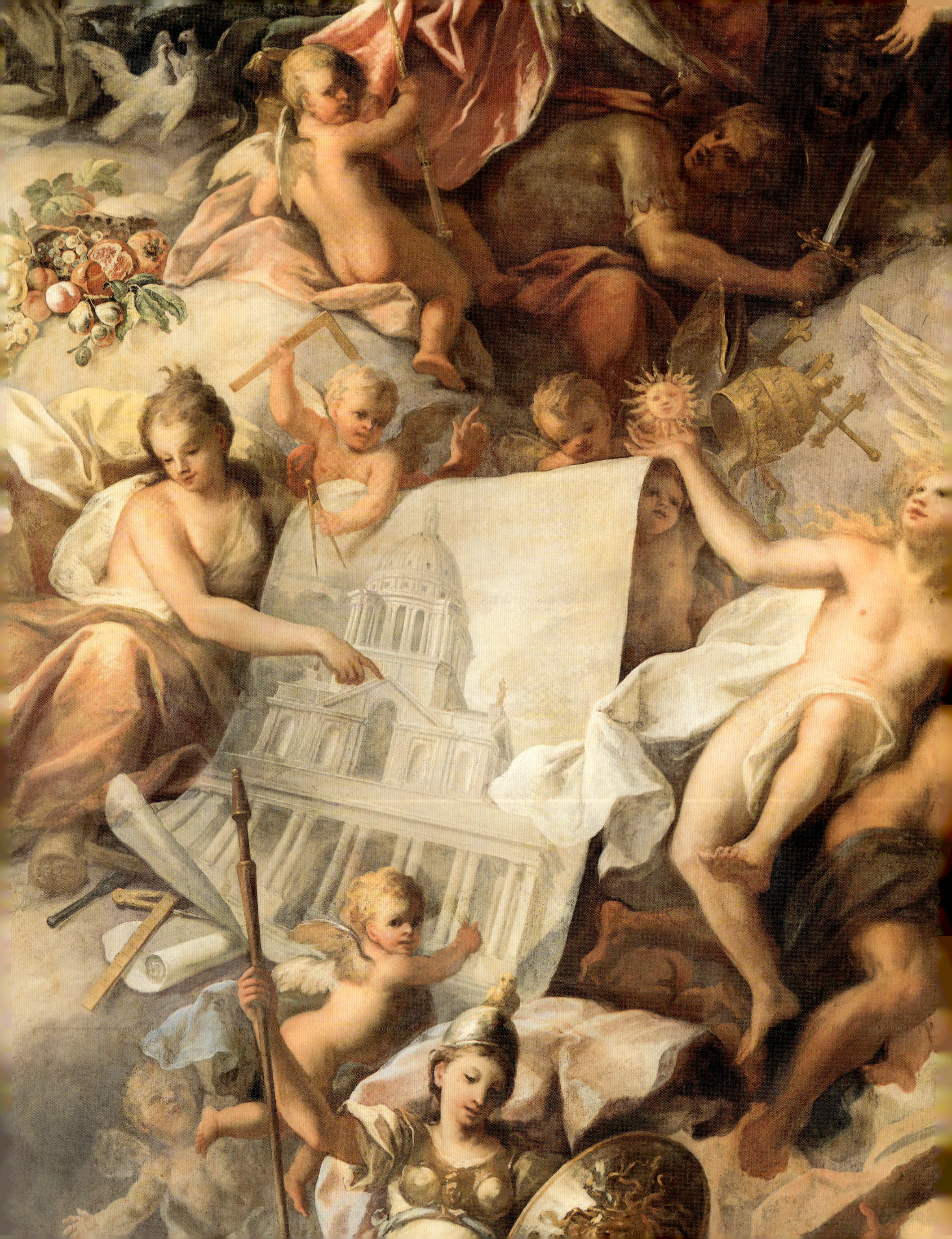

ANYA LUCAS

Her Majesty's fixt Intention for Magnificence

THE FOUNDATION, DESIGN AND CONSTRUCTION OF GREENWICH HOSPITAL

The year 1672 is an important one in the story of the Royal Hospital for sick and injured seamen at Greenwich. The idea of establishing such an institution was not yet even embryonic, and the start of construction on its buildings was more than two decades off. Nevertheless, the year saw two unrelated developments that were highly significant for the Hospital's later realization, from the laying of the first stone in 1696 to the decoration of its Great Hall between 1708 and 1726, and its final completion in 1751.

First, it was in 1672 that Charles II abandoned his ambitious vision to rebuild a royal palace at Greenwich[1] – a ceremonial gateway to the Stuart kingdom for lavish ambassadorial welcomes[2] – to rival Louis XIV's Versailles. The Office of Works had demolished most of the red-brick Tudor palace buildings in 1662 to make way for this replacement three-range complex on classical lines, but only the shell of a single range designed by John Webb had been completed by the time of the architect's death in October 1672.[3] Precarious royal finances made continuation of the costly new palace of stone impossible, and building activity shifted to Windsor Castle for the rest of the reign. The sole product of Charles II's abortive scheme, the Portland stone 'King's House' (1664–69), now stood marooned like a gleaming white question mark at this visually striking and strategically important bend on the River Thames (figs. 3 and 4). Two decades later, Greenwich Hospital would provide the answer to the question that the abandoned building posed, and would indeed deliver aspects of Charles II's vision for an English Versailles. For now, at least, the future use of this royal building-plot was in doubt.

The second significant occurrence in the year 1672 was the arrival in England of the decorative history painter Antonio Verrio (fig. 2).[4] Born in Lecce in southern Italy, Verrio (*c.* 1639–1707) had risen to prominence in Paris by way of commissions in Naples and Toulouse, and was talent-spotted by the English ambassador in France, Ralph Montagu. It was chiefly Verrio who supplied the European glamour and French taste favoured in the art of the Restoration, and he did more than any other artist to assist Charles II in his rivalries with his cousin

Fig. 1 The Spirit of Architecture points to a drawing of the Hospital on the Lower Hall ceiling.

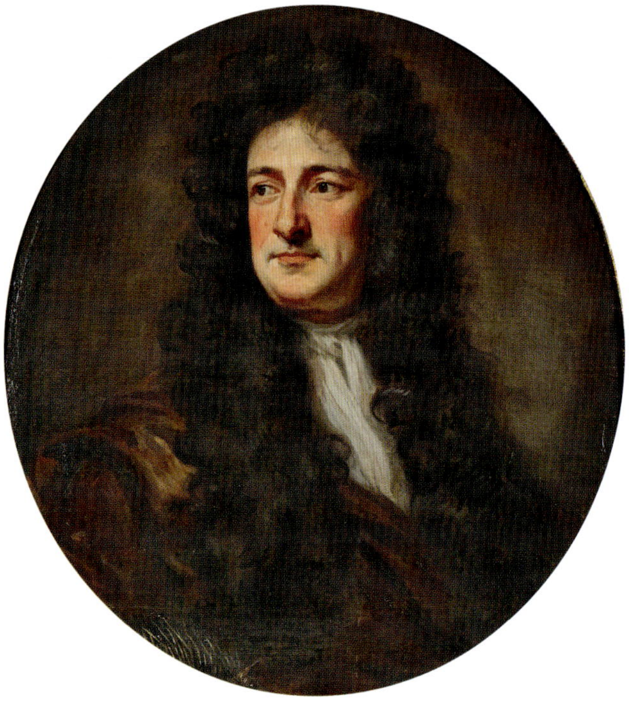

Fig. 2 Godfrey Kneller, *Portrait of Antonio Verrio*, oil on canvas, *c.* 1688.

Louis XIV. Most importantly for our purposes, it was this southern Italian who imported the style of unbounded allegorical mural painting that would be used to such extraordinary effect in the decoration of Greenwich Hospital's Great Hall. The so-called Painted Hall is the masterpiece of a native painter, James Thornhill (1675–1734), and its political message in support of Britain's constitutional monarchy is delivered with unabashed patriotic triumphalism. The visual language that it uses to trumpet Protestant Britishness is that of Roman Catholic Europe, however, and that language arrived most decisively on these shores with Verrio.

The Royal Hospital at Greenwich and its Painted Hall can be traced back to both the failed architectural patronage and the fruitful artistic patronage of Charles II, and to the pivotal year that saw the Greenwich Palace proposals abandoned and the arrival on English soil of an exuberant painter from Puglia.

As Simon Thurley has observed, 'A visitor to Greenwich in the 1670s would have seen the boarded up hulk of the king's block, set amidst piles of demolished brick and stone from the Tudor palace and the Queen's House surrounded by half-dug foundations.'[5] The Queen's House – the low, square classical building to the left of the taller King's House in the Danckerts and Vorsterman views – had been constructed for James I's queen, Anne of Denmark, from 1616 to designs by Inigo Jones. It was completed for Charles I's queen, Henrietta Maria, in the 1630s. The building was repaired and extended in the 1660s as part of Charles II's palace vision; most importantly, the demolition of the Tudor palace had liberated it visually.[6] The harmonious and restrained north elevation of the white Queen's House had emerged from behind a forest of red brick and was now visible from the Thames. The emergence by the 1670s of this new visual axis across the palace site to the water was to be another important element of the Greenwich Hospital project years later: royal insistence that it be preserved forced Sir Christopher Wren to develop a cloven rather than a centralized scheme – and generated the twin-domed bilateral plan that makes the complex instantly and famously recognizable today (pp. 12–13).[7] The Queen's House, like the King's House, was as yet unanchored by Wren's weighty masterplan for Greenwich Hospital, and floated uncertainly to the south of the palace building site.

In the seventeenth century, as now, architecture was intensely political, and it was regime change that provided the catalyst for renewed building activity at Greenwich. Charles II died in 1685 with no legitimate heirs and was succeeded by his brother, James, Duke of York. James had served Charles as Lord High Admiral from the Restoration in 1660 until 1673. A swaggering full-length portrait by Henri Gascar (fig. 5) conveys very powerfully James's idea of what it meant to rule – an autocratic concept of kingship that owed much to his deposed father, Charles I. James was excluded from office as Lord High Admiral under the Test Act of 1673 because he was a Roman Catholic. His increasingly hard-line Catholic sympathies triggered the so-called Exclusion Crisis of 1679–81, when the Earl of Shaftesbury's 'Country' (later Whig) party attempted to omit him from the succession to the throne on the grounds of his religion. Mock pope-burning processions were mounted by dissenting London citizens in support of the exclusion effort, but the rebellion was suppressed, and the Duke of York ascended the throne as James II with the approval of the Tory majority on 6 February 1685.

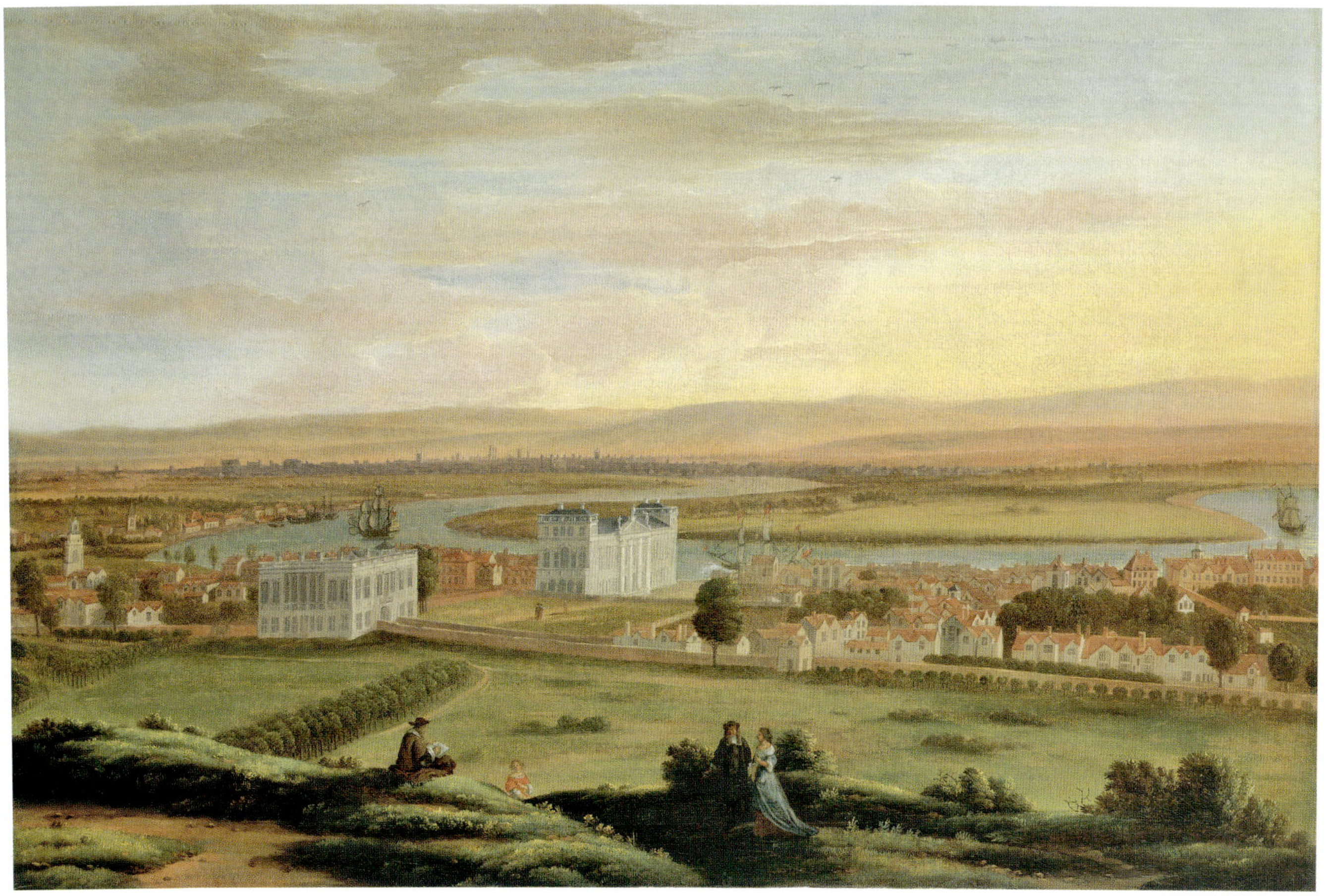

Fig. 3 Hendrick Danckerts, *View of Greenwich and the Queen's House from the South-East*, showing the new 'King's House' on the right in the middle distance and the City of London on the skyline, oil on canvas, *c.* 1670.

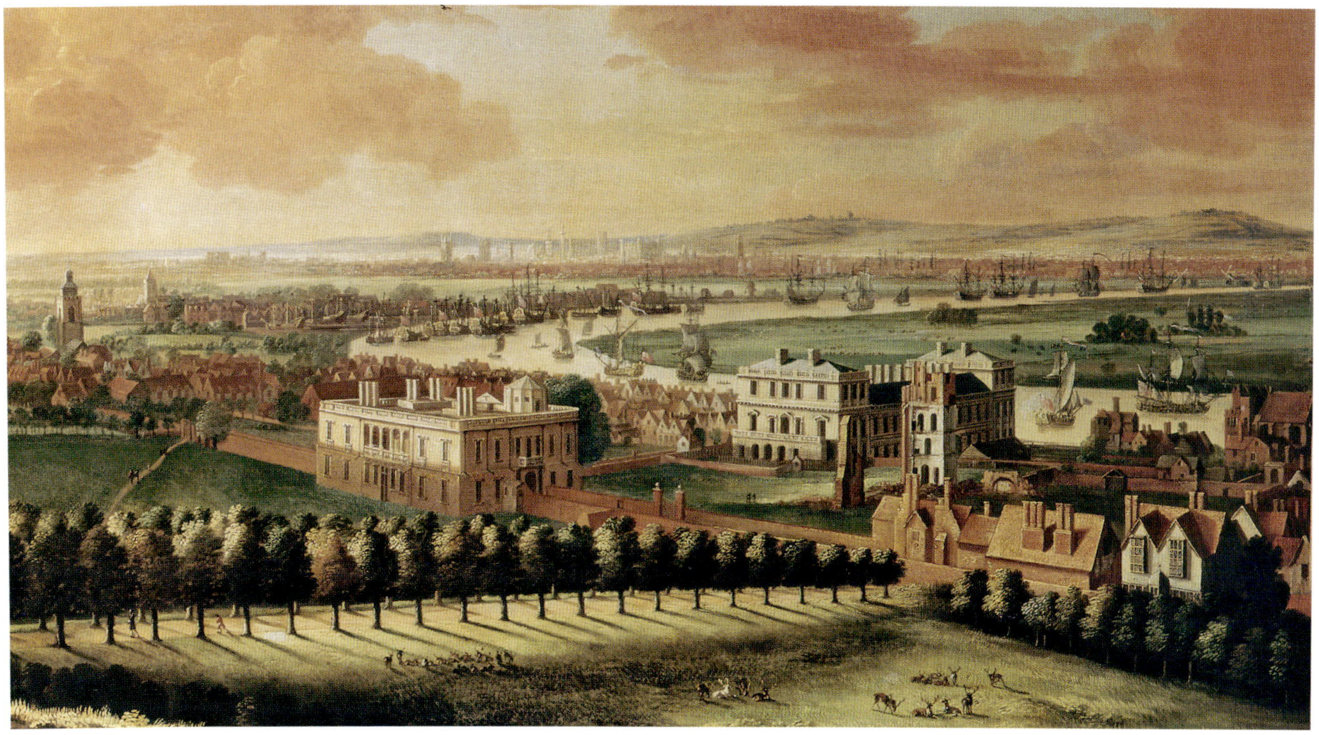

Fig. 4 Johannes Vorsterman, *Greenwich and London from One Tree Hill* (detail), oil on canvas, *c.* 1680.

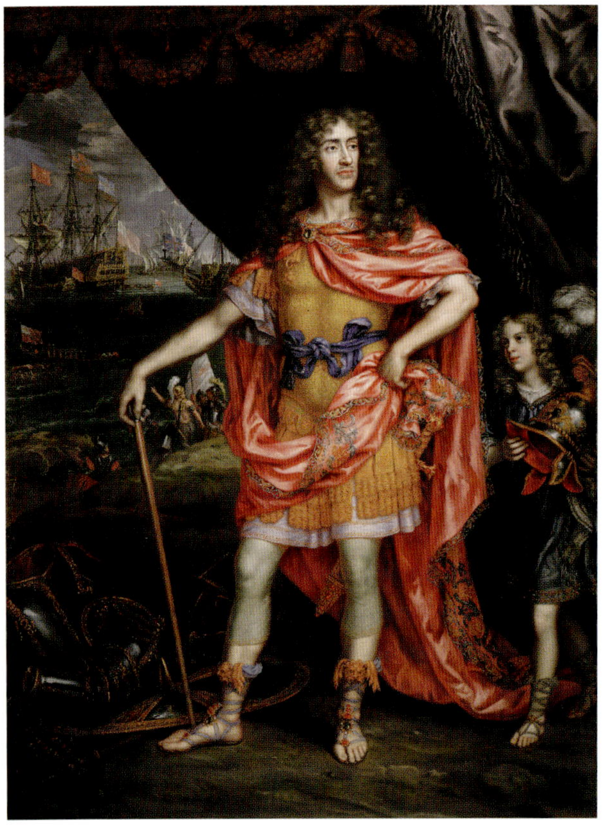

Fig. 5 Henri Gascar, *James, Duke of York, 1633–1701*, oil on canvas, 1672–73.

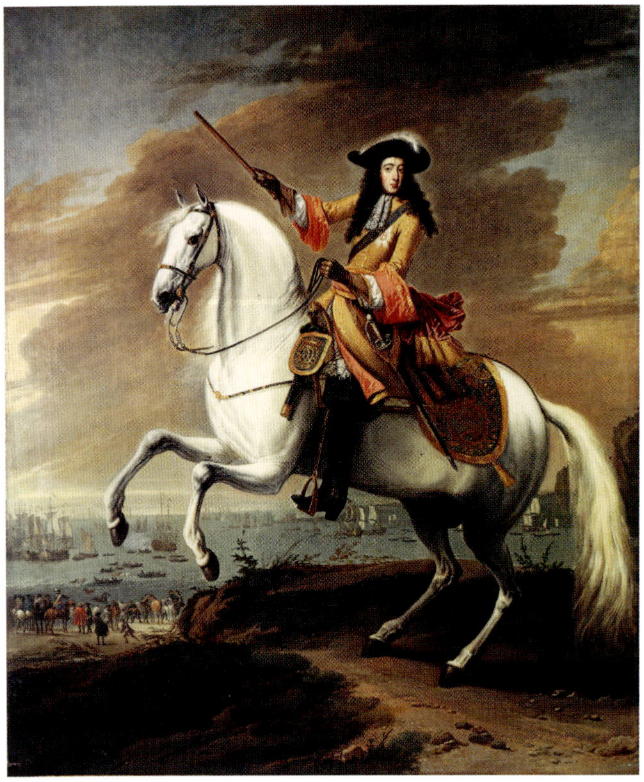

Fig. 6 Jan Wyck, *William III Landing at Brixham, Torbay, 5 November 1688*, oil on canvas, 1688.

James's reign was troubled and short-lived. First, Charles II's illegitimate son James, Duke of Monmouth, landed at Lyme Regis in Dorset with the intention of deposing his uncle. This Whig rebellion, supported by West Country dissenters, was defeated at the Battle of Sedgemoor by troops led by John Churchill, the future Duke of Marlborough, and Monmouth was executed in July of the coronation year. Three years later, however, a much bigger and better organized *coup d'état* succeeded. On 5 November 1688 (a date of significance as the anniversary of the failed Gunpowder Plot of 1605 and noted as a positive augury by Protestants), the Dutch Protestant ruler, William of Orange, landed at Torbay in Devon with a massive invasion force. William, who had married James's daughter Mary in 1677, had the support of members of the English elite who were sympathetic to the Whig cause – and even some Tories who were concerned that James's government was eroding rights and liberties. Most notable among these were the six nobles and one bishop, known as the Immortal Seven, who on 30 June had issued William with a letter of invitation to intervene in English politics. As William and his troops marched from Torbay and Exeter towards London, James II fled to France and William took the throne (fig. 6).

It is important to remember that in the decades of Charles II's reign, religious doctrines vied for control and provoked violent political disagreements: Puritans feared popery; Anglicans suspected dissenters and non-conformists. In the restored order, 'Exclusion replaced comprehension in the church; coercion replaced toleration in the state.'[8] Accordingly, the so-called Glorious Revolution of 1688 was defined by two competing narratives. The persuasiveness of the two narratives depended entirely on one's political and religious temper, and each was dramatized in highly partisan political broadsides and satires (fig. 7). For hard-line Tories loyal to James – whose second wife, Mary of Modena, had given birth to a legitimate healthy male heir in 1688 – William had seized the throne forcibly and unlawfully. For James's anti-Catholic Whig critics – who were fearful of a popish church settlement, baulked at perceived royal tyranny and sought to defend religious freedom and personal liberty – William was the 'great deliverer' who had taken up a vacant throne peaceably.

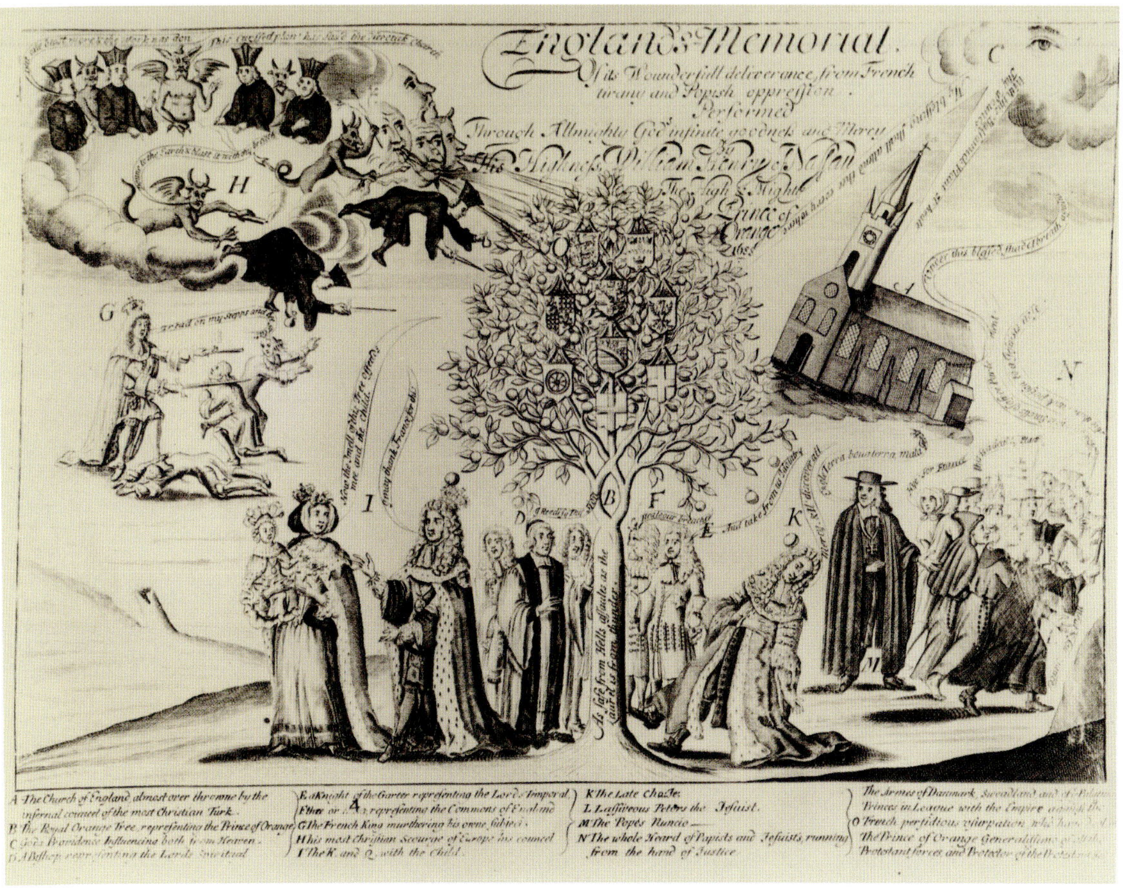

Fig. 7 *England's Memorial*, an etching made in about 1688, satirizing the flight of James II and the ascendancy of the House of Orange.

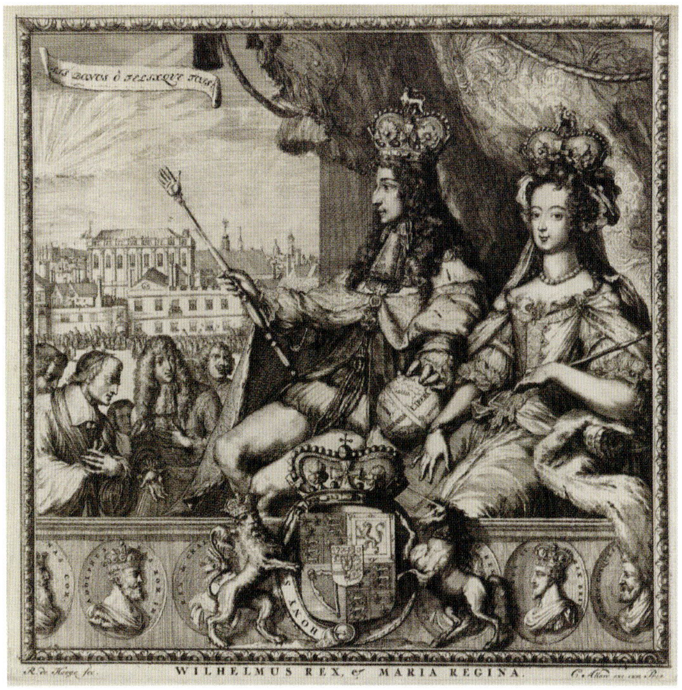

Fig. 8 Romeyn de Hooghe, an etching of King William III and Queen Mary II, made in their coronation year, 1689.

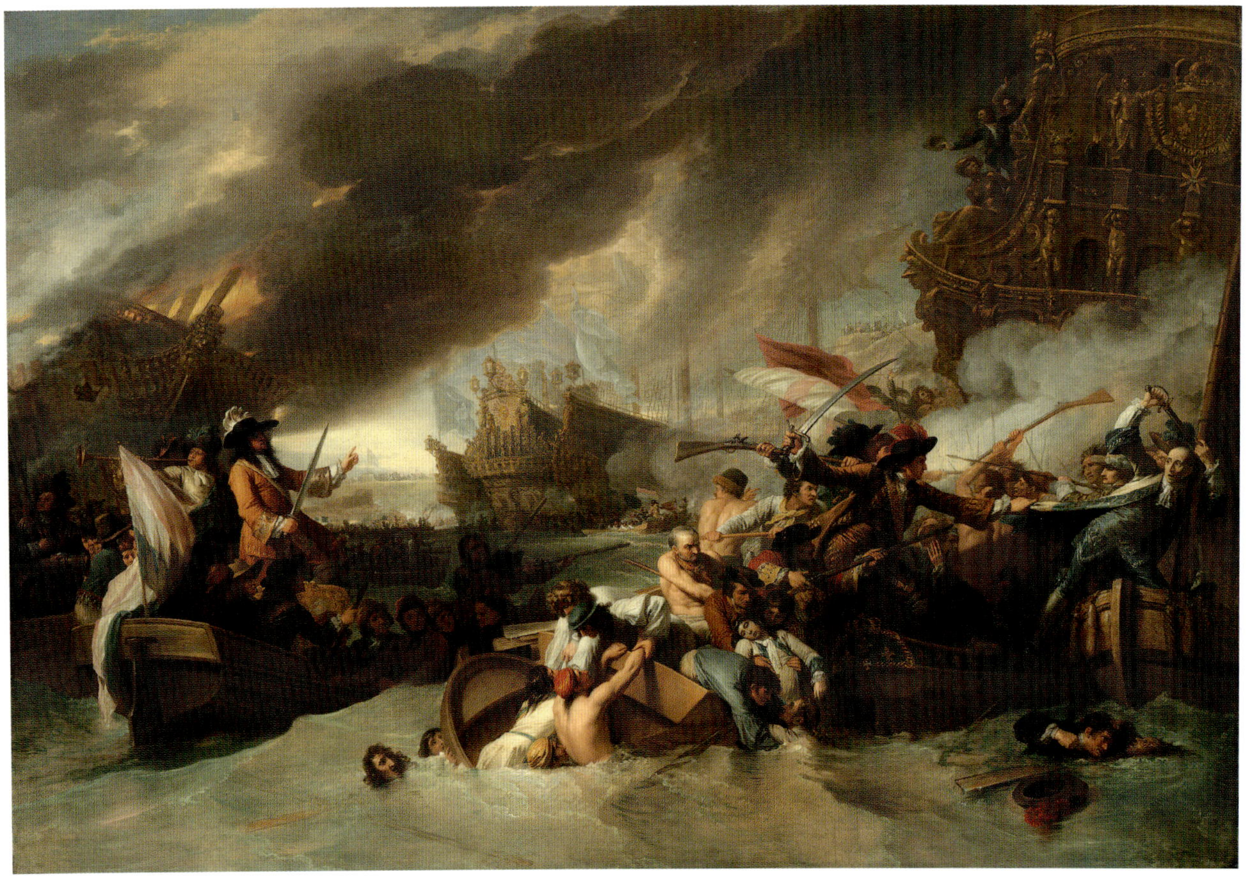

Fig. 9 Benjamin West, *The Battle of La Hogue* [1692], oil on canvas, *c.* 1778.

William III was crowned on 11 April 1689. That he ascended the throne jointly with his wife, Mary, James's eldest daughter, undoubtedly assisted the Whigs' 'bloodless' narrative (fig. 8).

It was events early in the entirely unprecedented co-regency that provided the impetus for a Royal Hospital for Seamen at Greenwich. In 1690 an uprising in Ireland led by Jacobites (those loyal to James II and his son James Francis Edward Stuart) ended bloodily but successfully for William's troops at the Battle of the Boyne. Further suppression of the Jacobite threat was necessary in 1692, however: as William was away fighting the French in the Low Countries, Louis XIV mounted an ill-fated attempt to return the exiled James to the English throne. Supported by her Dutch Protestant allies, England massed her fleets and engaged the enemy for five days off the northern French coast near La Hogue (fig. 9). The threat was overcome, but at huge cost. The casualties sustained by the Royal Navy prompted Queen Mary to send fifty surgeons to the aid of grievously injured seamen when the fleet returned to Portsmouth. Most importantly, news of the severe casualties gave fresh urgency to the idea conceived by James II in 1687 of a hospital for the care and accommodation of men who had served their country so bravely at sea.[9] Mary now pursued in earnest the 'grant of Greenwich as a hospital for seamen', and made such an institution 'the darling object of her life'; she had already signified to the Treasury Lords in 1691 that she wished the abandoned range of her uncle Charles's abortive palace to be converted for such a use.[10] In the wake of La Hogue, the King's Surveyor, Sir Christopher Wren (1632–1723; fig. 10), visited the site in January 1693. He inspected John Webb's building and offered to design, without charge for his services, a new hospital incorporating the abandoned range. Mary died in a smallpox epidemic on 28 December 1694, but William ensured that her wishes were executed posthumously by issuing a warrant, backdated to 25 October, in their joint names: this vested the King Charles block and adjoining lands in trust for the creation of a hospital 'for the reliefe and support of Seamen'.[11] The politics of the Glorious Revolution were now driving what would become one of the greatest achievements in English art and architecture.

The warrant issued, Wren began experimenting with a masterplan for the Hospital: no easy task, since the design had to be magnificent enough for its royal prefix, sufficiently capacious for 2000 pensioners (wounded or disabled seamen) and yet responsive to the constraints of the Greenwich site. No less a mind than a former president of the Royal Society, England's leading scientific institution, was required for such an intellectual challenge. Wren's amanuensis Nicholas Hawksmoor (1661–1736; fig. 11) assisted him closely in this task, being appointed his Clerk in June 1696 on a salary of £50, and then the Clerk of the Works in July 1698 for the nominal extra sum of 4*s.* a day (he held the latter post until 1733, when he was 'shabbily dismissed' under the surveyorship of Thomas Ripley).[12]

An account written by Hawksmoor provides us with the greatest insight into the way in which the Greenwich project developed and the preoccupations of those who commissioned the Hospital buildings.[13] In his *Remarks* of 1728 – a vigorous defence of the project at a time when political support was at a low ebb – Hawksmoor situates Greenwich Hospital in a wider European context, and in a long and noble building tradition, by invoking Les Invalides (fig. 12). He explains that the founding and finishing of the 'Hospital of the Invalids for Veteran Soldiers' in Paris, begun in 1671, was not only a useful philanthropic exercise but also the outstanding achievement of Louis XIV's reign. Hawksmoor credits the French king with beginning the great early modern European project of constructing residential institutions for sick and injured veterans, and explains that such establishments belong to a tradition of architecturally articulated philanthropy stretching back to antiquity: 'The great Men of the World heretofore, to perpetuate their own Memories, and their great Actions, among other Things had recourse to the liberal Arts; particularly to that of Architecture; sometimes by erecting useful Structures for the Good and Benefit of Mankind, and sometimes for their Grandeur only.'[14]

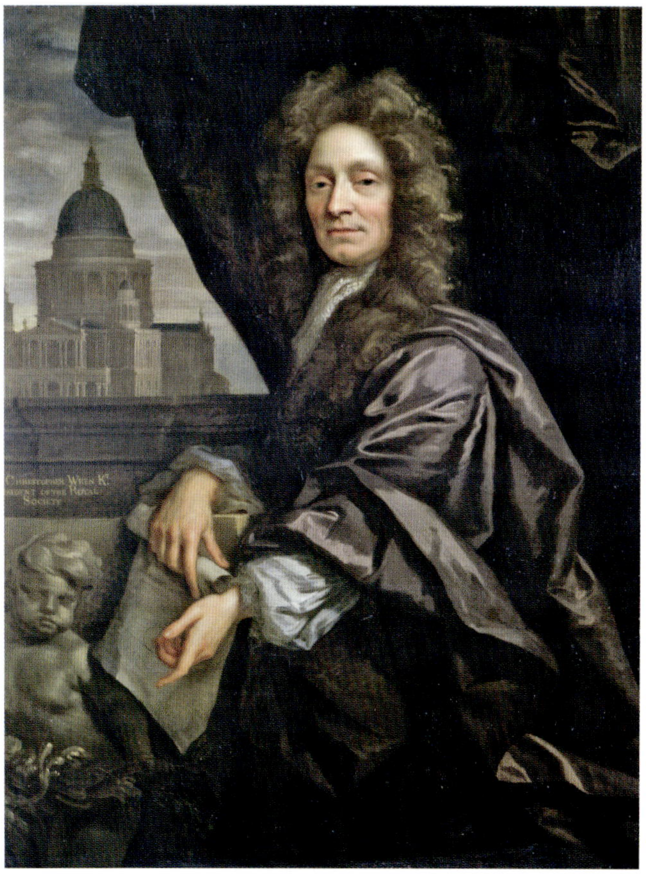

Fig. 10 John Closterman, *Portrait of Christopher Wren*, oil on canvas, *c.* 1690. Wren served as President of the Royal Society from 1680 to 1682.

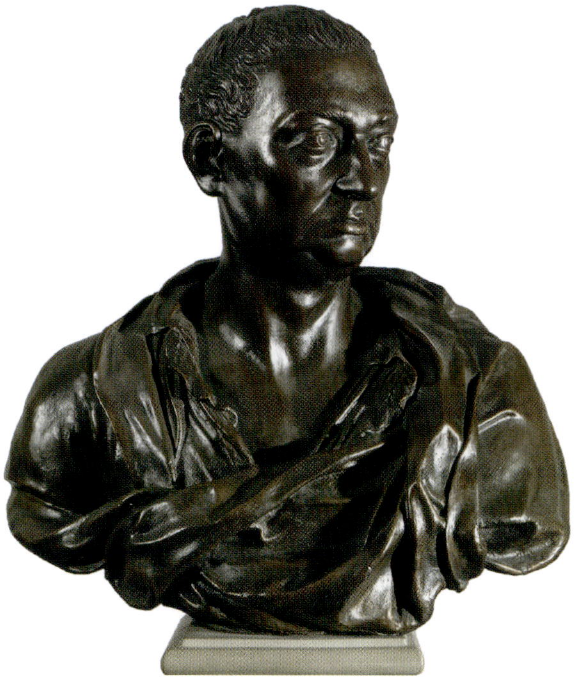

Fig. 11 Bronze bust of Nicholas Hawksmoor, cast 1962, after a bust attributed to Henry Cheere, 1736.

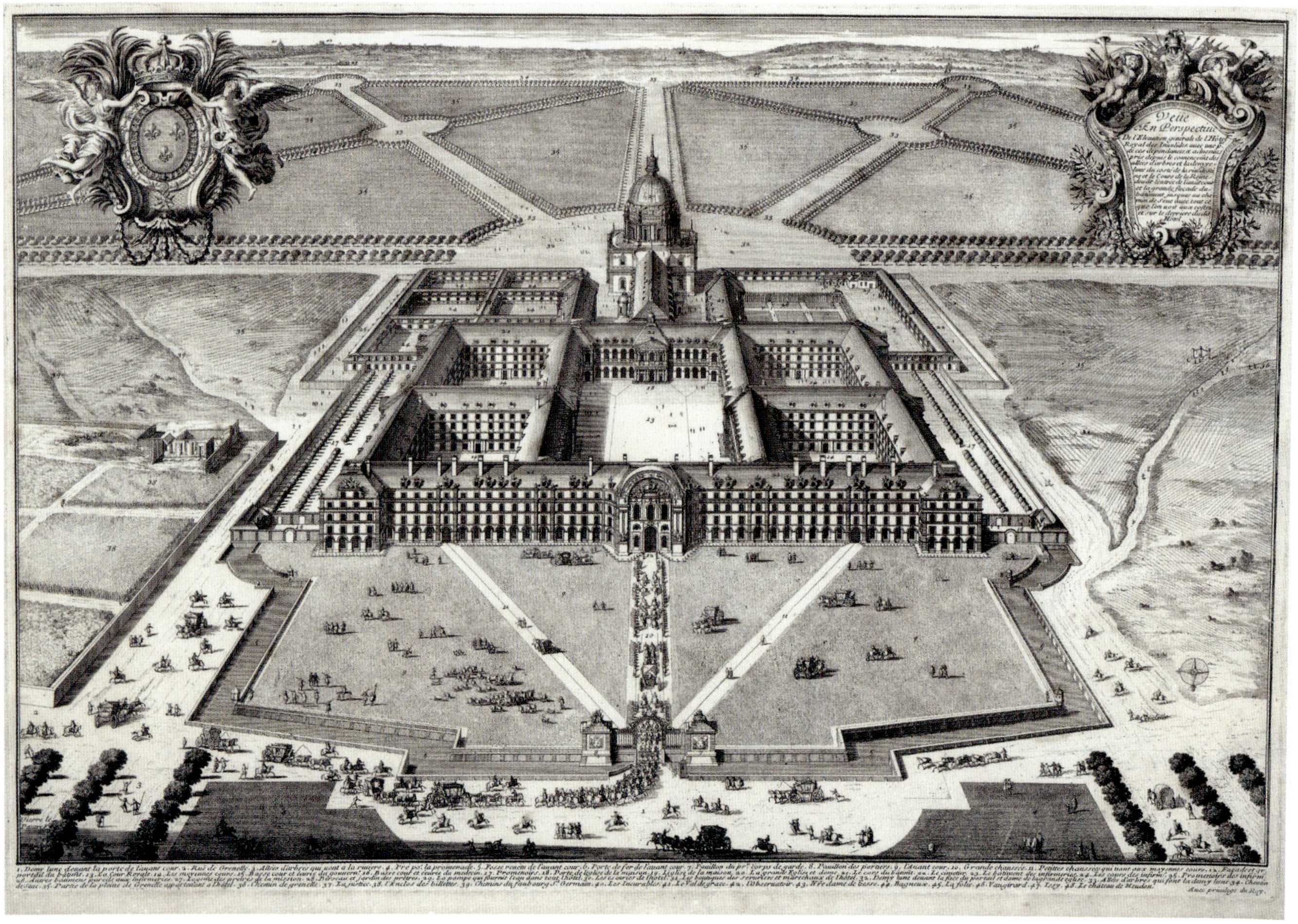

Fig. 12 Pierre Lepautre, bird's-eye view of Les Invalides (begun 1671) from the north, from Le Jeune de Boulencourt's *Description générale de l'Hostel Royal des Invalides*, published 1683.

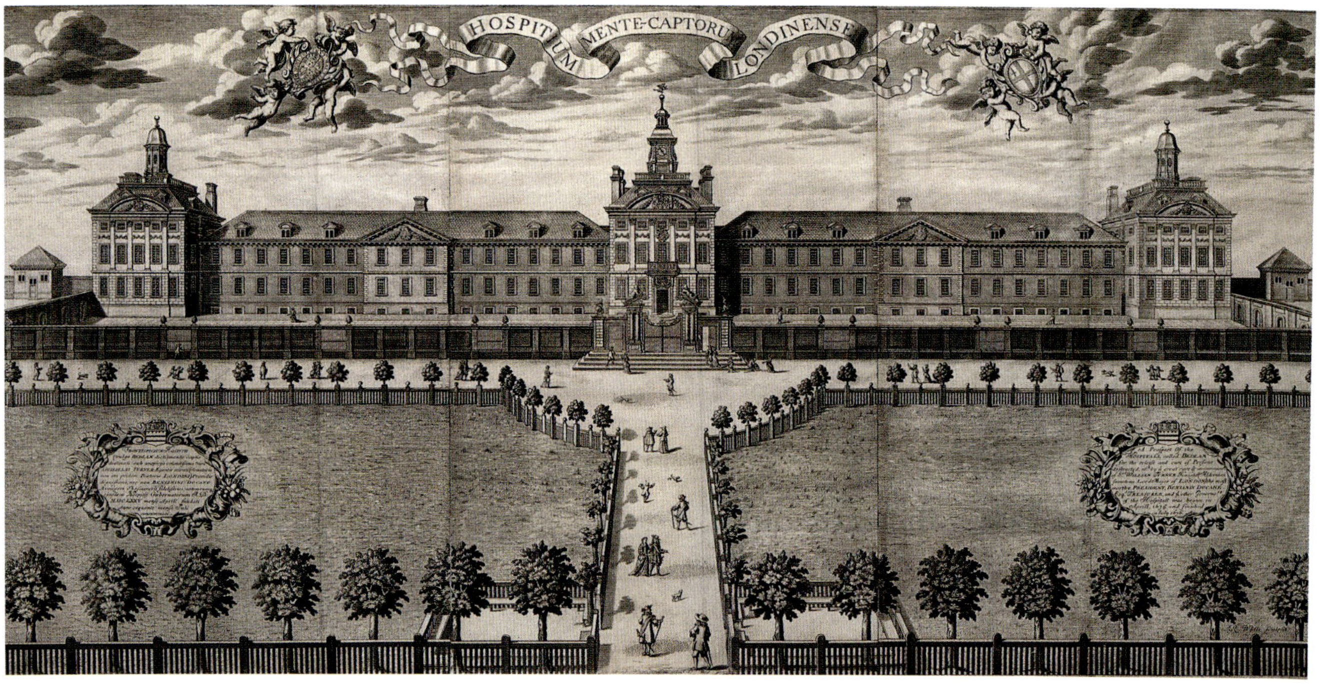

Fig. 13 Robert Hooke, Bethlem Hospital, built 1674–76; engraving by Robert White after Thomas Cartwright, 1677.

With these carefully chosen words, Hawksmoor takes us to the heart of the tensions inherent in projects such as the Greenwich Royal Hospital: the uneasy relationship between architectural magnificence and charitable purpose. It is a pairing that modern minds have particular difficulty accepting, and even in 1763 Samuel Johnson found the newly completed Hospital at Greenwich 'too magnificent for a place of charity'.[15] As Christine Stevenson has argued in relation to Bethlem (built in 1674–76 to designs by Wren's friend and colleague Robert Hooke; fig. 13), the key to understanding such projects lies in the distinction made between private luxury ('self-regarding ostentation') and public magnificence ('a noble liberality that scorned to calculate personal return'): 'Bethlem was meant to evoke different but simultaneous appreciations: magnificent beauty, charitable hospitality, good and healthful order. For each of these, the sight of the architecture, of carved stone fronts, great galleries, and tidy rows of airy cells was to be the stimulus.'[16]

This was an understanding of architectural decorum based on building type, not on the status of the people contained within the building: the hospitals and prisons of the seventeenth century were structures that had to convey the immense benign power of the state and the dignity of a particular authority. The practical benefit to the nation was at stake, but so, too, was its honour. In the case of Greenwich, the dignity of the Royal Navy had to be conveyed, as well as the state's willingness to discharge its duty of care to those who had suffered in its service. Thus, Edward Hatton, in his *New View of London* (1708), had no apparent difficulty in describing the Hospital, then still under construction, as 'one of the most sumptuous Hospitals in the World, much liker the Palace of a Prince than a Harbour for the Indigent'.[17] Similarly, in 1717, James Thornhill, the artist commissioned to decorate the institution's Hall, expressed a hope that 'this being an Hospital will make no difference [to the payment awarded to him], since Royal Hospitals are as well embellished as Palaces and with as much expense'.[18]

Thornhill's remark was self-serving but accurate: charitable works – especially those bearing the royal imprimatur – did not carry with them an expectation of economy, frugality or modesty. Indeed, in his *Remarks*, Hawksmoor makes it clear that maximum visibility and grandiosity were always the intention at Greenwich. He tells us that the site was chosen over others, including Winchester, because it was 'in the View of all the World' on a major route along the Thames into the City of London. It was an architectural spectacle designed to excite patriotic feeling and, in part, to encourage a new generation of men to serve their country at sea despite the lack of enticements. Hawksmoor leaves his reader in no doubt that it was '*her Majesty's* fixt Intention for Magnificence' – not the whim of the client or the architect – that generated the Hospital's 'beautiful and durable' fronts of Portland stone.[19] The same impulse towards magnificent charity (somewhat less dramatically and expansively expressed) had led to the creation in the 1680s of the Royal Hospital Chelsea, the military forerunner of Greenwich. This refuge for old and injured soldiers was also designed by Wren, but here he used the sober and martial Doric order (fig. 14).

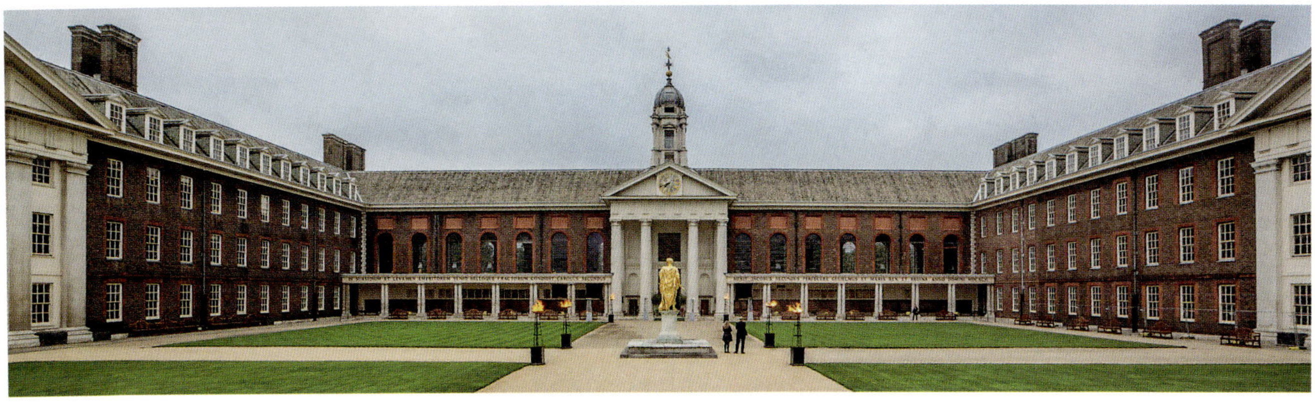

Fig. 14 Sir Christopher Wren, the Royal Hospital Chelsea for old and injured soldiers, completed 1692.

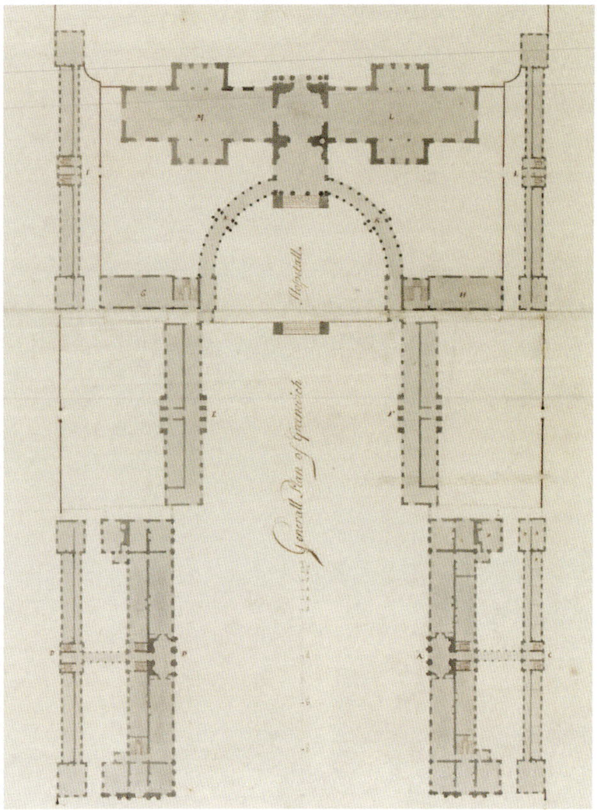

Fig. 15 Wren's 'Generall Plan' of a design for an enlarged Hospital with a central domed hall and chapel range, 1695.

For the columns and pilasters of Greenwich, he and Hawksmoor would enlist the more palatial and ornate Corinthian order (developing a theme begun by John Webb on the tetrastyle portico and end pavilions of the King's House).

Hawksmoor's *Remarks* shed light, too, on the design constraints of the Greenwich project and the extent of Mary II's active personal involvement before her death in 1694. In particular, they explain how Wren was compelled to treat the Queen's House axis and the King's House as non-negotiable components of the new Hospital's design:

Her Majesty, ever solicitous for the Prosecution of the Design, had several times honour'd Greenwich with her personal Views of the Building erected by King Charles II, as Part of his Palace, and that built by Mr Inigo Jones, called the Queen's House, & c. On which Views she was unwilling to demolish either, as was propos'd by some. This occasioned the keeping of an Approach from the Thames quite up to the Queen's House of 115 feet broad, out of the Grant that was made to the Hospital, that her Majesty might have an Access to that House by Water as well as by Land … And now as

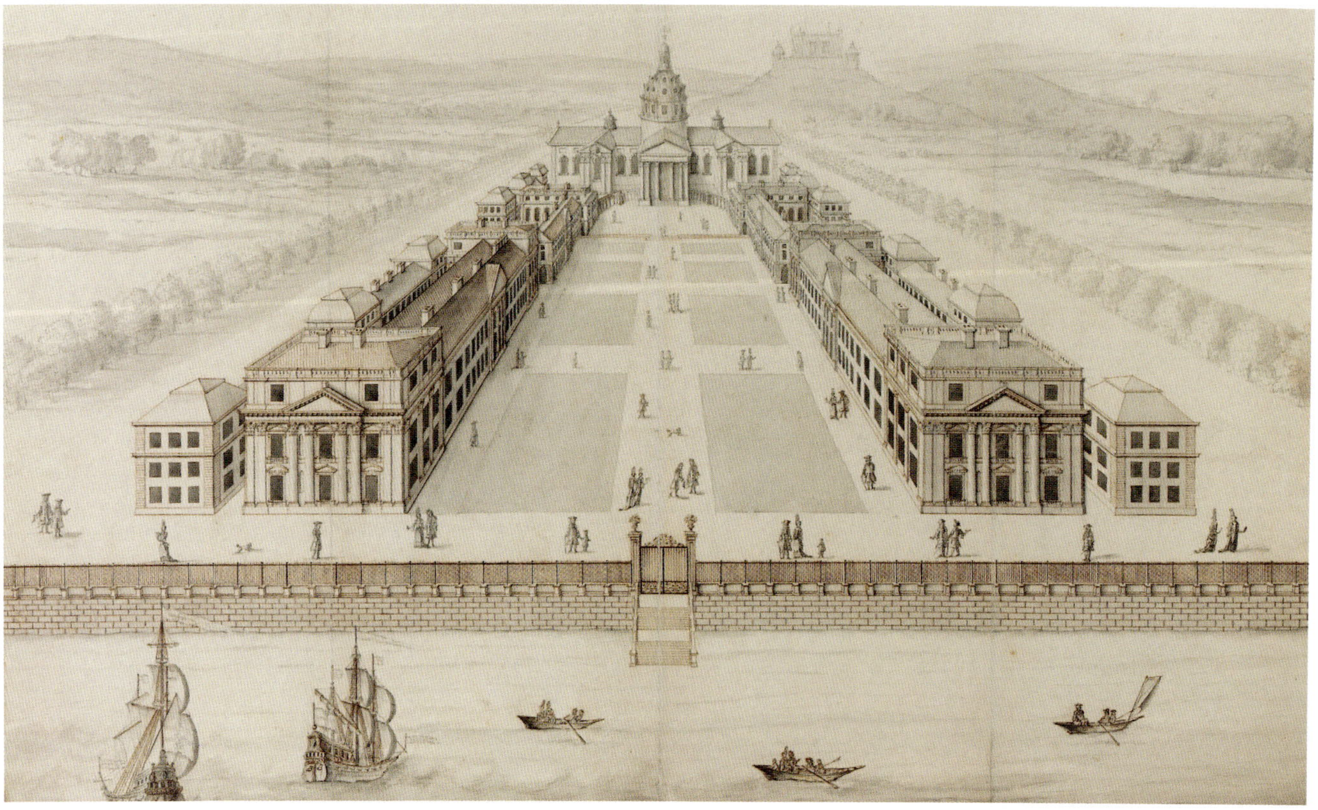

Fig. 16 Perspective of Wren's 'central domed scheme', drawn by Leonard Knyff, 1695.

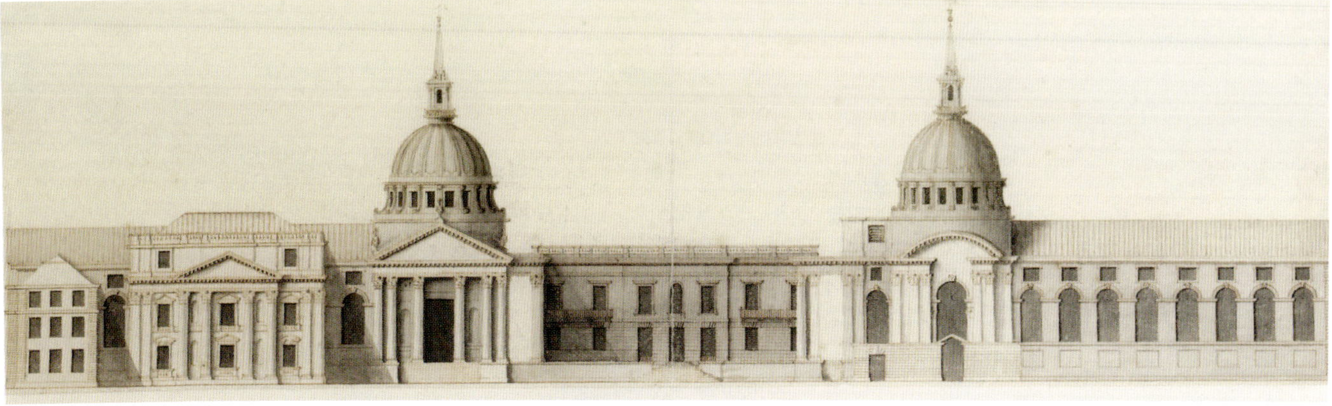

Fig. 17 Nicholas Hawksmoor, drawing for Wren's seven-block scheme, 1695: front elevation, showing the north elevation of the Queen's House and alternatives, left and right, for the design and positioning of the domes, dome vestibules, colonnades and porticoes of the hall and chapel ranges.

to the New Wing built by Charles II it was much debated by the Commissioners, whether it should be demolish'd or remain … But her Majesty received the Proposal of pulling down that Wing, with as much Indignation as her excellent good Temper would suffer her, order'd it should remain, and the other side of the Royal Court made answerable to it, in a proper Time.[20]

Among Wren's earliest proposals, in 1695, was a scheme to construct a new pendant range opposite the King Charles building, with wings extending southwards from each to a single domed cross-wing (figs. 15 and 16).[21] The cross-wing would, of course, have blocked the Queen's House approach, and the need to respect Mary's stipulations forced Wren to rethink. He next devised a seven-block scheme in which we see the emergence of the bilateral twin-domed solution that was eventually adopted (fig. 17). By 1698 this rather cluttered scheme of seven lateral ranges had been abandoned and the masterplan had settled into its final four-range form: the King Charles building, in the north-western corner of the site, would face a new pendant range named after Mary's sister and successor, Princess Anne, in the north-eastern corner (both were given linked base blocks); to the south-west was to be a new domed hall range named after King William, and to the south-east a domed chapel range named after Mary. Each of this second pair of twin buildings (William and Mary) was to form one wing of great courtyards facing each other through matching colonnades extending south towards the Queen's House. The bifurcation of the plan, along with the abandonment of the monolithic central dome, may have been driven by geography, but it was also uncannily reflective of the political situation: two constitutional monarchs had replaced a single absolutist one. John Summerson memorably likened these two domed blocks, which face each other across a dead end masquerading as a processional avenue, to 'two cats looking at each other in the absence of a king'.[22]

Hawksmoor clearly felt uneasy about this architectural 'overture without a drama', as Kerry Downes has described it, and as late as 1712 retained hope of adding a central visual emphasis in the form of an enormous domed chapel.[23] This enlarged scheme, which owed much to High Baroque Rome and the buildings of Bernini and Borromini, was never seriously entertained; presumably such Catholic visual associations would have precluded construction, even if lack of funds and the need to preserve the 115-foot-wide (35 m) Queen's House vista had not. Whether accidentally or intentionally, the centreless design adopted by January 1699 appeared to offer a new architectural language for a country then adopting a new kind of politics.

In addition to a three-part wooden model of the agreed scheme, for which he was paid £57, Hawksmoor produced a block plan with an explanatory key to the different buildings and their functions (fig. 18). At this stage, the intention – later dropped – was still to house the widows and orphans of inmates as well

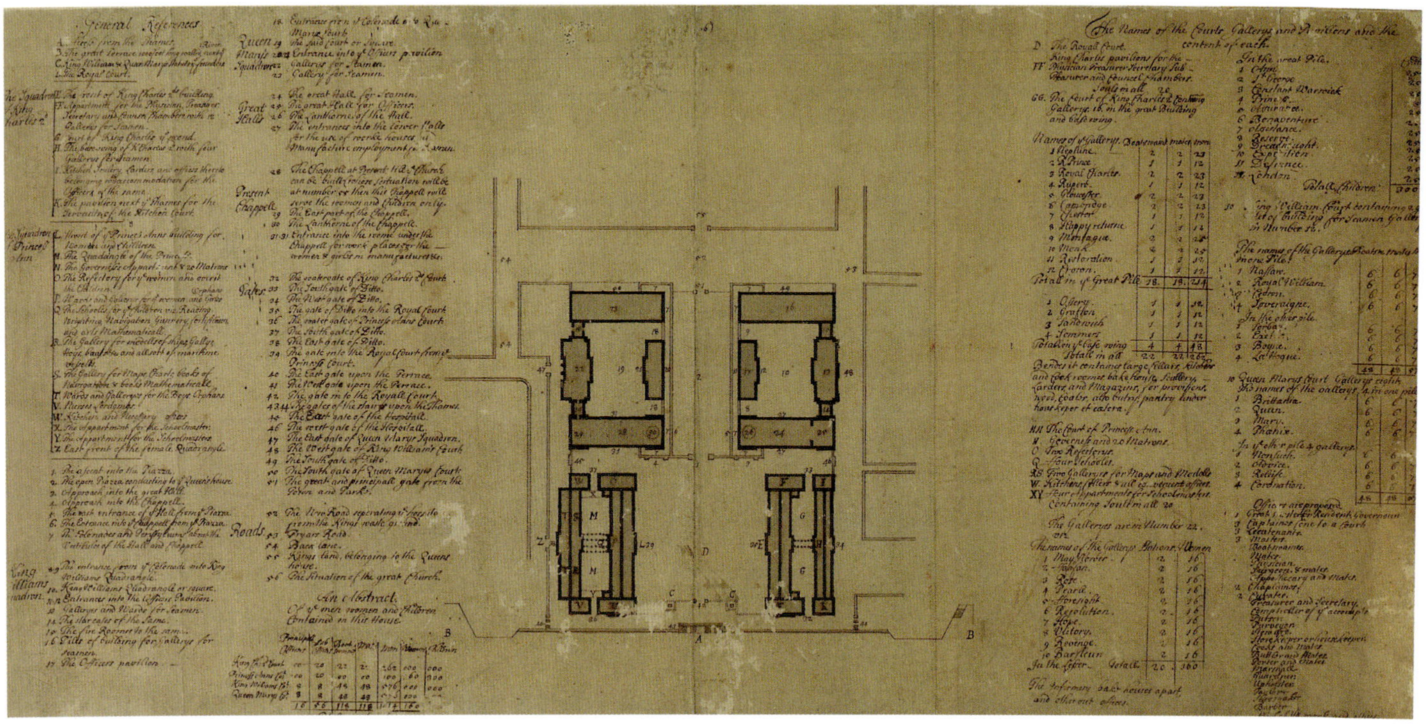

Fig. 18 Nicholas Hawksmoor, block plan of Greenwich Hospital, with explanatory key, *c.* 1700–1702.

as the seamen themselves. An engraved perspective, which was produced for fundraising purposes (a continual source of anxiety), takes the void at the heart of Wren's plan as its viewing point and shows the Queen's House framed by the proposed hall and chapel ranges named after William and Mary (fig. 19).

As John Bold has explained, it was through this series of logical steps that Wren developed the architecture of Greenwich 'towards ever greater articulation and magnificence, producing a far grander performance than he had essayed at Chelsea'.[24] The end result, Bold argues, was entirely appropriate given the Navy's pre-eminent status among the armed forces at the time and the political importance of the architectural enterprise. Greenwich Hospital was recorded soon after its completion in 1751 in a painting by Canaletto (fig. 20): a serene and seamless depiction that, of course, conceals a disjointed reality and is silent on the great difficulties that attended the project.[25]

While Wren and Hawksmoor were engaged in abstract design processes, a more worldly logistical and administrative effort was underway to establish the Hospital's management and constitution and, crucially, to raise funds for building. Looking at the Canaletto view of the finished complex, one can easily imagine that the project was a fully funded fait accompli in the 1690s. Although the Hospital turned out to be an architectural and political triumph, hindsight was not available to those in charge of the project in its early years. The Hospital's first commissioners and committee members needed huge reserves of energy to enlist political support and to elicit funds. Aside from Wren and Hawksmoor, the most effective and important figure in the Hospital's early years was the diarist and scholar John Evelyn (1620–1706; fig. 21). We learn from Evelyn's *Diary* that he was offered the role of Treasurer of Greenwich Hospital by the First Lord of the Treasury, Sidney Godolphin, in February 1695, just a couple of months after Queen Mary's death and the issuing of the royal warrant.[26] After some deliberation, Evelyn – who published or translated works on a huge range of subjects, including painting, architecture, forestry and London's air pollution – accepted Godolphin's offer. He was as practical as he was erudite, and his enthusiasm and efforts ensured that the ambitious enterprise was kept on track financially until he handed over the role to his

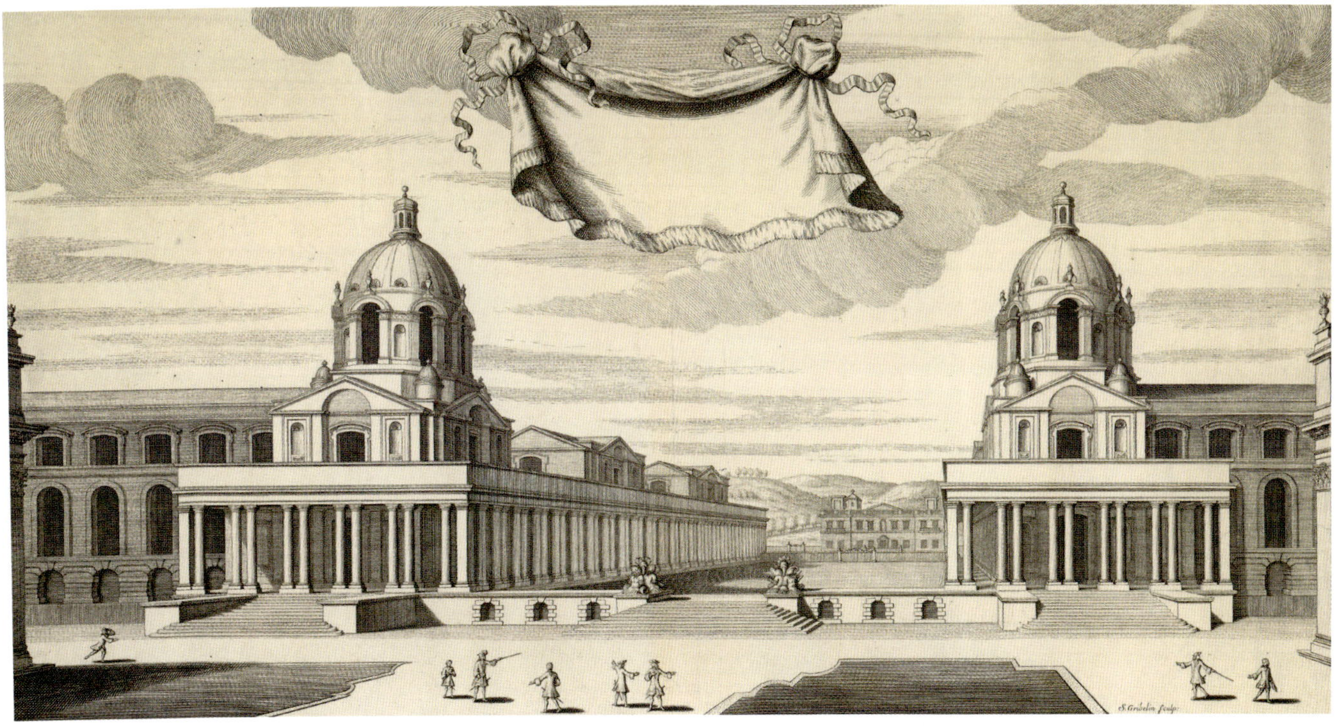

Fig. 19 Simon Gribelin, Greenwich Hospital, proof of an unpublished perspective showing the proposed King William block (right) and the Queen's House providing the end of the central axis, 1699.

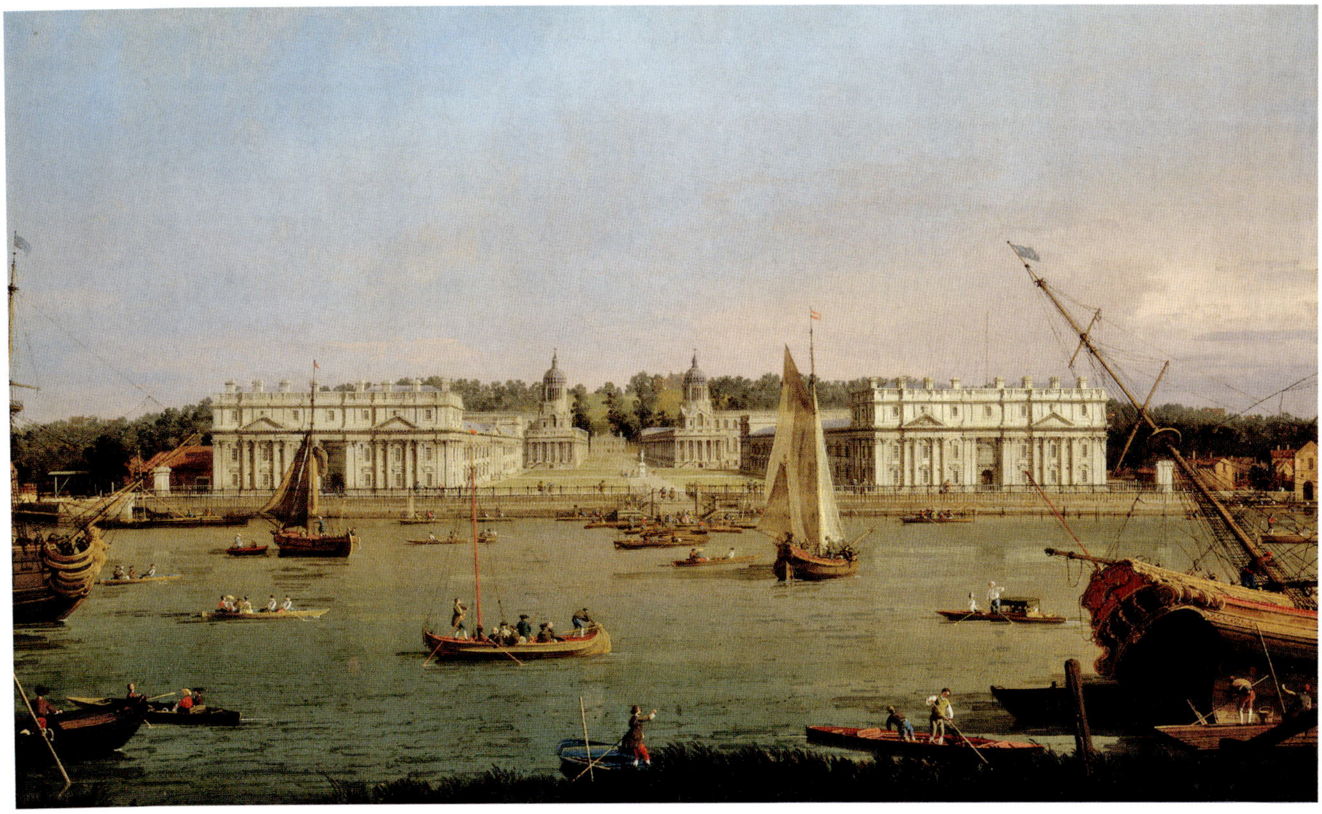

Fig. 20 Canaletto, *Greenwich Hospital from the North Bank of the Thames*, oil on canvas, *c.* 1752–53.

son-in-law, William Draper, in August 1703.[27]

In May 1695 Evelyn attended the first meeting of the Hospital commissioners at Guildhall. It is worth noting that meetings often took place in the City or Westminster (Scotland Yard) because Greenwich, 5 miles (8 km) downstream from London Bridge, was not always convenient for the men who sat on its committees, although it was more so for Evelyn, who lived at Sayes Court in neighbouring Deptford.[28] The list of attendees recorded by Evelyn provides some sense of the political weight and range of expertise that had been assembled in support of the project: among them were Thomas Tenison, Archbishop of Canterbury; Godolphin, Evelyn's initial contact on the project; the Duke of Shrewsbury; the Earl of Dorset; the merchant financier and former Lord Mayor of London Sir Robert Clayton; senior representatives of the Admiralty; and Sir Christopher Wren. Evelyn joined Clayton and Wren on a site visit to Greenwich on 17 May. At a follow-up meeting four days later, the Grand Committee discussed the preparation of the King Charles building in order to receive the first cohort of pensioners, and issued an order for the restoration of the water springs and conduits belonging to the Tudor palace.[29]

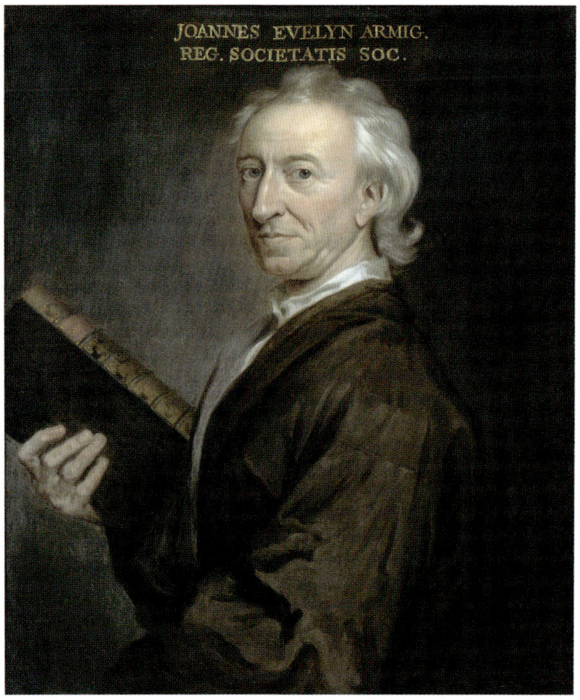

Fig. 21 Godfrey Kneller, *Portrait of John Evelyn*, oil on canvas, *c.* 1687. Evelyn was Treasurer of Greenwich Hospital from 1695 to 1703.

By December 1695 the Grand Committee had organized itself into a series of subcommittees for 'fabrick', 'constitution' and 'revenue', and by January 1696 the plans of the Fabric Committee (the most active and effective of the three) were approved for presentation to King William.[30] In early June, Evelyn notes that he and Wren 'made first agreement with divers workemen and for materials'; the latter contracts included one with 'a Mr Daniel [De]Foe' for the supply of bricks (the dissenting Whig and pamphleteer at this stage owned a pantile and brick factory at Tilbury and, in one of many links between this building project and contemporary politics, had supported Monmouth's rebellion of 1685).[31] Wren and Evelyn at this point also 'gave the first order for the proceeding on the foundations' (with weekly payments to workmen), and 'received orders from the Lords of the Treasury for the King's 2000 to be employed on that work'.[32] King William's promised endowment of £2000 per annum rapidly fell into arrears, however. The 1697 payment came in the form of 'mault tickets' (credits against the Malt Tax, which workmen were understandably reluctant to accept in place of cash),[33] and payments were missed completely in 1698 and 1699.

Evelyn's challenge was somehow to balance the books and ensure that workers were paid and materials acquired. In spite of the Hospital's royal imprimatur, it was ultimately the many small contributions of working men that provided this immense building project with the necessary financial ballast. As Wren's proposals were approved for presentation to the king in January 1696, the Grand Committee was urgently debating measures to finance the project, including deductions from seamen's wages, a new lottery and a cut of prizes taken at sea. In particular, members approved a report from the Revenue Committee that advocated requesting his Majesty to 'grant a general briefe for collecting the benevolence of all persons in England' and proposing to Parliament 'that a proportion … p[er] pound be paid out of all seamen's wages in merchant's imploy' (in addition to the sixpences deducted from the wages of Royal Naval seamen). The report also urged that 'a duty be laide on all persons getting their livelihood by water carriage in the rivers, ports, & harbors of England'.[34] The levy of sixpence on merchant and royal sailors' wages in fact proved the single most important source of funding in the Hospital's earliest days, accounting for three quarters of the money that Evelyn received and spent as Treasurer from the time of his appointment in 1695 until his retirement in the summer of 1703.[35]

Work began as these measures were put in place and, as Evelyn records, the key moment came on 30 June 1696 with a meeting of the Grand Committee at Greenwich for the laying of the first stone of the new complex (a cornerstone of the King Charles base block):

I went with a select committee of the Commissioners for the fabric of Greenwich Hospital and with Sir Chr Wren the Surveyor where with him I laid the first stone of that intended foundation: precisely at 5 o'clock in the Evening after wee had dined together: Mr Flamsteed the Kings Astronomical Professor Observing the Punctual time by instruments. Note that one of the workemen in helping to place the stone, being a large corner stone, grating his fingers against the gravelly bank, some drops of blood fell upon it.[36]

Here, the intellectual world of the Astronomer Royal, John Flamsteed, whose work to record the heavenly bodies was underway in the Royal Observatory overlooking the site (fig. 22), collides with the sublunar world. Those first drops of blood observed by Evelyn remind us of the visceral realities of building: the workmen sustained with 'hogsheads of good strong beer', and the huge physical effort to come.[37] The vignette serves to remind us, too, that endeavours by Flamsteed and others to map the stars had direct relevance to the Navy and therefore to the Hospital project: by establishing the fixed position of the stars, sailors could calculate longitude, pinpoint their position at sea and perfect the art of navigation. A royal warrant of 4 March 1675 had appointed Flamsteed as 'Astronomical Observer' to Charles II on a salary of £100 and provided for the building of the Observatory on the hill at Greenwich. The decision to fund the Observatory was part of the rivalry with

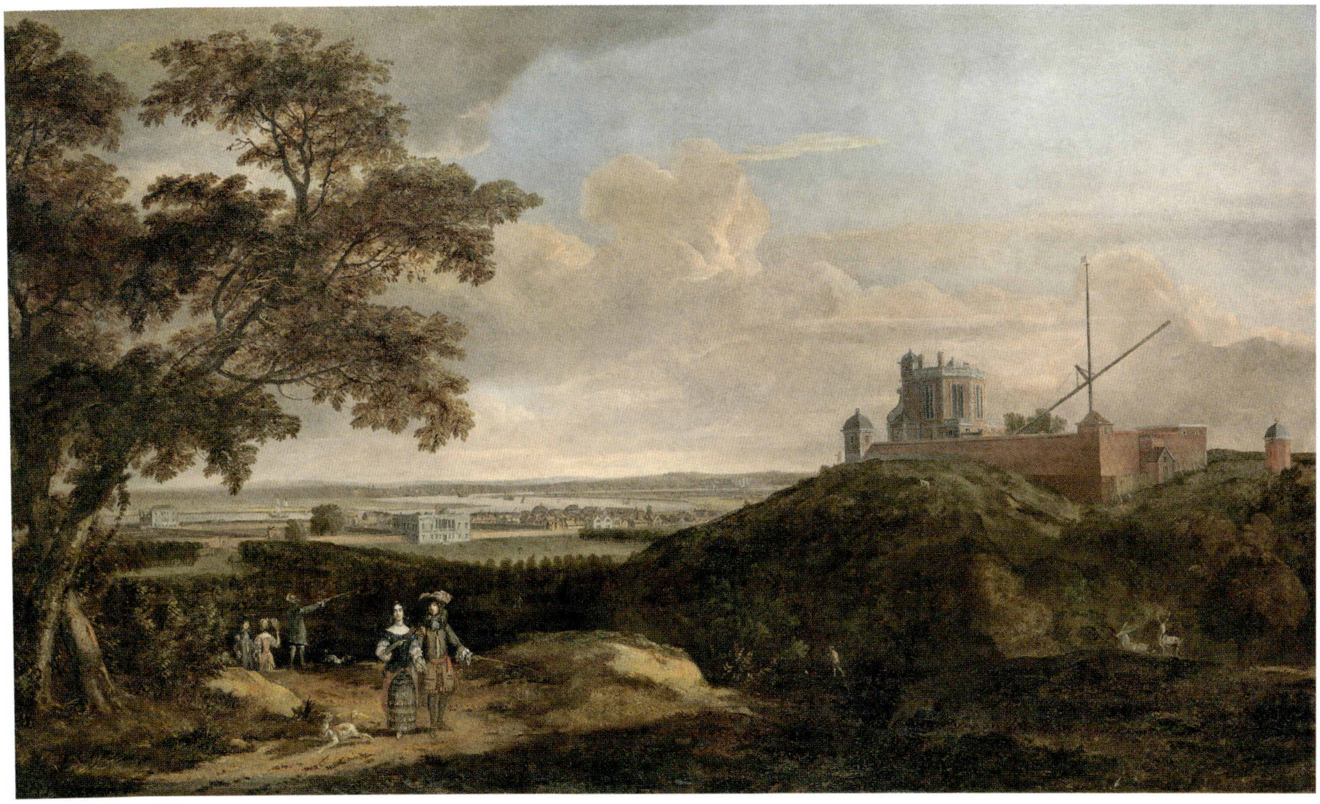

Fig. 22 English School, *The Royal Observatory from Crooms Hill*, oil on canvas, *c.* 1696, with the Queen's House and palace site in the far distance.

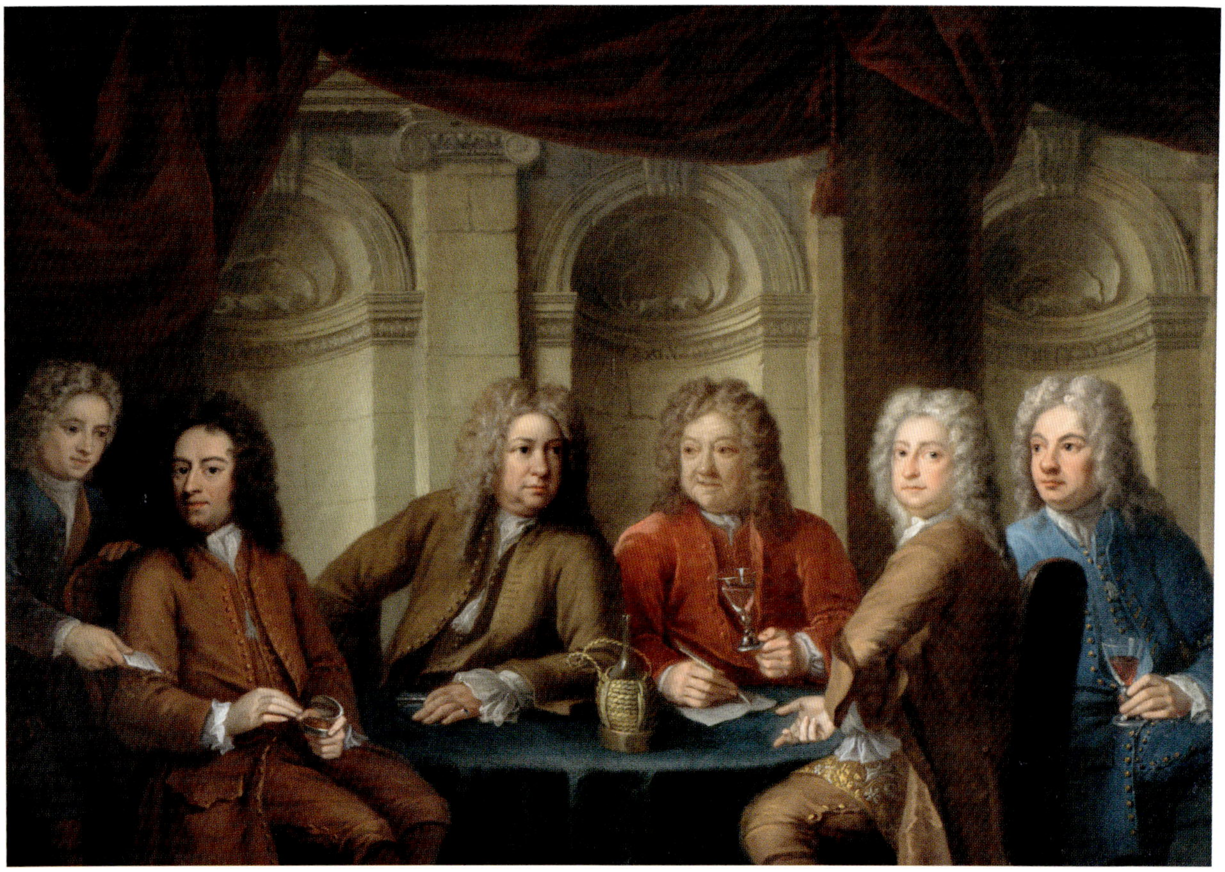

Fig. 23 James Thornhill, *Andrew Quicke in Conversation with the 1st Earl of Godolphin* [third from the right], *Joseph Addison, Sir Richard Steele and the Artist*, oil on canvas, *c.* 1711–12.

France to dominate the seas and also of the use of science in the service of patriotism and national prosperity. It was subject to the same fluctuations of political will and funding that subsequently dogged construction of the Hospital.[38] The relationship between the two buildings would be acknowledged later with the inclusion of Flamsteed's likeness in the painted ceiling decoration of the Hospital's Great Hall (fig. 19 on p. 86).

On 4 July, soon after the laying of the first stone, Evelyn notes that 'my Lord Godolphin was the very first of the subscribers who payed any money towards this noble fabric'.[39] Not all grandees who had promised money were as good as their word. The names of those elite supporters who did contribute meaningful sums are of great interest – not merely as one of many inventories in a major building project, but because they help us to understand Greenwich Hospital in its wider political context. Sidney Godolphin, depicted in a Dutch-style group portrait painted by James Thornhill in about 1711–12 (fig. 23), was a leading politician under James II, William III and Queen Anne, an art collector and, at the time of his overture to John Evelyn regarding the financial management of Greenwich Hospital, was personally responsible as First Lord of the Treasury for raising funds to sustain William's war with Louis XIV.[40] Often accused of retaining Jacobite contacts after 1689, Godolphin nevertheless managed to survive politically to become Lord Treasurer under Anne. The inaugural gift of £500 to which Evelyn refers is recorded on one of three fictive painted cartouches or tablets in the Vestibule of the Hospital's Hall (fig. 24). These list in gold the names of the principal individual benefactors to the construction effort, and were added to the Hall's immense decorative scheme around the time of its completion in 1726.[41]

Examination of the *trompe l'œil* tablets, which record forty-seven separate donations totalling a little over £100,000, takes us to the heart of the fickle political environment in which the Greenwich Hospital

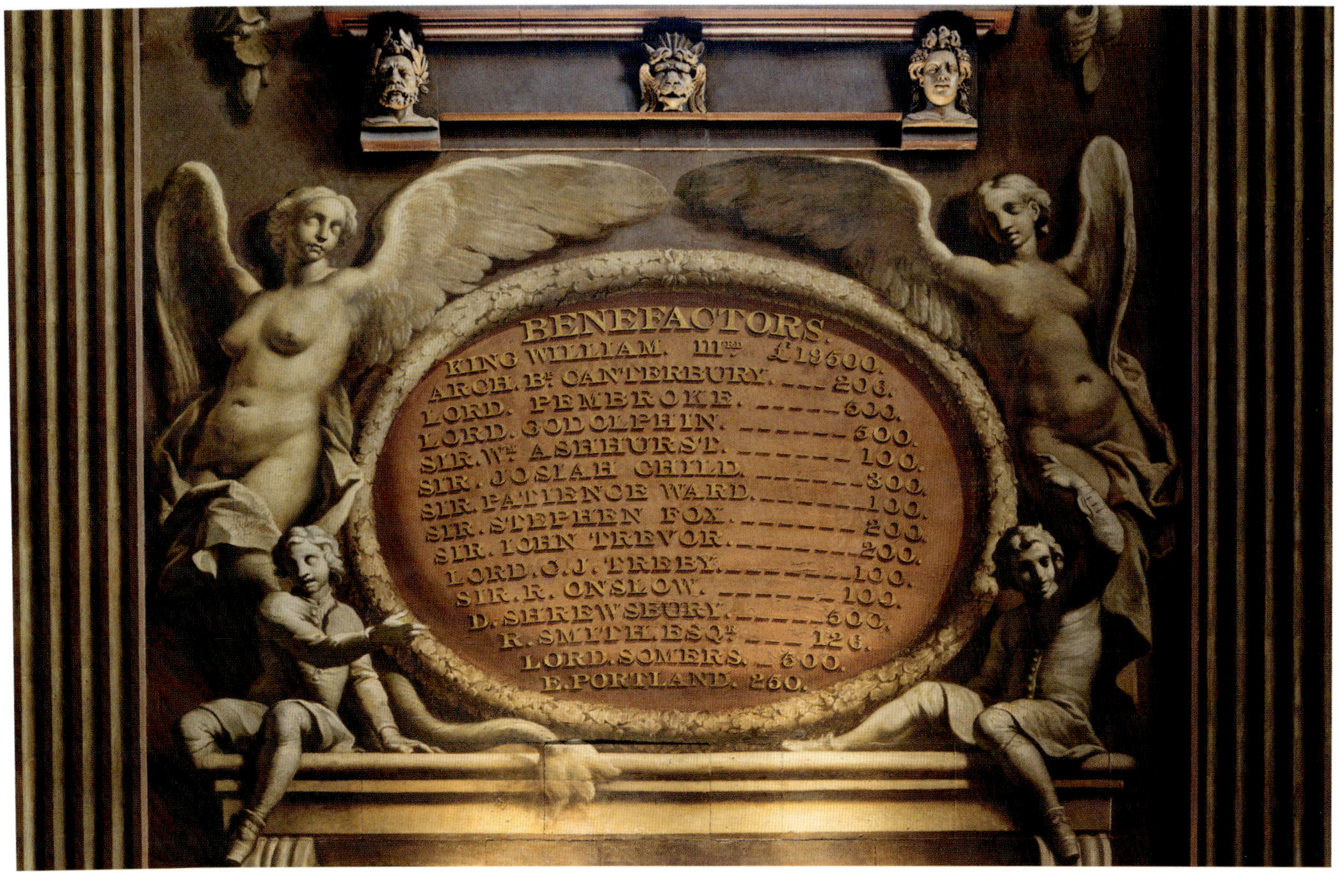

Fig. 24 Fictive tablet supported by winged figures and charity boys on the east elevation of the Painted Hall's Vestibule, recording the donations of King William III, Lord Godolphin and others, *c.* 1726.

project was forged. A wide range of religious and political tempers is represented side by side: Whig jostles with Tory, passionate anti-papist appears alongside High Church grandee, and proponents of hereditary succession and staunch supporters of the Protestant succession tolerate one other on the painted surface, if not in real life.[42] Aside from politics, the names, arranged (after those of the monarch) in no apparent order, also provide a fascinating insight into the confluence of commercial, cultural and intellectual interests behind this grand-scale architectural project: ebullient merchants and brash bankers find strange company among obscure antiquarians and reclusive mathematicians. Sharing a board with Godolphin, for example, we find Thomas Tenison, Archbishop of Canterbury, a passionate supporter of the Protestant succession and anti-papist; the Tory moderate Thomas Herbert, 8th Earl of Pembroke and First Lord of the Admiralty; Sir William Ashhurst (Ashurst), a London merchant with Puritan leanings, who had subscribed to a civic loan to William of Orange; Sir Josiah Child, a merchant and victualler to the Navy with strong East India Company links and Whig leanings; Sir Patience Ward, another London merchant and politician with dissenting sympathies, who had contributed to Monmouth's failed rebellion of 1685; the judge Sir John Trevor, who, by contrast, was one of the last Privy Counsellors loyal to James II; Charles Talbot, 1st Duke of Shrewsbury, one of the seven signatories on 30 June 1688 to the letter inviting William to intervene in English politics; and the Cambridge mathematician Robert Smith, who had particular interests in geometry, astronomy and Isaac Newton's work on optics (interestingly, all fields depicted in, or relevant to the design of, the Painted Hall's decorative scheme).

The two other donor tablets contain similarly eclectic and suggestive groups of names. To the north, headed by a donation 'from' Queen Anne of £6472 (a sum in fact confiscated from the estate of the

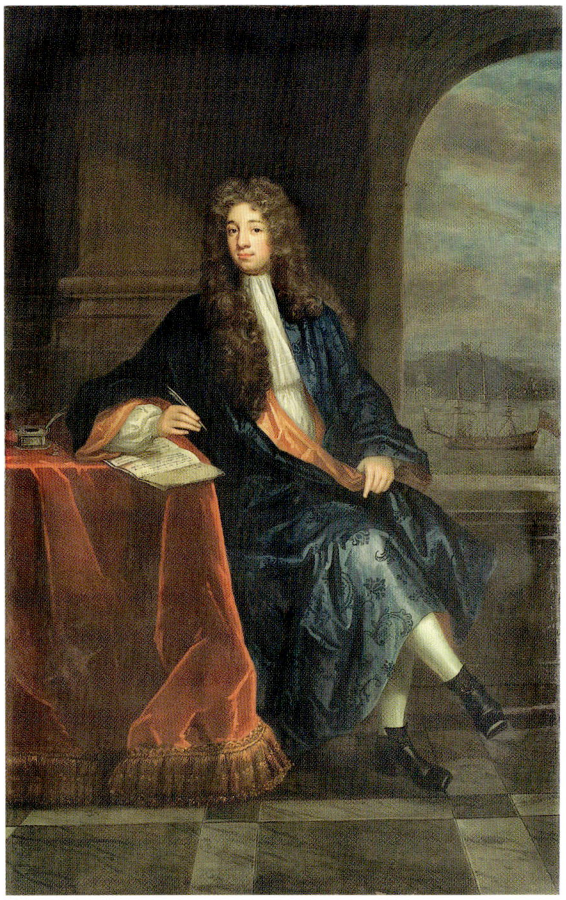

Fig. 25 Charles D'Agar, *Robert Osboldston*, oil on canvas, *c.* 1718.

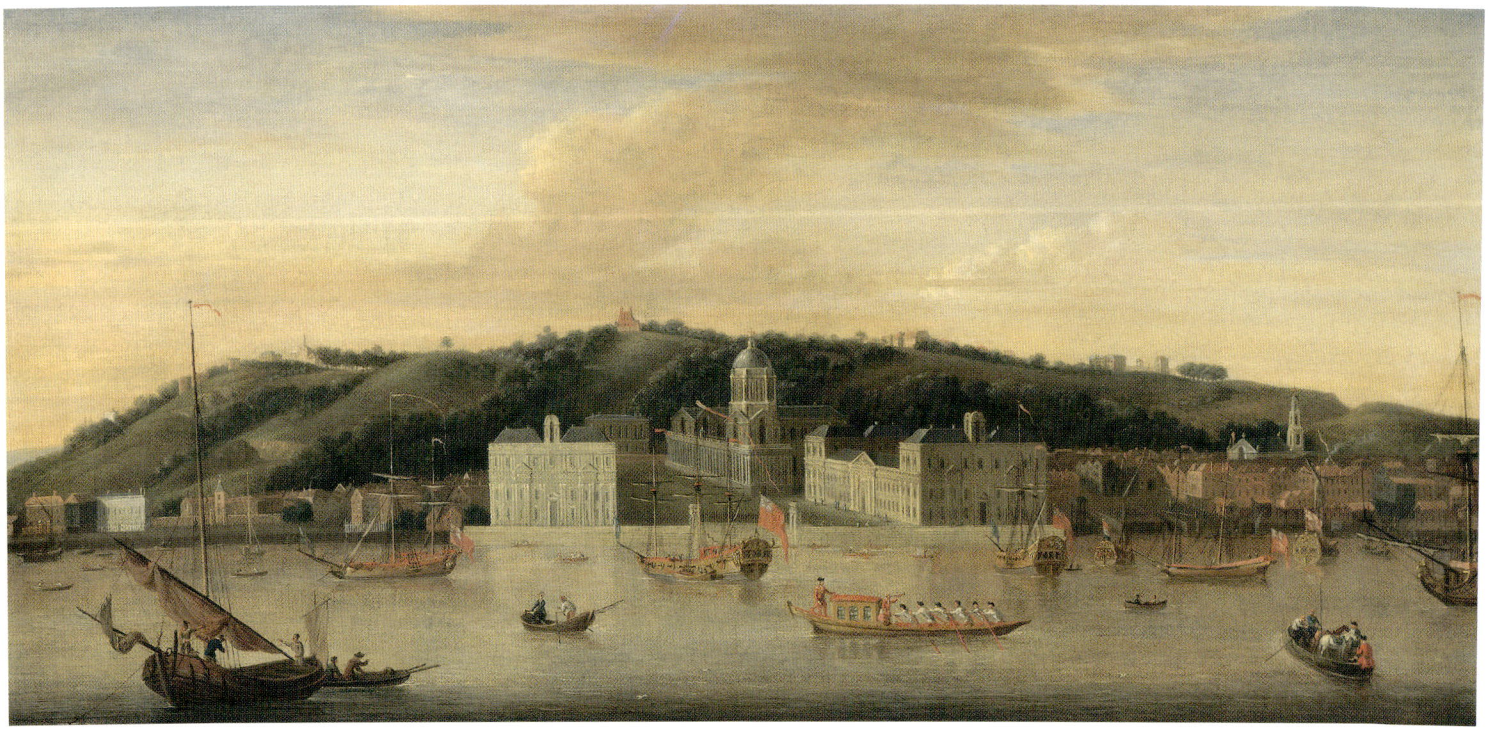

Fig. 26 Jan Griffier the Elder, *A View of Greenwich from the River with Many Boats*, oil on canvas, 1700–10.

executed buccaneer Captain William Kidd in 1706) and including one from John Evelyn himself (£1000), there are several figures of interest: Ralph Thursby (Thoresby), a Yorkshire antiquarian and Fellow of the Royal Society, who possessed a large collection of coins, medals, minerals, fossils and (perhaps significantly, given their prominence in the Hall's fictive decoration) instruments of war and shells;[43] the merchant Sir John Houblon, the first Governor of the Bank of England (established to fund the war effort against Louis XIV) and the successful Whig candidate for the mayoralty of the City of London in 1695; the great merchant financier Sir James Bateman, a City Whig whose recorded donation of £103 is decidedly modest, but who, as we shall see, played a central role in the Painted Hall commission; and Robert Osbolston (Osbaldeston), who at his death in 1715 left to the Hospital £20,000 of property, as well as the dues paid by ships passing his North and South Foreland lighthouses. The partially built Hospital to which he gave so generously can be glimpsed behind him in a posthumous portrait commissioned by the Hospital directors in 1717 (fig. 25). The mechanism for receiving such donations varied, but one instance is documented in the Fabric Committee minutes for August 1699, when 'being informd that Sir Josiah Child has left a legacy to Greenwich Hospital the Solicitor is ordered to attend the executor and desire to know what time he will pay the same'.[44] Moments such as these must have brought Evelyn and his fellow committee members some small respite from ongoing financial difficulties.

Both public and private funding for the Hospital project was, then, piecemeal and inextricably linked with contemporary politics. Work somehow proceeded with the help of the many sixpences and early individual donations such as Godolphin's, and, by April 1700, Wren and Evelyn were in a position to travel to Kensington Palace to present King William with 'the model and several draughts ingraved of the Hospital'. His Majesty, we are told, received the two men with 'greate satisfaction' and encouraged 'the prosecution of the work', although the meeting does not seem to have eased the passage of the thousands owing to the project from the royal purse.[45] By this point, the foundations of all the new blocks in Wren's design had been laid out – a shrewd piece of masterplanning that ensured his overall design was adhered to, even though completion would take five more decades under four different surveyors. The chief craftsmen had also been appointed: Edward Strong (1652–1724), who worked for Wren on other projects, including St Paul's Cathedral and Winchester Palace, and for John Vanbrugh on Blenheim Palace, took the first mason's contract in 1696; he was assisted on subsequent contracts for masonry by his son Edward (1676–1741), who became a close friend of the painter James Thornhill and worked on other prestige commissions, including the City churches and Marlborough House. The contract for bricklaying went to a Richard Billingshurst, while all carved work, external or internal, was awarded to Robert Jones (d. 1722).[46] The success of the project was due in no small part to the long-term commitment of skilled artisans such as Strong and Jones, who were also willing to wait for payment.[47]

By 1700 the King's House had also been remodelled and given a linked base wing in red brick on its western side. Together these comprised the new King Charles block, which can be seen at the centre of a painting of the incomplete Hospital by Jan Griffier the Elder (fig. 26). As at Bethlem Hospital, the new block was designed to evoke 'different but simultaneous appreciations' of magnificence and healthful order: rows of curtained cabins occupied wards that sat beneath a highly ornate stone pediment 30 feet (9 m) wide with carvings by Jones of 'Trophys and ornaments relating to Marine affairs'.[48] The first forty-two resident pensioners arrived in 1705, while building work continued. Throughout the Hospital these wards were given highly political names ('Restoration', 'The Boyne', 'La Hogue' and so on), once again underlining the relationship between the building project and the recent turbulent events that had precipitated it. Opposite King Charles to the east, Edward Strong was preparing the foundations for the new block that was to be named after Queen Mary's sister: the Princess (later Queen) Anne building. But it is to the south-western block – King William – that we now turn, and to the construction and decoration of the Hospital's Hall.

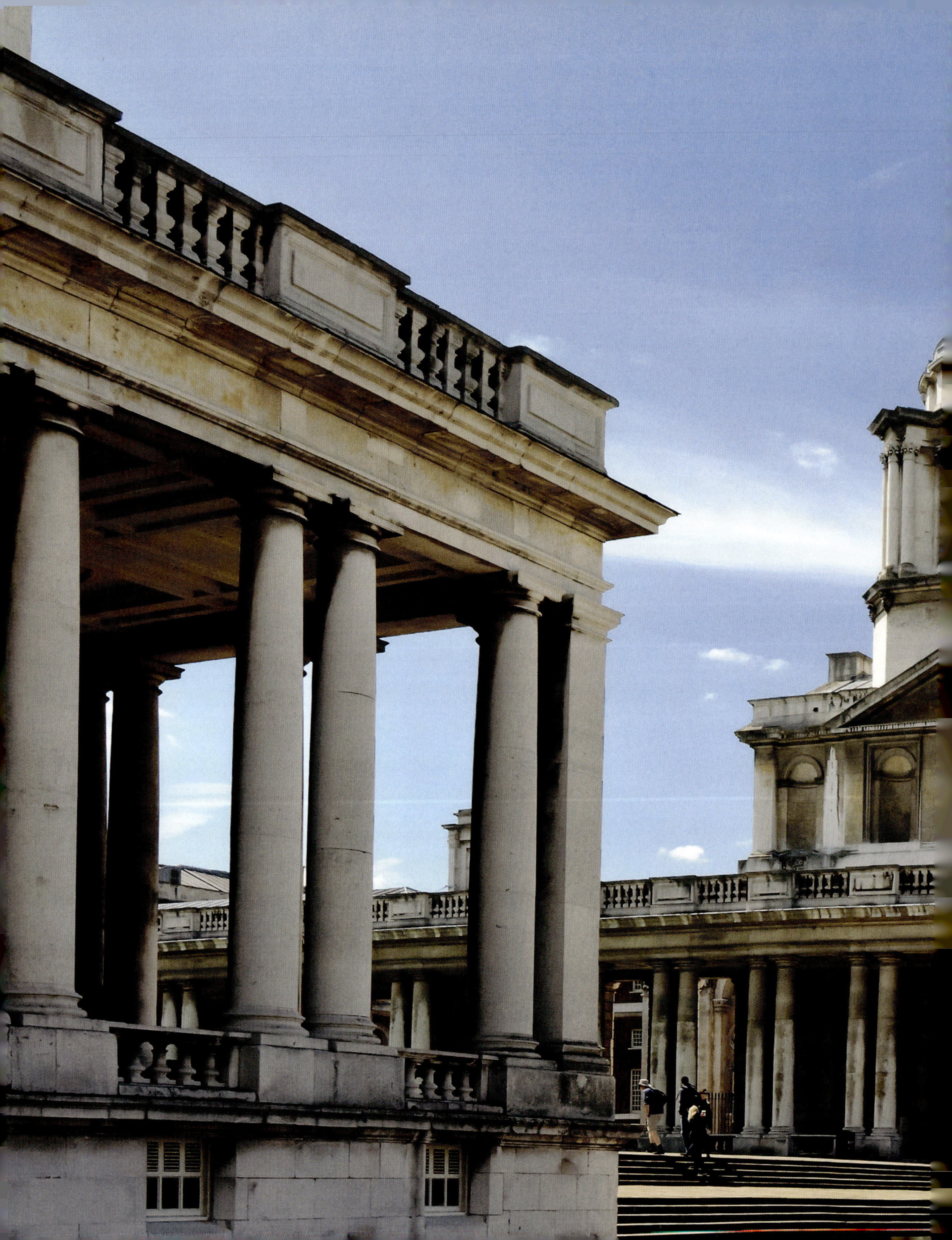

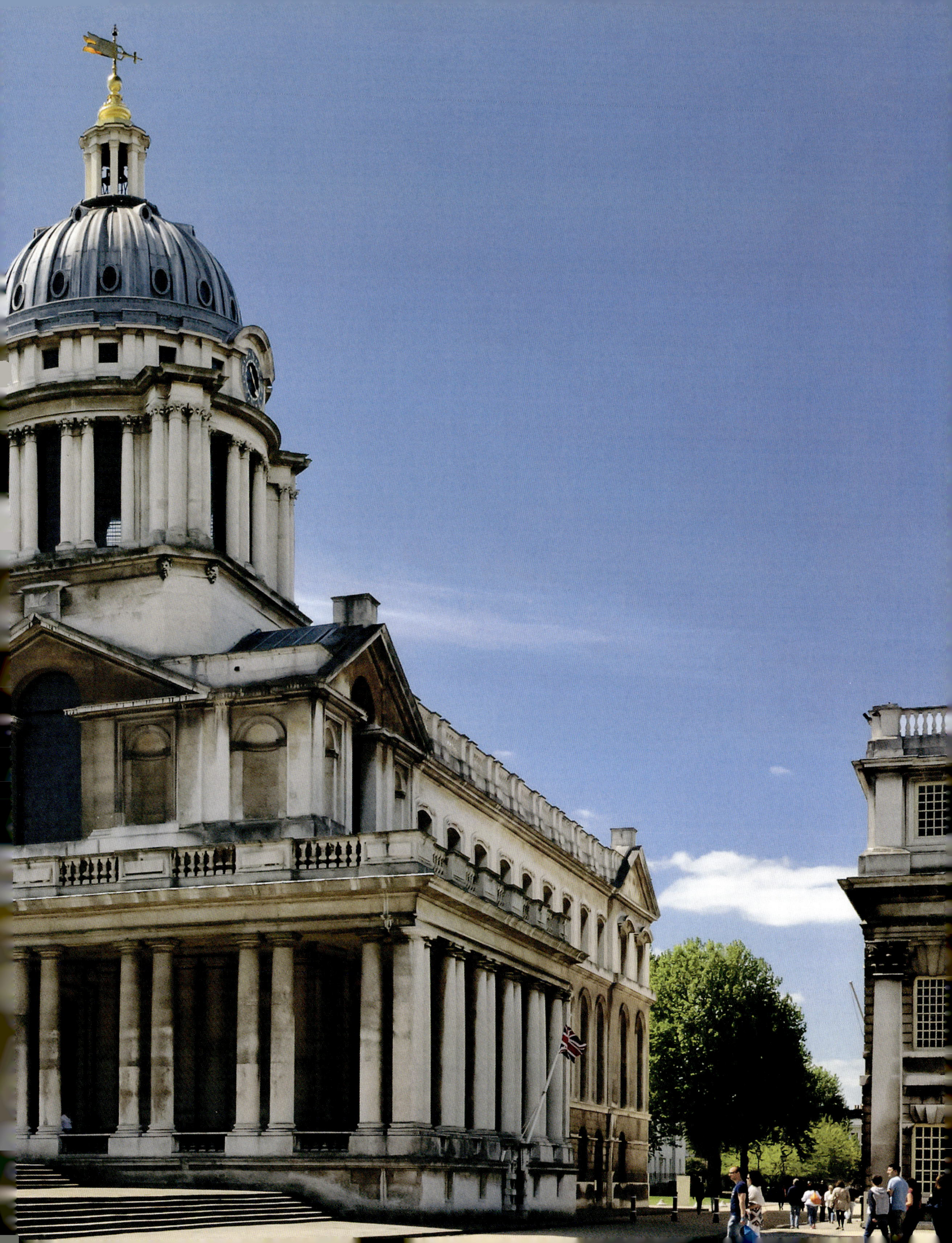

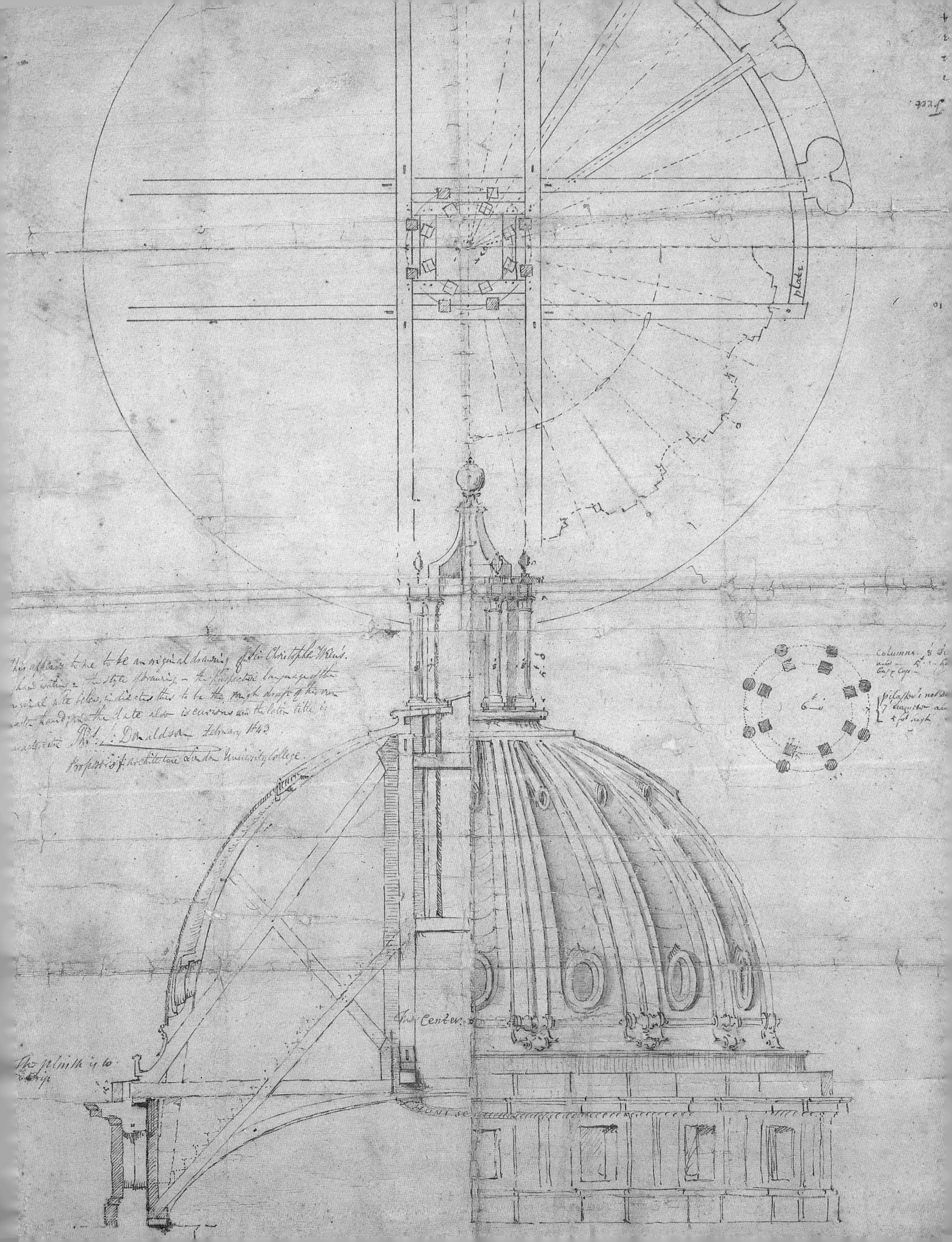

plate
This appears to me to be an original drawing of Sir Christopher Wren's.
J. Donaldson February 1843
Professor of Architecture London University College
The Center
Columns

Beautiful and durable

THE ARCHITECTURE, CONSTRUCTION AND PREPARATION OF THE PAINTED HALL

On 1 February 1698, Wren was formally instructed to prepare 'a draught & estimate of a Hall to be added to the present building, in pursuance of the general design'.[49] By 5 April, the Surveyor had obliged, and drawings had been presented to and approved by the Fabric Committee. In May, Hawksmoor was in a position to inform members that 'he had set out the ground for the Hall'.[50] The Hall in question was the domed structure forming the northern wing of the King William block, intended for a dining room, albeit for ceremonial occasions. This is the building pictured on the right-hand side of the 1699 perspective view (fig. 19) and visible in another view of the incomplete Hospital, painted by Jan Griffier the Elder in about 1705 (fig. 29).

Between the February and April 1698 meetings of the Fabric Committee, Hawksmoor began preparing the 'draughts' requested for the new Hall structure. A surviving pen-and-wash drawing for the north elevation of this date in Hawksmoor's hand sheds light on the evolution of the design (fig. 30). Hawksmoor begins to develop a much grander Hall than had been envisaged as part of the approved outline scheme; elaborate alternatives for the dome, front portico and steps are presented by means of several pasted overlays, which, Gordon Higgott suggests, were added to the sheet in 1699.[51] The overlaid elements replace a single flight of steps on the Hall's north side with a perron (a platform landing reached by two symmetrical flights), and present the option of a grander projecting portico of giant-order Composite columns. There is also a square overlay showing an option for a smaller dome: as Higgott suggests, Hawksmoor may have been experimenting with exaggerated recession to create increased drama. Through a series of amendments Hawksmoor takes the Hall design towards ever-greater magnificence, just as the overall masterplan had been. Given that this was to be the chief public space within the overall complex, it is unsurprising that he took a year to interrogate the design possibilities for its principal elevations and entrance. That the drawing is dignified with an inscription in Latin is also unsurprising. As his *Remarks* would later show, Hawksmoor understood Greenwich Hospital as part of an architectural tradition stretching back to antiquity. For him, this

Fig. 27 (*pages 34–35*) The colonnade and dome of the King William building.
Fig. 28 (*opposite*) Nicholas Hawksmoor, design for the dome (plan and elevation) of the Great Hall, *c.* 1700–1702.

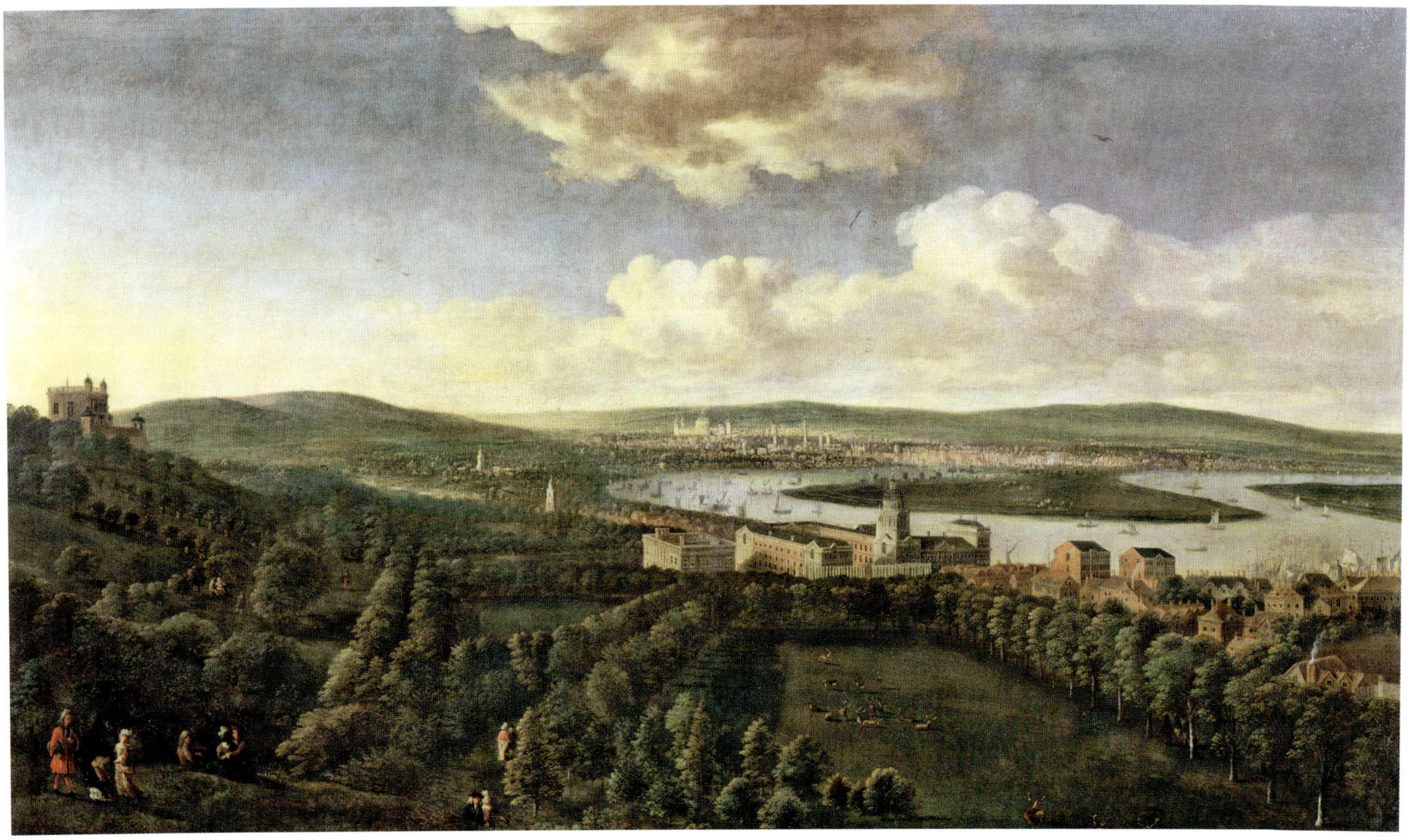

Fig. 29 Jan Griffier the Elder, *A Panorama of Greenwich and the River Thames*, oil on canvas, detail showing the incomplete Greenwich Hospital as construction of the domed Great Hall of the King William block was completed, *c.* 1705.

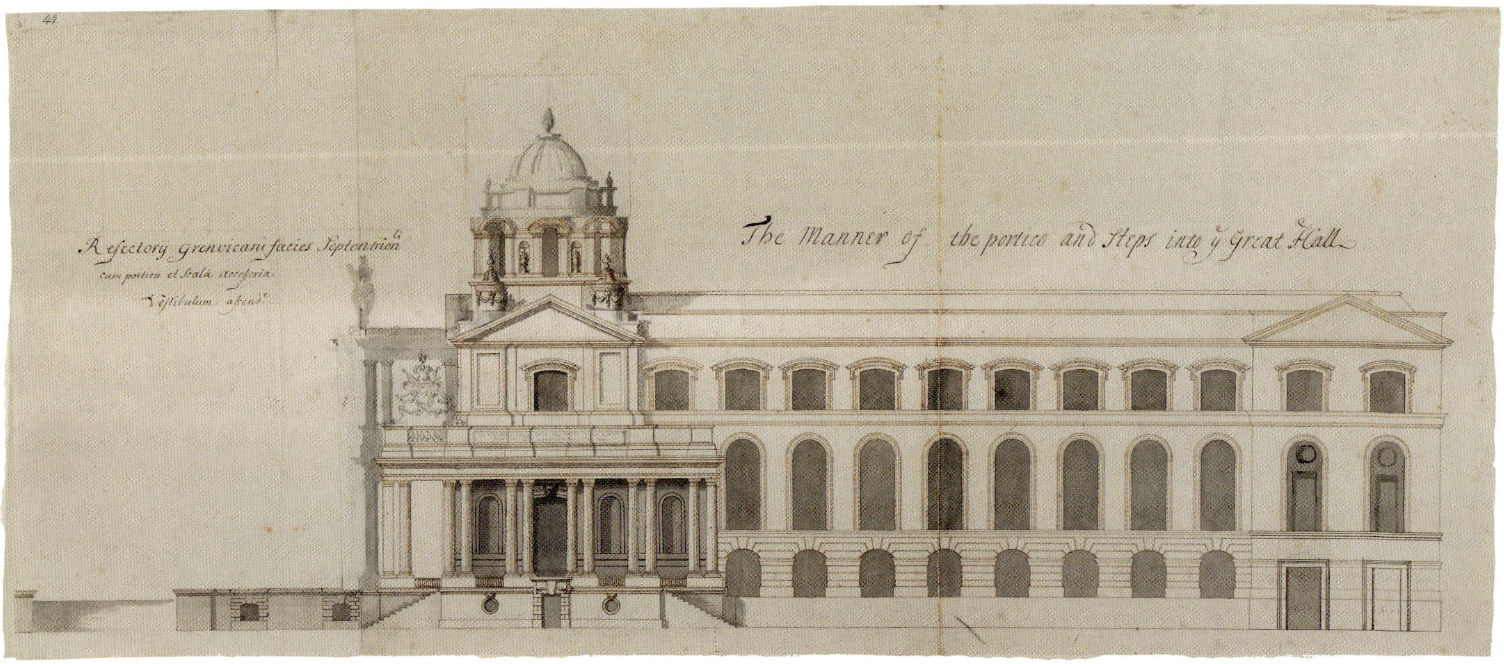

Fig. 30 Nicholas Hawksmoor, design for the Great Hall, 1698, incorporating revisions (probably 1699) for the dome, front portico and steps.

new structure, known to us today as the Painted Hall, was the 'Refectory Grenvicani'.

A second drawing, for the dome alone, also in Hawksmoor's hand, survives in the collection of the Royal Institute of British Architects (RIBA; fig. 28). As in the case of the Hall as a whole, designs for the dome became progressively more complex; the executed version is loftier and more elaborate than the diminutive cupola appended experimentally to the north elevation drawing. The RIBA drawing shows the dome almost as it stands and reveals the debt owed to Jules Hardouin-Mansart's Hôtel des Invalides, a building whose importance as a precedent for Greenwich Hospital cannot be overstated. However, Hawksmoor takes Mansart's dome a step further by using more sophisticated geometry. As John Bold has argued, small adjustments to the arrangement of the clustered Composite columns quartering the tambour bring a greater sense of movement and recession at Greenwich than in the Parisian prototype. Beneath the dome, Bold attributes the success of the executed Hall design to a 'sense of contained movement' and to the subtle interplay of triangular and segmental elements (fig. 27).[52]

Following the approval of designs for the Hall, attention turned to the sourcing of materials and to the appointment of craftsmen. In the summer of 1698 the Fabric Committee debated whether both the north and south elevations should be stone-clad and asked for an estimate from Wren.[53] Defective stone from the Portland quarries had begun to hamper progress on construction of the Hospital (as it had, too, at St Paul's Cathedral). Hawksmoor sourced alternatives by ordering parcels of stone from Ketton in Rutland and Roche Abbey in Yorkshire ('500 tuns' of each) in the spring of 1700.[54] In the event, only the Hall's north elevation was stone-clad. The south side, towards the great court, was left as brick with stone dressings, but not before Robert Jones had carved a series of fleshy but arrestingly beautiful stone heads to adorn the middle and upper windows of the Hall's two sides as they had originally been conceived. The accounts show that Jones submitted bills for sixteen lions' heads in 1700 and, appropriately for the maritime context, thirty-eight heads of Neptune, Galatea (a sea nymph who appears in Ovid's *Metamorphoses*) and tritons in

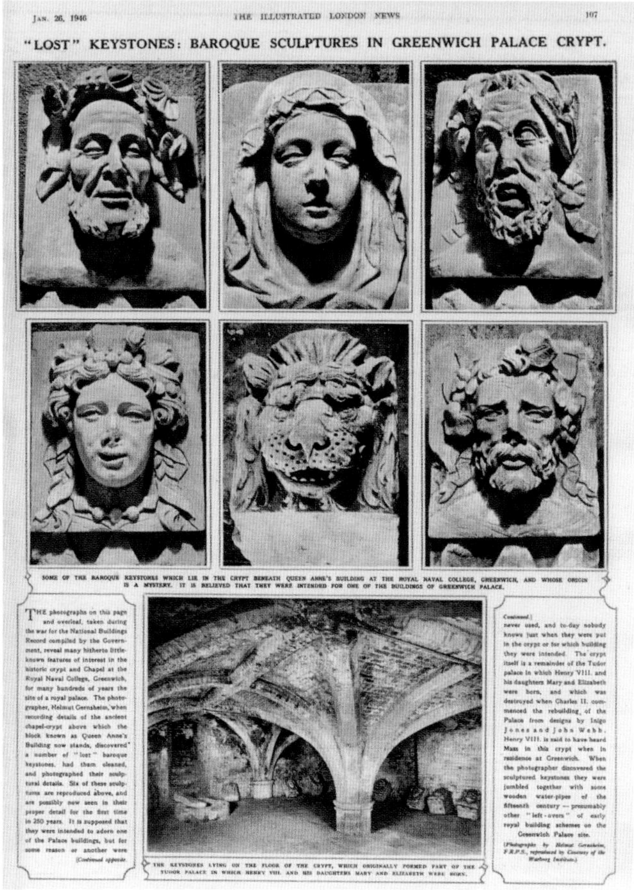
Jan. 26, 1946 THE ILLUSTRATED LONDON NEWS 107

"LOST" KEYSTONES: BAROQUE SCULPTURES IN GREENWICH PALACE CRYPT.

SOME OF THE BAROQUE KEYSTONES WHICH LIE IN THE CRYPT BENEATH QUEEN ANNE'S BUILDING AT THE ROYAL NAVAL COLLEGE, GREENWICH, AND WHOSE ORIGIN IS A MYSTERY. IT IS BELIEVED THAT THEY WERE INTENDED FOR ONE OF THE BUILDINGS OF GREENWICH PALACE.

THE photographs on this page and overleaf, taken during the war for the National Buildings Record compiled by the Government, reveal many hitherto little-known features of interest in the historic crypt and Chapel at the Royal Naval College, Greenwich, for many hundreds of years the site of a royal palace. The photographer, Helmut Gernsheim, when recording details of the ancient chapel-crypt above which the block known as Queen Anne's Building now stands, discovered a number of "lost" baroque keystones, had them cleaned, and photographed their sculptural details. Six of these sculptures are reproduced above, and are possibly now seen in their proper detail for the first time in 250 years. It is supposed that they were intended to adorn one of the Palace buildings, but for some reason or another were [Continued opposite.

Continued.] never used, and to-day nobody knows just when they were put in the crypt or for which building they were intended. The crypt itself is a remainder of the Tudor palace in which Henry VIII. and his daughters Mary and Elizabeth were born, and which was destroyed when Charles II. commenced the rebuilding of the Palace from designs by Inigo Jones and John Webb. Henry VIII. is said to have heard Mass in this crypt when in residence at Greenwich. When the photographer discovered the sculptured keystones they were jumbled together with some wooden water-pipes of the fifteenth century — presumably other "left-overs" of early royal building schemes on the Greenwich Palace site.

[Photographs by Helmut Gernsheim, F.R.P.S., reproduced by Courtesy of the Warburg Institute.]

THE KEYSTONES LYING ON THE FLOOR OF THE CRYPT, WHICH ORIGINALLY FORMED PART OF THE TUDOR PALACE IN WHICH HENRY VIII. AND HIS DAUGHTERS MARY AND ELIZABETH WERE BORN.

Fig. 31 Carvings by Robert Jones, featured in an article in the *Illustrated London News*, 26 January 1946.

1704.[55] Jones's now superfluous carvings were stored in the undercroft of the Queen Anne building and forgotten about until the Second World War, when they were photographed by Helmut Gernsheim for the Warburg Institute and then published in an *Illustrated London News* article in January 1946, '"Lost" Keystones: Baroque Sculptures in Greenwich Palace Crypt' (fig. 31).[56] Robert Jones discovered, as John Webb had before him, that this Greenwich building site could dispose of proposals just as easily as it invited them.

An agreement was made with James Grove the carpenter for the 'floor and roofe of the New west Hall' in 1699,[57] and he was in a position to start work by summer 1700, when the masonry of the main walls was complete. His chief task was to erect the nineteen 58-foot-long (18 m) trusses that form the roof structure. Edward Strong, meanwhile, began work on the masonry drum that supports the dome. The dome was completed and covered with ribs of lead in September 1703 and topped with a copper vase and ball in 1704;

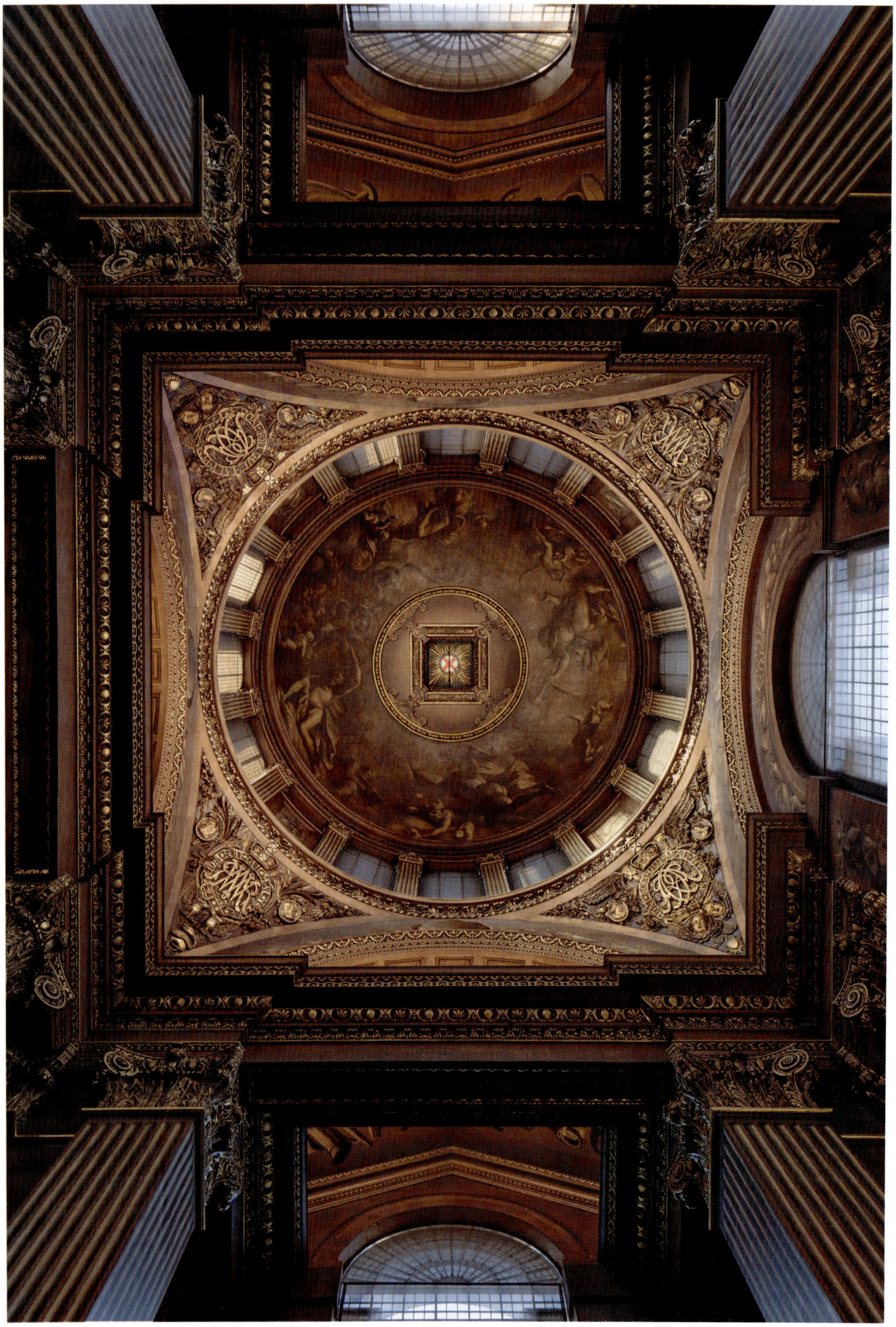

Fig. 32 (*above*) View looking upwards into the interior of the Vestibule dome.
Fig. 33 (*opposite*) View from the Vestibule into the Lower Hall, with the proscenium arch and Upper Hall beyond.

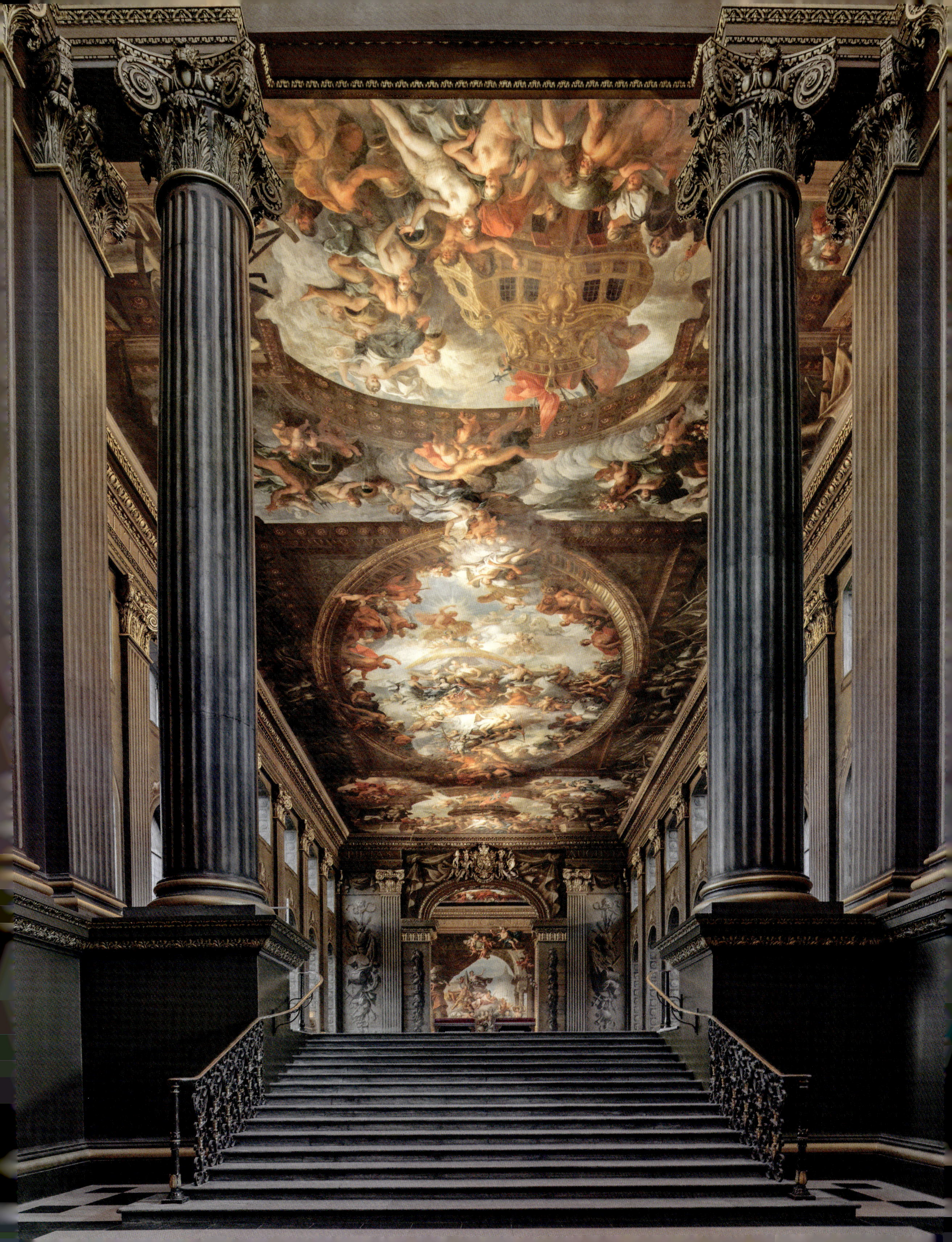

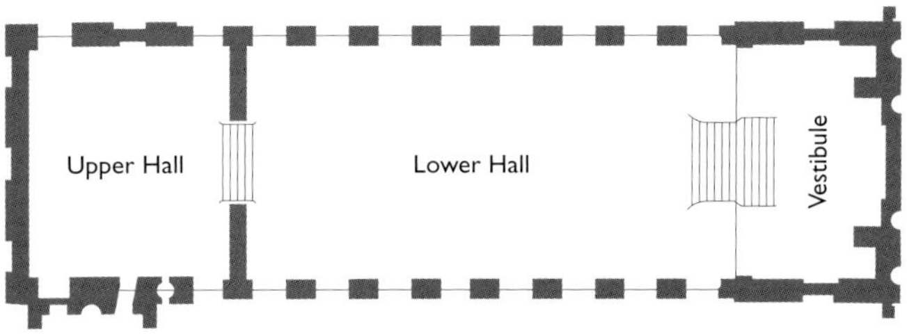

Fig. 34 Plan of the Painted Hall, comprising Vestibule, Lower Hall and Upper Hall.

this arrangement was replaced with a smaller, lighter weather vane in 1726.[58] Robert Jones was responsible for the architraves and other ornament (including the tritons' heads that nestle beneath the projecting clusters of columns quartering the drum).[59] By 1703 the Hall structure was complete and covered, however, and it was at this stage that Jones's skills were diverted to the interior carving.

The Hall as built comprises three distinct spaces, all 50 feet (15 m) wide but of differing height and length (fig. 34). On entering at the great east doors from the colonnade,[60] one first encounters the Vestibule, which soars 90 feet (27 m) to the building's inner saucer dome. This is supported by a drum of sixteen gilded pilasters lit by twelve windows, beneath which the carved and gilded ciphers of William and Mary or of Queen Anne are set within four triangular pendentives (fig. 32). A flight of steps and giant screen of Composite columns leads to the Lower Hall, the length of which roughly corresponds to the height of the Vestibule. Giant Composite pilasters with gilded capitals divide the room into eight bays on each side (fig. 33). These are heightened with fictive fluting and gilding, and support an enriched and heavily gilded entablature some 40 feet (12 m) above the floor. At the west end of the Lower Hall, six steps raise the viewer once again, this time through a proscenium-type arch (with carved and gilded signs of the zodiac on its underside) to the smaller Upper Hall – a near cube measuring 50 feet wide, 45 feet deep and 42 feet high (15 × 14 × 13 m; fig. 37). An absence of columns and pilasters in this space, as well as fewer windows, leaves the wall surfaces clear for painted decoration; this replicates the Hall's real architecture in fictive form. *Trompe l'œil* columns frame the Hall's west wall, just as real ones introduce the Lower Hall earlier in the sequence (fig. 36). The use of the Composite order for both the solid and painted columns is essential to the overall illusion; the eye is confounded and rendered more suggestible. As we shall see, this sophisticated ensemble was the work of a skilled decorative painter who himself produced competent architectural designs and enjoyed a close professional relationship with Nicholas Hawksmoor; an artist who regarded the planes of a building not merely as fields on which to paint, but as active agents in the construction of grand-scale historical and allegorical narratives.

The Hall's capitals and carved entablature (fig. 35) are ornamented with carefully chosen mouldings and motifs; some derive from classical structures known to Hawksmoor and his chief workmen from engravings in Renaissance architectural treatises.[61] The main Composite capitals (see fig. 33), which are fluted above the line of their curling acanthus leaves, derive from the Porta Leoni in Verona. An engraving of this ancient and noble structure was available to Hawksmoor in the third book, published in 1540, of Sebastiano Serlio's highly influential *Tutte l'opere d'architettura et prospetiva*.[62] Unlike the Roman prototype, the Greenwich capitals have painted rather than carved fluting. The decision to paint this element no doubt made the carver's job easier and cheaper, but it was also part of the conscious effort to blur boundaries between the Hall's real and fictive architecture.

The wooden entablature that these capitals support contains a frieze painted with a Latin inscription honouring William and Mary's role in the founding of the Hospital. Translated, it reads:

By Royal piety, under the auspices of Mary, the Palace of Greenwich is dedicated to seamen needing help, so that they may dwell securely and be publicly maintained, who have watched over the public security, in the reign of William and Mary, 1694.[63]

There are further references to classical antiquity for the entablature of the 'Refectory Grenvicani', too. The curious arch-headed motif in the cornice was commonly found on Roman triumphal arches. A specific example was available to the designer of the Greenwich entablature in the fourth book of Andrea Palladio's *I quattro libri dell'architettura* (1570): an illustration of the portico of the Temple of

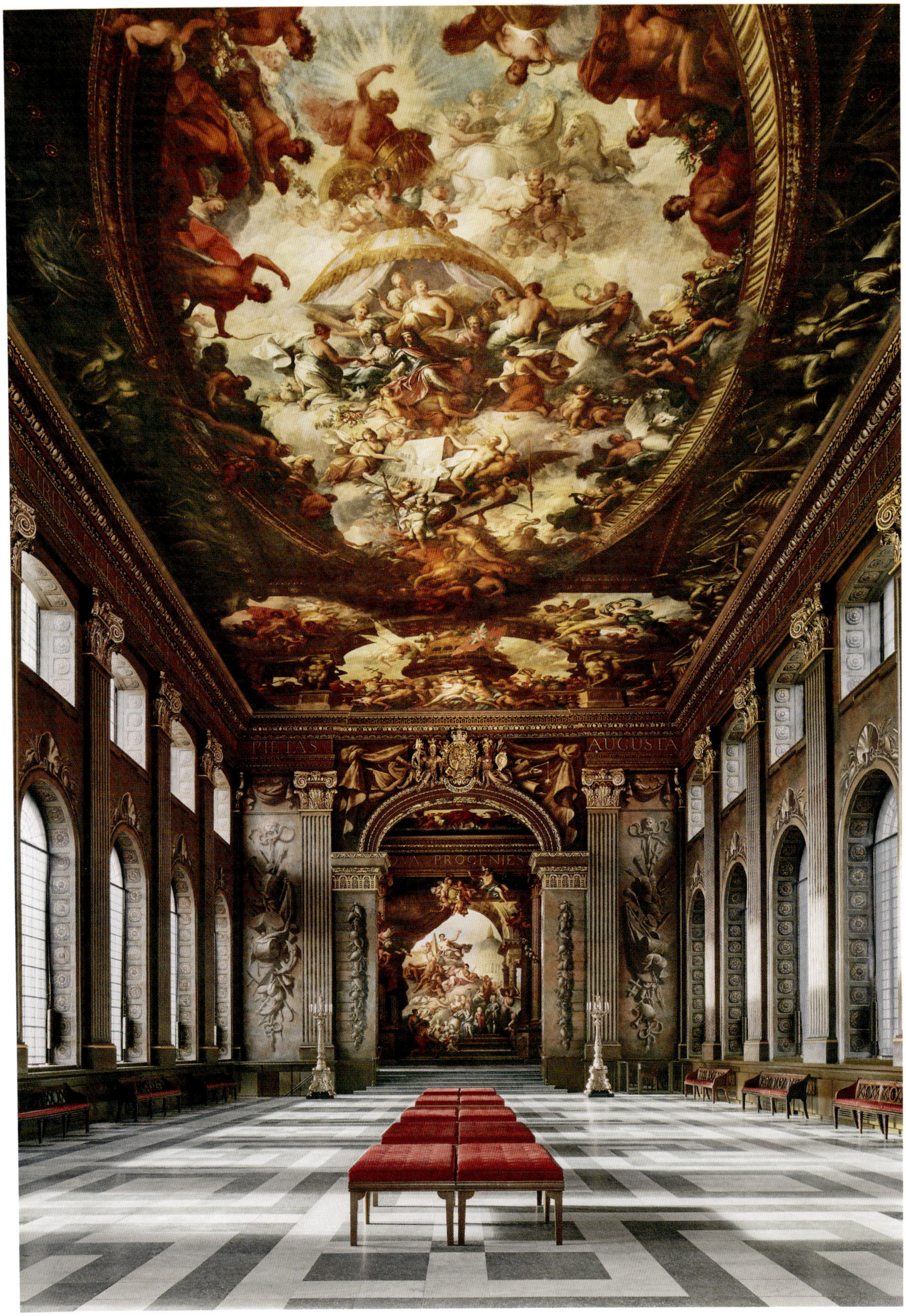

Fig. 35 View of the pilasters and entablature in the Lower Hall.
Fig. 36 (*overleaf*) The west wall of the Upper Hall, framed by fictive Composite columns.
Fig. 37 (*pages 46–47*) View from the Upper Hall into the Lower Hall, with the Vestibule beyond.

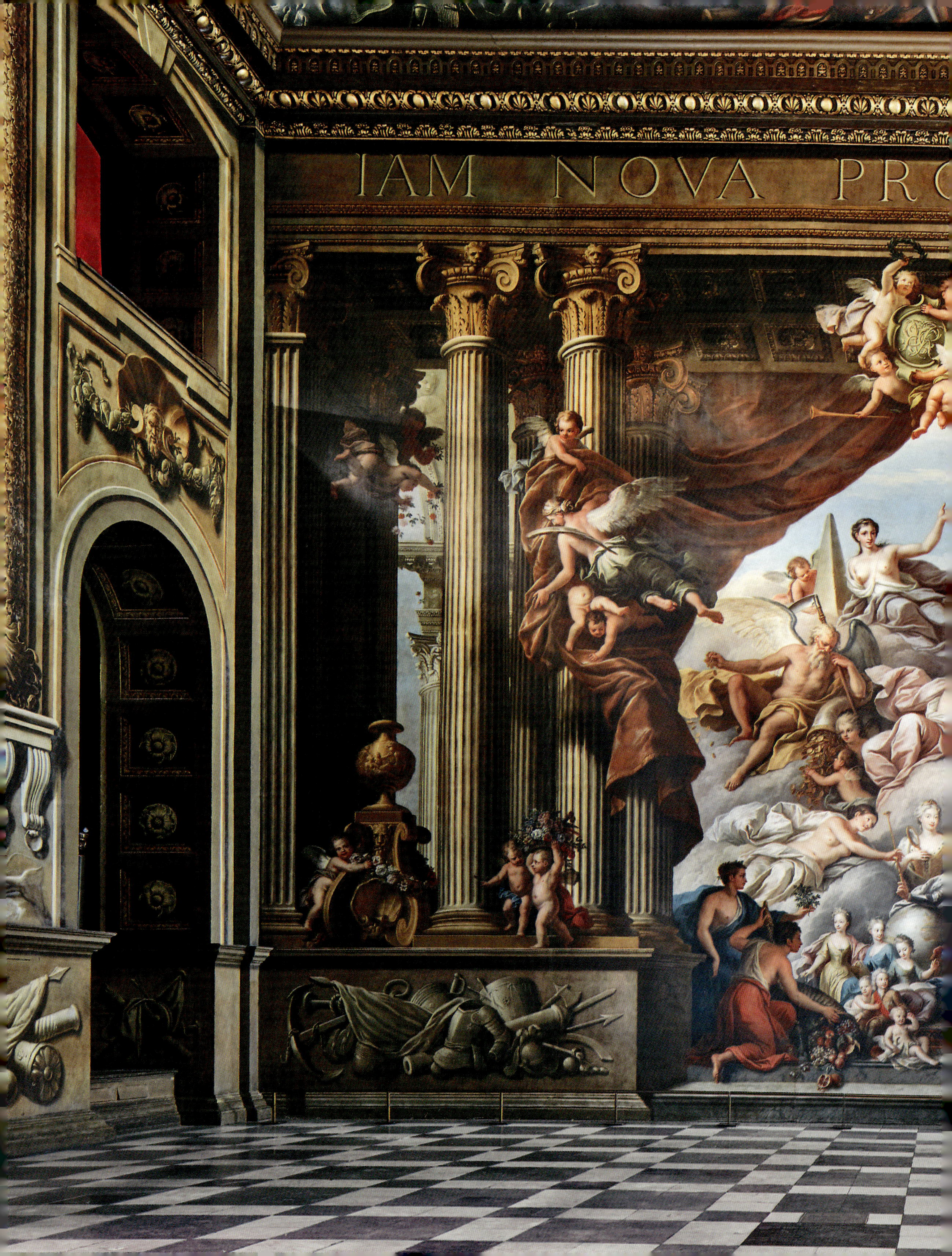
IAM NOVA PRO

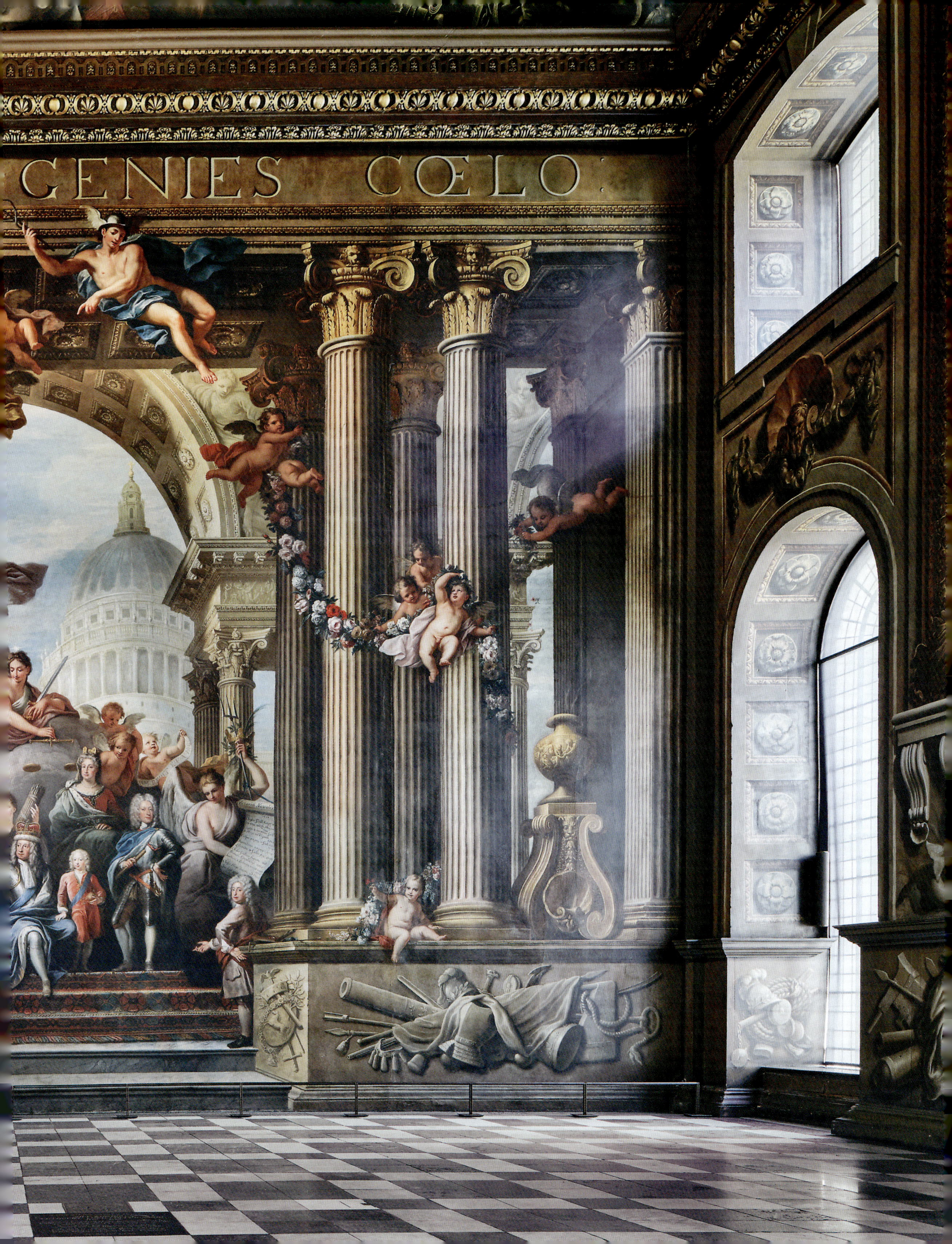
GENIES COELO

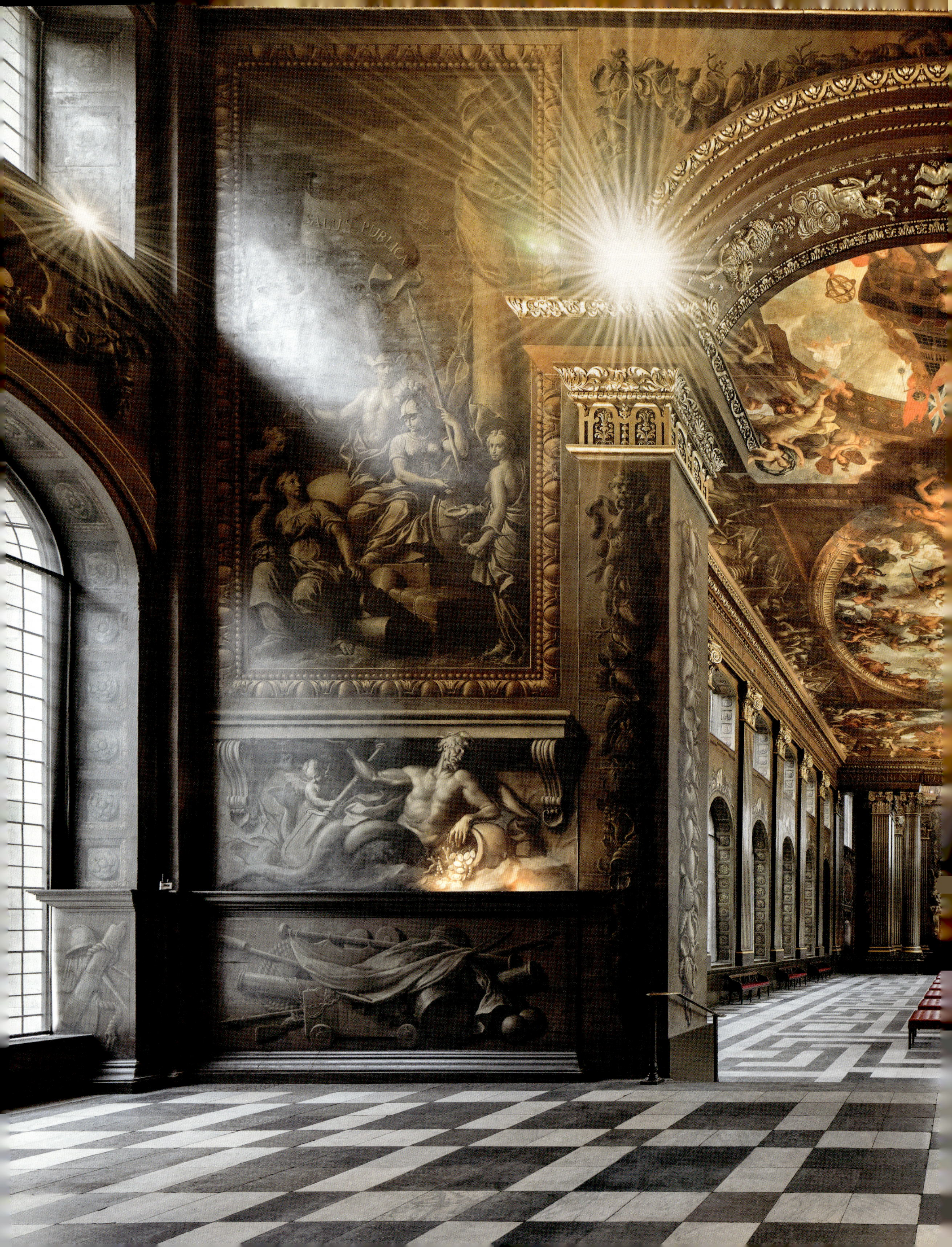
SALUS PUBLICA

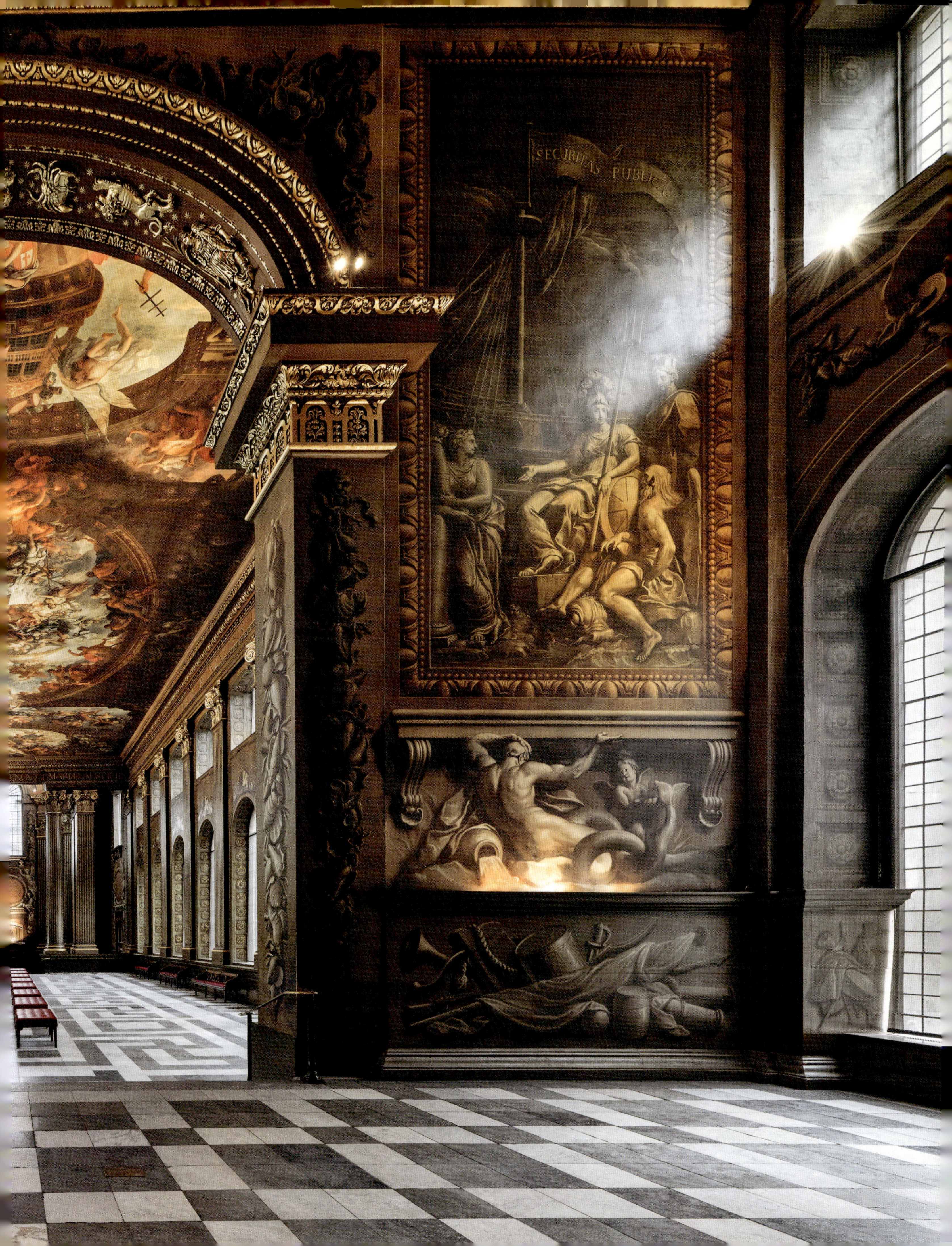
SECURITAS PUBLICA

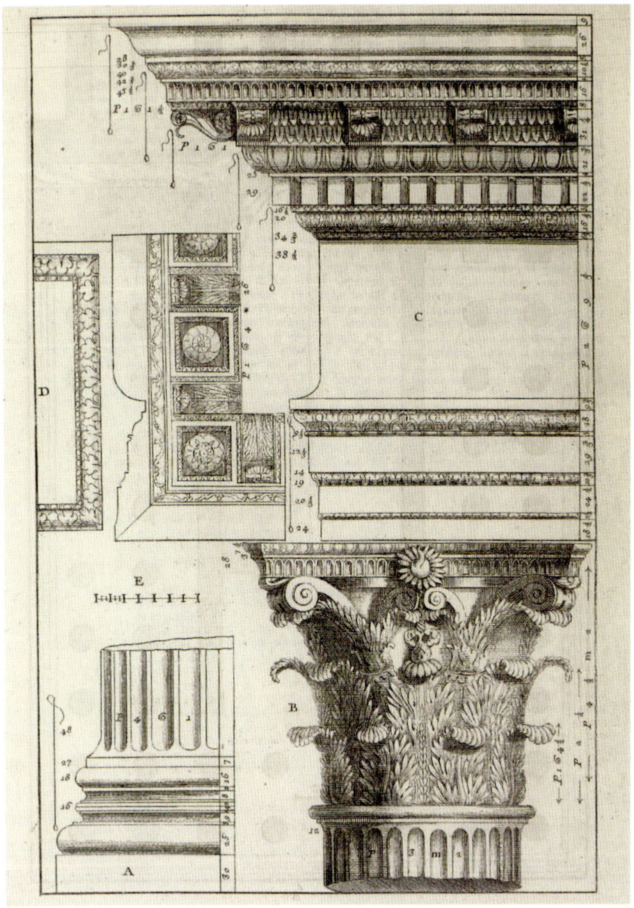

Fig. 38 Andrea Palladio, details of the portico of the Temple of Jupiter the Thunderer in Rome, including the arch-headed moulding adapted for the Hall at Greenwich. From Book IV of *I quattro libri dell'architettura*, first published 1570.

Jupiter the Thunderer, which stood at the foot of the Capitoline Hill.[64] In his commentary, Palladio praises the temple's ornaments, 'exquisitely cut with beautiful carvings' (fig. 38). The Greenwich moulding has not been lifted from this classical source without adaptation: the arches have been spaced out with horizontal linking elements and filled with foliate motifs. Maritime elements are also introduced in the entablature, as they are in almost every area of the Hospital's decorative programme: scallop shells playfully usurp some of the ovolos in the egg-and-dart moulding (see fig. 39).

The rejection of the decorative carving planned for the Hall's exterior elevations makes this lavish interior ornament all the more striking. The building's relative exterior restraint would certainly have pleased the architect of the neighbouring Queen's House. Inigo Jones advocated a clear distinction in the decorative treatment of exterior and interior in a now famous passage from his Italian sketchbook of 1615:

and to saie trew all thes composed ornamentes, the w[hi]ch proceed out of ye aboundance of dessignes and wear brought in by Michill Angell and his followers in my oppignion do not well in sollid Architecture and ye facciati of houses ... for as outwar[d]ly every wyse ma[n] carrieth a graviti in Publicke Places, whear ther is nothing els looked for. & yt inwardly hath his Immaginacy set free, and sometimes liccenciously flying out ...[65]

In precisely the manner described by Jones, the Hospital's solid and weighty architecture starts to dissolve inside the Hall and, with the assistance of painting, to become part of a game of imagination and illusion.

Heraldic and other informative carving also assists the interior decorative programme. The Vestibule's deep pendentive carvings of the royal ciphers of William, Mary and Anne are complemented by a large royal coat of arms over the proscenium leading to the Upper Hall. These are the arms of William and Mary supported by the seated figures of Mars, god of war, and Pallas Athene (aka Minerva), goddess of war and wisdom (fig. 39). Again, the carving was by Robert Jones, who submitted a bill of £70 for the work in December 1707.[66]

It is very easy to be dazzled by carved, gilded and painted surfaces without giving thought to the craft processes that made the Hall fit to receive such elaborate decoration. As the title of this section reminds us,[67] for Hawksmoor and Wren, durability and strength were attributes as important to a building's success as beauty and regularity (hence the preoccupation with inferior materials and the former's endeavours to source the best stone, bricks and lime). Plaster, an often-overlooked element of a building project, performs a particularly vital role here as the substrate or support for the Hall's complex painted scheme. As Geoffrey Beard has remarked: 'Plasterwork is anonymous stuff, rarely signed, and few plasterers' names appear in the conventional, or unconventional, literature of art history about it. Thus the attribution of plasterwork to particular dates and craftsmen is a more than usually hazardous task.'[68]

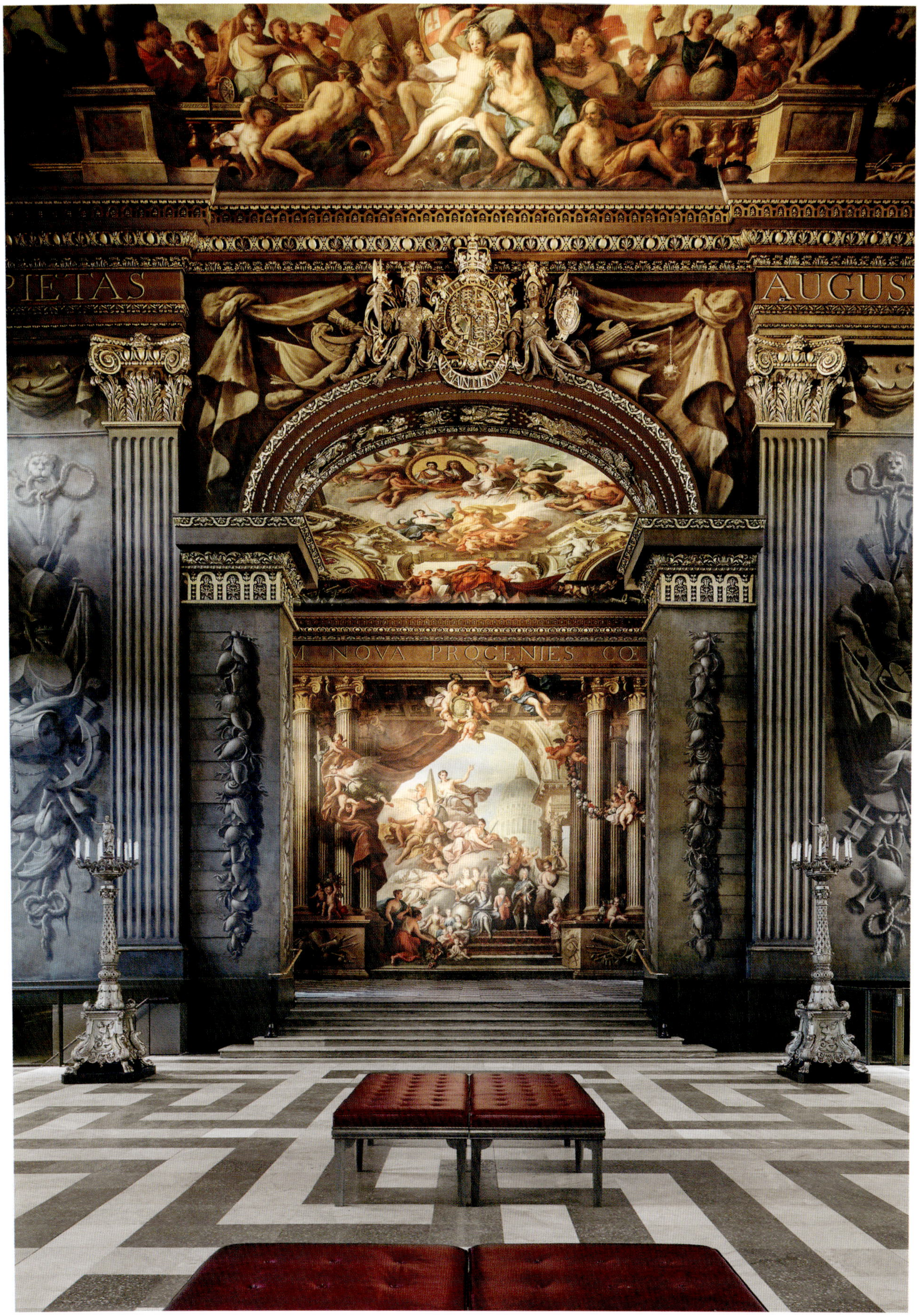

Fig. 39 View looking west through the proscenium arch to the Upper Hall, with the carved royal coat of arms by Robert Jones above.

At Greenwich, however, the names do survive. Alongside the initial 1696 contracts with Edward Strong, James Grove, Roger Davis and Robert Jones for masonry, carpentry, joinery and carving, we also find agreements with the plasterer Henry Doogood (later succeeded by Robert Weatherill and James Ellis) and with Richard Woods and Thomas Steers for the provision of lime and sand (the key components of the type of plasterwork found at Greenwich). Doogood's business partner was John Grove, brother of the carpenter James, and it is worth noting that these craftsmen had worked together in various combinations on a number of other high-status projects. The first agreement with Doogood at Greenwich was on 14 August 1696, and his first involvement with the Hall came in June 1704, when he was awarded the contract for plastering the cupola (at rates agreed for other areas of the site).[69] Two months later, the Fabric Committee ordered that a notice be placed in the *London Gazette* 'for Plasterers to offer their proposals for the work of the Great Hall' (i.e. the walls and ceiling), with Hawksmoor instructed to provide all those tendering with 'a Scheme of the parts of the same to be performed when they come to view'.[70] Henry Doogood, along with others, submitted his proposition, and in the following summer it was resolved that 'the Great Hall be finished as follows: the finishing of the Walls To be with shell lime after the best manner and the Ceiling after the best manner fit for painting, with kid's hair, well trowelled and floted and that it be performed by Mr Doogood.'[71]

Doogood's rate was agreed at 2*s*. 4*d*. per yard for plastering the ceiling and 2*s*. 6*d*. for 'finishing the walls with hard stone lime and sharp sand'. Hawksmoor was requested to enquire about rates for the hire of scaffolding.[72] An illustration of the tools of the plasterer's trade from Joseph Moxon's *Mechanick Exercises* of 1703 – including a laying trowel, a setting trowel, wooden floats for flatwork and mouldings, 'streight rules', a pocket for lathing nails, and a bucket for water or whitewash – gives us some sense of what Doogood's labours entailed (fig. 40).

The Fabric Committee could not have picked a better craftsman for the job. Doogood, born in 1644, was from a prominent family of London plasterers.

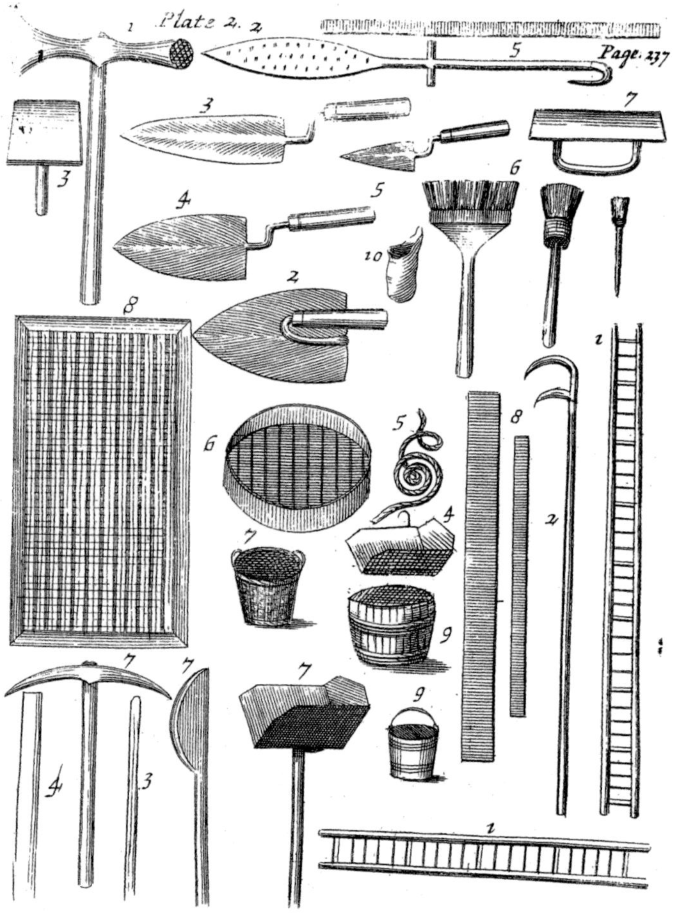

Fig. 40 Plasterer's tools, as shown in Joseph Moxon's *Mechanick Exercises*, published 1703.

With his business partner, John Grove, he had worked for Wren on the library at Trinity College, Cambridge, and executed a particularly fine plaster ceiling at the church of King Charles the Martyr in Tunbridge Wells, Kent, in 1679–90. But it was in London that Doogood rose to prominence. He and Grove worked on forty-three City churches for Wren after the Great Fire of 1666. This work included the spectacular 'fretted' fan vault of St Mary Aldermary (1679–82), a very different skill indeed from the seamless flatwork of the Hall at Greenwich. Doogood also worked at St Paul's Cathedral from 1687 and became Master of the Plaisterers' Company in 1700.[73]

The lime plasterwork provided by Doogood for the Hall's interior is composed of two coats applied to a lath-and-timber-framed support (see fig. 11 on p. 116). Elsewhere the substrate is stone or brick. Lime plaster is made by burning stone in a kiln at great heat; it is then slaked with water, and the resulting putty is cut with sand and sometimes seashells. The making of lime plaster had preoccupied architectural treatise writers since antiquity, and indeed it was a matter of interest to Wren, who had particular requirements about the kind of strengthening aggregate that should be used (washed river sand) and the kind of lime (stone lime from Maidstone in Kent, rather than chalk lime). The Office of Works lime kilns had moved to Deptford in the seventeenth century, a relocation that was convenient for the Greenwich Hospital project.[74]

The lime plaster is applied in 1-inch-thick (2.5 cm) coats, with several days allowed between each coat for shrinkage and strengthening. Careful tending is required to ensure that the plaster does not set too fast and crack. Most importantly for the Greenwich project, painting on lime plaster is not possible for at least a year. Cattle hair was often used as a strengthening binder, but, in high-status projects, shorter and finer goat or kids' hair was employed (as stipulated in Doogood's contract). The lime plaster is applied to laths, which are affixed by the plasterer to a timber structure provided by the carpenter. The laths are flat strips of wood typically measuring 1 inch wide and around 48 inches (122 cm) long. The woods used were typically oak (as at Greenwich, where Doogood supplied finest heart-of-oak laths), sweet chestnut, white pine or beech. The two layers comprised a render or pricking-up coat, and a floating or setting coat. The first layer created a key by seeping between the wooden laths, while smooth perfection was the goal with the second (or sometimes even third) coat, which was formulated with much finer, softer sands and the finest, shortest hair.[75]

Two years after his agreement for plastering the Hall, Henry Doogood was dead and Robert Weatherill applied to be employed in his place for plastering work in other parts of the King William block. Doogood had completed his work to the highest possible standard, however, and the Hall's interior plasterwork had dried and set hard. Hawksmoor was now ordered to erect scaffolding once again, this time 'for the painter to proceed upon primeing'.[76] It was at this stage that the attention of the Hospital directors turned to the question of what would be applied to the fine plaster surfaces supplied by Doogood, and that the name of James Thornhill, Painter-Stainer, first appears in Hospital records.

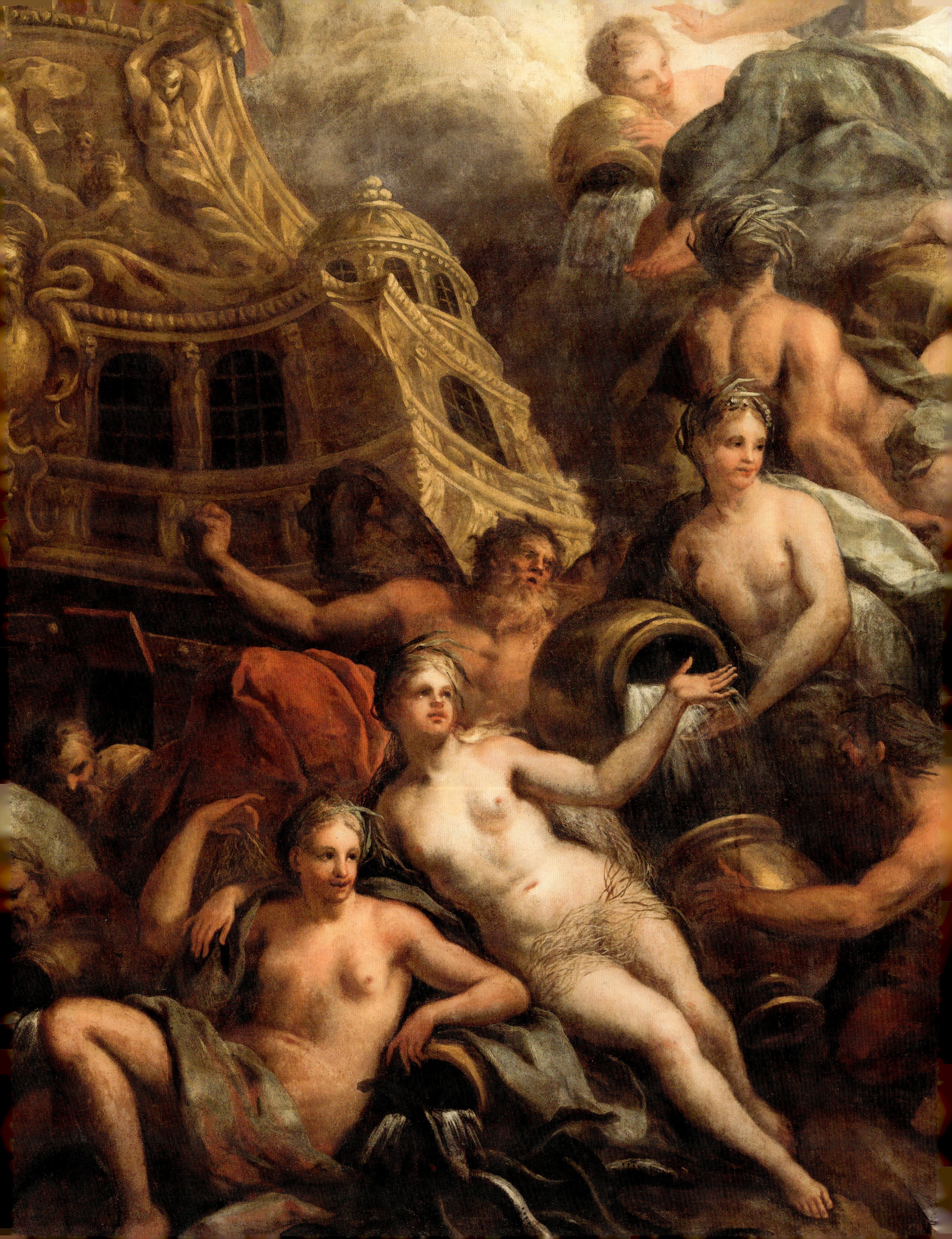

An Historical Painter, Native of our own Soyl

SIR JAMES THORNHILL AND THE PAINTED HALL COMMISSION

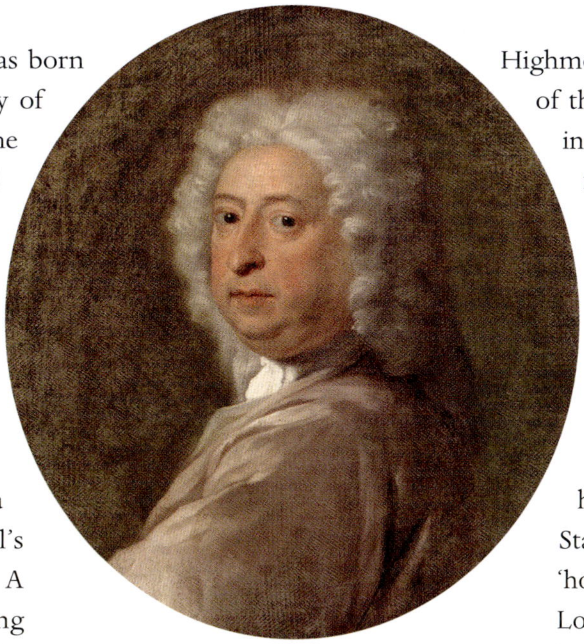

Fig. 42 Dietrich Ernst Andreae (attr.), *Sir James Thornhill*, oil on canvas, *c.* 1724–26.

James Thornhill (fig. 42) was born in 1675 into the squirearchy of Dorset and grew up amid the political tumult described in the foregoing sections. He was ten years old at the time of the Monmouth Rebellion, which began at Lyme Regis in his native county, and just thirteen when, in 1688, William III landed down the coast at Torbay. Despite a genteel background, Thornhill's family were impecunious. A means of earning a living (apparently a relatively humble one) was provided, however, when Thornhill's great-uncle Dr Thomas Sydenham, an eminent physician in London, left £30 for him to be apprenticed to a trade or profession.[77] Thornhill's apprenticeship began at the age of fourteen in 1689, when he was bound for seven years to another (distant) relative, Thomas Highmore. Highmore was a successful member of the Painter-Stainers' Company in the City of London and a future Serjeant-Painter to William III (a post that occasioned work decorating the sovereign's palaces, coaches and barges, and which Thornhill would one day assume from his master).[78] As Richard Johns has argued, the Painter-Stainers' Company – a guild for 'house' painters in and around London who were skilled in heraldic work, the gilding of leather, and effects such as the graining of wood in imitation of marble and porphyry – was an important professional focus for Thornhill throughout his career.[79] His apprenticeship was not time wasted, nor was his master, Highmore, lacking in talent or contacts, as Thornhill's earlier biographers suggested (perhaps

Fig. 41 (*opposite*) A captured Spanish galleon and personifications of the rivers Avon (centre) and Severn (pouring lampreys from an urn), at the east end of the Lower Hall ceiling.

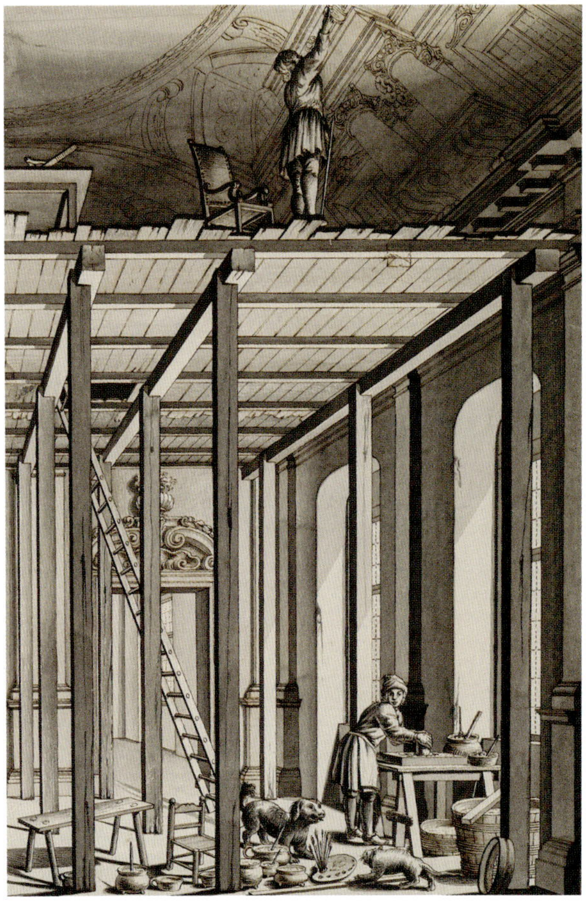

Fig. 43 A painter supported by scaffolding prepares to decorate a ceiling with fictive architecture; below, an apprentice grinds pigment while surrounded by painting equipment, *c.* 1700. This rare depiction of a decorative painter working at height gives us an idea of how Thornhill worked on site at Greenwich.

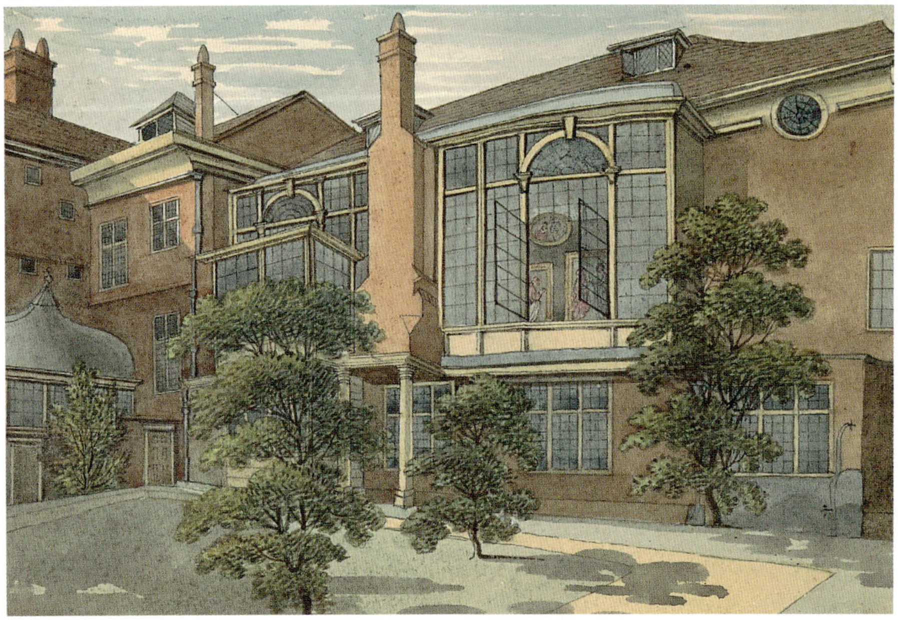

Fig. 44 Samuel Ireland, *Painters' Hall, Little Trinity Lane*, watercolour with pen and black ink, *c.* 1794.

because of a connoisseurial aversion to his trade-based route into painting and a reluctance to associate an artisanal training with artistic achievements of great note). Johns has contended that membership of this City of London livery company in fact brought meaningful professional and social associations, and that an apprenticeship with Highmore taught Thornhill the vital practical skills he would later need, from handling a brush, mixing pigments and working at height (see fig. 43 for a rare contemporary evocation[80]) to managing his own apprentice as well as teams of specialist artists on huge projects such as Greenwich.[81]

In 1704, just as Hawksmoor's refectory at Greenwich Hospital was newly built, Thornhill was granted the freedom of the Painter-Stainers' Company and entered the burgeoning art world of early eighteenth-century London. Although he lived outside the City walls, first in the new western suburb of Soho, then later in Covent Garden, Thornhill retained a career-long association with the Square Mile, and Painters' Hall on Little Trinity Lane (fig. 44) remained an important professional focus; he ultimately became Master of the Company in 1720. It is clear, however, that although Thornhill owed a significant debt to Highmore, he was also heavily influenced by the foreign artists whose works he made close studies of in a sketchbook begun in 1699, when he was twenty-four years old (fig. 45). Having the confidence and independence of mind to assimilate both his native artisanal training and the work of continental painters was essential to Thornhill's success as a British artist at the start of the eighteenth century.

Of the continental artists Thornhill studied, he was particularly drawn to the work of Antonio Verrio (see fig. 2). Verrio's dramatic style of mural painting rapidly attracted royal patronage on his arrival in England in 1672. For a decade from 1675, he was employed at Windsor, where he painted twenty ceilings, three staircases, the King's Chapel and a scheme glorifying Charles II and the Order of the Garter in St George's Hall – a prototype, along with Peter Paul Rubens's earlier Banqueting House ceiling, for the Painted Hall (see figs. 15 and 16 on p. 82).[82] The subsequent decade saw Verrio working on a series of sumptuous murals in a suite of five state rooms at Burghley House in Lincolnshire for John Cecil, 5th Earl of Exeter.

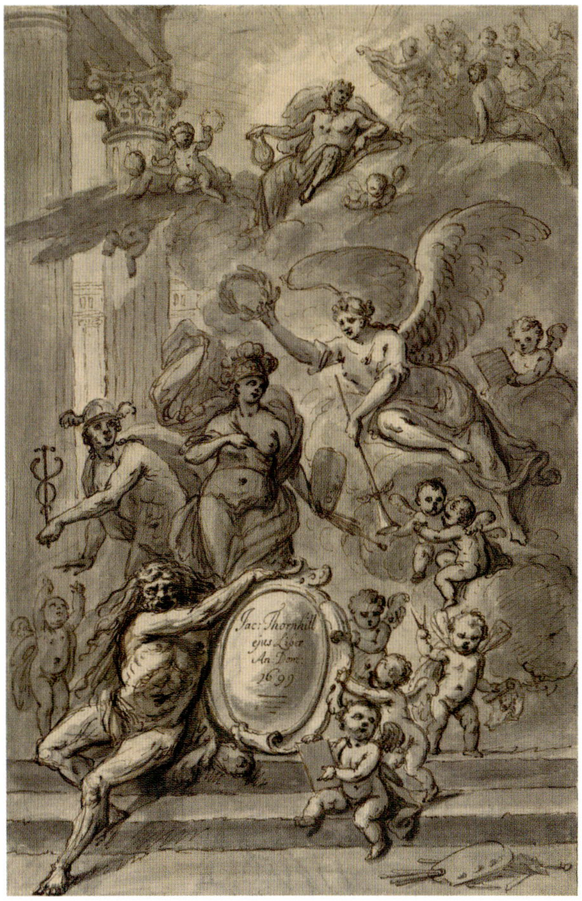

Fig. 45 Frontispiece to Thornhill's sketchbook, begun 1699.

The 'Heaven Room' at Burghley, a scheme in which mythological figures disport themselves within a fictive architectural framework, again shows the importance of Verrio's work to Thornhill and to the Greenwich commission that would make his name (fig. 46).[83] Louis Laguerre (1663–1721) was a significant influence on both Thornhill and his competitor. He arrived in London in 1684 and became one of the most in-demand grand-scale mural artists of his time. Laguerre, like Verrio, was much influenced in turn by the artist Charles Le Brun (1619–1690), who specialized in the grandiose decoration found at Versailles.[84] As Richard Johns has observed, what Le Brun achieved as a designer and artist furthering the political agenda of Louis XIV, Verrio carried out for Charles II and James Thornhill delivered for William III.[85] Thornhill copied such artists as Le Brun and Verrio, then, but also made important innovations of his own. As his career progressed, he was praised as often for his capacity to invent schemes as for his correctness and dexterity in executing them.[86]

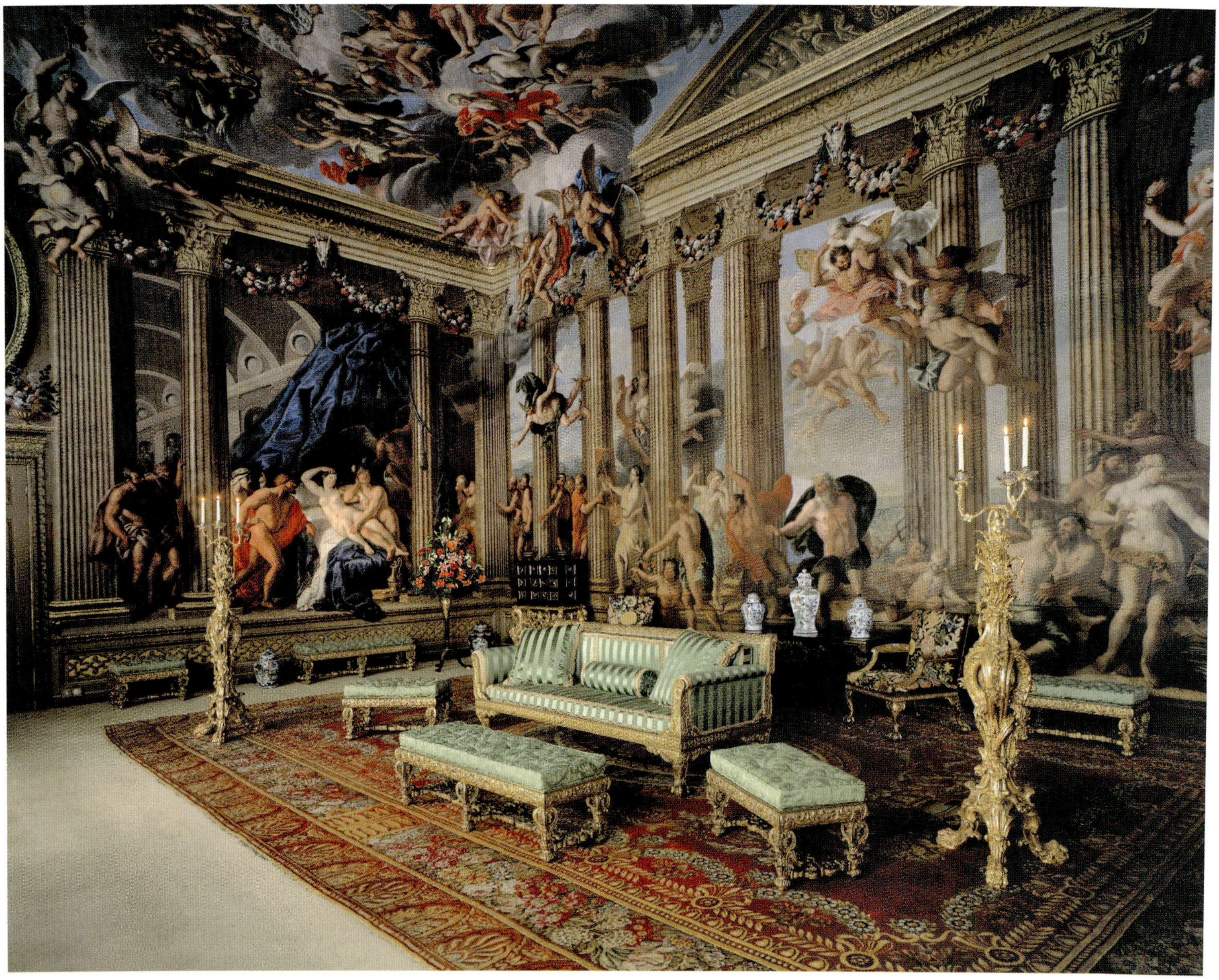

Fig. 46 Antonio Verrio, Heaven Room at Burghley House, Lincolnshire, 1693–94.

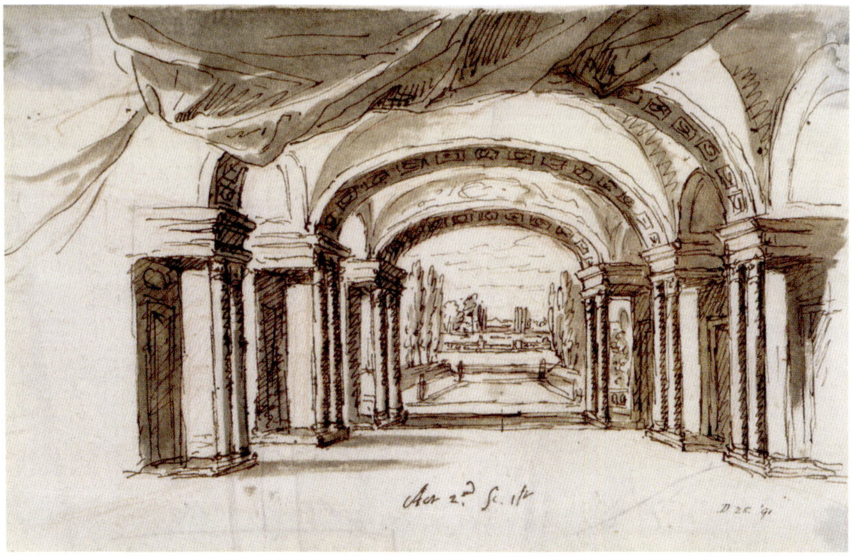

Fig. 47 James Thornhill, design for a stage setting (a great hall looking into a garden), Act II, scene I of the opera *Arsinoë, Queen of Cyprus*, pen and ink with wash, 1705.

One of Thornhill's earliest commissions, in 1705, was scenery design for Thomas Clayton's opera *Arsinoë, Queen of Cyprus*, performed at the Theatre Royal, Drury Lane. These designs show the artist already developing a flair for the dramatic and a fascination with perspective that would come to the fore with his work on the Painted Hall a few years later (fig. 47). In the same year, Thornhill completed one of his first independent commissions for a large decorative scheme. This was for Thomas Foley MP and comprised the decoration of the hall, staircase and overmantels at Stoke Edith in Herefordshire.[87]

In 1706 Thornhill won his biggest early (pre-Greenwich) commission: the painting for the 1st Duke of Devonshire of the saloon and staircase and other rooms at Chatsworth in Derbyshire. It was the prestige assignment of his career to date and was followed by a number of important commissions for other leading elite patrons: these included a staircase scheme depicting the early life of Achilles for the Whig lawyer Thomas Vernon at Hanbury Hall, Worcestershire (1710); a hall ceiling painting glorifying the military triumphs of John Churchill, 1st Duke of Marlborough, at Blenheim Palace, Oxfordshire (1716); and the chapel of Wimpole Hall, Cambridgeshire, for the patriotic Tory patron Edward Harley, 2nd Earl of Oxford (1724). It is not difficult to imagine the professional pride felt by the thirty-one-year-old Thornhill arriving at Chatsworth to work alongside schemes by Antonio Verrio and Louis Laguerre (fig. 48). Here, finally, was an English artist able to compete with glamorous continental rivals. Highly connoisseurial writers of the preceding century, such as William Aglionby, had lamented England's inferiority in the arts compared to the continent and the absence of 'an Historical Painter, Native of our own Soyl' to equal or surpass Italian and French counterparts.[88]

It is worth noting that, despite an extraordinarily busy career, Thornhill travelled to the continent twice: to the Low Countries in 1711, and to Paris in 1717. He documented his journeys in great detail, obsessively sketching the buildings he saw along the route and making memoranda of art collections to visit. He viewed works of art in his capacity as an artist but also as a collector of paintings himself, as an agent and as a director of the Great Queen Street Academy in London (a fledgling institution that helped to forge the way for the Royal Academy in 1768).[89]

As Thornhill arrived in Derbyshire, the wait for a native school of history painting – and a dynamic young artist to lead it – appeared to be over. His principal work at Chatsworth, in the Sabine Room, is his most substantial early surviving work. Executed in what Croft-Murray describes as his distinctive 'happy palette of clear blues, pinks, crimsons, and warm browns', the scheme, which depicts Hersilia, wife

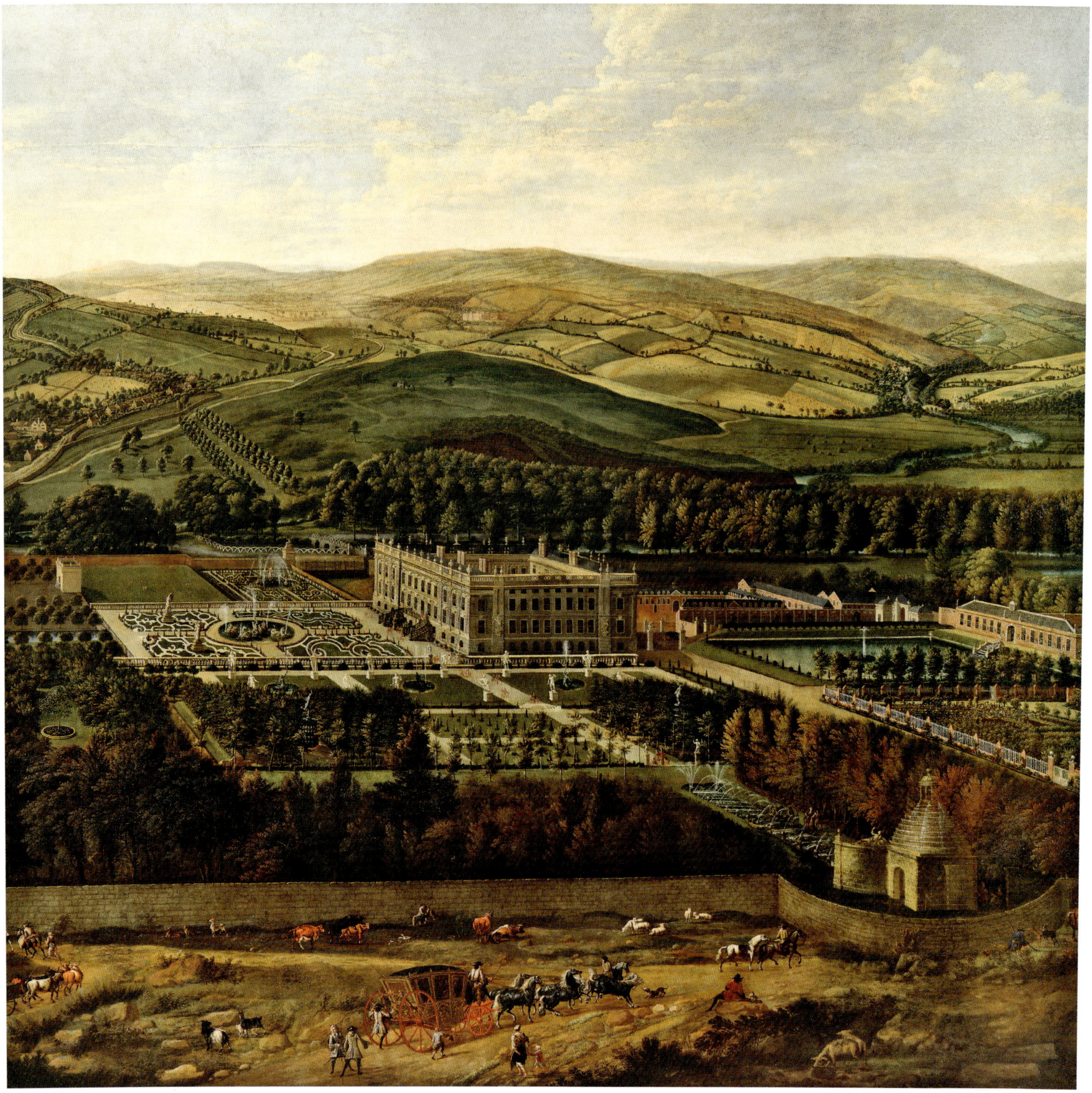

Fig. 48 Jan Siberechts, *A View of Chatsworth*, oil on canvas, *c.* 1703.

of Romulus, shows Thornhill already at ease both with classical sources and with combining form and narrative action.[90] In a preparatory sketch for the room, we see evidence that, just as his continental rivals did, Thornhill thought of design (drawing) as the basis of painting, and that he had developed a mastery of pen and wash in order to produce these studies (fig. 49). We see, too, the importance of fictive architecture to Thornhill's compositions and his ability to conceive of architecture and painting as an ensemble.

As Thornhill arrived at Chatsworth, the plasterwork of the Hall at Greenwich Hospital was completed. The Hospital directors – a collection of aristocrats and churchmen familiar with the elite art form of decorative history painting – appear to have wasted no time in registering the talents of this young artist or the desirability of using a native painter on a patriotic public project. The nature of their first contact with Thornhill and the mechanics of his engagement are unknown; we simply have a first mention of the artist in the directors' minutes of July 1707, with an instruction to him to amend a design 'by inserting what more he can relating to maritime affaires'.[91] Thornhill's response was probably one of the early pen-and-wash studies for the main ceiling of the Lower Hall in which the sterns of ships have been introduced at each end beneath fictive arches (fig. 29 on p. 93).

There is no record of any sort of competition for the Greenwich scheme, as there would be for another major public commission a few years later: the decoration of the interior of the newly completed dome of St Paul's Cathedral, which Thornhill won in 1715 with a Raphaelesque scheme based on the life of that apostle.[92] The Greenwich commission could easily not have come about at all. In an account of the newly decorated lower part of the Hall in 1714, the essayist and politician Richard Steele states that, of the Hospital directors, it was the aldermanic merchant financier Sir James Bateman who first suggested that the Hall should be painted, and that he acted as the scheme's first benefactor as well as proposer.[93] Interestingly, Thornhill experimented with including Bateman in his allegorical scheme for the Painted Hall; he was to represent Merchandise, as an unexecuted drawing

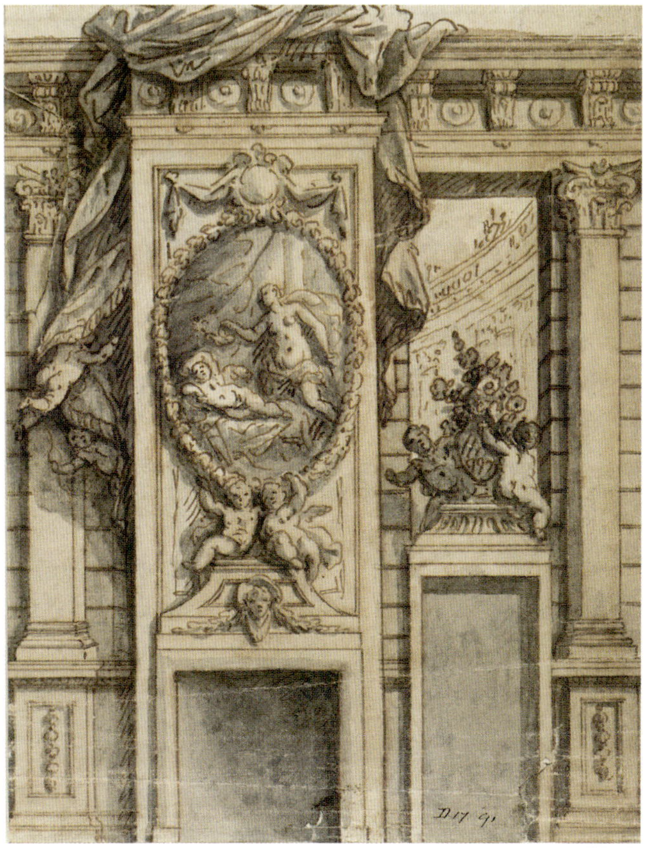

Fig. 49 James Thornhill, design for the Sabine Room at Chatsworth, Derbyshire, pen and ink with wash, *c.* 1706.

for one of the ceiling's fictive balconies shows (fig. 50, bottom left, with the coins).

Once Bateman had proposed the idea of a grand-scale painting, the question of an artist must have been discussed. There were at least two existing connections to Thornhill among the commissioners of Greenwich Hospital. Thornhill's work at Chatsworth lasted until 1707, and his patron was the Greenwich director and Whig grandee the 1st Duke of Devonshire. It seems highly likely that Thornhill was awarded the Painted Hall commission at least in part on the basis of his work at Chatsworth. Indeed, Thornhill's earliest ideas for the Painted Hall appear to have been conceived in the hills of Derbyshire: a topographical sketch of the Peak District by the artist (today in the Bodleian Library, Oxford) is dated 22 July 1707 – just five days after that instruction to him to amend his design for the Hall ceiling at Greenwich by inventing new maritime content. Perhaps less relevant, although still of importance, is a link to the first Treasurer of Greenwich Hospital, John Evelyn. One of Thornhill's

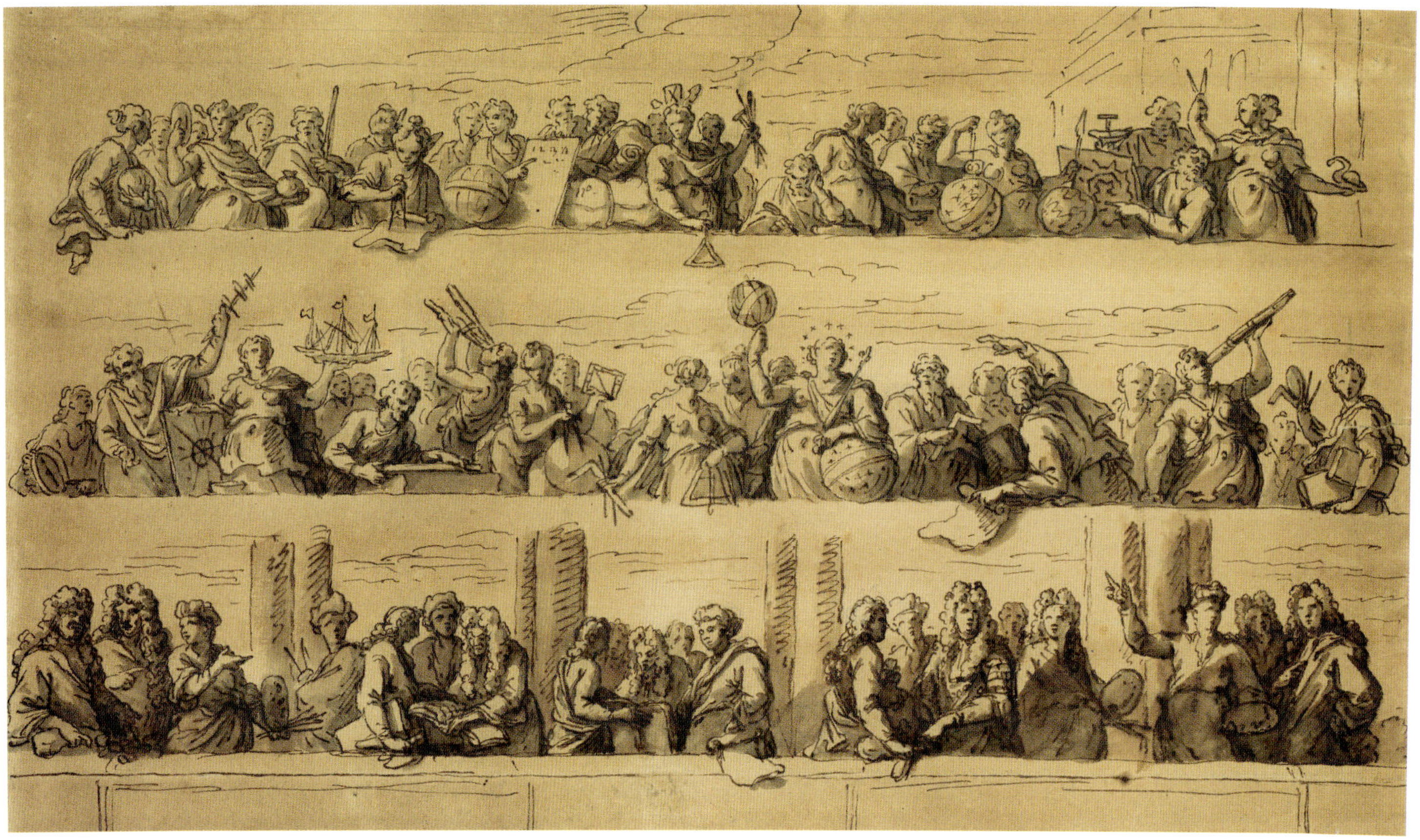

Fig. 50 James Thornhill, figure studies for the balconies of the Lower Hall ceiling, pen and brown ink with grey and brown wash over pencil, *c.* 1707. Thornhill's inscription on the reverse is a key to some of the figures: *Arithmetique Jn James/Merchandize Sr J Bateman/Surveying Sr Chr Wren/Archit Hawksmoor/Painting J Thornhill/Astronomy Flamstead/Ticho Brahe/Archimedes.*

earliest small commissions, in 1703, was to paint the staircase and saloon at Addiscombe House in Surrey for Evelyn's son-in-law, William Draper. Draper succeeded Evelyn as Treasurer of Greenwich Hospital in the year Thornhill was working for him in a private capacity. As with artistic patronage more generally in the eighteenth century, such intricate professional and social networks were central to the workings of the Painted Hall commission. Frustratingly, almost nothing of Thornhill's communication with the Hospital directors is documented, but from around thirty surviving sketches it is possible to piece together the evolution of his design for the Painted Hall, which unfolded over the course of nineteen years and thousands of square feet. Although unrecorded, the interaction between artist and patron on such an epic and politically sensitive scheme must have been intensive. The little-known Painted Hall sketches are testament to Thornhill's exceptional skills as a draughtsman, and show the way in which the artist conceived and organized the opulent and complex painted scheme.[94]

Thornhill's talents as both a draughtsman and a painter meant that from 1707 – the year in which he was awarded the Painted Hall commission – until the late 1720s he was in high demand and, as we have seen, working on decorative schemes in private houses, churches and institutions for some of the most powerful men in the country. In June 1718 Thornhill was officially recognized as the foremost decorative painter in England by his appointment as History Painter to the king. In March 1720 he became Serjeant-Painter, and in May of that year he was knighted – the first British artist to be so honoured. The Painted Hall commission, which occupied the central two decades of Thornhill's career, was key to establishing the reputation of a talented artist, hailed in his day as 'our Ingenious Countryman'.[95]

NOTE ON DATES

Until 1752, the civil calendar began on Lady Day (25 March). To avoid ambiguity, dates between 1 January and 24 March are given in the notes using both the old-style and the new-style year, e.g., 20 January 1695/96; dates in the essay are new style.

1 The Tudor Greenwich Palace had a scale and magnificence comparable to those of Hampton Court. Refaced in red brick under Henry VII, it had been the principal residence of Henry VIII and the birthplace of Mary I and Elizabeth I, and remained an important royal palace under the Stuarts until the Civil War.

2 Simon Thurley, 'Architecture and Diplomacy: Greenwich Palace under the Stuarts', *The Court Historian*, vol. 11, no. 2, December 2006, pp. 125–33.

3 H.M. Colvin (ed.), *The History of the King's Works*, vol. 5: 1660–1782, London (HMSO) 1976, pp. 140–52.

4 On Verrio, see Edward Croft-Murray, *Decorative Painting in England, 1537–1837*, vol. 1: *Early Tudor to Sir James Thornhill*, London (Country Life) 1962, pp. 50–60, 236–42; Cécile Brett, 'Antonio Verrio (*c.* 1636–1707): His Career and Surviving Work', *The British Art Journal*, vol. 10, no. 3, Winter/Spring 2009–10, pp. 4–17; and Richard Johns, '"Those wilder sorts of Painting": The Painted Interior in the Age of Antonio Verrio', in *A Companion to British Art: 1600 to the Present*, ed. Dana Arnold and David Peters Corbett, Chichester (Blackwell) 2013, pp. 79–104.

5 Thurley, 'Greenwich Palace under the Stuarts', p. 133.

6 John Bold, *Greenwich: An Architectural History of the Royal Hospital for Seamen and the Queen's House*, New Haven, Conn., and London (Yale University Press) 2000, pp. 77–79.

7 Sir Christopher Wren first became involved in the creation of the Hospital in 1693; see p. 20. In 1696 he was appointed Surveyor of the Royal Hospital for Seamen in Greenwich.

8 Gary S. De Krey, *London and the Restoration, 1659–1683*, Cambridge (Cambridge University Press) 2005, p. 15.

9 Bold, *Greenwich*, p. 95; Colvin, *History of the King's Works*, vol. 5, p. 151.

10 Bold, *Greenwich*, p. 95; Pieter van der Merwe, *A Refuge for All: A Short History of Greenwich Hospital*, London (Greenwich Hospital) 2010, p. 4.

11 Bold, *Greenwich*, p. 95; Philip Newell, *Greenwich Hospital: A Royal Foundation, 1692–1983*, London (Trustees of Greenwich Hospital) 1984, p. 8.

12 The National Archives, Kew (hereafter TNA), ADM 67/1, 30 June 1696; ADM 67/2, 22 July 1698; Kerry Downes, *Hawksmoor*, London (Thames & Hudson) 1996, p. 43.

13 Nicholas Hawksmoor, *Remarks on the Founding and Carrying on the Buildings of the Royal Hospital at Greenwich*, London 1728.

14 *Ibid.*, p. 6.

15 James Boswell, *The Life of Samuel Johnson*, 2 vols., London (J.M. Dent) 1906, vol. 1, p. 284.

16 Christine Stevenson, 'Robert Hooke's Bethlem', *Journal of the Society of Architectural Historians*, vol. 55, no. 3, September 1996, pp. 268, 269. See also by Stevenson, *Medicine and Magnificence: British Hospital and Asylum Architecture, 1660–1815*, New Haven, Conn. (Yale University Press) 2000.

17 Edward Hatton, *A New View of London; or, An Ample Account of That City*, 2 vols., London 1708, vol. 2, p. 746.

18 TNA ADM 67/5, James Thornhill's Memorial of 24 August 1717.

19 Hawksmoor, *Remarks*, p. 13; my italics.

20 *Ibid.*, pp. 12–13.

21 For a detailed commentary on Wren's and Hawksmoor's proposals for Greenwich Hospital and the associated drawings, see Gordon Higgott, 'Greenwich Royal Hospital', Sir John Soane's Museum English Baroque Drawings catalogue, 2009, available online: collections.soane.org (accessed June 2019). See also *The Royal Hospital for Seamen at Greenwich, 1694–1728*, Wren Society 6, Oxford 1929; Bold, *Greenwich*, pp. 95–132; and Anthony Geraghty, *The Architectural Drawings of Sir Christopher Wren at All Souls College, Oxford: A Complete Catalogue*, Aldershot (Lund Humphries) 2007.

22 John Summerson, *Architecture in Britain, 1530–1830*, 9th edn, New Haven, Conn., and London (Yale University Press) 1993, p. 275.

23 Downes, *Hawksmoor*, p. 96. Drawings by Hawksmoor for this unbuilt scheme survive in the collections of the Royal Institute of British Architects, the Courtauld Gallery and Worcester College, Oxford.

24 Bold, *Greenwich*, p. 104.

25 *Ibid.*

26 John Evelyn, *The Diary of John Evelyn*, ed. by E.S. de Beer, 6 vols., Oxford (Clarendon Press) 1955, vol. 5, p. 203.

27 *Ibid.*, p. 544.

28 *Ibid.*, p. 209.

29 *Ibid.*, p. 210; TNA ADM 67/1, 21 May 1695.

30 TNA ADM 67/1, 23 December 1695 and 20 January 1695/96.

31 Evelyn, *Diary*, vol. 5, p. 244; TNA ADM 67/2, 5 June 1696. The same records reveal that agreements were also made with James Hurst for digging the foundations and clearing the site, Richard Billingshurst for bricklayer's work, and Richard Woods and Thomas Steers for the provision of lime and sand. An order was sent to the stationer to provide two large store books, one daybook and a dozen pocketbooks, as well as a bottle of ink and 200 Dutch quills, so that payments for materials and labour could be carefully logged. Contracts with Mr Thomson for painting, Henry Doogood for plasterer's work, and Roger Davis for joiner's work (including the design and production of 'shash windows') followed on 14 August 1696. On Defoe, see Eveline Cruickshanks, 'Religion and Royal Succession: The Rage of Party', in *Britain in the First Age of Party, 1680–1750: Essays Presented to Geoffrey Holmes*, ed. Clyve Jones, London and Ronceverte, W. Va. (Hambledon Press) 1987, p. 22.

32 Evelyn, *Diary*, vol. 5, p. 244.

33 TNA ADM 67/2, 7 August 1697. Evelyn was instructed to sell these devalued malt tickets in April 1698 'by reason of the great want of mony to carry on the work'.

34 TNA ADM 67/1, 31 January 1695/96. See also Bold, *Greenwich*, p. 112.

35 Bold, *Greenwich*, p. 121.

36 Evelyn, *Diary*, vol. 5, p. 249. TNA ADM 67/1, 30 June 1696, records the event more prosaically: 'the foundations of the new building were begun, a corner stone being laid by the Committee and gratuitys being given to the workmen by each person present'.

37 For such workmen's provisions, see, for example, TNA ADM 67/2, 26 July 1698.

38 Bold, *Greenwich*, pp. 21–22.

39 Evelyn, *Diary*, vol. 5, p. 249.

40 Biographical information on Godolphin and other donors is drawn from the *Oxford Dictionary of National Biography*.

41 Comparison of the painted tablets as they read today with lists printed in an 18th-century topographical account – the 1733 edition of John Stow's *Survey of London* (vol. 1, pp. 213–14) – indicates that the lists were revised, reordered and enlarged. Traces of the earlier fictive lettering were observed during conservation work carried out in 2017–18.

42 On the civic Whig interests represented, see Gary Stuart De Krey, *A Fractured Society: The Politics of London in the First Age of Party, 1688–1715*, Oxford (Clarendon Press) 1985.

43 Thoresby visited the Hospital in 1714 to view the first completed phase of work on the painted ceiling. See Ralph Thoresby, *The Diary of Ralph Thoresby*, ed. Rev. Joseph Hunter, 2 vols., London 1830, vol. 2, entry for 14 July 1714, p. 236; and Richard Johns, 'James Thornhill and Decorative History Painting in England after 1688', PhD thesis, University of York, 2004, pp. 180–81.

44 TNA ADM 67/2, 1 August 1699.

45 Evelyn, *Diary*, vol. 5, p. 399.

46 Bold, *Greenwich*, p. 108. On Strong senior and junior, see Howard Colvin, *A Biographical Dictionary of British Architects, 1600–1840*, 4th edn, New Haven, Conn., and London (Yale University Press) 2008, pp. 936–38. On Jones, see Rupert Gunnis, *Dictionary of British Sculptors, 1660–1851*, Cambridge, Mass. (Harvard University Press) 1954, p. 221. For Jones's contract, see TNA ADM 67/2, 28 October 1696.

47 See, for example, TNA ADM 67/2, 8 October 1697, when the Fabric Committee noted 'the considerable sums of mony due to some of the chiefe workmen imployd about the Hospitall'. James Grove the carpenter (first appointed in 1696) and Edward Strong senior were both owed £200 at this stage.

48 Stevenson, 'Robert Hooke's Bethlem', p. 269; Bold, *Greenwich*, p. 113. The original plan had been for fully wainscoted cabins 'as near the manner, as may be, as Chelsea college is', but this was later abandoned. TNA ADM 67/2, 3 September 1697 and 22 October 1698.

49 TNA ADM 67/2, 1 February 1697/98.

50 *Ibid.*, 5 April and 3 May 1698.

51 For a detailed analysis of the drawing, see Higgott, 'Greenwich Royal Hospital'.

52 Bold, *Greenwich*, pp. 125–26.

53 TNA ADM 67/2, 26 July 1698.

54 *Ibid.*, 26 March 1700.

55 Bold, *Greenwich*, p. 119.

56 Of these carvings, twenty-three remain in the undercroft and seven are on display in the Old Royal Naval College Visitor Centre.

57 TNA ADM 67/2, 4 April 1699.

58 Bold, *Greenwich*, p. 121.

59 *Ibid.*, p. 135.

60 This was the entrance used by visitors until the start of the recent conservation project. Visitors today enter the Painted Hall via the King William Undercroft, a route adopted for conservation reasons; see p. 131.

61 I am grateful to Gordon Higgott for his help in identifying these sources.

62 Sebastiano Serlio, *Sebastiano Serlio on Architecture*, vol. 1: *Books I–V of 'Tutte l'opere d'architettura et prospetiva'*, translated from the Italian with an introduction and commentary by Vaughan Hart and Peter Hicks, New Haven, Conn., and London (Yale University Press) 1996, p. 227, Book III, fol. 116r. Books I–V of Serlio's treatise were translated into English in 1611.

63 This translation is taken from William R. Osmun, 'A Study of the Work of Sir James Thornhill', PhD thesis, Courtauld Institute of Art, University of London, 1950, p. 252.

64 Andrea Palladio, *The Four Books on Architecture*, trans. Robert Tavernor and Richard Schofield, Cambridge, Mass., and London (MIT Press) 1997, p. 282. No English translation of Book IV was available as the Hall's decoration was being planned in 1703, but there was a complete French translation by Roland Fréart de Chambray (Paris 1650).

65 Edward Chaney, *Inigo Jones's 'Roman Sketchbook'*, 2 vols., London (Roxburghe Club) 2006, vol. 2, pp. 167–68.

66 Bold, *Greenwich*, p. 134; TNA ADM 68/682, December 1707.

67 Hawksmoor, *Remarks*, p. 14.

68 Geoffrey Beard, *Decorative Plasterwork in Great Britain* [1975], Abingdon (Routledge) 2015, p. xxix.

69 TNA ADM 67/3, June 1704.

70 *Ibid.*, 31 August 1704.

71 *Ibid.*, 12 July 1705.

72 *Ibid.*, 9 August 1705.

73 Beard, *Decorative Plasterwork*, pp. 113–14. The Doogoods appear also as Toogoods in many records. Beard fails to make the connection between Henry (listed as Doogood) and his father, Arthur (listed as Toogood), as a result. I am grateful to Claire Gapper for additional biographical information on Henry Doogood.

74 TNA E 351/3269, Royal Works Accounts, 1635–36.

75 I am grateful to Richard Ireland and Jenny Saunt for technical information on the lime plaster at Greenwich. The explanation of materials and processes is taken from Ireland's introduction to the 2015 edition of Beard's *Decorative Plasterwork*.

76 TNA ADM 67/3, 12 June 1707. Plasterers were allowed to apply distempers to the plastered surface, but they were confined to 'whiting, blacking, redlead, redoker, yellow oker, and russet' mingled with size (a kind of animal glue), according to an Act of 1606 passed after a long-running dispute between the Painter-Stainers' and Plaisterers' Companies. See James Ayres, *Art, Artisans and Apprentices: Apprentice Painters and Sculptors in the Early Modern British Tradition*, Oxford and Philadelphia (Oxbow Books) 2014, p. 264.

77 James Thornhill has been the subject of renewed interest among art historians in recent years, thanks in large part to the work of Dr Richard Johns, author of the second part of this volume. Much of the biographical information in this section derives from Johns's thesis, 'James Thornhill and Decorative History Painting' – the basis also for Johns's forthcoming monograph on Thornhill. Other important sources for Thornhill's life and work include Osmun, 'A Study of the Work of Sir James Thornhill' and Croft-Murray, *Decorative Painting in England*, vol. 1. I am also very grateful for the insights and information provided by Jeremy Barker, who has written and lectured widely on Thornhill and, in particular, Thornhill's Dorset and West Country roots and commissions. See, for example, 'Sir James Thornhill's Obelisk at Thornhill', *Proceedings of the Dorset Natural History and Archaeological Society*, vol. 121, 1999, pp. 140–42.

78 On Highmore, see Croft-Murray, *Decorative Painting in England*, vol. 1, p. 264.

79 Johns, 'James Thornhill and Decorative History Painting', pp. 35–52.

80 I am grateful to Jenny Saunt and Richard Ireland for bringing this image – reproduced in Christine Casey, *Making Magnificence: Architects, Stuccatori and the*

Eighteenth-Century Interior, New Haven, Conn., and London (Yale University Press) 2017, p. 91 – to my attention.

81 Richard Johns, 'J. Thornhill, Painter and Decorator', talk given at the Old Royal Naval College, Greenwich, December 2017.

82 Wolf Burchard, 'Illusion and Involvement: The Lost Baroque Architecture of St George's Hall at Windsor Castle', *Immediations*, vol. 2, no. 4, 2011, pp. 99–119.

83 On Verrio's Heaven Room, see Johns, 'The Painted Interior in the Age of Antonio Verrio'.

84 On Laguerre, see Lydia Hamlett, 'Rupture Through Realism: Sarah Churchill and Louis Laguerre's Murals at Marlborough House', in *Court, Country, City: British Art and Architecture, 1660–1735*, ed. Mark Hallett, Nigel Llewellyn and Martin Myrone, New Haven, Conn., and London (Yale University Press) 2016, pp. 195–216; and Laurel O. Peterson, 'Making Spaces: Art and Politics in the Whig Country House Interior, 1688–1745', PhD thesis, Yale University, 2018. On Le Brun, see Wolf Burchard, *The Sovereign Artist: Charles Le Brun and the Image of Louis XIV*, London (Paul Holberton Publishing) 2016.

85 Johns, 'J. Thornhill, Painter and Decorator'.

86 See, for example, Colen Campbell's assessment of the Painted Hall in *Vitruvius Britannicus; or, The British Architect*, vol. 1, London 1715, p. 6: 'I can't neglect mentioning that excellent Cieling in the great Hall, by Mr Thornhill, to his eternal Honour, and his Country: Here Foreigners may view with Amaze, our Countrymen with Pleasure, and all with Admiration, the Beauty, the Force, the Majesty of a British Pencil! Rich in Invention, correct in Design, noble in Disposition, in Execution admirable.'

87 Jeremy Barker, 'James Thornhill, Thomas Foley and the Decoration of Stoke Court, Herefordshire', in *Essays in Honour of Jim and Muriel Tonkin*, ed. Rosalind Lowe, Herefordshire (Woolhope Club) 2011, pp. 93–112.

88 William Aglionby, *Painting Illustrated in Three Dialogues*, London 1685, preface.

89 Both of Thornhill's travel notebooks are in the collection of the Victoria and Albert Museum, London. See Tamsin Lee-Woolfe, 'James Thornhill's Travel Diary to Paris, 1717', *Volume of the Walpole Society* 80, 2018, pp. 202–61; and Ilaria Bignamini, 'The "Academy of Art" in Britain Before the Foundation of the Royal Academy in 1768', in *Academies of Art Between Renaissance and Romanticism*, ed. Anton W.A. Boschloo *et al.*, 's-Gravenhage, The Netherlands (SDU) 1989, pp. 434–50.

90 Croft-Murray, *Decorative Painting in England*, vol. 1, p. 170.

91 TNA ADM 67/3, 17 July 1707.

92 On the St Paul's scheme, regarded along with Greenwich as one of the public proofs of Thornhill's ingenuity, see Richard Johns, '"An Air of Grandeur & Modesty": James Thornhill's Painting in the Dome of St Paul's Cathedral', *Eighteenth-Century Studies*, vol. 42, no. 4, Summer 2009, pp. 501–27. Thornhill's growing interest in Raphael as his career progressed – culminating in 1729 with the Herculean endeavour of producing painted copies of Raphael's tapestry cartoons at Hampton Court Palace – cannot be discussed here, but is of great relevance to the second part of his Greenwich commission, completed after 1717. See *Apostles in England: Sir James Thornhill and the Legacy of Raphael's Tapestry Cartoons*, exhib. cat. by Arline Meyer, New York, Miriam and Ira D. Wallach Art Gallery, Columbia University, October–December 1996.

93 [Richard Steele], *The Lover. To which is added, The Reader*, London 1715, p. 229.

94 *'A Great and Noble Design': Sir James Thornhill's Painted Hall at Greenwich*, exhib. cat. by Anya Matthews, London, Stephen Lawrence Gallery, University of Greenwich, September–October 2016.

95 [Steele], *The Lover*, p. 223.

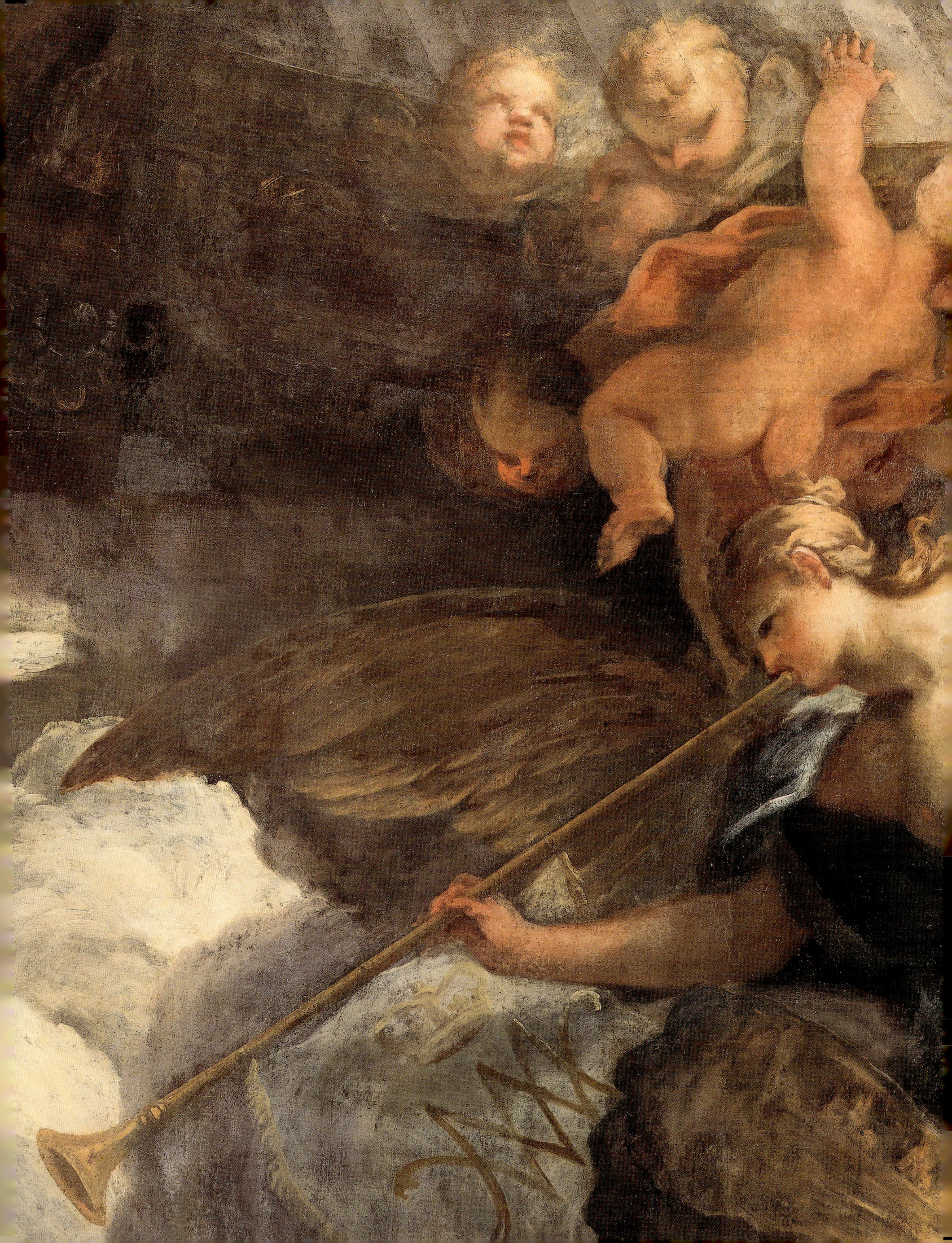

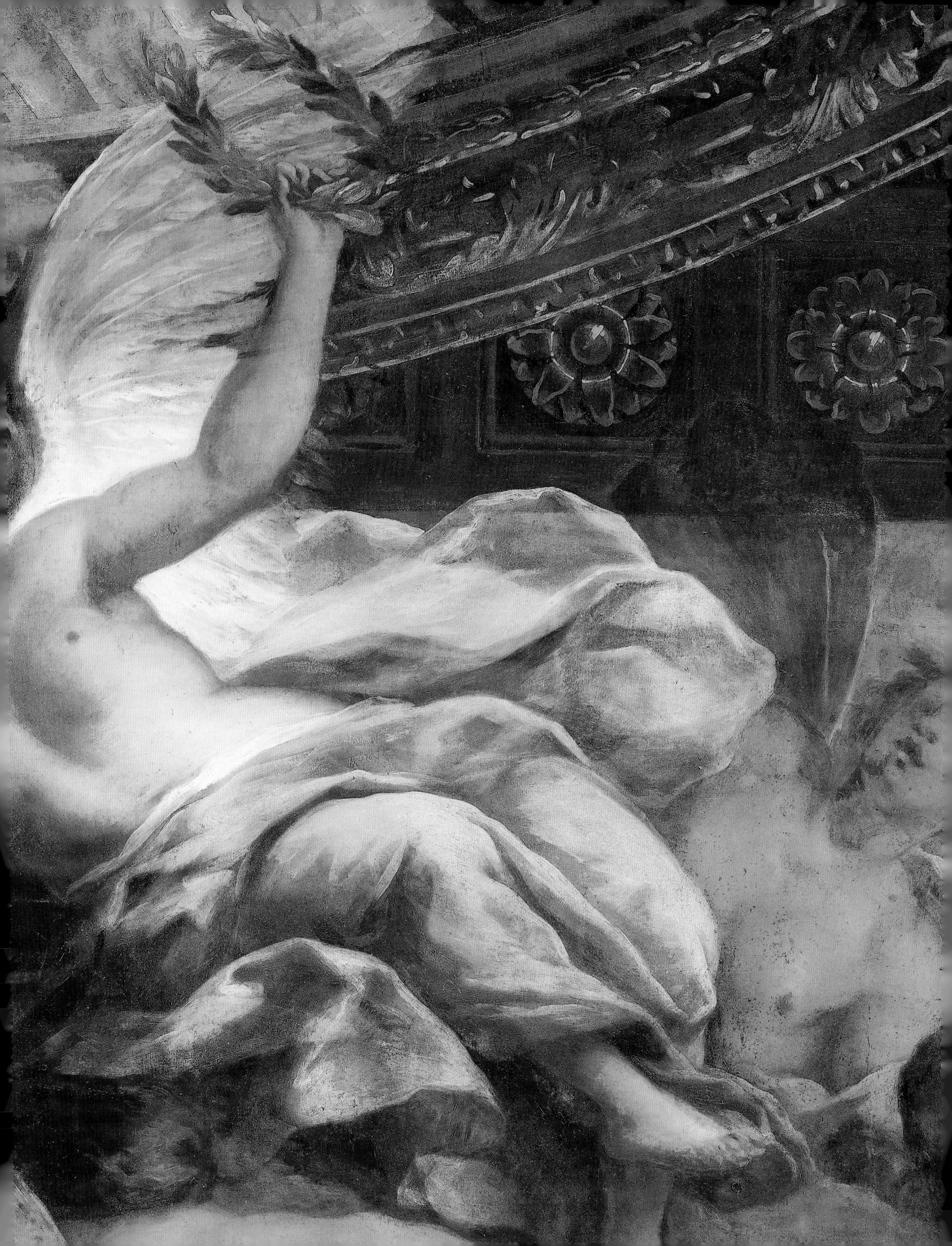

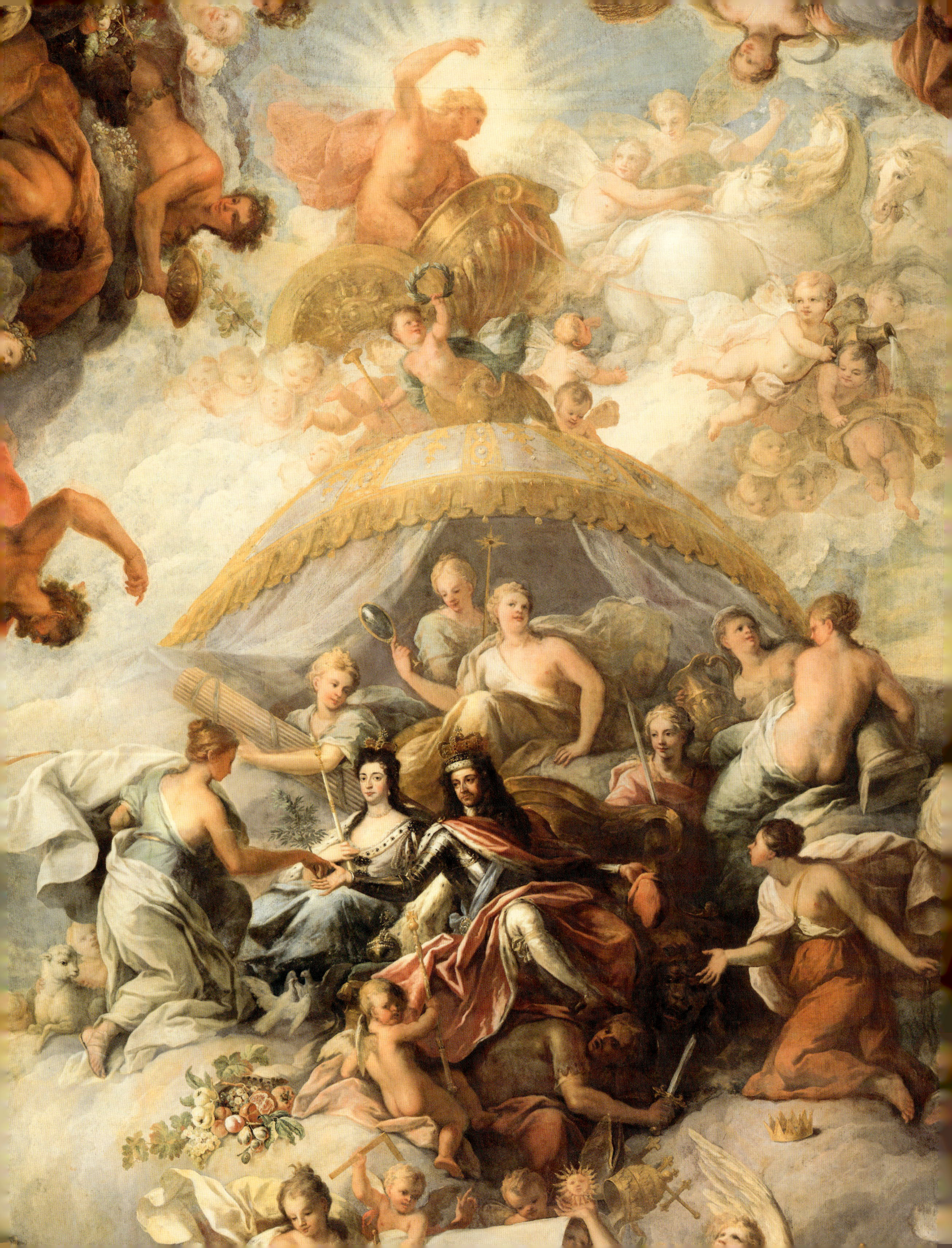

RICHARD JOHNS

IMAGE AND MEANING

An Explanation of the Painting in the Royal Hospital at Greenwich

The spectacle of the Painted Hall at the Royal Hospital for Seamen in Greenwich has changed little since it was completed almost 300 years ago. On entering the Hall from the colonnaded porch of the King William building in the south-west quarter of the Hospital site, or climbing the stairs from the Undercroft, the visitor arrives at an impressive Vestibule with a high drum and dome supported by a giant order of Composite columns and pilasters enriched with feigned fluting and gilded capitals (fig. 2). Inside the dome, arranged around the points of a compass that used to hang from the centre, are winged figures representing the four winds, painted the colour of stone. On each of three sides of this antechamber is a large painted tablet with the names of the Hospital's early donors in gold letters – an impressive roll of royals, nobles, politicians and bankers (fig. 3). Each tablet is flanked by more winged figures and by two smartly dressed '*Charity-Boys*', painted to look as if carved in white marble. One of these boys, on the eastern wall (see fig. 24 on p. 31), points towards an arched window above the entrance, where a larger-than-life figure of Charity once stood.[1] Thus oriented, by the compass and by the Hospital's charitable objectives, the visitor ascends a short flight of steps into one of the most richly decorated spaces of the eighteenth century, where James Thornhill's painted decoration centres on an elaborate posthumous glorification of the joint monarchs William III and Mary II (fig. 4).

In the Middle of the great *Oval*, under a Canopy of State, and attended by the four *Cardinal* VIRTUES, are *King William* and *Queen Mary*, *Concord* sitting between, *Cupid* holding the Scepter …

The larger Lower Hall is configured as an open pavilion on a grand scale, with a fictive ceiling supported by eight stone figures and pierced by a large oval. At its centre, William and Mary are enthroned beneath a purple canopy of state and surrounded by a panoply of Virtues and other attributes of good government, including Prudence

Fig. 1 The centre of the Lower Hall ceiling, with William and Mary enthroned beneath a canopy of state and surrounded by a panoply of Virtues and other attributes of good government.

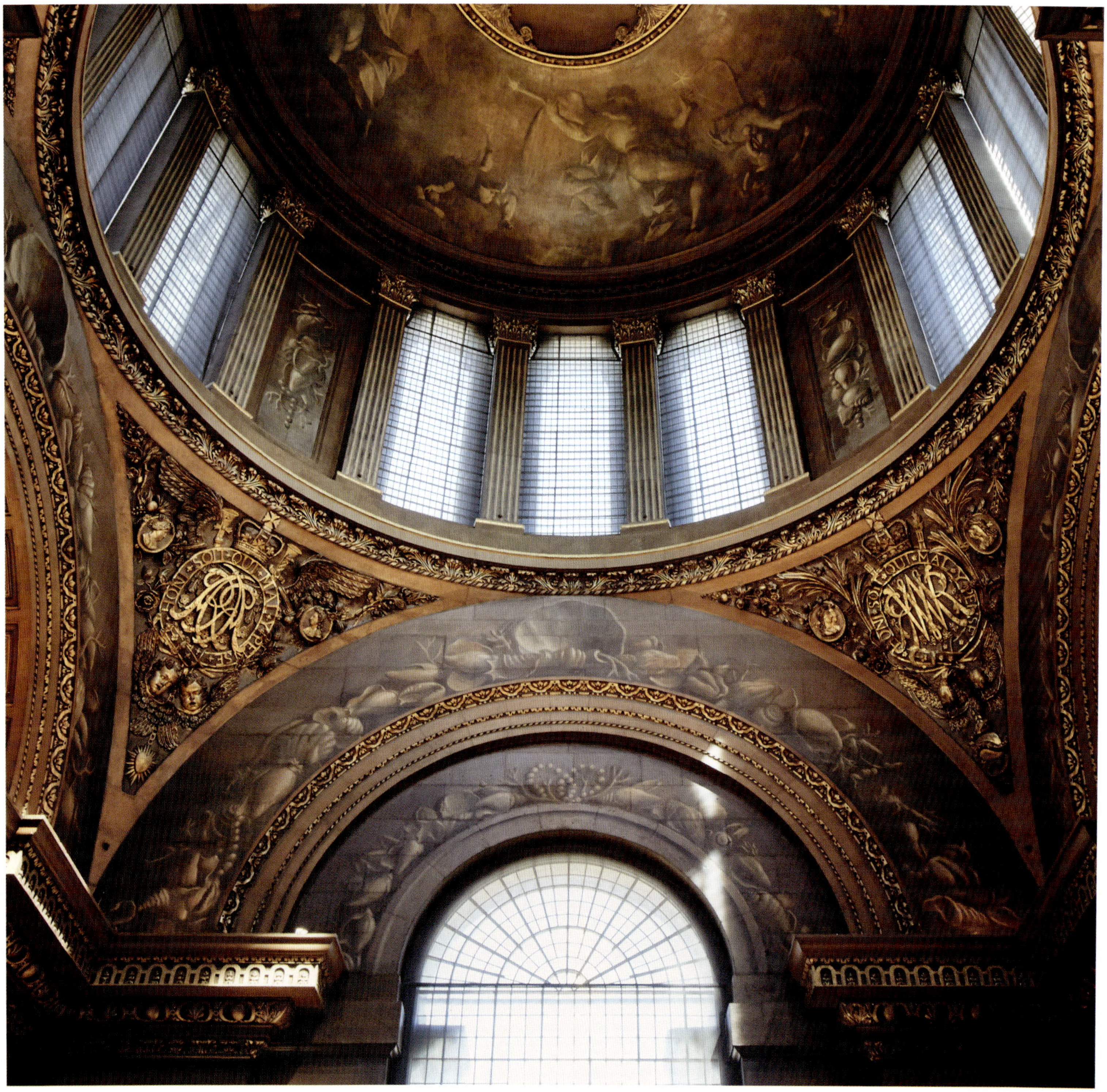

Fig. 2 (*above*) Interior view of the high drum and dome of the Vestibule.
Fig. 3 (*opposite*) Fictive tablet of donors above the south door of the Vestibule; to the right are the steps leading to the Lower Hall.

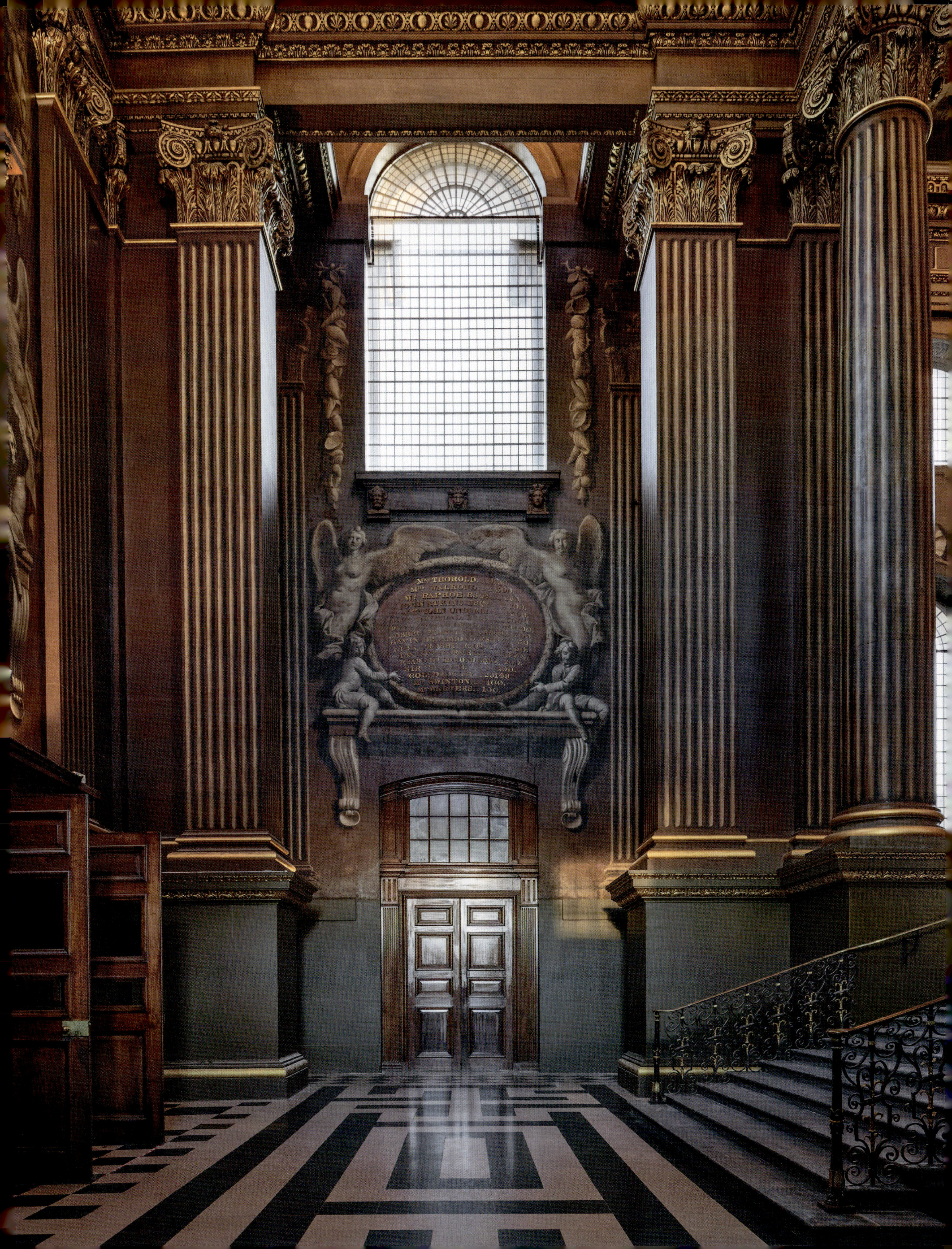

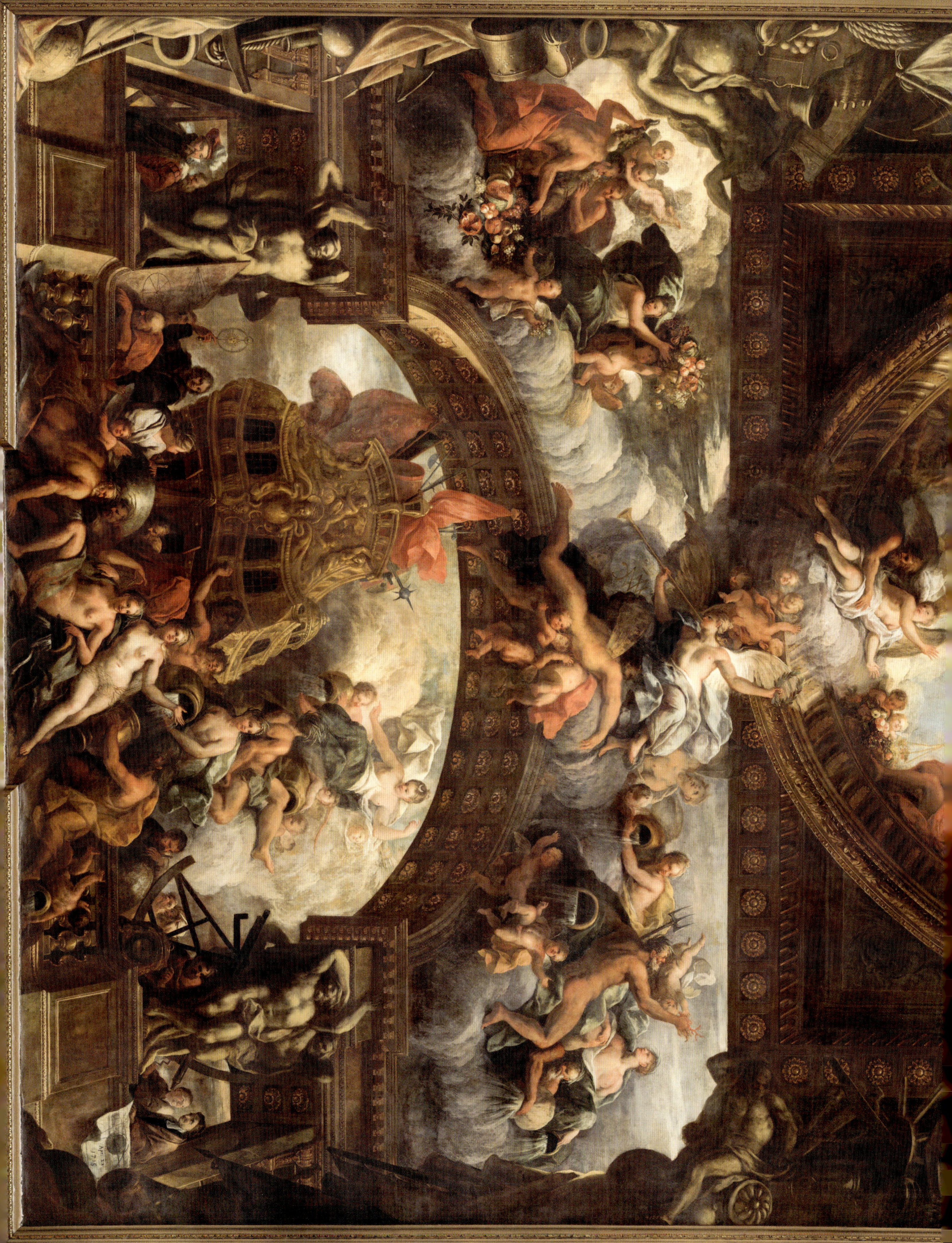

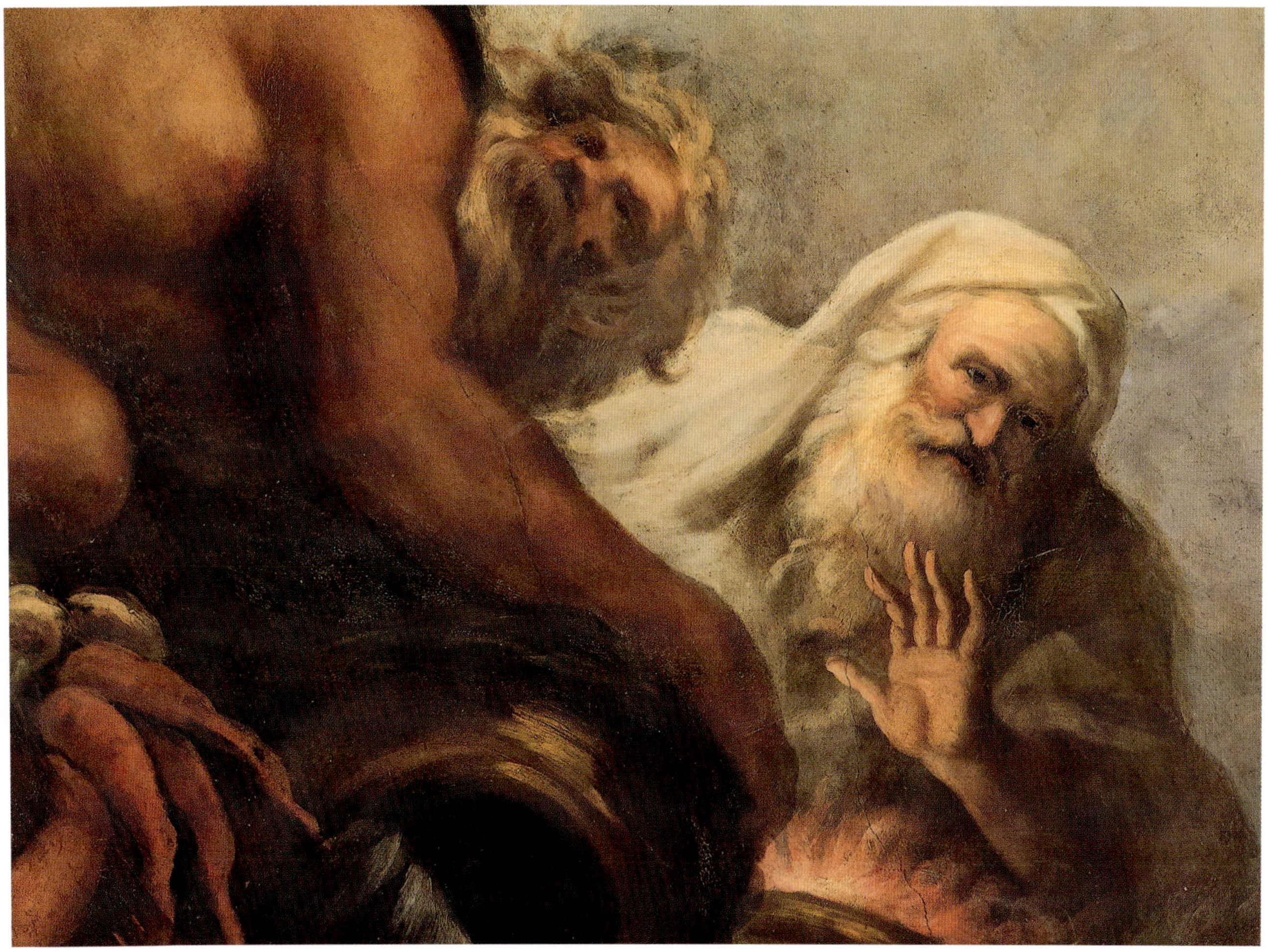

Fig. 5 John Worley, one of the first pensioners to be admitted to Greenwich Hospital in 1705, is depicted as Hyems, the personification of winter.

(holding a mirror) and Justice (with a sword; fig. 1). William accepts an olive branch from the personified figure of Peace, while offering a red cap of Liberty to Europe as he stamps on a cowering figure, identified for early visitors as '*Tyranny* and *Arbitrary Power*'. A papal crown and mitre tumble from the scene, and, in case of any doubt that this was an allusion to the religion and policies of the French king Louis XIV, the vanquished enemy holds a broken sword decorated with fleurs-de-lys.

Below the royal entourage, Pallas Athene (aka Minerva) and a club-wielding Hercules, representing '*Wisdom* and *Virtue*' respectively, do battle with a group of Vices (fig. 6). Among the contorted bodies and anguished faces of those expelled from the ceiling in a cloud of black smoke are '*Calumny*, *Detraction*, and *Envy*'. Looking on from the perimeter of the central oval are the twelve signs of the zodiac, accompanied in their rightful place by the four seasons (fig. 5). And all within are illuminated by the sun god, Apollo, who charges across the ceiling in a chariot drawn by four powerful white horses. The remaining spaces, to the east and west of this central oval, are each decorated with a large elliptical arch extending upwards from the pilasters of the supporting wall. In the angles, or quadrants, over the arches are the four elements – Fire, Air, Earth and Water – represented by Jupiter (or Zeus), Juno, Cybele and Neptune. Under each arch, a balustrade is painted along the width of the ceiling to form a gallery, busy with figures. Here also are two of the most visually striking elements of the whole scheme: projecting from both ends of the ceiling is the stern of a ship, near life-size and laden with trophies. At the west end of the Hall, half a dozen more steps lead the visitor through a proscenium arch and into a third painted chamber (fig. 7).

Fig. 6 (*opposite*) Pallas Athene and Hercules represent Wisdom and Virtue.

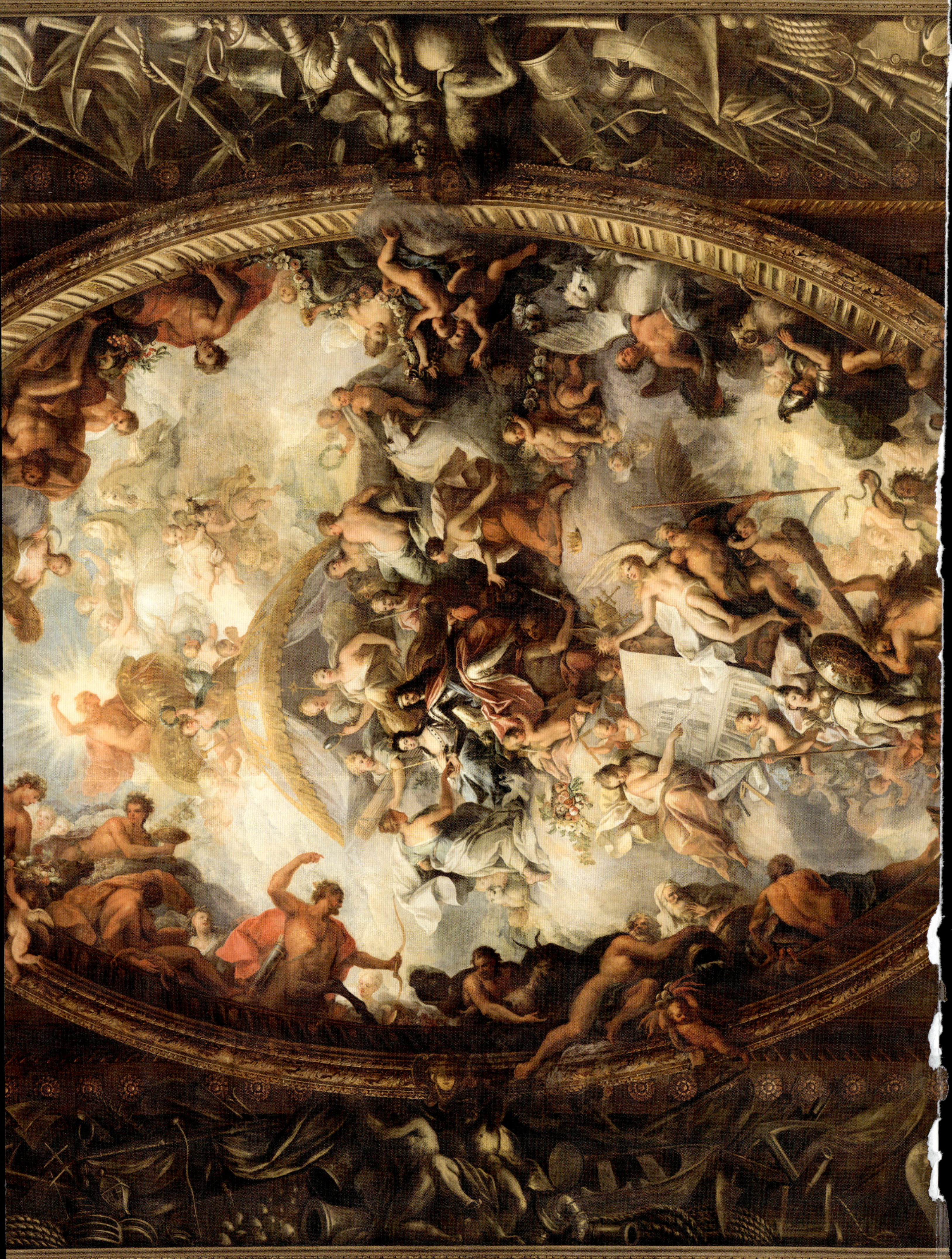

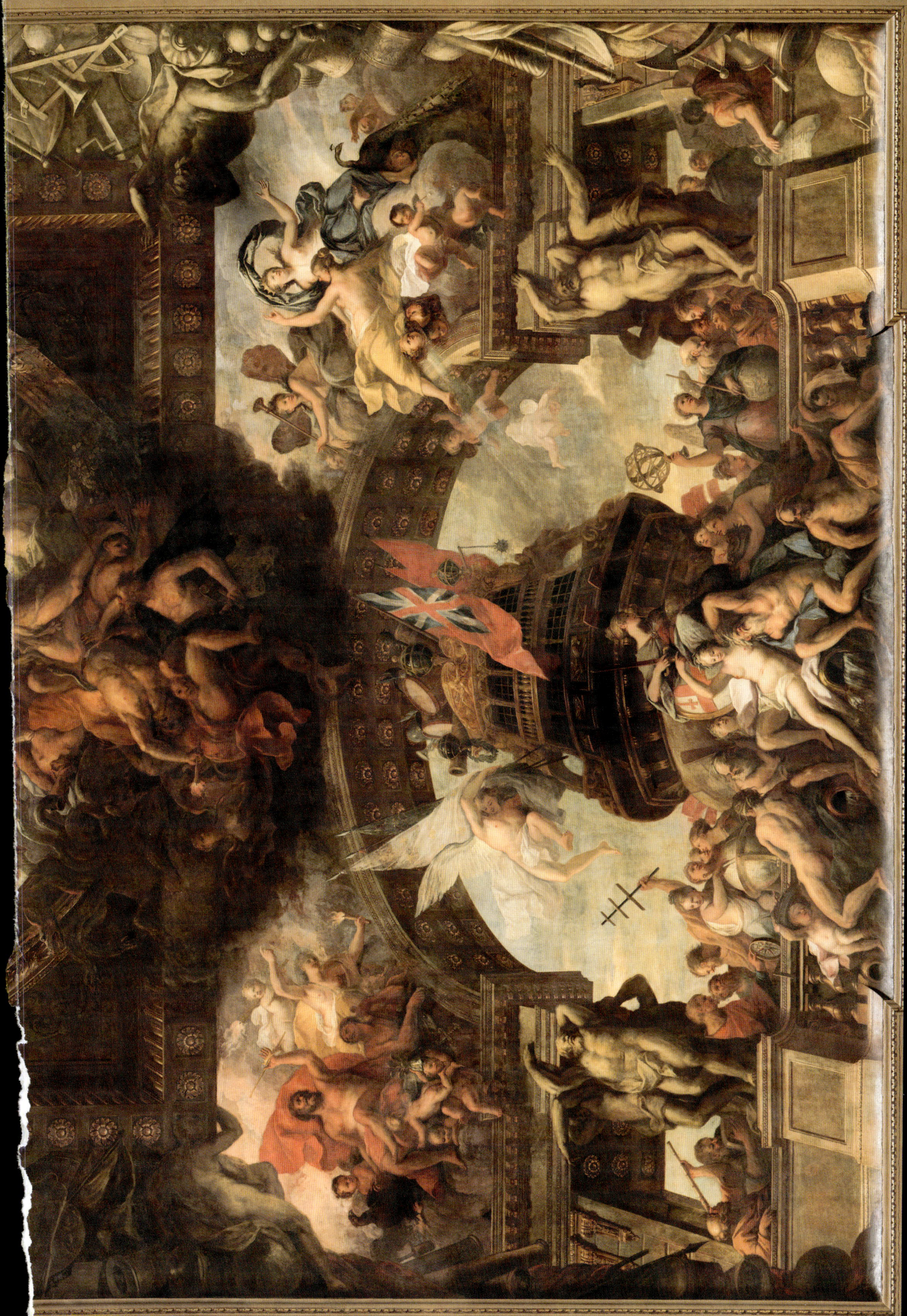

Fig. 4 (*gatefold*) The Lower Hall ceiling.

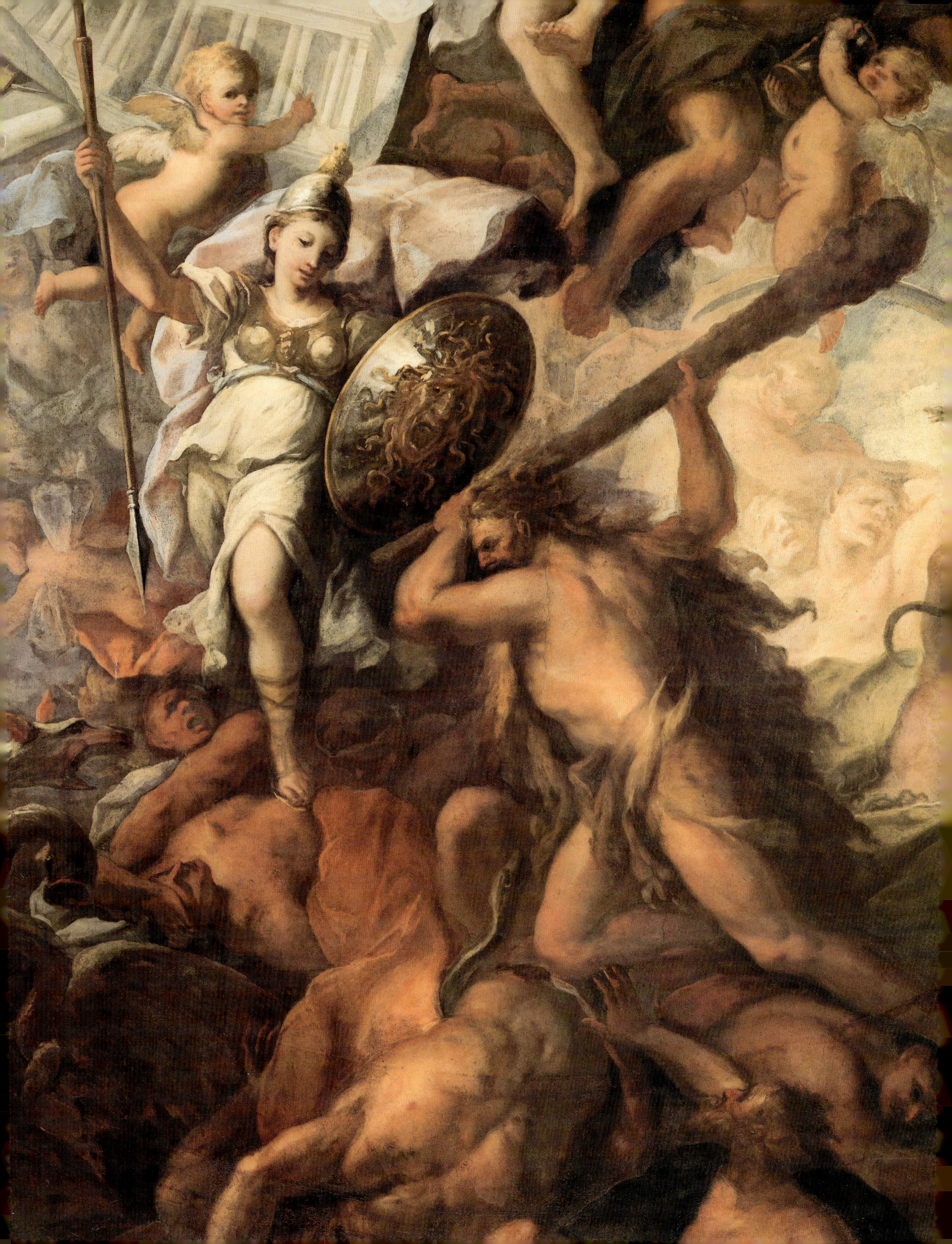

Fig. 7 View from the Lower Hall towards the proscenium arch and the steps to the Upper Hall.

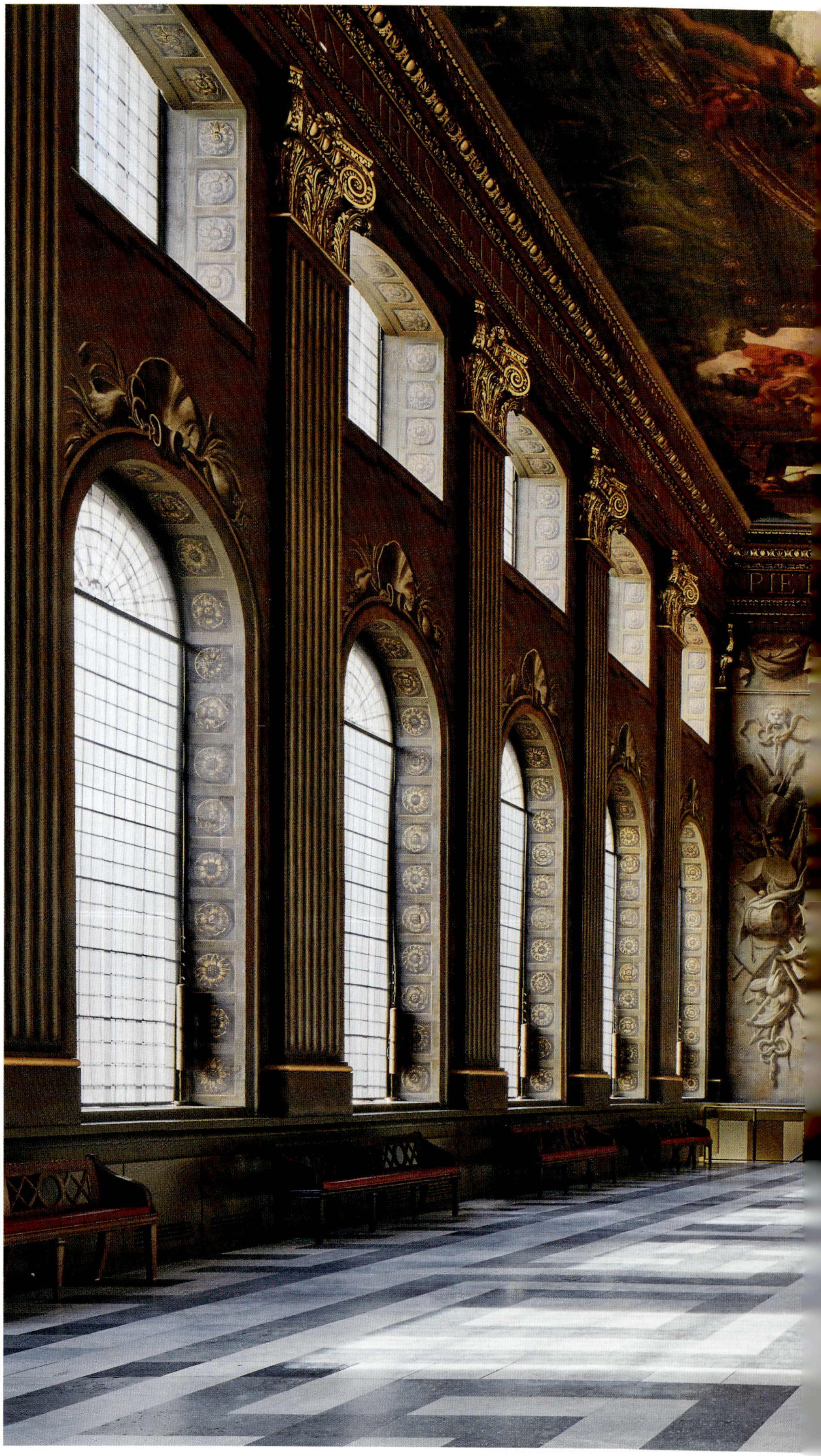

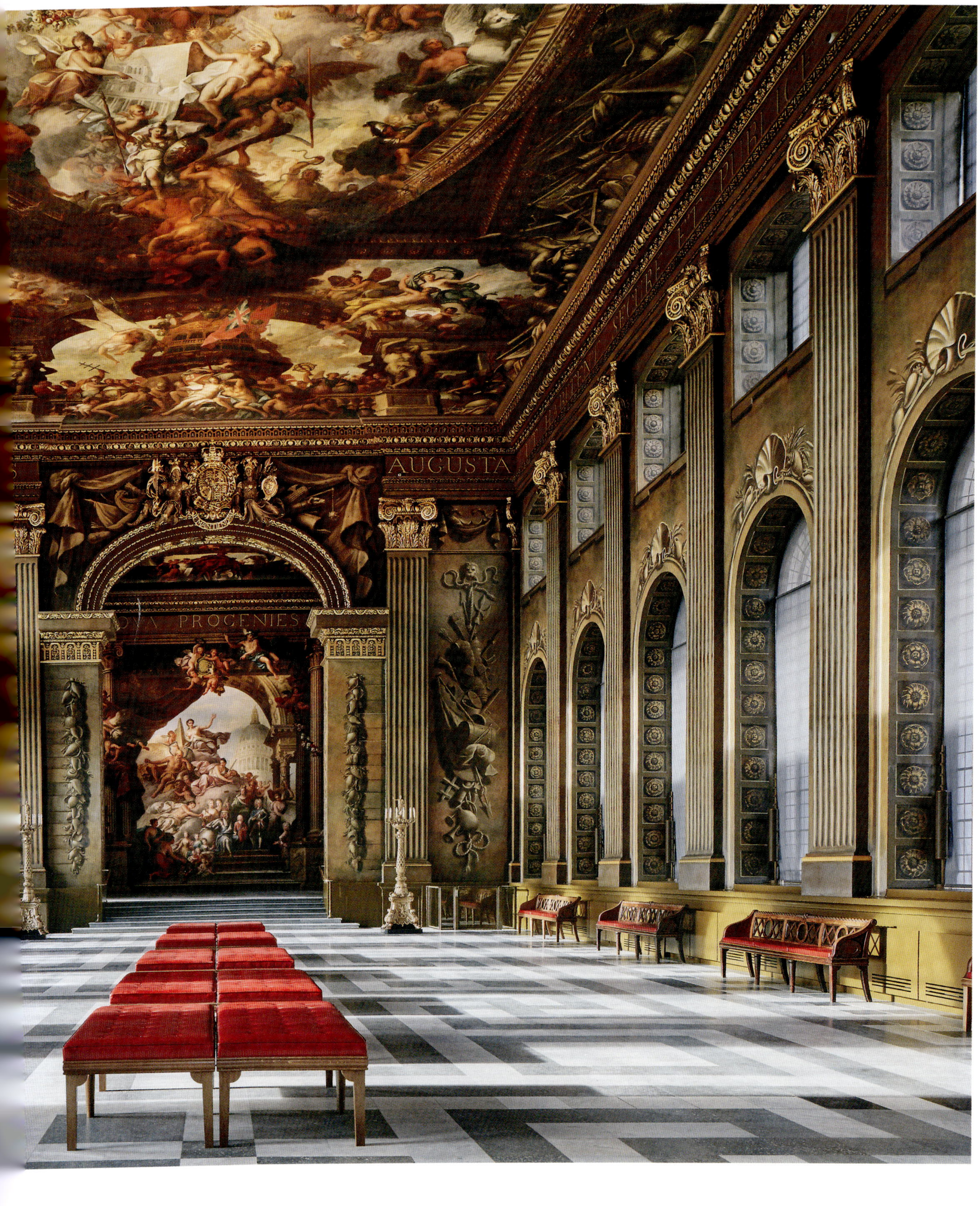
AUGUSTA
PROGENIES

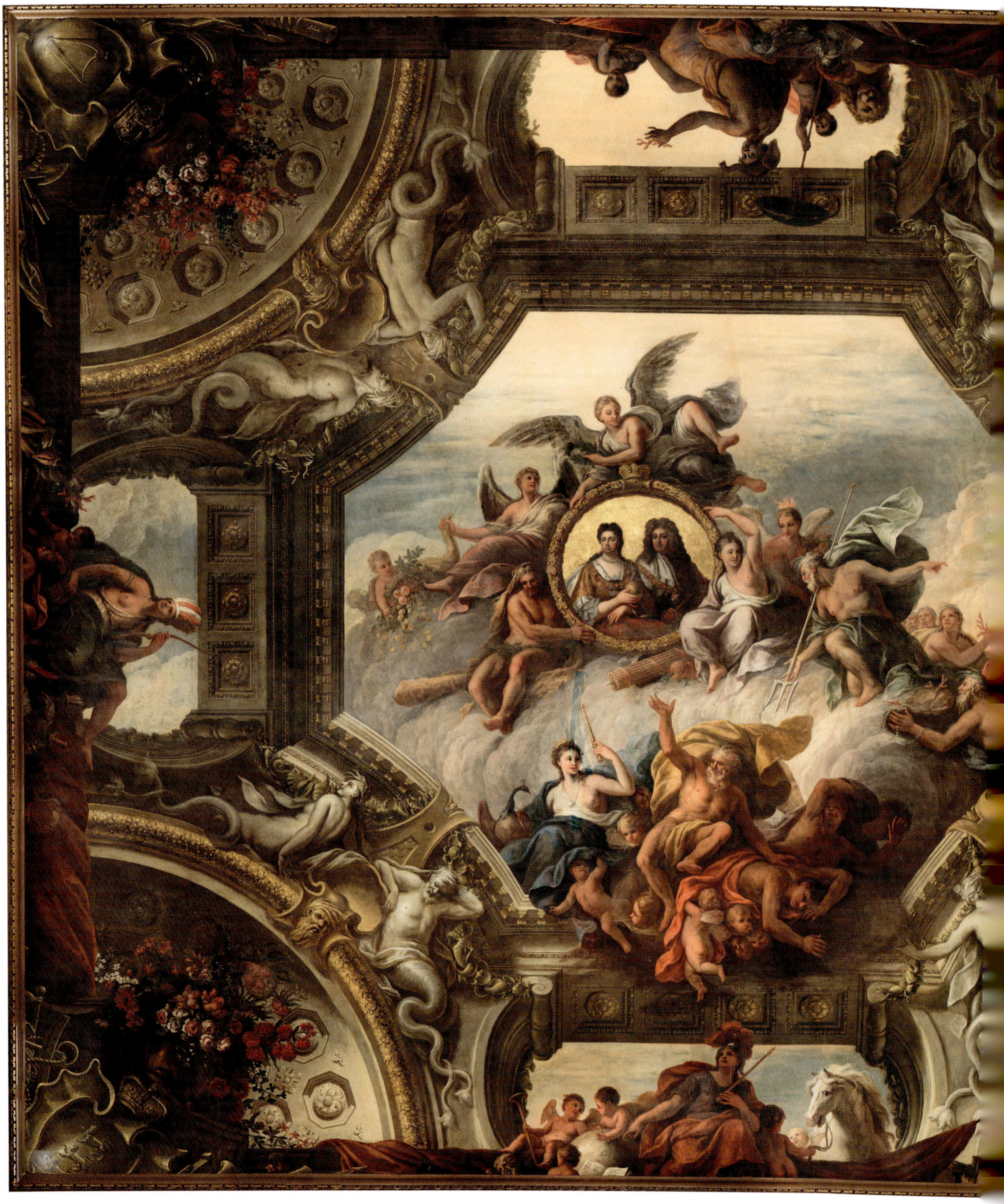

Fig. 8 The ceiling of the Upper Hall, with a double portrait of Queen Anne and Prince George of Denmark.

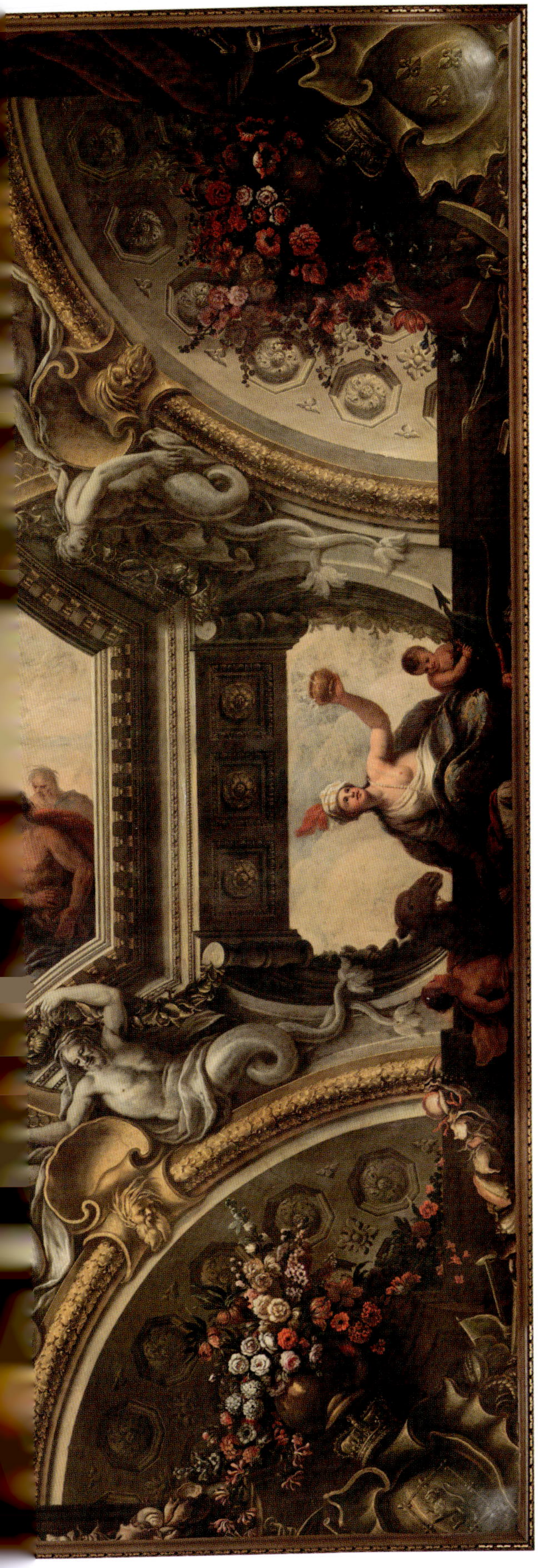

In the Cieling, which is elevated in Perspective, is *Queen Anne* with *Prince George* of *Denmark*, supported by *Virtue* HEROICK, *Concord* Conjugal, *Liberality*, *Piety*, *Victory*, &c.

On the Upper Hall ceiling is a double portrait of Queen Anne and Prince George of Denmark surrounded by a gilt frame and, in comparison with the Lower Hall, a more modest gathering of allegorical figures (fig. 8). Seated to the left is Hercules in his usual guise as Heroic Virtue; to the right, '*Concord* Conjugal'. Prince George assumes an unusual prominence in this painting as Lord High Admiral, and it is to him as much as to the Queen that Neptune offers his trident, signalling the supremacy of the Royal Navy. The winged figures of Liberality, or Plenty, Victory and Piety (with her crown of flames) complete the group around the royal couple.[2] Looking on are personifications of the four continents, set within the deep coving of an impressive octagonal pavilion replete with shells from every part of the world and flowers from every season.

The painted decoration continues along the same axis on the west wall of the Upper Hall with a glorification of Britain's Hanoverian princes. George I is seated at the centre, with the Prince of Wales (later George II) and his son, a young Prince Frederick, to his left. They are accompanied by other members of the royal family, and by a further array of allegorical bodies – some descending from the sky, others assembling at the feet of the royal party. The theme of maritime power, so prominent elsewhere in the Hall, continues with a winged figure of Naval Victory holding a trident from which hangs a scroll recording Britain's military triumphs at sea, including most recently the British defeat of the Spanish fleet off the coast of Sicily in 1718 at the Battle of Cape Passaro (an event also commemorated in oil by Thornhill's contemporary Peter Monamy; fig. 9).

Viewed in this sequential way, from the entrance to the west wall, Thornhill's complex scheme seems a coherent and unified whole, representing no fewer than five successive monarchs (six if we include Prince Frederick, who died before his father). Important in

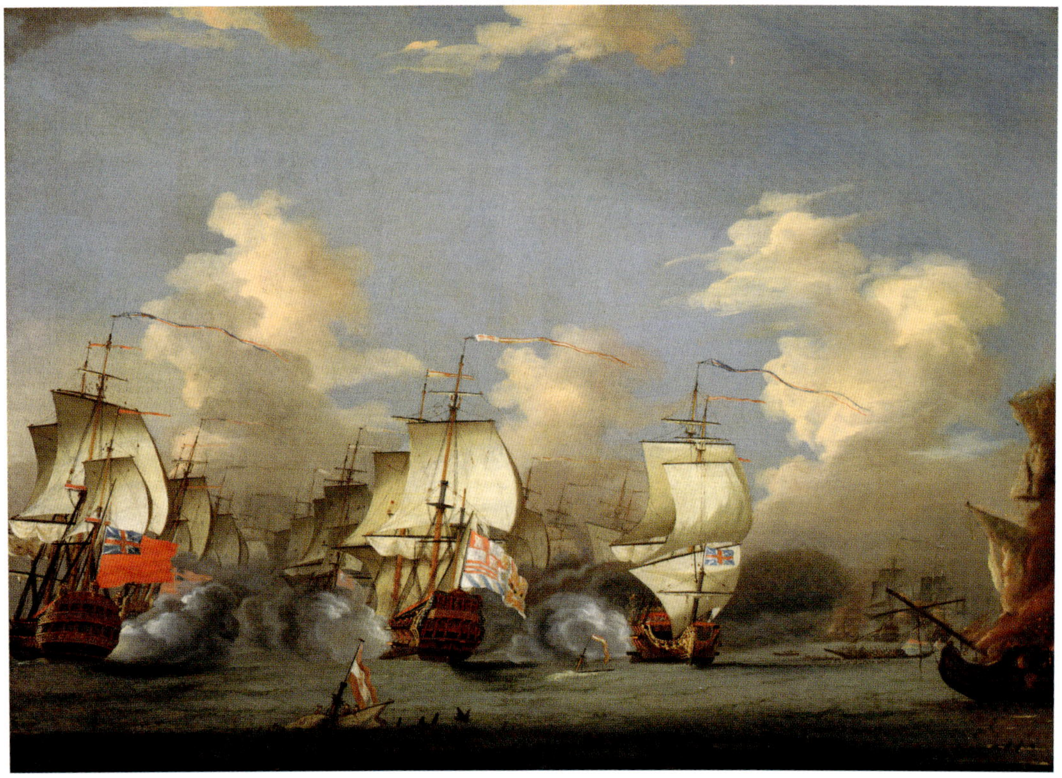

Fig. 9 Peter Monamy, *The Battle of Cape Passaro, 11 August 1718*, oil on canvas, early 18th century.

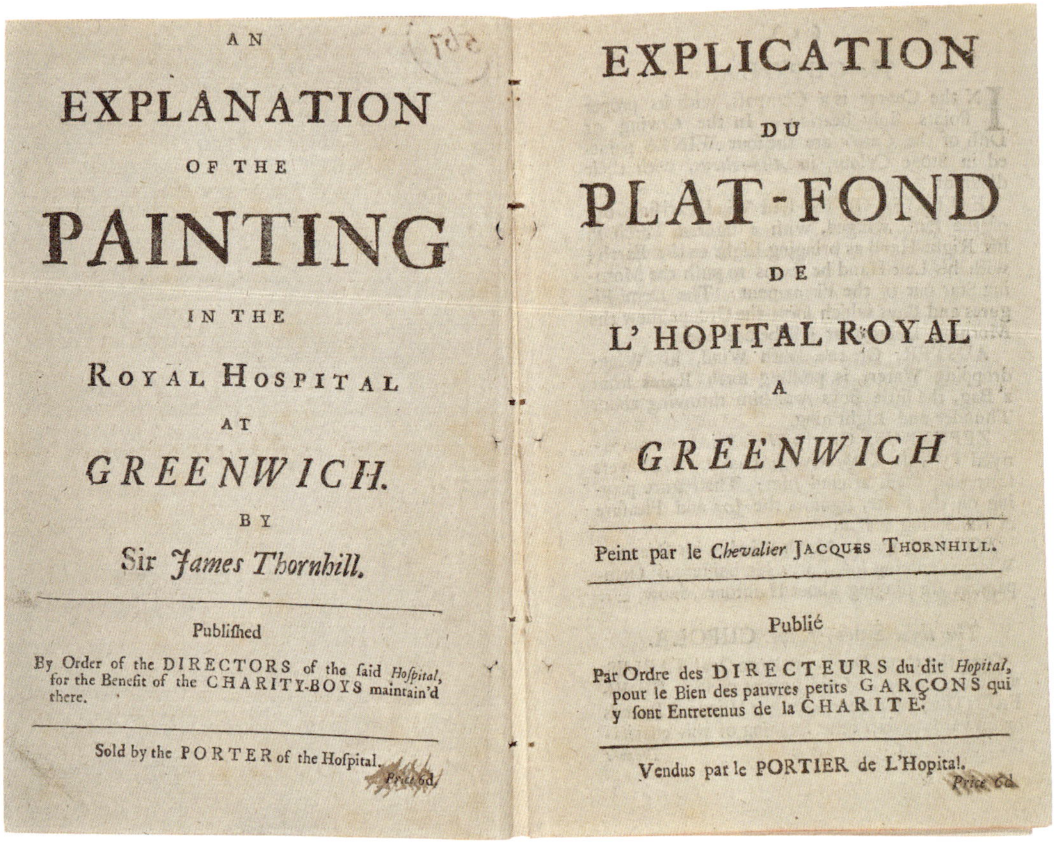

AN
EXPLANATION
OF THE
PAINTING
IN THE
ROYAL HOSPITAL
AT
GREENWICH.
BY
Sir *James Thornhill.*

Publiſhed
By Order of the DIRECTORS of the ſaid *Hoſpital*, for the Benefit of the CHARITY-BOYS maintain'd there.

Sold by the PORTER of the Hoſpital. *Price 6d.*

EXPLICATION
DU
PLAT-FOND
DE
L' HOPITAL ROYAL
A
GREENWICH

Peint par le *Chevalier* JACQUES THORNHILL.

Publié
Par Ordre des DIRECTEURS du dit *Hopital*, pour le Bien des pauvres petits GARÇONS qui y ſont Entretenus de la CHARITE.

Vendus par le PORTIER de L'Hopital. *Price 6d.*

Fig. 10 *An Explanation of the Painting in the Royal Hospital at Greenwich by Sir James Thornhill*, published 1726.

creating this impression of pictorial and political unity are the chorus of Virtues and other personifications that appear at each stage of the scheme, and the small army of helpful putti, or winged infants, busily shifting scenery and props into place (the allusion to a chorus and stage hands is deliberate; the Painted Hall may be likened to an operatic production of the most ambitious kind). These characters supply the recurring motifs – the cornucopias and laurel crowns, the scales and swords – that forge a continuous allegory of good government from one monarch to the next.

The visual coherence of the scheme is reinforced by the non-figurative elements of the decoration: by the use of a single order for both the real and the *trompe l'œil* architecture throughout; by the uniform details of the painted mouldings, trophies and inscriptions in both the Lower and Upper Halls; and not least by the soft architecture of the clouds, which roll across the two ceilings before tumbling down to Earth on the west wall, allowing the illusion of a single pictorial space broken only by the supporting framework of the building. In this way, the scheme progresses without interruption from one painted surface to another, from a glorification of William and Mary on the Lower Hall ceiling to Queen Anne on the Upper Hall ceiling and finally to the Hanoverian princes on the far wall.

That is certainly the impression that was encouraged by an early explanation of the Hall, first published by the Hospital directors to coincide with the completion of Thornhill's work in 1726 (fig. 10). Incorporating redrafted elements of an earlier description of the Lower Hall by the essayist and politician Richard Steele into a detailed account of the Vestibule and Upper Hall,[3] *An Explanation of the Painting in the Royal Hospital at Greenwich* provided the first official, inexpensive guide to the completed scheme. It made the complex iconography of Thornhill's painting comprehensible to the thousands who visited the Hall during the initial few years after its completion, many of whom would never have previously encountered this type of sprawling allegory.

The official *Explanation* still offers one of the best introductions to Thornhill's painting. Written with the close cooperation of the artist, it offers a rare insight into an eighteenth-century world of political allegory that can seem wilfully obscure to visitors today. It is also a useful reminder that, from the beginning, the Painted Hall at Greenwich was not supposed to be difficult to understand. Early visitors could buy a copy for sixpence, and for a shilling or two more could be shown around the Hall by one of the resident pensioners (fig. 11). But if the official *Explanation* gives visitors access to the vocabulary and grammar of grand-scale decorative painting, it also exercises a high degree of control over that experience, guiding us from one part of the Hall to another, giving cause to dwell on some parts of the painting while glossing over other details with a cursory '&c.'. It encourages the viewer to read the scheme in a particular order (roughly in the sequence in which it has just been described), and therefore to understand the whole as a seamless celebration of the nation's recent royal past, united by the common themes of national prosperity and military success.

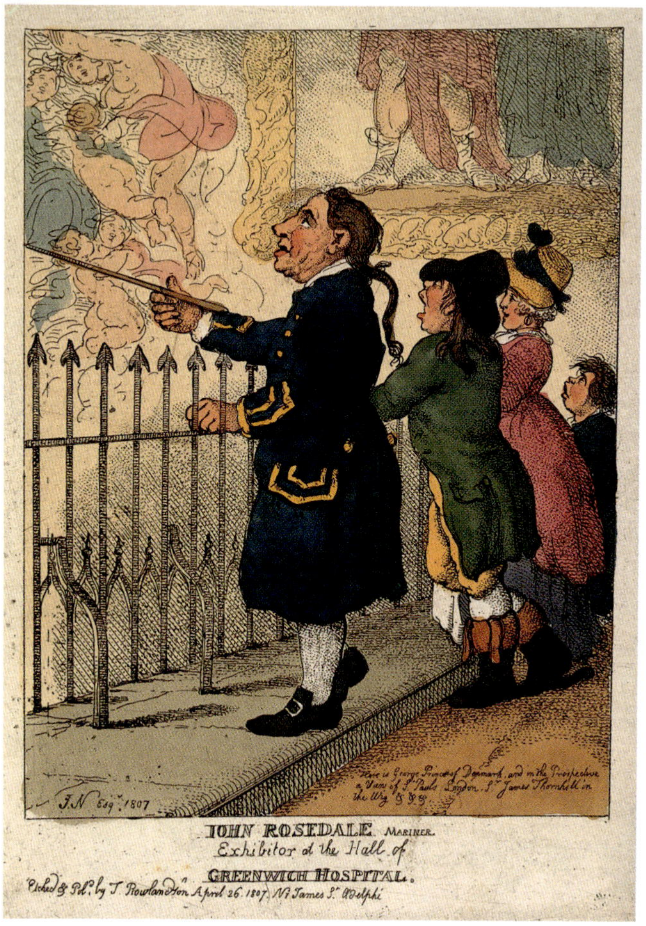

Fig. 11 Thomas Rowlandson, *John Rosedale, Mariner, Exhibitor of the Hall of Greenwich Hospital*, hand-coloured etching, 1807.

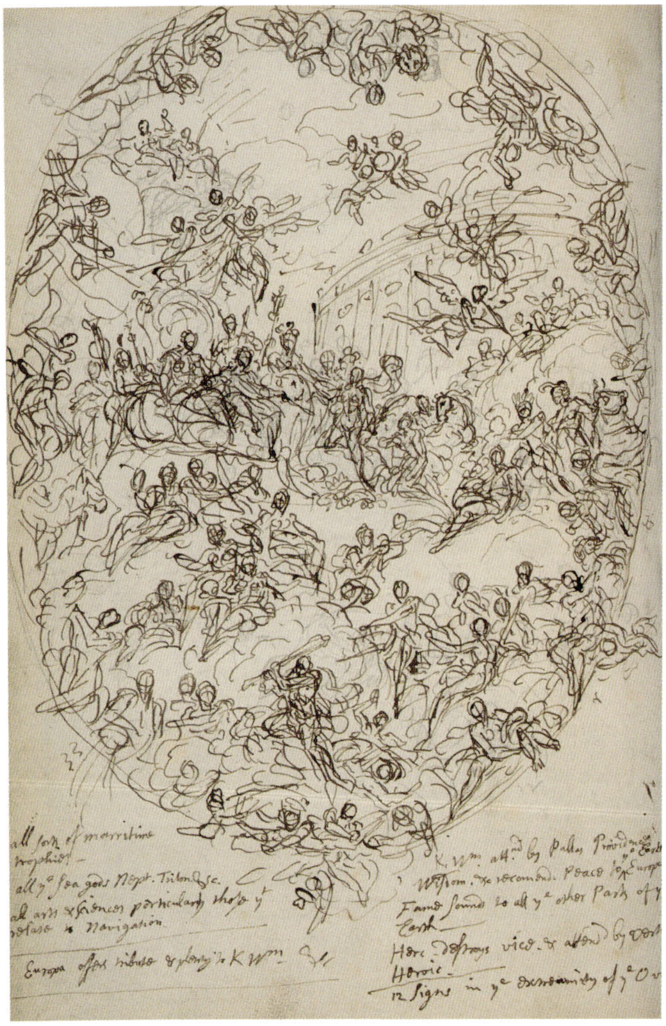

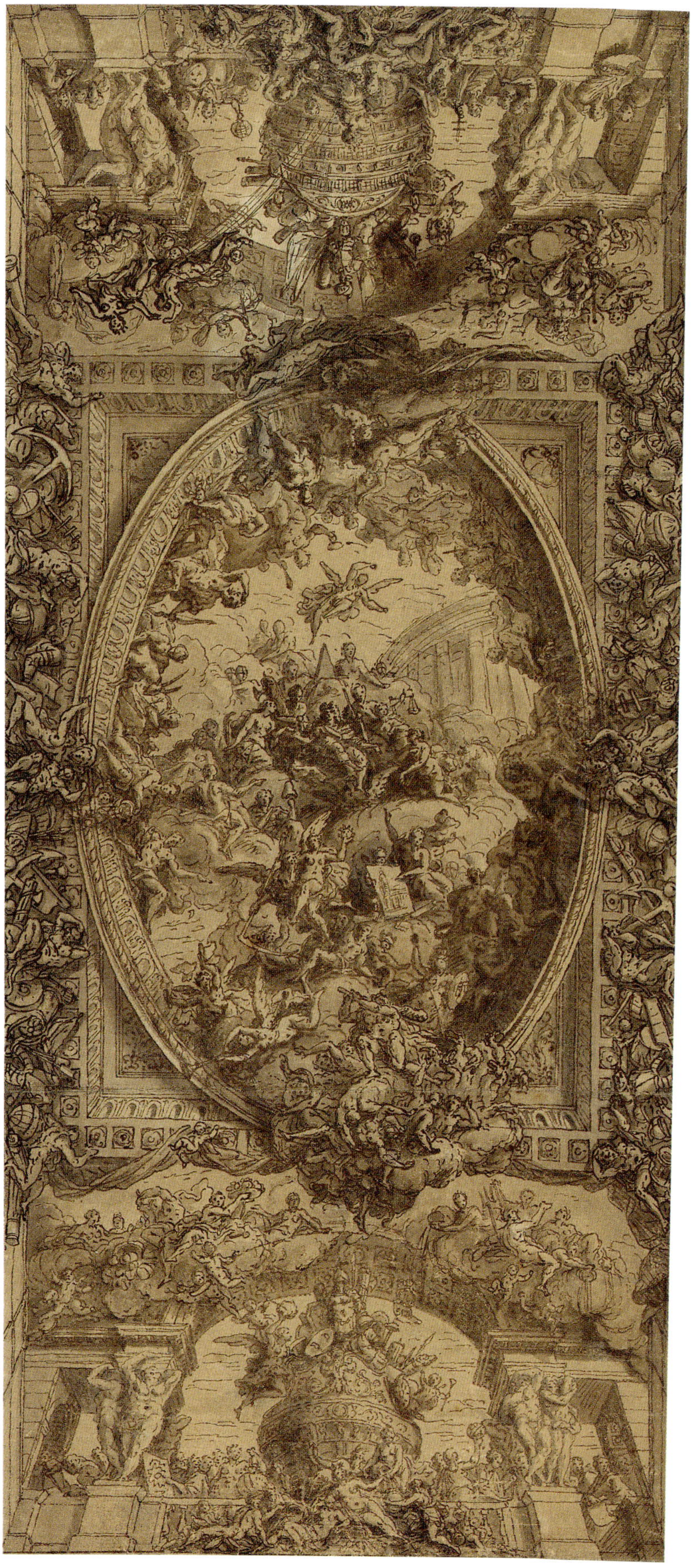

Fig. 12 (*above*) James Thornhill, preliminary design in the artist's sketchbook for the central oval of the Lower Hall ceiling, pen and brown ink over pencil, *c.* 1707.

Fig. 13 (*right*) James Thornhill, full ceiling design for the Lower Hall, pen and brown ink with brown and grey wash over pencil, *c.* 1707.

Over all is a *Figure* holding a PYRAMID, which signifies *Stability*, or the Glory of Princes.

It is a powerful illusion, one that belies the more disjointed and unpredictable way in which the painting itself and the events emplotted on its walls and ceilings came about. For example, the minutes of the Hospital's Fabric Committee reveal that the Vestibule, the first part of the scheme to be encountered and the first to be described in the 1726 *Explanation*, was in fact the last to be painted, almost two decades after work in the Lower Hall had begun.[4] The same records also reveal that the Lower and Upper Halls, the two main components of the decoration, were distinct projects initiated by separate commissions under very different circumstances. Painting began in the Lower Hall in 1708, several years after the death of its main subjects, King William (who died in 1702) and Queen Mary (who died in 1694). It was completed by 1714, at which point the west wall still contained two windows. Early designs reveal plans for an elaborate allegorical portrait of Queen Anne for the west wall. However, by the time Thornhill was formally requested to extend the decoration into the Upper Hall, Anne's death had brought the German-speaking George I to the throne – an event that could hardly have been imagined when work on the first phase of decoration began.

Thornhill's name first appears in the official records on 17 July 1707, when he was asked to prepare the ceiling by priming it himself as soon as the scaffolding was ready, and to make 'such Alterations in his designe by inserting what more he can relating to maritime affaires'.[5] It is clear from the directors' instructions that there had already been several meetings with the artist, and that the overarching theme of the decoration had been discussed. Several preliminary designs for the Lower Hall provide an eloquent visual record of the to-and-fro between artist and patron as a final design emerged during the course of about a year, from early annotated ideas on the pages of the artist's sketchbook to larger and more intricate drawings in which the relationships between figures, and their interaction with the

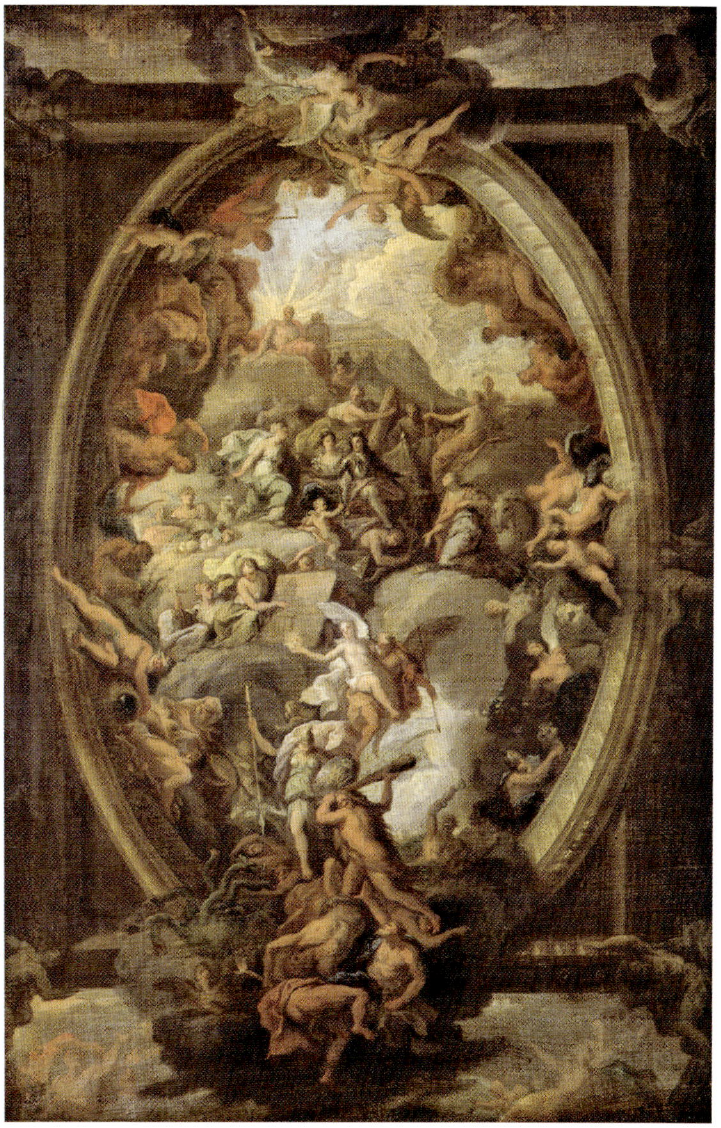

Fig. 14 James Thornhill, design for the central oval of the Lower Hall ceiling, oil on canvas, 1707–1708.

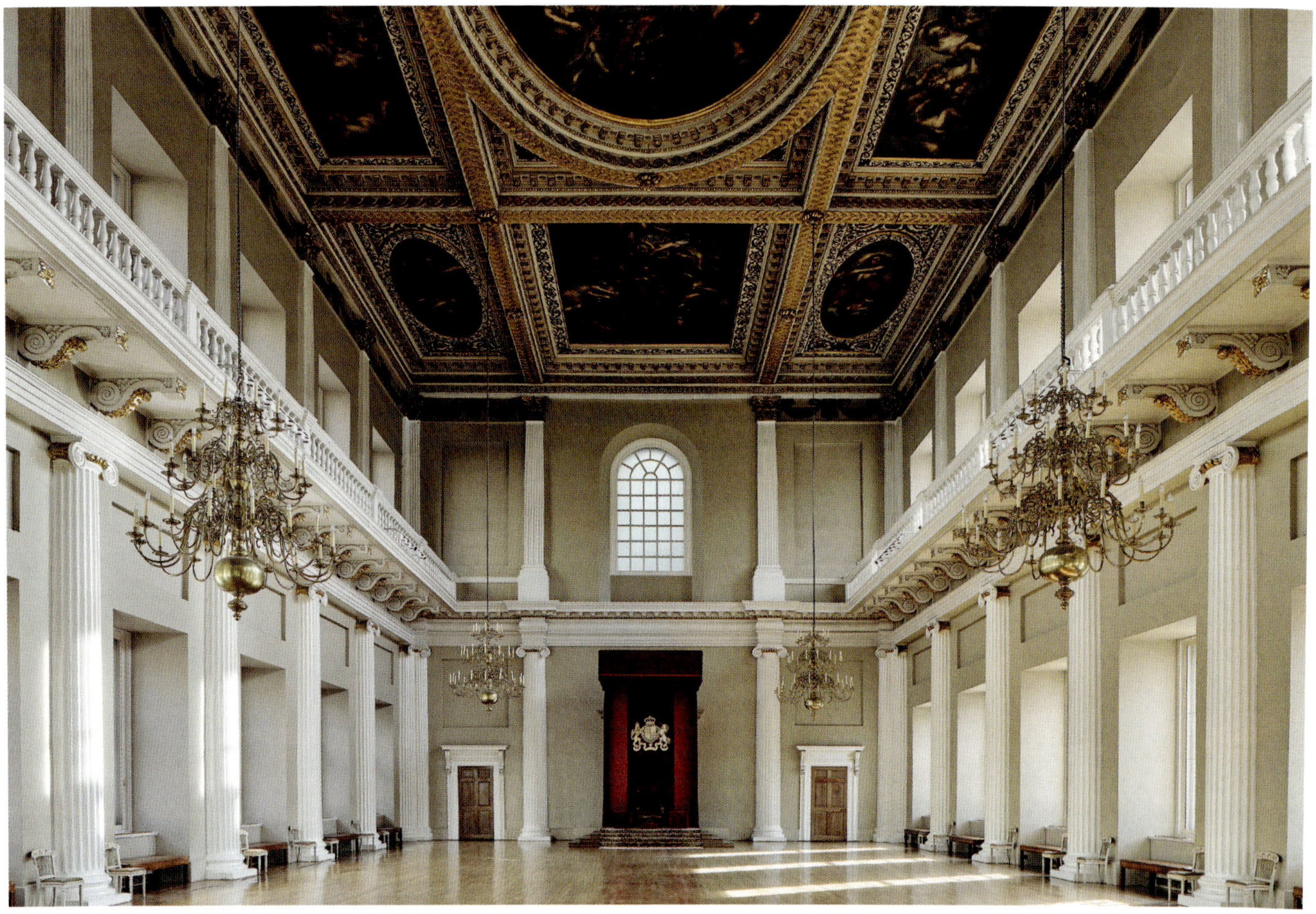

Fig. 15 The Banqueting House, Whitehall, with paintings by Peter Paul Rubens, installed 1636.

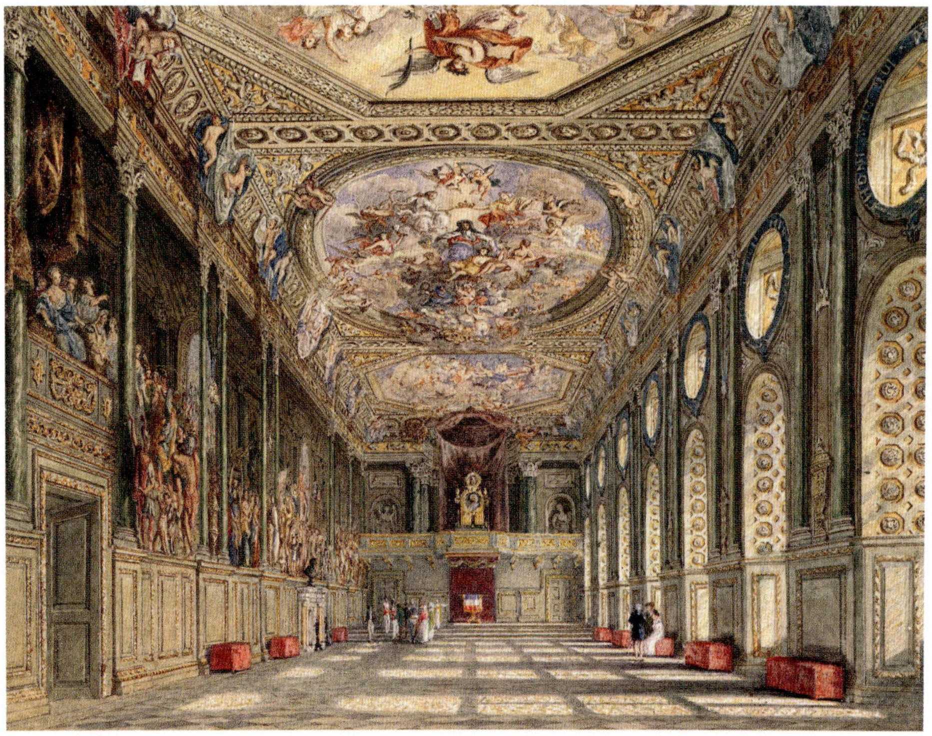

Fig. 16 Charles Wild, *St George's Hall, Windsor Castle*, pencil and watercolour, *c.* 1816.

surrounding architecture, are worked out in more detail (figs. 12 and 13). Painting on such a grand scale was necessarily a collaborative enterprise that required the coordination of many highly skilled artists and craftsmen. But these drawings tell us something more specific about Thornhill's role as the inventor of the pictorial scheme at Greenwich. In each of these preparatory designs, William III is at the centre of things (though not, until the final stages, accompanied by Mary), and Hercules is always nearby. From the outset, the decoration of the Painted Hall placed at its centre the figure of William as the Protestant hero of an aristocratic Whig 'revolution'.

An oil sketch, which was made shortly before work on the ceiling began, shows the central section close to its final design, and gives the earliest indication of the chromatic range of the ceiling (fig. 14). One important detail of this sketch deserves a special mention. Just below the royal couple is a large drawing of the King William building, supported by a female personification of Architecture, who gestures towards the king with her left hand while pointing to the structure named in his honour with her right. To the right of the drawing is the winged figure of '*Time* bringing *Truth* to Light', providing a subtle reminder to the Hall's early visitors that another, equal part – the Queen Mary building – had still to be built. In the final painting, Thornhill added a putto at the bottom of the drawing. The infant's task was clear: to cajole the visitor into following the example of the Hospital's royal founders by contributing towards its completion (fig. 1 on p. 14).

Underneath is a Figure of *Architecture* holding a DRAWING of Part of the *Hospital*, and pointing up to the Royal Founders.

Three years after the Lower Hall ceiling had been completed, Thornhill petitioned the Hospital directors for what money he was still owed for his work in the Lower Hall. Before agreeing a figure, the directors instructed the Clerk of the Works at Greenwich, Nicholas Hawksmoor, and the Clerk, John James, to investigate the cost of other painted schemes around the country. Among those identified as suitable comparisons were Thornhill's own recently completed decoration for the Duke of Marlborough at Blenheim Palace, Robert Streater's earlier painting on the ceiling of the Sheldonian Theatre in Oxford, and Antonio Verrio's royal commissions at Windsor and Hampton Court. Thornhill himself was rather more ambitious, adding Peter Paul Rubens's work at the Banqueting House (fig. 15) to his own list, which he submitted to the same board of directors in the following month.[6]

The artist's inclusion of the Banqueting House was not wholly unjustified. After all, the type of royal panegyric that Thornhill painted on the ceiling at Greenwich had been established in England by Rubens at Whitehall nearly a century before. Moreover, it was a scheme that Thornhill knew well and referred to often, not least of all in his early designs for Greenwich. However, in terms of subject matter and style, both the artist and his employers would have agreed that there was a more immediate precedent for the artist's work in the Lower Hall: Verrio's painting on the ceiling of St George's Hall at Windsor Castle. The scheme was destroyed when much of the palace was remodelled during the nineteenth century, but a watercolour of the hall made a few years earlier (fig. 16) gives a good indication of its former splendour, showing Charles II as the gravitational centre of the design, around whom all else revolved. The ceiling painting was in keeping with Verrio's decoration in the other rooms at Windsor, in which the king was portrayed in a variety of god-like roles, each one reinforcing the divine assumptions of the Restoration monarchy.

King William presents PEACE and LIBERTY to *Europe*, and tramples on *Tyranny* and *Arbitrary Power*.

The architectural historian Howard Colvin once described Verrio's work at Windsor as 'fulsomely and unrealistically propagandist in the manner accepted throughout Europe in the seventeenth century' – a response that applies equally well to Thornhill's work at Greenwich.[7] However,

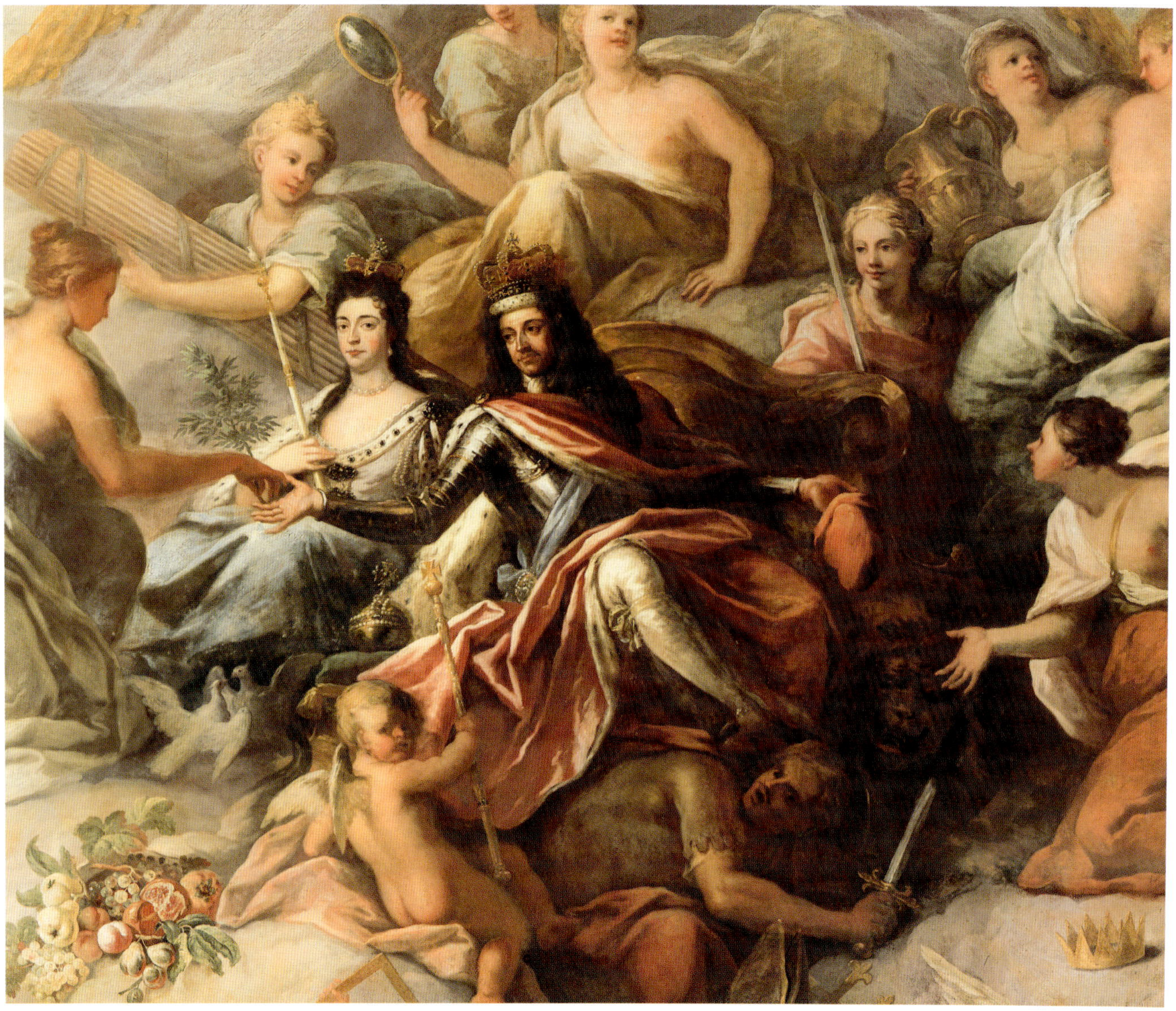

Fig. 17 William III negotiates between the figures of Peace (left) and Europe (right).

while working within the same recognizable format, Thornhill's scheme differs from Verrio's in a number of ways that combine to project a subtly different image of William and Mary's reign. While drawing on the powerful precedent at Windsor to give his design an appropriate sense of grandeur (and, importantly, an air of continuity with the previous regime), Thornhill also sought ways to distinguish the Williamite narrative that plays out in the Painted Hall from the visual culture of the Restoration court by staging William's rule as a triumph of Protestant 'liberty' over the perceived twin evils of popery and arbitrary government.

Leaning backwards, his arms outstretched as he negotiates between the personified figures of Peace and Europe, William exudes an air of natural command in his assumed role as the defender of Protestant internationalism (fig. 17). His self-appointed task, restoring the balance of power between Europe's warring nations, seems almost effortless, conveyed on the ceiling as a gloriously simple exchange between a handful of well-disposed figures. William's open-armed posture and averted gaze not only convey a powerful idea of the king's political character, they also serve to direct our attention away from the royal bodies at the centre, inviting visitors to explore the outward parts of the ceiling, where the narrative of the Painted Hall continues in ways that extend beyond the lifetime and immediate concerns of its royal protagonists.

On the Right in this Gallery is the celebrated *English* Astronomer the Reverend Mr *Flamsteed*, who holds the Construction of the great Eclipse which happen'd *April* the 22d, 1715.

The readiness with which the royal couple at the centre of the ceiling became subsumed within a wider patriotic spectacle at Greenwich is suggested by the testimony of one early visitor, Ralph Thoresby (fig. 18), a Leeds antiquarian who visited the Painted Hall with some friends a few weeks after the last of the scaffolding used by Thornhill and his assistants had been cleared from the Lower Hall. Thoresby recorded his impression of the newly completed ceiling in his diary:

We viewed the Royal Hospital, fitter, indeed, for a Royal residence, than poor mariners, &c: the hall is admirably painted, by Mr Thornhill; ... in the centre of the oval, upon the roof, are the pictures of King William and Queen Mary, with the Liberal Arts, &c. All the several apartments of the said ceiling are delicately performed: amongst the Astronomers is Dr Flamstead, with the scheme of an almost total eclipse of the sun, with the date April 22, 1715.[8]

Thoresby was mistaken on one point of detail: the 'Liberal Arts' are among the few allegorical regulars that do not appear on the ceiling at Greenwich. However, this apparent oversight contrasts with the rest of his short account, which is notably precise, focusing on a single event – a solar eclipse calculated to take place on 22 April of the following year. The way in which Thoresby's brief account moves from a general, if inaccurate, recognition of the royal couple's entourage at the centre of the ceiling to the specific, contemporary detail of the eclipse in the corner – giving equal importance to both – is suggestive of the novel kind of viewing that Thornhill's painting at Greenwich encouraged.

Of all the figures represented in the Lower Hall, it is significant that Thoresby should single out John Flamsteed (1646–1719), the first Astronomer Royal, for special attention (fig. 19). He appears in the south-eastern corner of the ceiling, almost hidden from view, with his assistant Thomas Weston. In the astronomer's hand is a large piece of paper with a measured and beautifully simple diagram of a solar eclipse. And there is a date, just as Thoresby recorded, and a little to the left a large table clock set at approximately two minutes past nine. Painting on such a scale is rarely so exact in its detail.

Flamsteed is one of several earthly and allegorical figures on the ceiling representing the history of astronomy. Others include Tycho Brahe, the celebrated sixteenth-century Danish star-gazer, and Copernicus, who holds a model demonstrating the orbit of the Earth around the Sun. Flamsteed was a worthy successor to these astronomers of old. After his appointment as Astronomer Royal in 1675, he spent the next forty years mapping the northern stars from the newly founded Royal Observatory in Greenwich, a short walk from

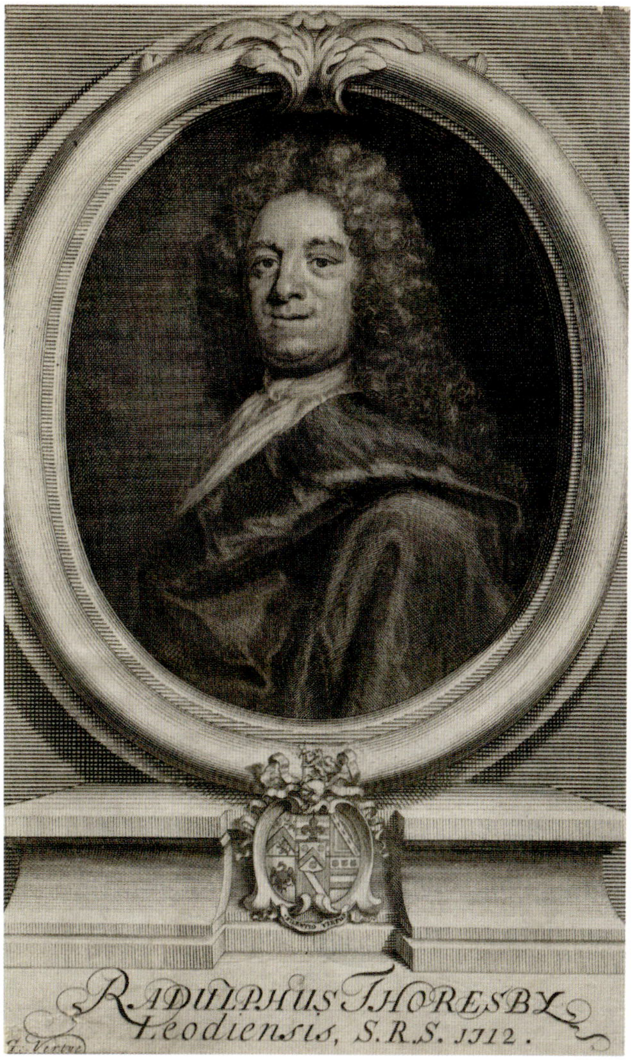

Fig. 18 George Vertue, *Radulphus Thoresby Leodiensis* (Ralph Thoresby of Leeds), engraving, 1712.

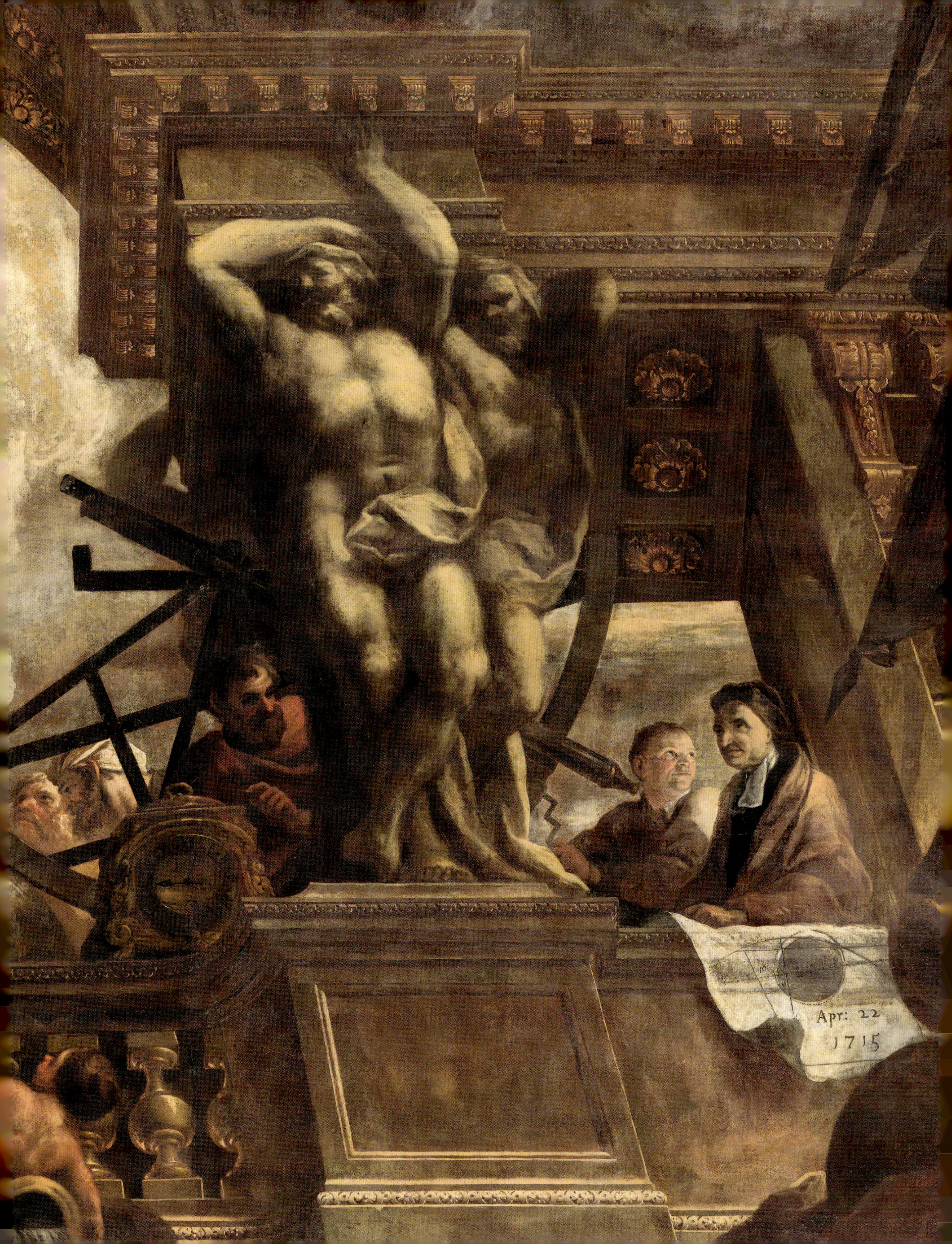
Apr: 22
1715

the Painted Hall. The mural arc telescope that he designed in 1689 (fig. 20) was an astonishingly accurate instrument for its time, used to measure the position and magnitude of any visible star as it passed a fixed north–south axis, or meridian. The resulting data, when cross-referenced with the observatory's two pendulum clocks and adjusted for atmospheric refraction, allowed Flamsteed and his assistants to document the northern night sky more fully and accurately than ever before.[9]

The ultimate goal of Flamsteed's Herculean task at the Royal Observatory was to provide a reliable means to determine a ship's longitude at sea.[10] The strategic and commercial advantages of being able to pinpoint a ship's position anywhere on the globe were immense, but for centuries sailors had relied on a combination of experience and folklore to find their way between continents, using methods that were at best inefficient and at worst disastrous. Accurate navigation depended on the ability of a ship's captain to keep time relative to a fixed position on land (thereby using the time difference and the speed of the Earth's rotation to calculate the longitudinal distance between the two points). Before the development of reliable chronometers later in the eighteenth century, the best hope of doing that rested on Isaac Newton's new theory of the Moon's orbit (represented on the ceiling by a pair of 'Mathematical Figures', or diagrams), coupled with an accurate understanding of the position and movement of the stars – in effect, turning the night sky into a universal timepiece. Thornhill also painted Newton's portrait around the same time for Trinity College, Cambridge (fig. 21).

The ability of astronomers to calculate the cycle of the eclipse to within a few seconds was a powerful demonstration of Newton's lunar theory and a testament to the accuracy of Flamsteed's observations. The symbolic importance of the eclipse was heightened by the fact that its path of totality passed over London – an event so rare that the last occurrence had been during the reign of King Alfred (the next is expected on 21 July 2726). The nearest comparable event within recent memory was on 11 August 1999, when the path of totality of a solar eclipse passed over the western end of Cornwall. The moment of unfamiliar darkness was anticipated for months. Excitement grew in the weeks

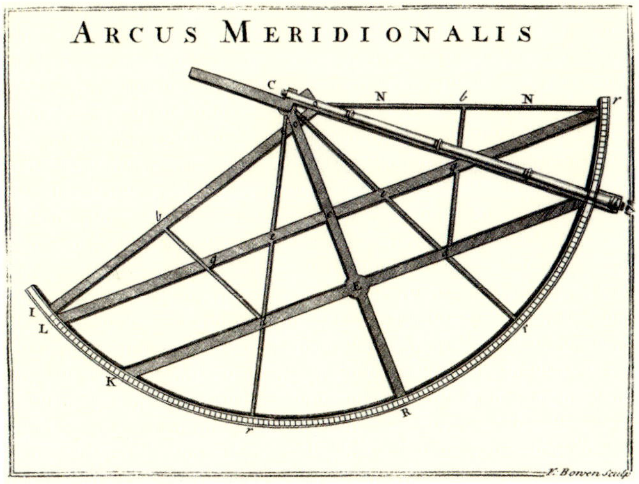

Fig. 20 John Flamsteed's mural arc, engraving from *Historia Coelestis Britannica*, vol. 3, published 1725.

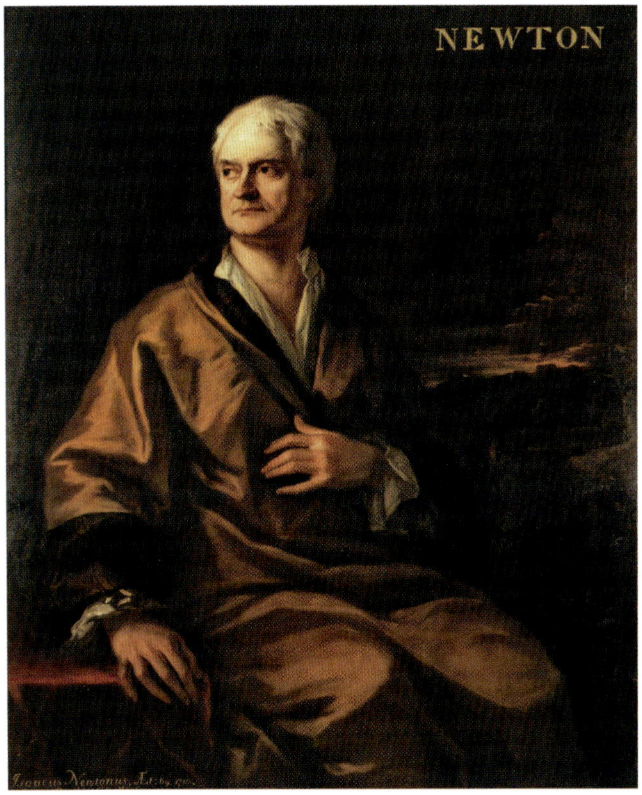

Fig. 21 James Thornhill, *Isaac Newton*, oil on canvas, 1709–11.

Fig. 19 (*opposite*) John Flamsteed, the first Astronomer Royal, appears in the south-eastern corner of the Lower Hall ceiling with his assistant Thomas Weston and with a mural arc telescope. The mural arc is directed towards Diana, goddess of the Moon (see frontispiece).

and days leading up to the event, prompting souvenirs of all kinds and a surge in interest in popular astronomy. Boffins were introduced on every television channel to explain the science, while celebrity astrologers predicted what it all might mean for the future. The next morning, the moment of 'totality' was front-page news (fig. 22). No less in Flamsteed and Thornhill's time: as 22 April 1715 approached, publishers exploited the commercial possibilities of the event with new poems and sermons that variously interpreted the impending darkness, either as a heavenly portent of the nation's triumphs or as a sure sign of imminent doom. *Mr Flamsteed's Figure of the Eclipse of the Sun* (fig. 23), drawn up by the astronomer's assistant Joseph Crosthwait, was one of several broadsides that offered a more scientific analysis of the eclipse. Edmond Halley and William Whiston issued their own calculations (also relying on Flamsteed's data), as members of the public were encouraged to become amateur astronomers for the day by comparing their own eye-witness observations with the scientists' predictions.

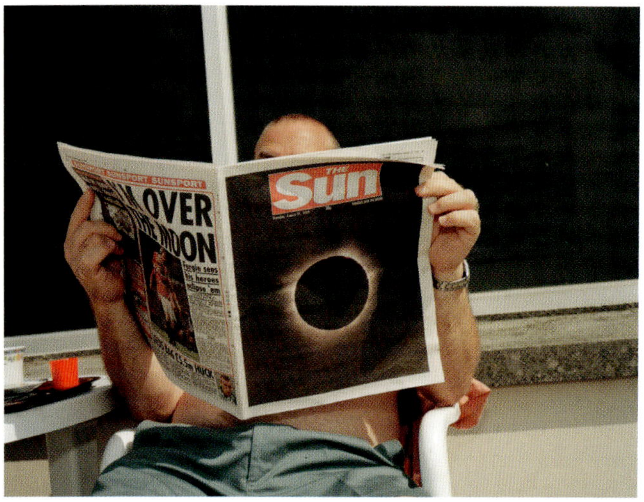

Fig. 22 Martin Parr, *GB. England. Cornwall. Reading about the solar eclipse in The Sun newspaper the next day.* 1999.

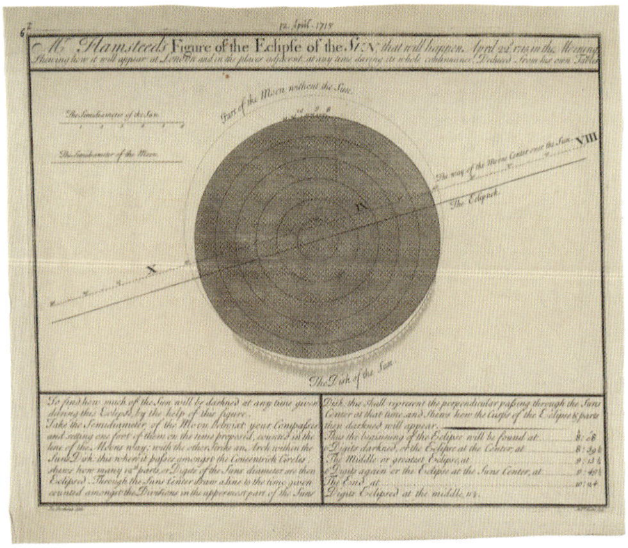

Fig. 23 *Mr Flamsteed's Figure of the Eclipse of the Sun*, 1715.

In the Circumference of the Oval are the twelve *Signs* of the *Zodiack* with their proper Attitudes, over which preside the four *Seasons* of the Year …

Through the application of modern scientific ways of looking, the conventional language of courtly allegory became co-opted into a visual celebration of Britain's modern maritime identity. Viewed through the lens of Flamsteed's mural arc, the goddess of the Moon, Diana, is interpreted not as an abstract divinity, but in relation to the ebb and flow of the tides and the potential dangers that they hold for sailors (Flamsteed had pioneered the use of tide tables in the 1680s). In the words of the official *Explanation*, the astronomer is observing 'the Moon's Descent upon the SEVERN, which at certain Times when she is in her *Perigee*, makes such a Roll of the Tides, call'd the *Eagre*, as is very dangerous to all in its Way'.

Thornhill's decision to include such precise details on the ceiling at Greenwich was not only a public gesture of faith in the work of the Royal Observatory, it also projected into the future the grand narrative of imperial splendour that plays out across the Lower Hall, encouraging early visitors to contemplate what was still to come. Long after the eclipse had faded from memory, Flamsteed's diagram remained visible in the Painted Hall as a powerful reminder of the greater promise of the astronomer's labours. In 1720, a year after Flamsteed's death, Thornhill agreed to provide the figures for the constellations that were to be included in the first atlas based on the astronomer's 'catalogue of the heavens' (fig. 24). Thornhill abandoned the project after completing only a handful of the projected twenty-seven designs, and financial problems caused further delays, but when the *Atlas Coelestis* was finally published in 1729 by Margaret Flamsteed and Crosthwait, it was the largest and most accurate portrayal of the night sky to date, plotting the relative positions of almost 3000 stars and setting a new standard in professional astronomy.

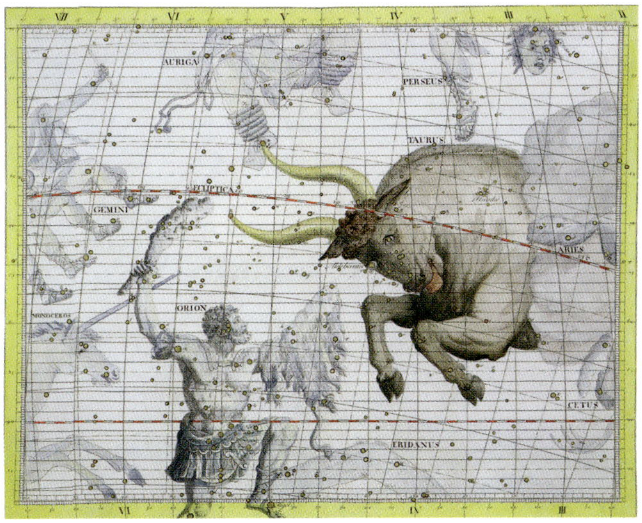

Fig. 24 Taurus, from John Flamsteed's *Atlas Coelestis*, published 1729, with figures designed by James Thornhill.

In the Middle of the Gallery next the upper Hall, is the Stern of a *British* Man of War, with a Figure of VICTORY filling her with *Spoils* and *Trophies* taken from the Enemy.

Dominating the east end of the Hall is the stern of a captured Spanish galleon filled with trophies (fig. 26). Beneath this we find two of England's major waterways: 'the SEVERN with her *Lampreys*' and 'the HUMBER with his *Piggs of Lead*'. This eye-catching display of British military and commercial power is echoed at the other end of the Hall (fig. 27), where Thornhill painted a British man-of-war, identified by Steele as 'the *Blenheim*',[11] a ninety-gun ship of the line, built at Deptford and launched in 1679 as the *Duchess* and later renamed after Marlborough's most famous land victory during the War of the Spanish Succession in 1704 (fig. 25). Approaching the vessel from the left is a winged figure of Victory, carrying an armful of captured French colours. Underneath, surrounded by a myriad of other allegorical and earthly figures, is the personified City of London, held aloft on the shoulders of the rivers Thames and Isis. She carries what appears to be a bundle of wool under her left arm and receives

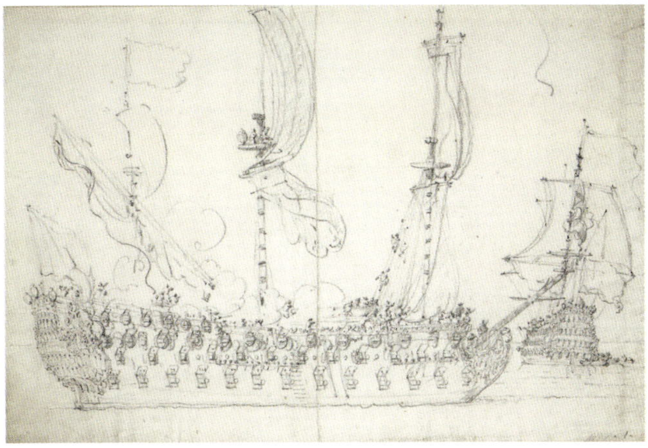

Fig. 25 Willem van de Velde the Elder, *The 'Duchess' before a Light Breeze*, pencil, *c.* 1681. The *Duchess* was later renamed the *Blenheim* and was identified by Richard Steele as the ship depicted at the west end of the Lower Hall.

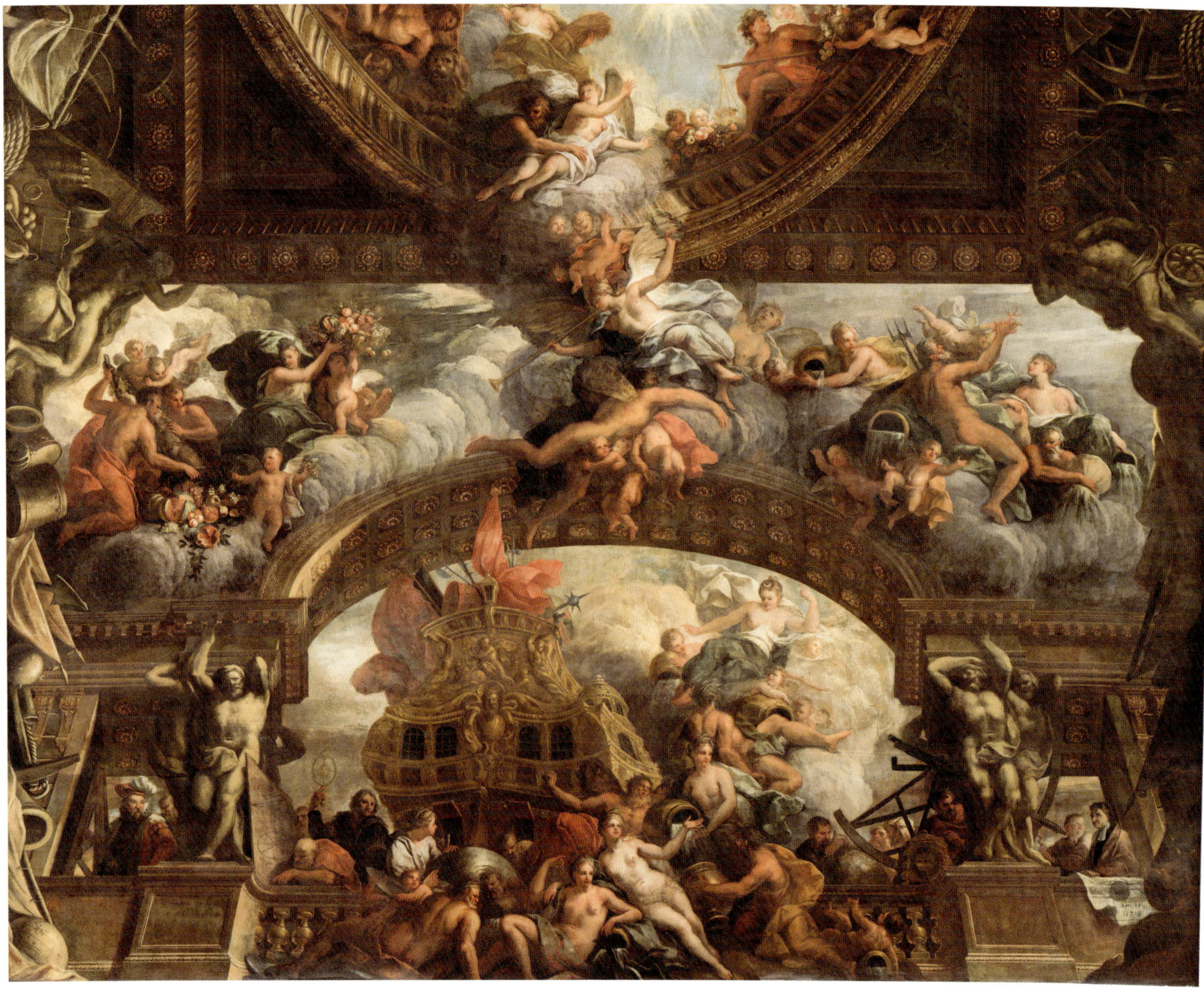

Fig. 26 A captured Spanish galleon at the east end of the Lower Hall, with the rivers Severn and Humber beneath (see key on p. 138).

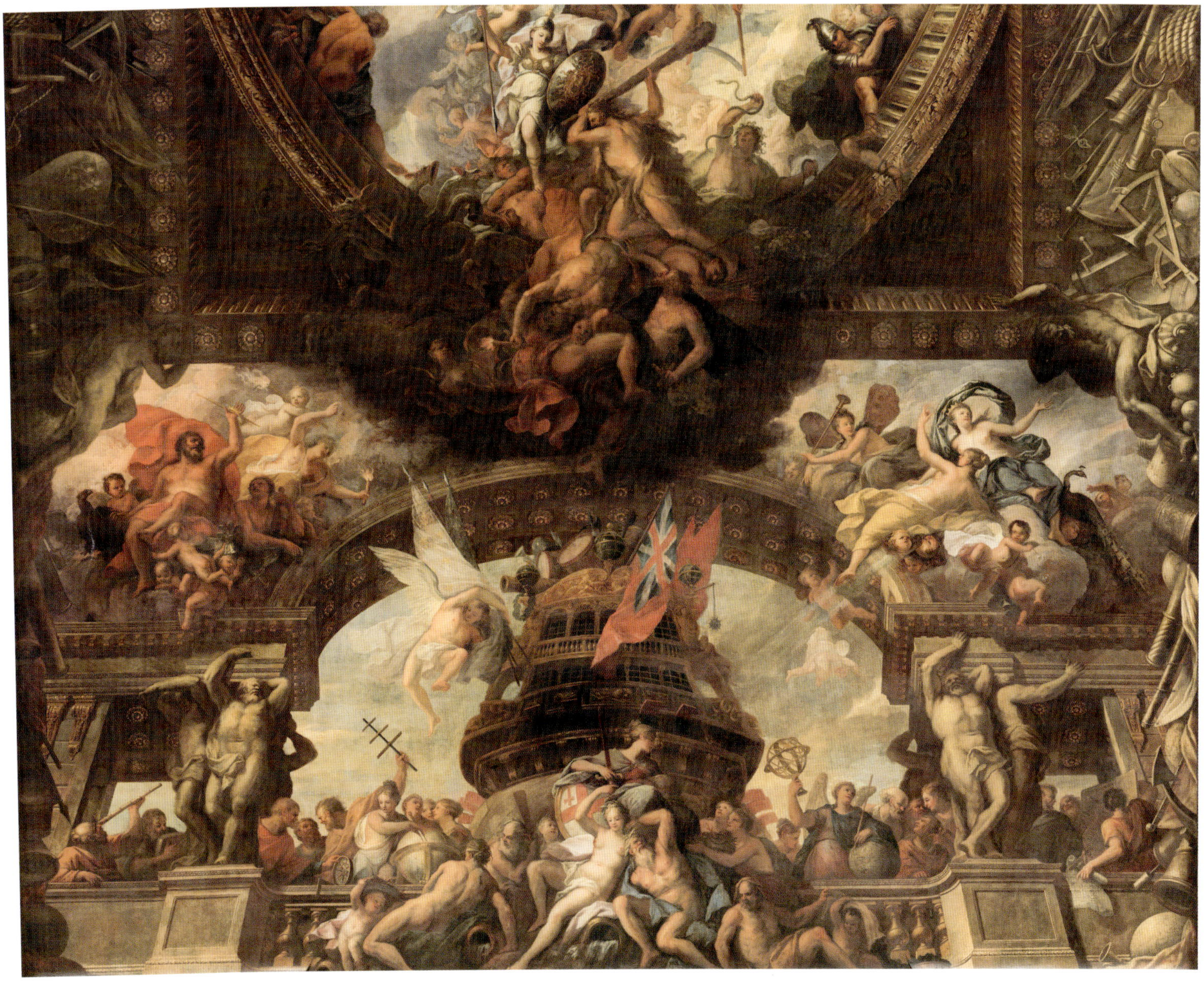

Fig. 27 A British man-of-war at the west end of the Lower Hall, with the winged figure of Victory carrying an armful of captured French colours.

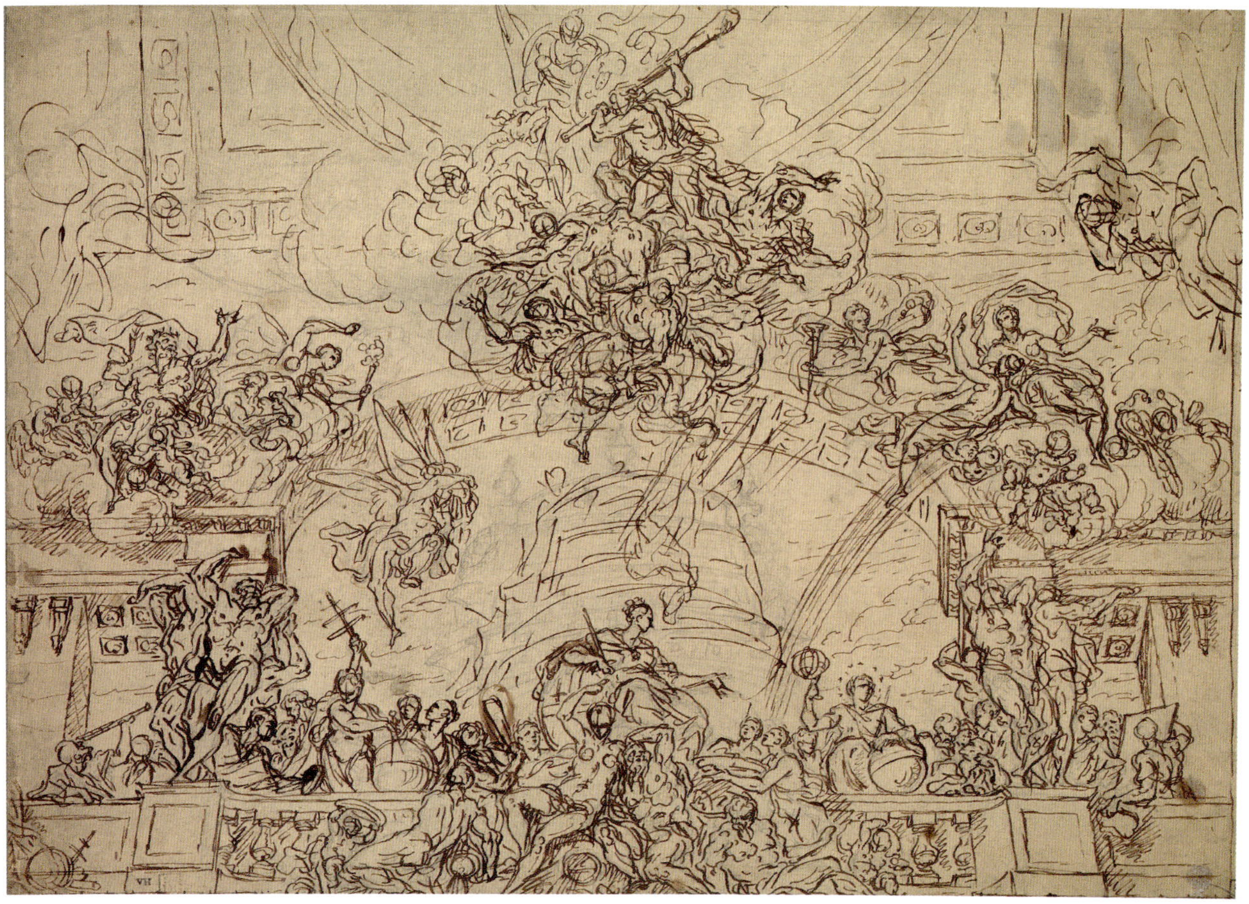

Fig. 28 James Thornhill, design for the west end of the Lower Hall ceiling, pen and brown ink over pencil, *c*. 1707.
Fig. 29 (*opposite*) James Thornhill, design for the Lower Hall ceiling, pen and brown ink with grey wash over pencil, *c*. 1707.

a basket full of seafood from another female figure, while beneath is the Tyne, 'pouring forth his Plenty of *Coals*'.

Under the *Man of War* is a Figure that represents the CITY of LONDON sitting on THAME, and ISIS, with the smaller *Rivers* bringing Treasures unto her.

The likes of fish, coal and wool are not the usual stuff of allegory, but here they form an integral part of the decoration alongside Flamsteed and the more conventional cast of allegorical figures. In this way, Thornhill allegorizes the powerful relationship between trade, finance and military power by emphasizing the critical role of the City of London in providing the capital for Britain's voracious colonial exploitation during the eighteenth century. The Thames enables the trade that brings great riches to the City, which in turn supports the Royal Navy, whose firepower secures the commercial advantage of England's merchant fleet, bringing ever greater riches to the City, and on it goes. Navigating the Painted Hall with the official *Explanation* in hand, early visitors to Greenwich were invited to steer a course between the allegorical language of courtly virtue emanating from the centre and another set of 'virtues' driving the modern state, focused on trade, money and maritime power.

We can usefully understand such details in the light of the directors' request for more in the way of 'maritime affaires' when handing the task to Thornhill. One of the largest preparatory drawings of the Hall to survive – a wonderful demonstration of Thornhill's ability to bring figural arrangements into being – shows this important configuration coming into view for the first time (fig. 28). Earlier drawings reveal the lengths to which Thornhill went in search of an appropriate mythology of modern maritime Britain. One of these

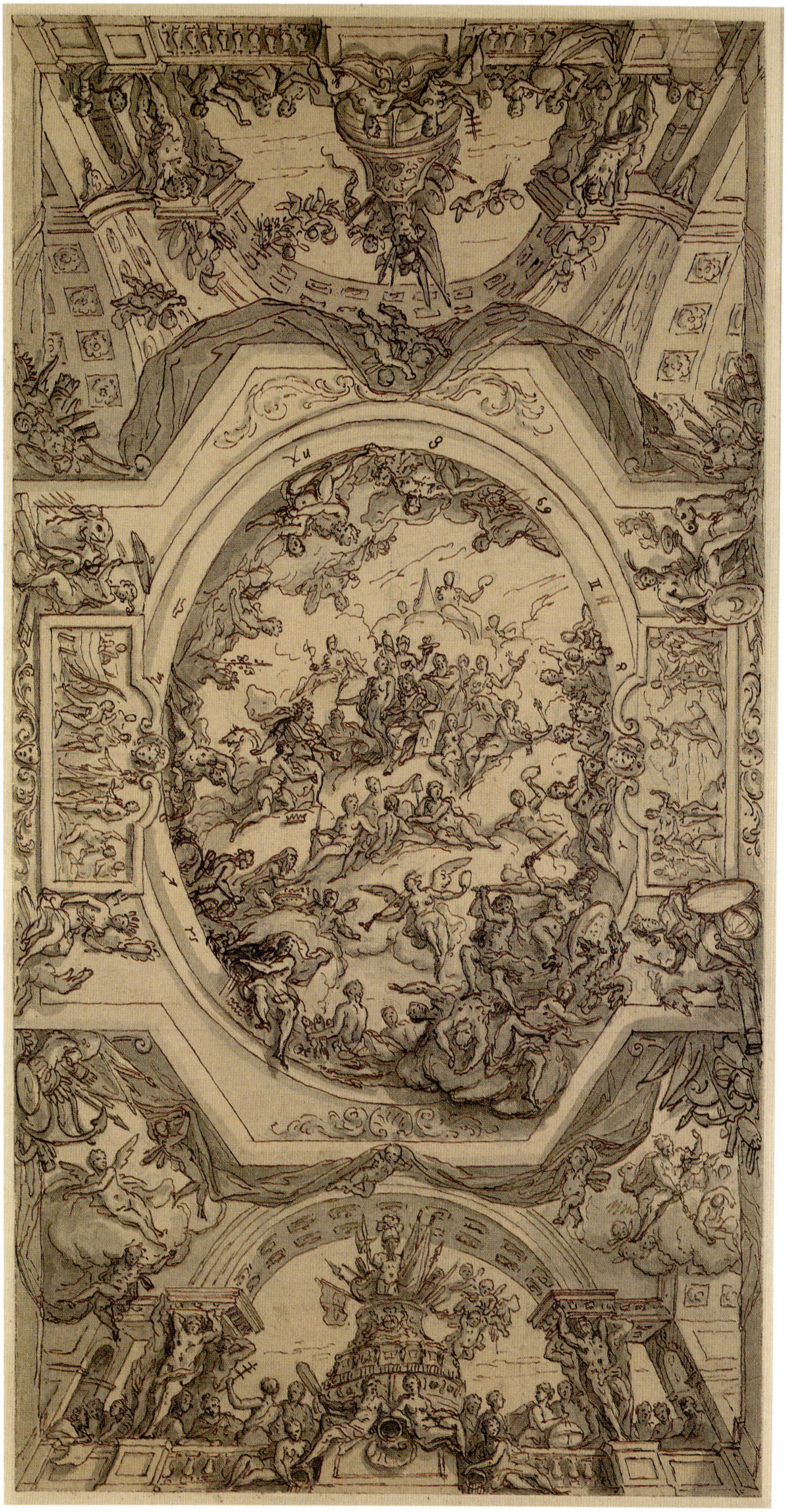

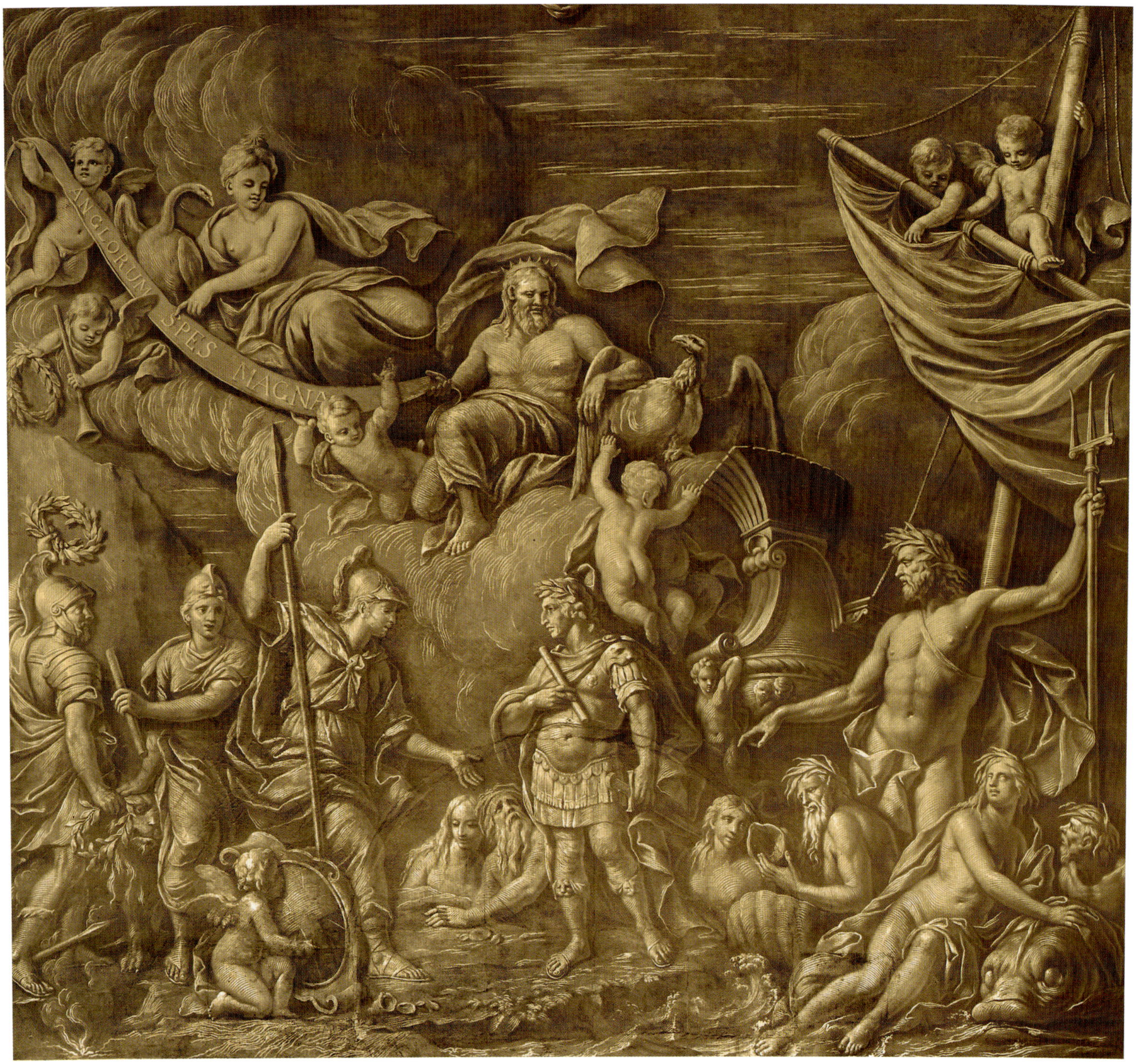

Fig. 30 The south wall of the Upper Hall depicts William of Orange being welcomed ashore by Britannia at Torbay in 1688.

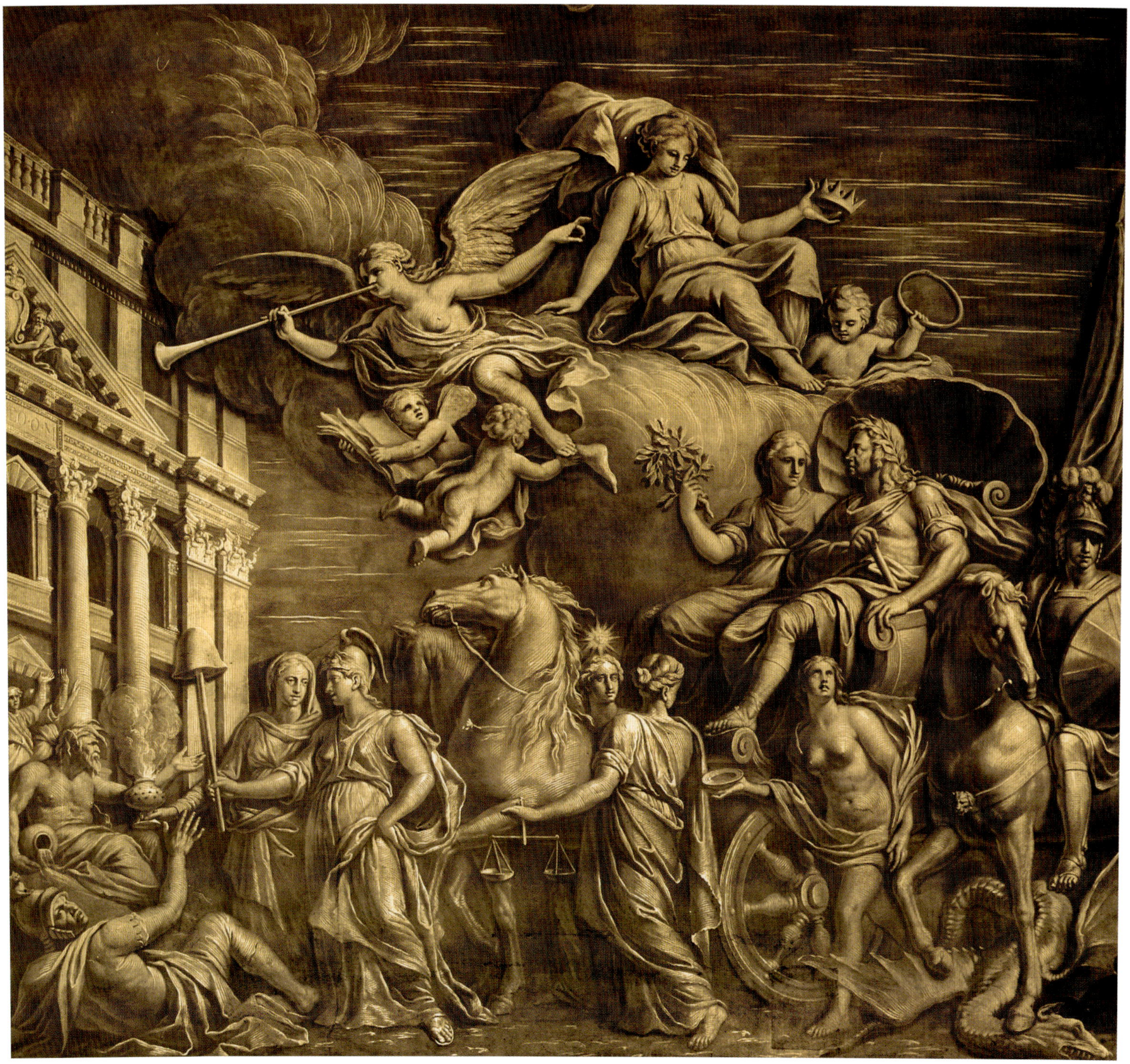

Fig. 31 The north wall of the Upper Hall portrays the arrival of George I at Greenwich in 1714.

(fig. 29), helpfully annotated on the reverse, includes a pictorialization of 'the origin of Shipping' in the long margin near what would have been the coving of the north wall. On the opposite side is a more current shipbuilding scene, described by the artist as 'Shipping as it now is in perfection'. The former detail alludes to an ancient myth, today forgotten by all but the most ardent classicists, that identified the origins of seacraft with 'Typhis' (or Tiphys), helmsman of the *Argo*. It may have been judged too obscure even for an eighteenth-century audience, but Thornhill's drawing remains of interest as possibly the earliest known representation of surfing in Western art, made long before anyone had the idea of 'swimming on a plank' for fun.

Some indication of the success of Thornhill's painting in the Lower Hall can be suggested by returning to the example of Ralph Thoresby, whose impressions of the Hall we encountered earlier. It was the prospect of seeing Thornhill's painting that drew Thoresby to the Hospital, and it seems that he was sufficiently impressed by what he saw. The same 'R^P.H^ Thursby' is commemorated among the great and the good on one of the three tablets of benefactors painted in the Vestibule twelve years later, after he gave a substantial £500 towards the cost of completing the Hospital. As one of the very first visitors to the Painted Hall, Thoresby himself became a part of the spectacle for subsequent viewers. If his example is anything to go by, decorative painting had never before been called upon to appeal to such a diverse public, nor been so successful in inciting visitors to part with their money.

On the Right-hand over the Chimney is the ACCESSION or *Landing* of *King* GEORGE at *Greenwich*; On his Right-hand is PEACE, on his Left-hand HAPPINESS …

George I stepped foot on English soil for the first time at Greenwich, at around six in the evening on 18 September 1714. For the architects of the succession, George's arrival represented the triumph of those principles and interests first inscribed in the Declaration of Rights in 1689 and confirmed twelve years later by the Act of Settlement (1701), the law designed to 'settle' the Protestant succession once and for all. But not everyone welcomed the new king's arrival. George's coronation on 20 October 1714 was greeted by riots in some parts of the country; and during the autumn of 1715, the Jacobite Rebellion in Scotland and northern England served as a violent reminder that many people across the islands – not only disaffected Catholics – continued to hold a flame for the Stuart cause. For opponents of the new regime, George's arrival in September 1714 was an aberration, and marked the imposition of yet another unwelcome foreign king over the claims of the exiled Stuart princes (by some accounts, there were fifty or more candidates with a stronger hereditary claim to the throne than George, though none was Protestant).

Without the Hanoverian monarchy winning the cultural as well as the legal argument for the succession, its future and, with it, the perceived liberties safeguarded by the Glorious Revolution could not be assumed safe. The job of reconciling the nation's Stuart past with its Hanoverian future required the energies of those writers, preachers and artists who worked on behalf of the Crown: in the press, from the pulpit, in the realm of music and, not least of all, in the visual arts. In 1717 Thornhill was asked to prepare a further set of designs for paintings in the Upper Hall at Greenwich that would, in the words of the Hospital directors, 'make the whole appear uniform'.[12] The demands for pictorial and political uniformity implied in the directors' carefully worded instructions were inseparable. On the one hand, any new work that did not cohere visually with the painting in the Lower Hall would risk undermining the earlier decoration by accentuating the dynastic complications brought about by the Glorious Revolution. On the other hand, a scheme that successfully incorporated the Hanoverian succession within an extended, visually harmonious display of the nation's Protestant history would go a long way in smoothing over the ideological fault lines of the previous three decades.

Thornhill's response to these challenges can be seen in two of the lesser-known paintings at Greenwich, which face each other on the north and

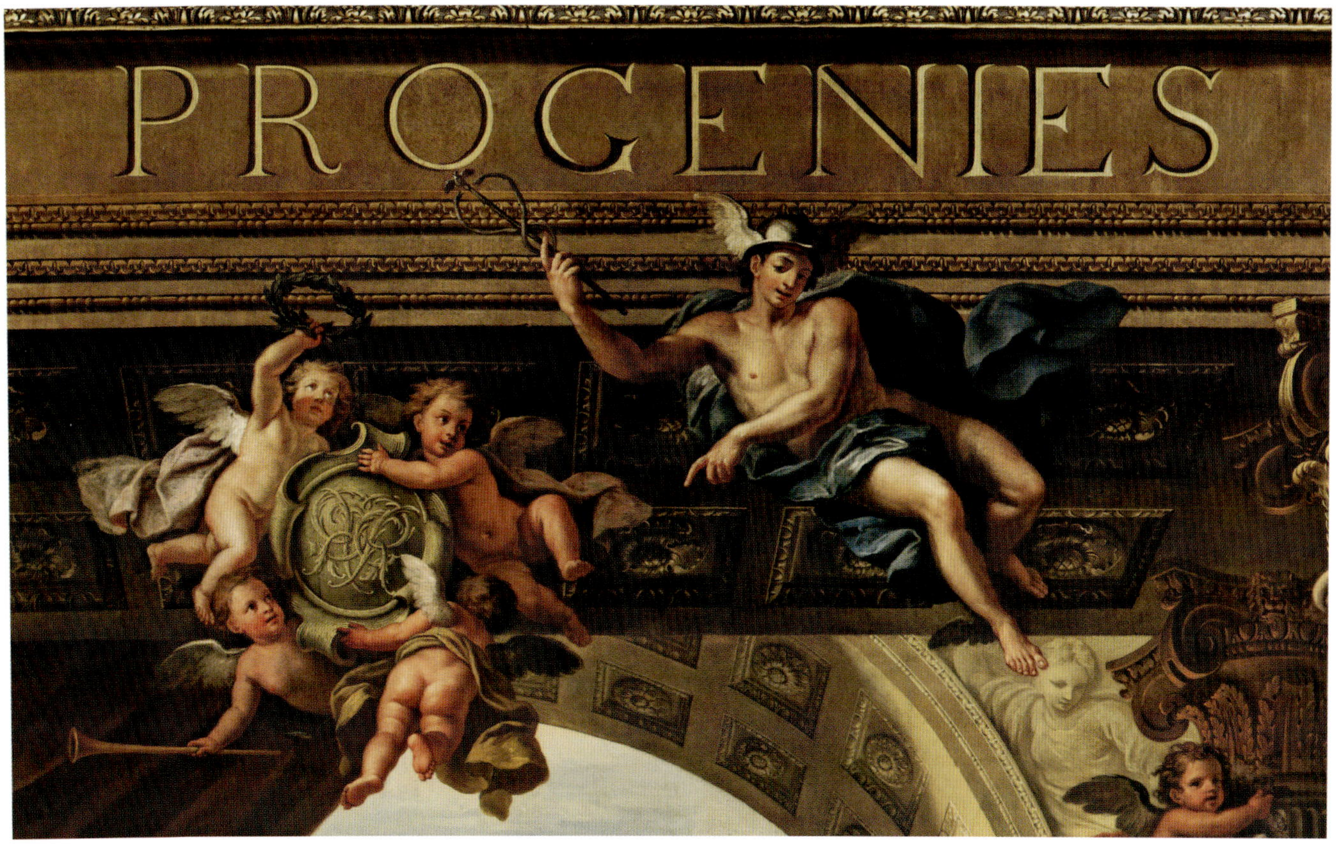

Fig. 32 Part of the inscription above the west wall of the Upper Hall, with the messenger god Mercury. The inscription translates as 'A golden Progeny from Heav'n descends.'

south walls of the Upper Hall (figs. 30 and 31). Both are around 20 feet (6 m) wide; they are painted in stone-like colours with gilded highlights and surrounded by a painted gold frame. The first painting, on the left as you enter the Upper Hall, is an allegory of William's arrival at Torbay in 1688, described succinctly in the official *Explanation* as 'the REVOLUTION, or the *Landing* of the *Prince* of *Orange*'. It portrays William welcomed ashore by Britannia and two other figures, identified as '*Reason* of *State*, and *Love* of her *Country*'. Jupiter observes from above, accompanied by Juno, who points eagerly to a scroll with the motto 'ANGLORUM SPES MAGNA' ('England expects great things'). On the opposite wall, above a fireplace, Thornhill painted 'the ACCESSION or *Landing* of *King* GEORGE at *Greenwich*'. Here the new Hanoverian king is shown in a horse-drawn chariot escorted by St George on horseback and by a train of allegorical figures led by Religion, Liberty, Truth and Justice. The river front of the King Charles building at Greenwich is clearly visible in the background. In the lower left corner of the painting, beneath the personification of the Thames, an unarmed soldier representing the Jacobite uprising of 1715 cowers before the royal procession.

The triumphal symbolism of both compositions is heightened by Thornhill's use of grisaille, an allusion to the monumental bas-relief carvings of ancient Rome, and by the Roman military costume worn by both princes. In addition, the artist exploits the spatial organization of the Hall to suggest an equivalence between the events depicted, using the double portrait of Anne and her consort, Prince George, on the ceiling as an additional link between William and George. The result is a remarkably neat interpretation of the nation's most recent royal past, one that harnesses the architectural symmetry of the room to present William's landing in 1688 as a precedent for and, by implication, a validation of the subsequent accession of George I a quarter of a century later.

If the Hanoverians could offer anything to Britain's ruling elite, it was a narrative of stability: an assurance that the Protestant monarchy had finally settled on a predictable, hereditary course. So much, at least, is heralded by the Virgilian inscription across the top of the west wall that heralds the arrival of a new dynasty: 'IAM NOVA PROGENIES CŒLO', translated by John Dryden as 'A golden Progeny from Heav'n descends' (figs. 32 and 33).[13] Beneath this inscription the messenger god, Mercury, gestures towards an assembly of characters that includes a female figure holding a large stone pyramid, identified to visitors at the time as '*Stability*, or the Glory of Princes'. Further down are two more familiar characters: Justice (Astraea) with sword and scales; and Time with his scythe, here in the role of 'the *Golden Age* restored … pouring forth *Riches*, &c. from a *Cornucopia*'.

Immediately behind the king stands Princess Caroline, here both as mother to the royal grandchildren and as a personification of Prudence (echoing the figure behind William in the Lower Hall). Caroline is accompanied to her left by the king's daughter, Sophia Dorothea, Queen of Prussia, as Concord, and by the king's mother, the Electress Sophia of Hanover, who makes a posthumous appearance as Cybele, the goddess of nature. In these dual roles, the women of the Hanoverian dynasty play an important role in Thornhill's quest for visual and political unity, mediating between the celestial allegory above and the earthbound, interior realm of dynastic family portraiture.

Great Variety of *Cupids* are flying with vast *Festoons* of *Flowers* wreathing them round the COLUMNS: Some bringing Baskets, others throwing Flowers …

This spiralling cascade of bodies is given an additional twist with the inclusion of six more of the king's grandchildren, four of whom are identified in a preparatory drawing for the west wall (fig. 34). In this rapid sketch, likely the result of a few minutes of intense activity, we see the artist's mind at work as the allegory is outlined on the page. Like the overflowing cornucopia held by the adjacent figure of Plenty, the royal offspring spill on to the floor in

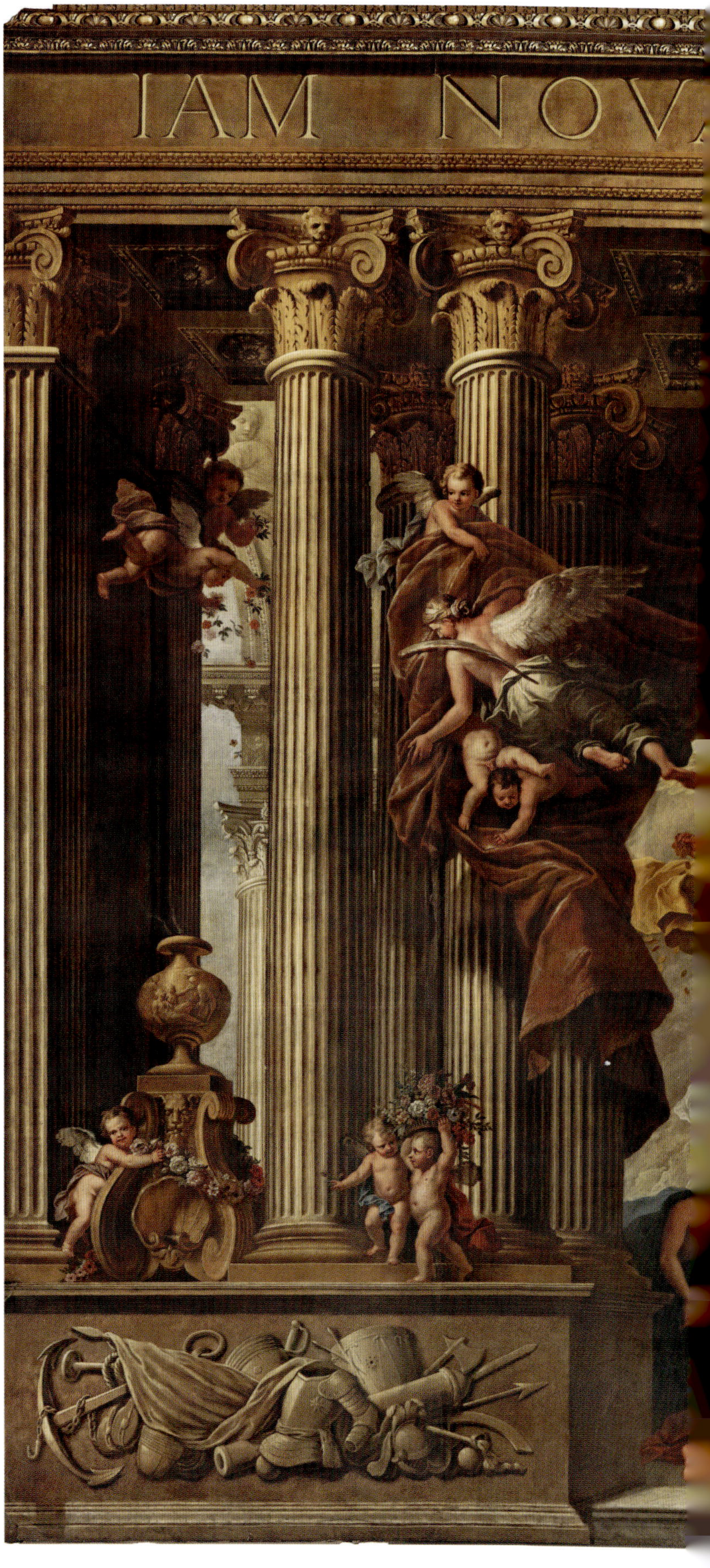

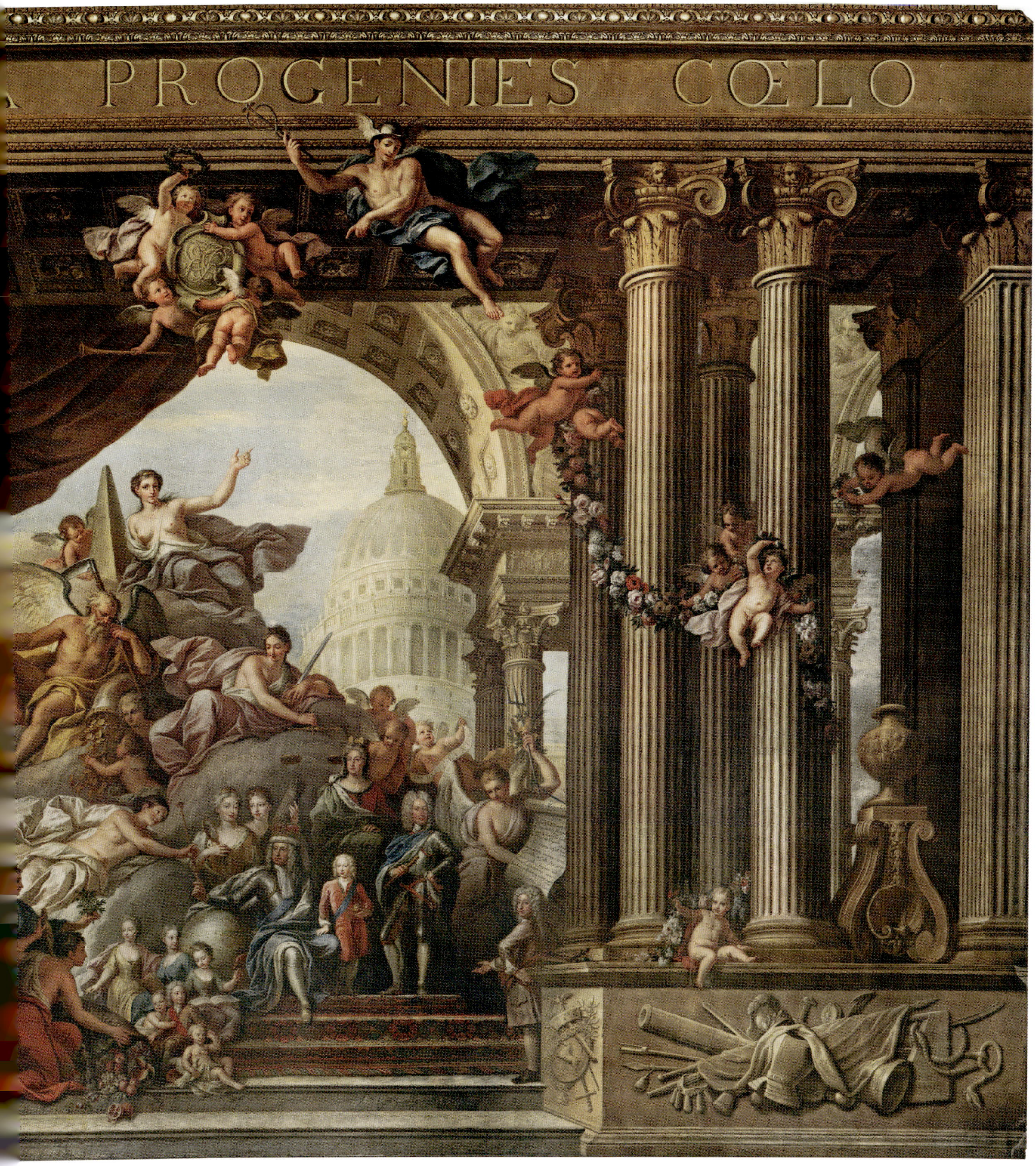

Fig. 33 The west wall celebrates the arrival of the Hanoverians, with George I at the centre of a large family group portrait.

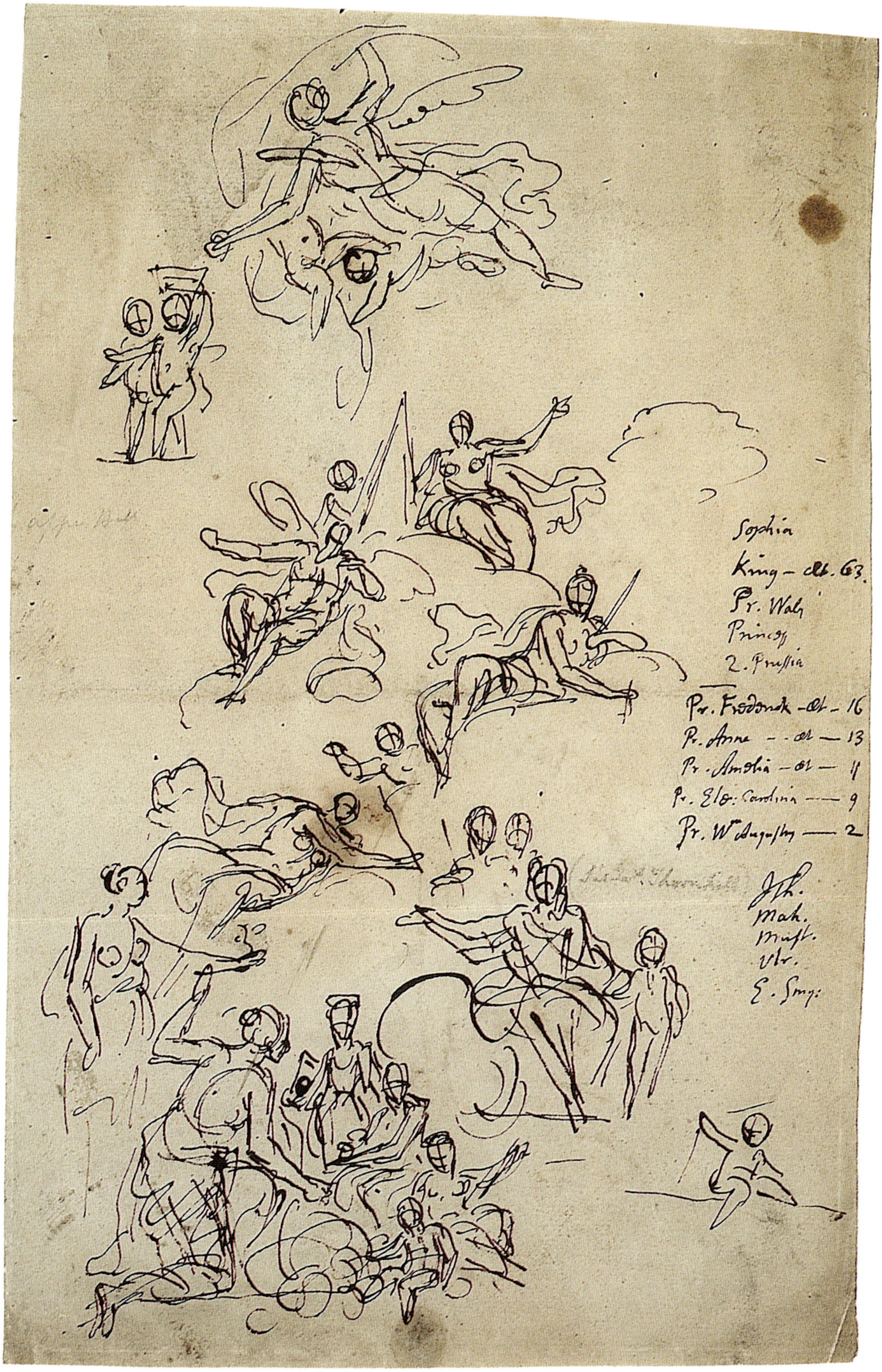

an impromptu demonstration of royal fecundity. But there is nothing accidental about the appearance and attitude of these royal children. Unusually, it is possible to calculate fairly precisely when this drawing was made from the artist's annotations along the right-hand side of the page, which register the ages of the king and each of his grandchildren. At the same time, the drawing reveals how Thornhill has manipulated the age of George's eldest grandson, who at the time, at sixteen, was too old for his grandfather's knee. In the final design, two more grandchildren have arrived, but the small child who barely reaches the seated king's shoulder belies the appearance of a young man of seventeen or eighteen. In fact, at the time of painting, Frederick had never even been to England (he did not arrive until 1728, after the death of George I). But his prominent inclusion becomes an essential part of the elaborate constitutional fiction of the Painted Hall, his presence unifying and making sense of the complex and troubled sequence of events that had gone before. Meanwhile, the king's former wife and mother of the Prince of Wales, Sophia Dorothea of Celle, is conspicuous by her absence (she had been imprisoned outside Hanover for the previous thirty years at the king's behest).

Thornhill was keenly aware of the political function of decorative painting and of the propaganda value of the role that he performed. His job, simply put, was to make the accidental and temporary appear inevitable and permanent; to craft a vision of modern Britain as a plentiful, pious and victorious nation, well governed by the right people. And it was a grand illusion that Thornhill wilfully entered into, skilfully using painting to serve his own interests as much as those of his patrons. So much so, that the two are often difficult to separate: for celebrating the perceived achievements and virtues of his countrymen, Thornhill himself was called 'our celebrated Country-man'.[14]

The interconnected narratives of national prosperity and artistic identity converge at Greenwich most directly around the artist's own likeness on the west wall (fig. 35). Here, Thornhill assumes the attitude (and wears the wig and long coat) of an eighteenth-century gentleman as he gestures towards the king and his family. What makes this such a remarkable addition to the Hall is not the fact that Thornhill has included his own likeness within the scheme, or even that this and the other portraits on the west wall were painted by another artist (the portrait painter Dietrich Ernst Andreae), but that he positions himself within such close proximity to the royal family. No other British artist had become so intimate with the nation's political and cultural elite.

The Painted Hall of the Royal Hospital for Seamen at Greenwich was one of the first great undertakings of Thornhill's career, and also one of the last. The intervening years had been productive in many ways. As well as working intermittently on the Painted Hall, Thornhill undertook major commissions at numerous palaces, country houses and other public buildings, including work that can still be seen today: at Hampton Court, at Blenheim Palace in Oxfordshire, at Hanbury Hall in Worcestershire, and in another monumental scheme on the inner dome of St Paul's Cathedral, begun in 1715. Thornhill's professional success led to a degree of official recognition never before achieved by a British artist. In 1718 he was appointed History Painter to the king (a post that had last been held by an Italian), and two years later he became the first English-born painter to receive a knighthood. When the final touches were made to the painting at Greenwich, in August 1726, he was, for a short time at least, the most celebrated British artist who had ever lived.

Fig. 34 James Thornhill, figure studies for the west wall, pen and brown ink, 1723.

NOTES

The title of this section and the displayed quotations are taken from Thornhill's *Explanation of the Painting in the Royal Hospital at Greenwich*, published in 1726.

1 The large figure of Charity is visible in the print of the Painted Hall produced for Rudolph Ackermann's *Microcosm of London*, 3 vols., London 1808–10, vol. 3, pl. 97.

2 Concord Conjugal, Liberality and Piety are included in a longer list of attributes identified in a preparatory drawing of 1717 for the Upper Hall ceiling (now in the Huntington Library, California, inv. no. 63.52.257) under the heading 'Vertues reciprocal to both Princes'.

3 Richard Steele, *The Lover*, no. 33, 11 May 1714; reprinted in [Richard Steele], *The Lover. To which is added, The Reader*, London 1715, pp. 223–29.

4 The minutes of the Hospital directors and the various committees responsible for the building and related works are collected among the Admiralty papers at the National Archives, Kew (hereafter TNA). For the Vestibule, see ADM 67/7, 28 May and 23 July 1726. The entries relating directly to Thornhill's work have been collected by William Osmun in 'A Study of the Work of Sir James Thornhill', PhD thesis, Courtauld Institute of Art, University of London, 1950, esp. pp. 273–97. The chronology of the commission is also discussed in some detail in John Bold, *Greenwich: An Architectural History of the Royal Hospital for Seamen and the Queen's House*, New Haven, Conn., and London (Yale University Press) 2000, pp. 145–53.

5 TNA ADM 67/3, 17 July 1707.

6 See Edward Croft-Murray, *Decorative Painting in England, 1537–1837*, vol. 1: *Early Tudor to Sir James Thornhill*, London (Country Life) 1962, p. 75. Other schemes chosen by the directors included work by Sebastiano Ricci at Burlington House on Piccadilly and by the French painters Charles de Lafosse, James Parmentier and Jacques Rousseau at Montagu House in Bloomsbury.

7 H.M. Colvin (ed.), *The History of the King's Works*, vol. 5: 1660–1782, London (HMSO) 1976, p. 322.

8 Ralph Thoresby, *The Diary of Ralph Thoresby*, ed. Rev. Joseph Hunter, 2 vols., London 1830, vol. 2, entry for 14 July 1714, p. 236. See also p. 33 of Anya Lucas's text.

9 The mural arc telescope was used to make more than 28,000 observations between 1689 and 1719. See Graham Dolan, 'Telescope: Flamsteed's Mural Arc (1689)', [2014], on the Royal Observatory Greenwich website: www.royalobservatorygreenwich.org/articles.php?article=1045 (accessed April 2019).

10 For more on the history of longitude, see Richard Dunn and Rebekah Higgitt, *Finding Longitude: How Clocks and Stars Helped Solve the Longitude Problem*, Glasgow (Collins) 2014.

11 [Steele], *The Lover*, p. 227.

12 TNA ADM 67/5, 27 July and 30 November 1717.

13 From Virgil's Fourth Eclogue (1st century BCE). The standard English version of Virgil was John Dryden's *Works of Virgil*, first published by Jacob Tonson in 1697.

14 *Weekly Packet*, no. 155, 18–25 June 1715.

Fig. 35 Thornhill on the west wall, painted by Dietrich Ernst Andreae.

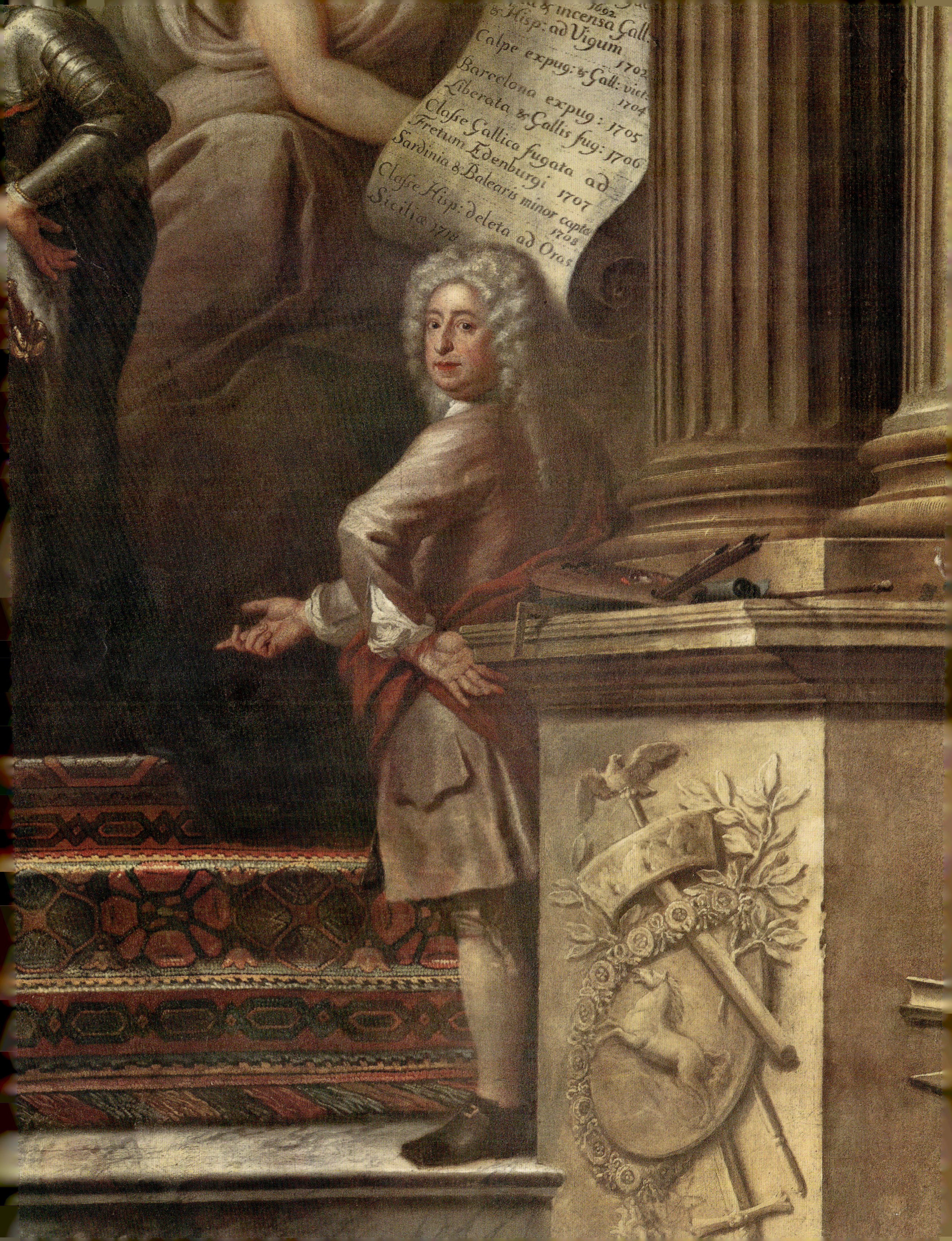
& Hisp: ad Vigum
Barcelona expug: 1705
Liberata & Gallis fug: 1706
Classe Gallica fugata ad
Fretum Edenburgi 1707
Sardinia & Balearis minor capta 1708
Classe Hisp: deleta ad Oras
Siciliæ 1718

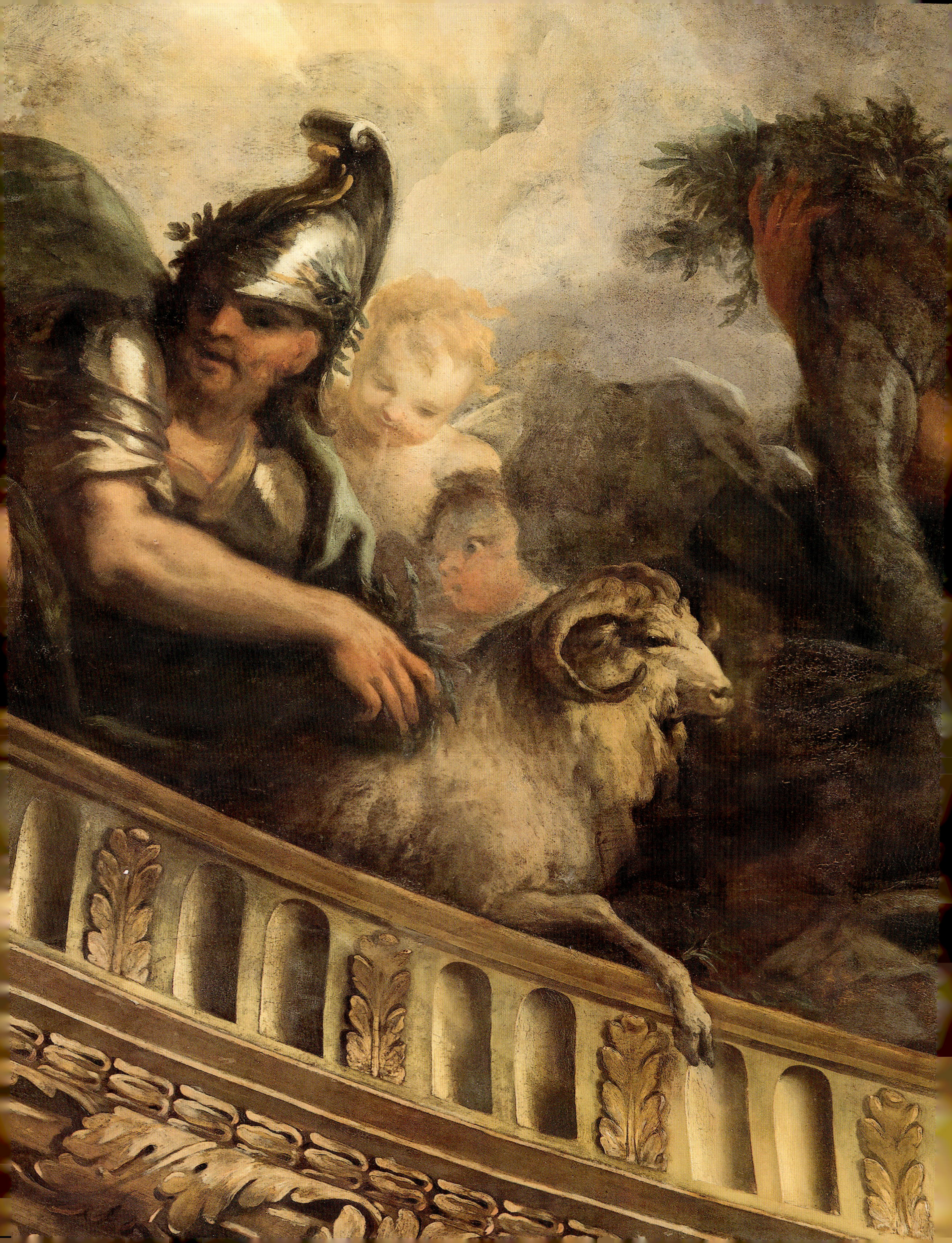

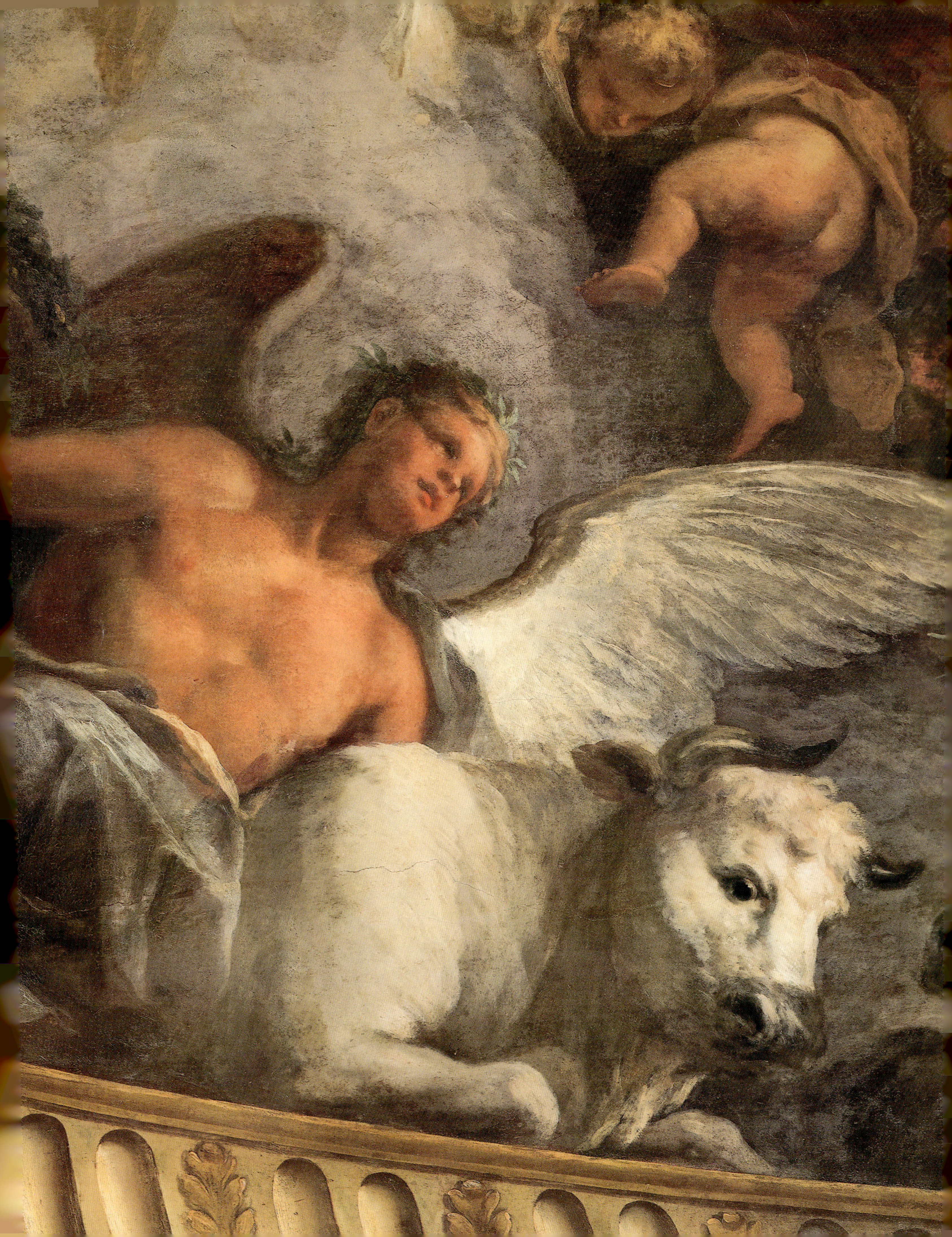

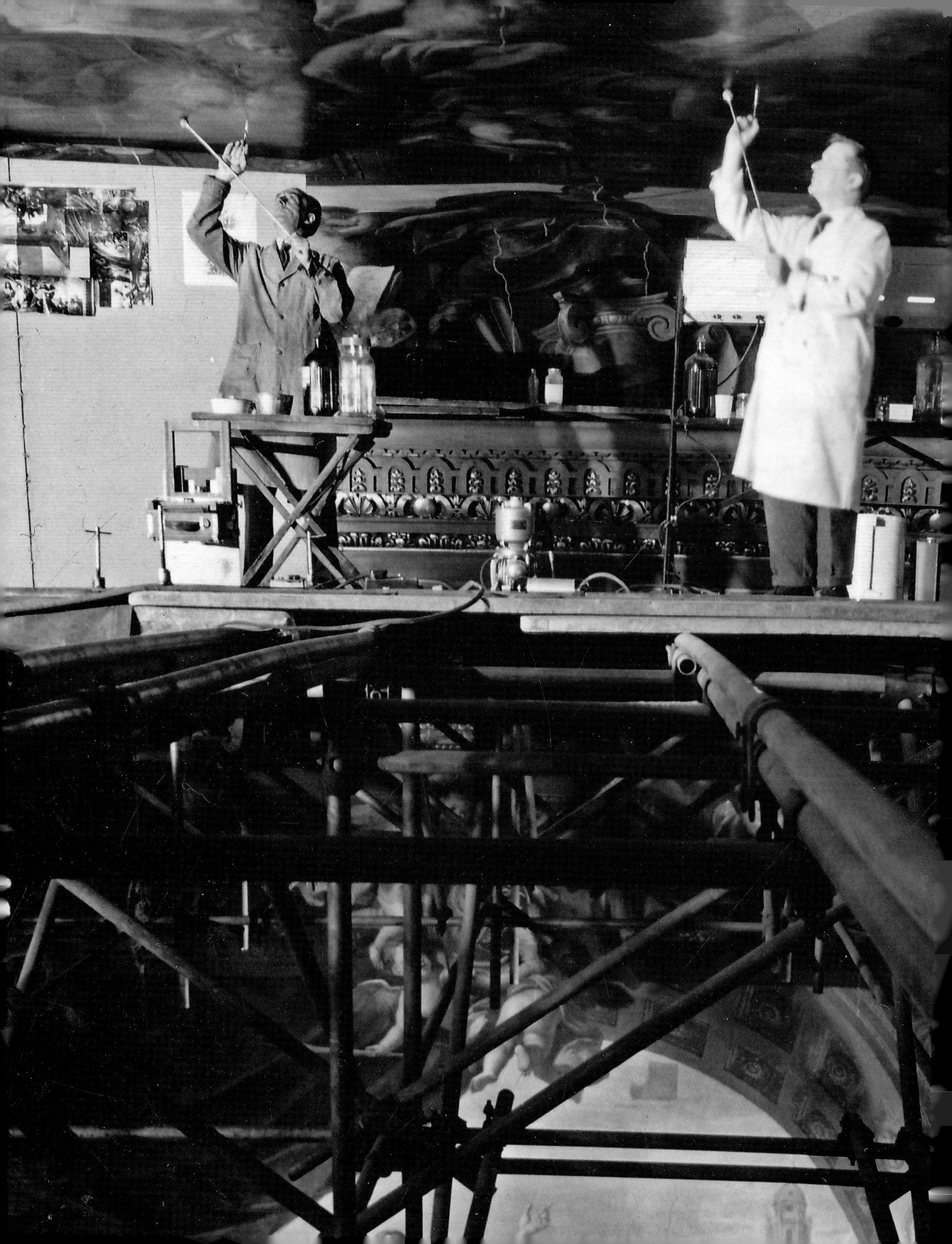

SOPHIE STEWART & STEPHEN PAINE

FROM OLD RESTORATIONS TO A NEW CONSERVATION

I have to say that there is no secret of any relevance or of any useful consideration in the process of retouching and cleaning, for whether or not one is able to carry out any process depends upon the original preparation of the painting ... even when it is possible, the operation is more likely to result in deterioration than in improvement of the painting.
FRANCISCO DE GOYA, 1801[1]

A review of the physical history of any wall painting invariably reveals the continual hazards to which it has been subjected throughout its existence, primarily owing to its innate relationship with the fabric of the building in which it resides. In contrast to an easel painting, which is able to exist in a relatively secure and controlled environment, a wall painting is at constant risk from either direct mechanical damage or the effects of moisture and light entirely because of its location. In the case of English Baroque decorative schemes, these problems are magnified still further. First and foremost, such schemes are often vast in size (the Painted Hall scheme is over 45,200 sq. ft / 4200 sq. m), covering large expanses of wall or ceiling in inaccessible areas, and so the likelihood of a failure in an unreachable part of the building, or of exposure to uncontrollable environmental conditions, is increased (fig. 3).

This vulnerability is exacerbated by the standard techniques of wall and ceiling painting of the late seventeenth or early eighteenth century. Such paintings comprise a succession of fragile films of pigments mixed with a medium of a drying oil binder, applied in multiple layers over either a stone or a plaster support. Delicate glazes and areas of gilding further complicate the situation.

In the past, when direct damage or general deterioration occurred, the response frequently resulted in a heavy-handed restoration, misguidedly undertaken in an attempt to improve the appearance and presentation of a painted scheme considered of great prestige and artistic value. These interventions typically involved haphazardly applied coatings of natural resin varnishes that were intended as a 'quick fix' to revive the appearance of the paintings

Fig. 1 A photograph of work in progress on the ceiling of the Upper Hall in 1958 shows contemporary conservation practice.

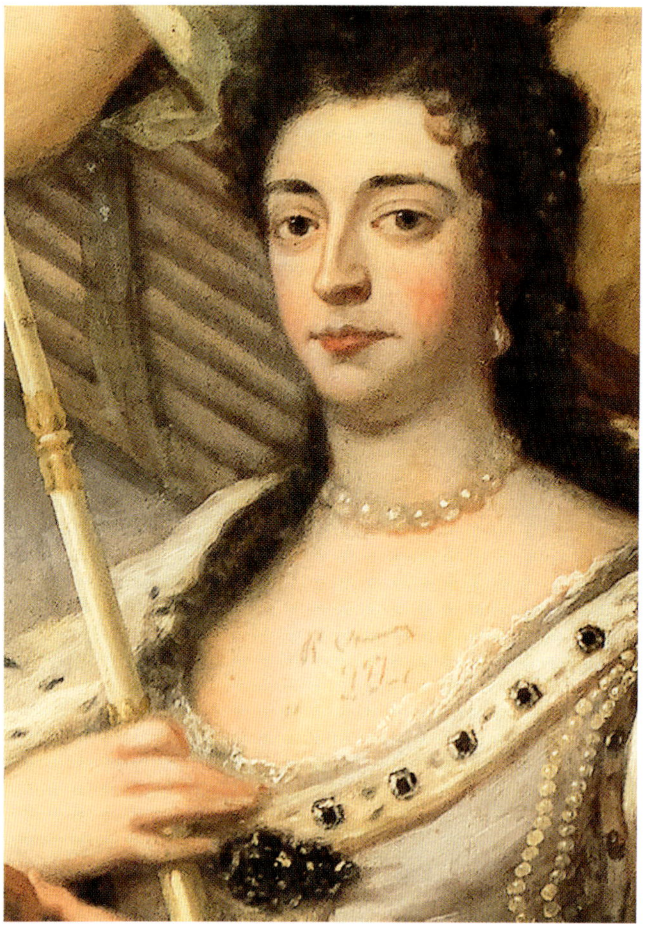

Fig. 2 Dated signatures reference past restoration campaigns. In 1777 a restorer applied his signature to the décolletage of Queen Mary, at the centre of the Lower Hall ceiling.

by increasing saturation, darkening colours and intensifying gloss. Extensive repainting was often undertaken at the same time. The efficacy of such restorations tended to be short-lived, however, and further repeated cycles of invasive treatment became necessary as the coatings deteriorated and darkened over time, requiring their removal, often with aggressive solvents, followed by the reapplication of a new varnish layer. Early cleaning materials might have included vinegar, purified nut oil, oil of turpentine, water, potash, spirit of wine and even essence of lemons.[2]

The detrimental impact of these past treatments on English Baroque wall paintings is often considerable, for, as noted by Jane Davies,

The essence of Baroque mural painting is its extravagance and flamboyance. The paintings are characterized by the use of trompe l'œil *architecture, illusionistic spatial recession, implied dynamic movement, vivid colour, steep perspectives, complexity of form and ornament. Their dependence upon illusion and spatial deceit means that their fragile visual balance is easily spoiled by crude retouching and/or damages. The vibrant palette of the best Baroque paintings – luscious organic glazes, blue skies, colourful drapery, extensive gilding – is quickly obliterated by the repeated application of deteriorating varnishes and overlying discoloured retouching. In this sense they are also particularly 'visually vulnerable'.*[3]

All of these factors apply directly to the magnificent scheme of early eighteenth-century wall paintings by Sir James Thornhill in the Painted Hall of the Old Royal Naval College. The entire scheme of decoration throughout the three internal chambers of the Hall, from the Vestibule through to the Lower and Upper Halls, has suffered from 300 years of adverse environmental conditions, as well as multiple restorations. Not only are most restorations documented in the directors' minutes of the Hospital, but also many of the individuals responsible for the works signed their names directly on to the paintings. In the 1950s, the conservator Westby Percival-Prescott noted that twenty-two names had been added to the Lower Hall ceiling since 1733, and a further ten have recently been found.[4] Some are particularly brazen, such as that applied in 1777 to the décolletage of Queen Mary herself at the centre of the Lower Hall ceiling (fig. 2).

Thornhill completed his work at Greenwich in 1726, but as early as 1733 – a mere seven years later – it was considered necessary to instigate the first of many surface cleanings of the paintings, or as it was referred to at the time, 'refreshing of the paintings'. In 1742 John Bouttats 'repaired the blemishes' for eighteen guineas and agreed to 'mend all the defects and clean and varnish the whole Hall and restore it to its former beauty for £50'.[5] Further restorations followed in 1752 and in 1777, the latter by a Mr Davies, when the paintings were described as 'dirty'.[6] It is interesting to note that the contract sum of £1000 (excluding scaffolding and materials) was awarded to Davies without any price tendering, and, perhaps unsurprisingly, a squabble broke out over the immense

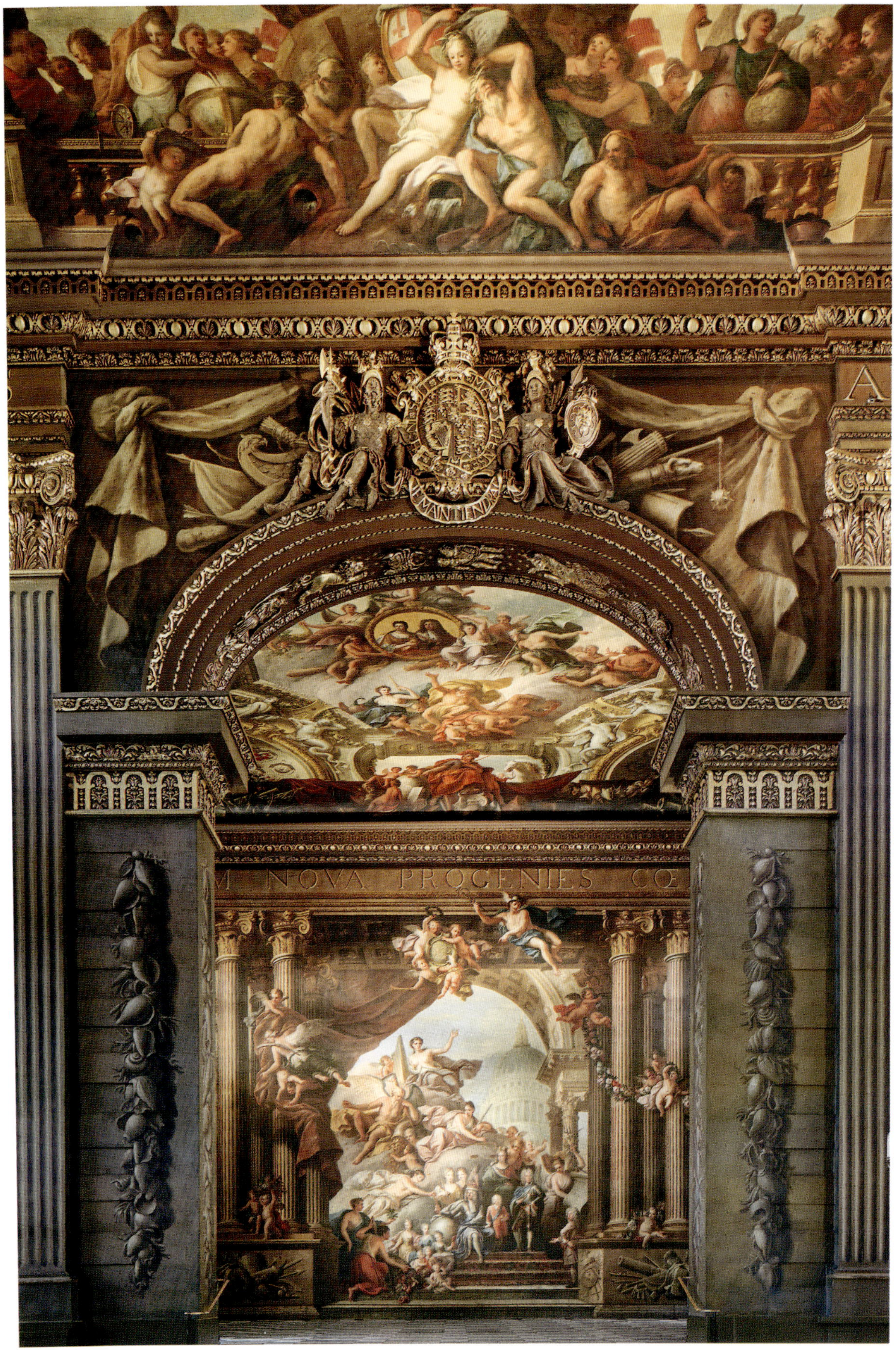

Fig. 3 Thornhill's scheme – the largest ever painted in 18th-century Britain – looking from the Lower Hall into the Upper Hall.

fee. The artist and restorer Giovanni Battista Cipriani was subsequently asked for an opinion at an inquiry into the management of Greenwich Hospital, and commented that he 'thought the work done well and reasonable'. He compared the Greenwich project with his work restoring the Rubens paintings in the Banqueting House, Whitehall, for which he considered that he had been underpaid.[7]

In 1779, in a parliamentary motion after the inquiry, the Duke of Richmond made an interesting observation on the process of restoration at that time:

[P]ainting and cleaning pictures are two very different sorts of work; that little more than care, and some practice, is necessary for the latter; while genius, and great art, to be acquired by long study, are requisite to make a painter. If proper economy had been attended to … at Greenwich, some careful picture-cleaner, at moderate wages, would have been employed to remove the dirt, with which time had covered the paintings …, and Mr Cipriani, or some great master, might have retouched such parts as had received any damage.[8]

Fig. 4 A 'witness patch' retained during the 1950s campaign indicates the level of darkening that had occurred to the multiple varnish coatings applied since the 1730s.

Further campaigns were recorded in 1797, 1807, 1824 and 1846, so that by the time of a major restoration of the paintings in the 1950s, Westby Percival-Prescott (who was to lead this campaign) noted more than fifteen individual layers of varnish on the ceiling. A small section of the ceiling was left untreated as a 'witness patch', to demonstrate for future reference just how discoloured the scheme had become (fig. 4). According to Percival-Prescott, these varnishes were 'composed of various hard and soft resins and oils', which 'together with the layers of repaint and grime which lay between them, formed a stubborn barrier which resisted most solvents'.[9] Some of these previous restorations had been particularly brutal, as exhibited by the abrasion of the paint layer in certain areas of the Lower Hall ceiling, in some of the most prominent and iconographically significant parts of the scheme.

A similar frequency of past treatments can also be noted in other contemporary wall paintings, such as the scheme painted between 1682 and 1684 by Antonio Verrio in St George's Hall, Windsor Castle. By 1724 Daniel Defoe was already referring to its significant deterioration, and William Kent carried out a series of interventions between 1730 and 1747. Work was again recorded in 1750 (by William Oram and Stephen Wright) and in 1778 (by Giovanni Battista Cipriani and John Richards). Restoration ceased only when the scheme was all but obliterated as part of a remodelling during the reign of George IV.

The repetition of treatment at Greenwich almost certainly indicates the occurrence of some specific cause of deterioration. Moisture can be presumed to be a continual threat, either from direct infiltration of water as a result of a failure in the building fabric, or from high levels of humidity. Indeed, in 1752 the directors of Greenwich Hospital noted that 'the painting in the Painted Hall is in danger of being damaged by the dampness of the weather'.[10] There is also evidence of various types of heating having been used in the Hall. It is recorded that, before the 1797 campaign, an iron stove was removed from the Hall in order to facilitate the cleaning programme. As a replacement, a Buzaglo stove was installed 'for the purpose of keeping the hall dry during the winter months for the preservation of the paintings'.[11] It may

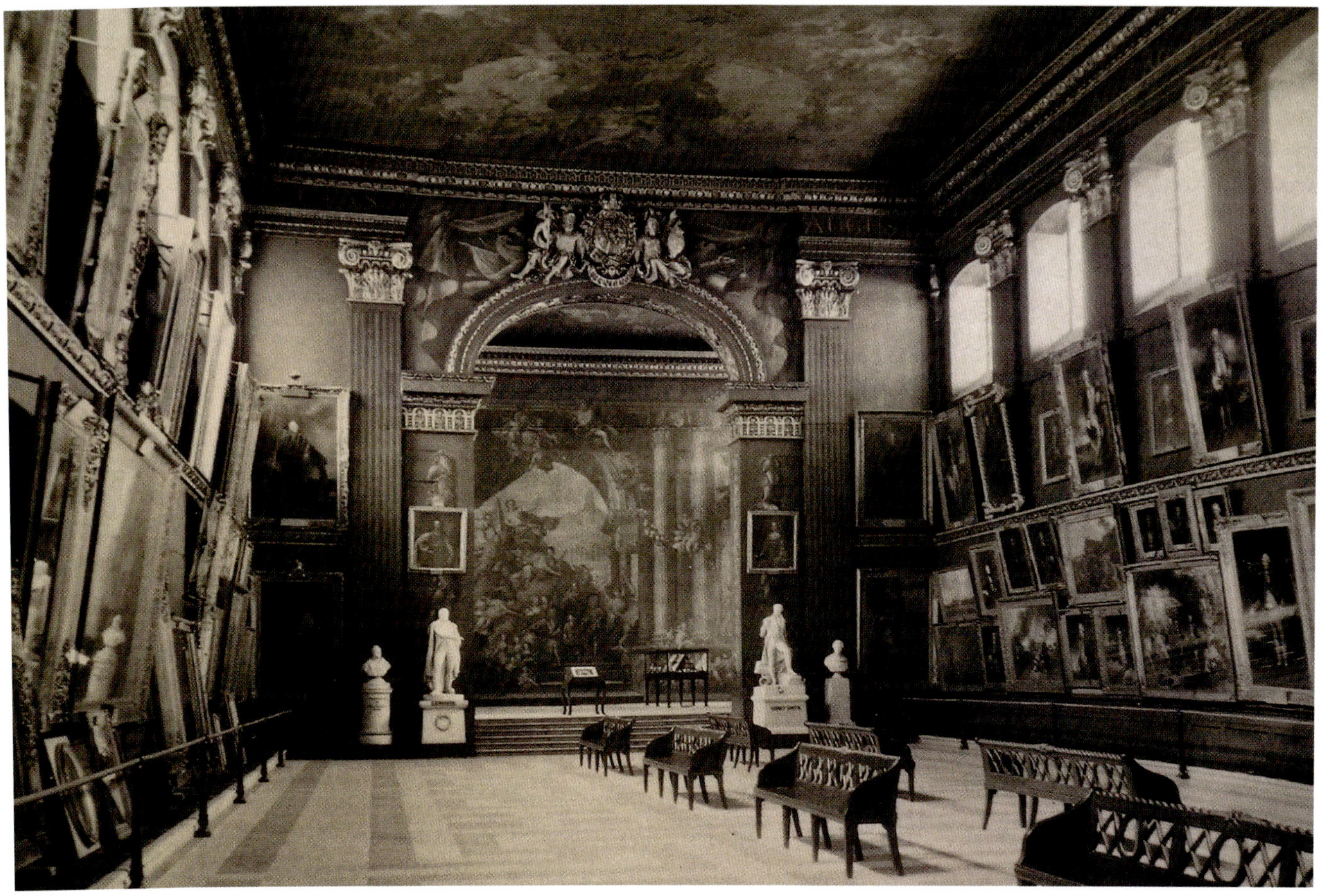

Fig. 5 In order to become the National Gallery of Naval Art in 1824, the Painted Hall underwent structural changes, such as the bricking-up of the lower windows in the Lower Hall.

be presumed that the coal-burning stoves deposited significant pollutants directly into the interior of the building and on to the surfaces of the paintings. The large open fireplace on the north wall of the Upper Hall and the fire-driven cooking appliances in the Undercroft below the Hall may have also been contributing factors. To the effects of heating and cooking should be added that of smoke from tobacco and from the vast quantity of candles used for illumination. This toxic mix must surely have accounted in large part for the need for such frequent cycles of restoration as the paintings deteriorated and darkened.

The Painted Hall also underwent various changes of use over time. First, a proposal was made in 1795 to transform the Hall into a gallery for the display of naval paintings, which required that its lower windows be bricked up; it opened in the spring of 1824 as the National Gallery of Naval Art, better known as the Naval Gallery (fig. 5). This was one of the first 'national' collections of art in Britain, preceding the foundation of the National Gallery by a matter of weeks. The gallery closed in 1936, and in 1937 the paintings were removed for exhibition in the new National Maritime Museum; in 1939 the Hall was restored as an officers' mess for the Royal Naval College (figs. 6 and 7). Contemporary photographs provide evidence of the extensive work undertaken on the walls of the Lower Hall at this time, with the clerestory windows being partially bricked in to reduce the original angled sill to a horizontal base, so as to allow for the positioning of electric lights. The lower windows were then opened up by removing the previously installed bricks, thereby revealing the original Thornhill soffit design of fictive coffering with rosettes. However, as part of the earlier infilling of the windows, a coating of lead white paint had been applied, possibly as a form of protection, and its removal proved very difficult. Consequently, in 1938 much of this lower soffit decoration was either entirely

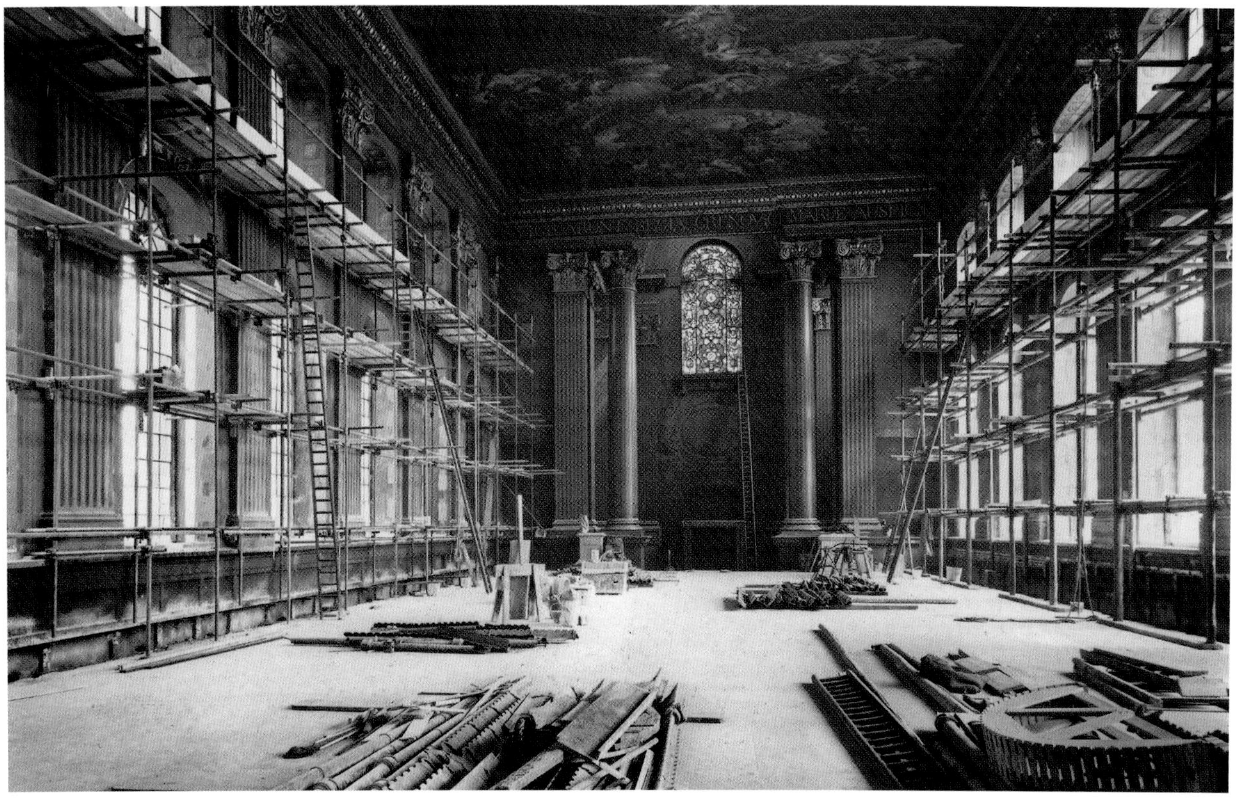

Fig. 6 In 1937 work began to reconvert the Hall from a picture gallery to a dining room for naval officers.

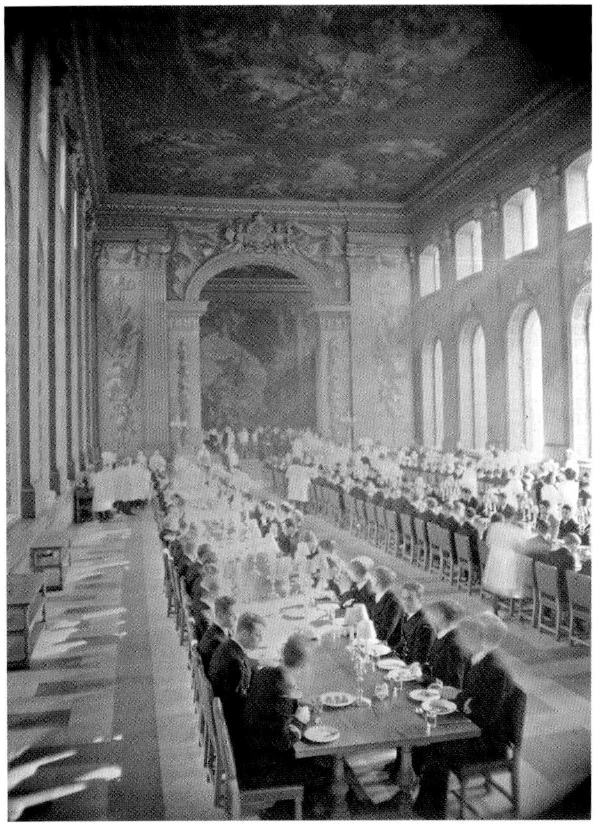

Fig. 7 Trainee naval officers eating in the dining hall of the Royal Naval College in February 1948.

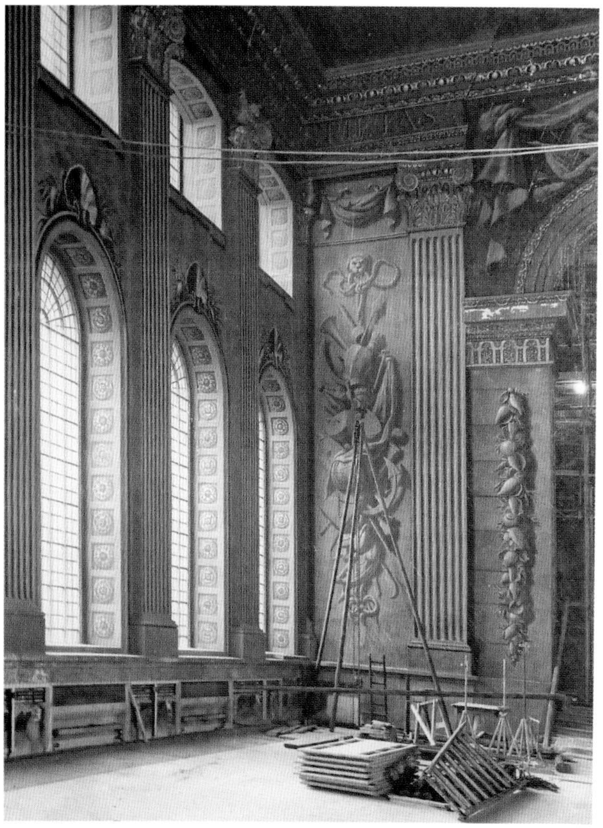

Fig. 8 In 1938, after the lower windows were unblocked, artists reconstructed the fictive coffering within the soffits.

re-created or significantly restored by students from the Royal Academy (fig. 8).

Perhaps the most important moment in the physical history of Thornhill's paintings came in the late 1950s, more than two centuries after their completion and over a hundred years since their last extensive restoration, in 1846. Between 1957 and 1960, all areas of decoration were comprehensively conserved by a team of restorers from the Ministry of Works. Concern about the condition of the main schemes had been raised in 1956, and in August of that year a number of areas within the Painted Hall had been selected for the purposes of carrying out a series of cleaning trials. The treatment successfully removed a material described as a hard covering over a discoloured varnish, although the use of extremely robust solvents and cleaning methods had proved necessary to achieve this result (fig. 9). The ceiling painting had also clearly suffered directly as a result of its use as a refectory, since its surface in the area above the serving hatches at the west end of the Hall was found to be in a very grimy and darkened condition.

The highly ambitious restoration project commenced early in 1957 and took three and a half years to complete. Work started in the Vestibule, continued into the Lower Hall and culminated in the Upper Hall, which was finally finished in June 1960. The interventions were principally undertaken by five restorers from the Ministry of Works Conservation Department, but credit for the vision and overall success of the project undoubtedly belongs to the remarkable conservator Westby Percival-Prescott (1923–2005), who designed and directed the overall treatment programme.[12]

In an obituary, Percival-Prescott was described as 'one of the last surviving members of a pioneering group of paintings conservators in the era after the Second World War that took the old empirical craft tradition of picture restoration and made of it an ethical profession'.[13] Before the Painted Hall project, he had participated in a series of large-scale restoration projects with the Ministry of Works team, including at Lancaster House and Hampton Court and on the Rubens ceiling in the Banqueting House in Whitehall. He was thus well versed in coordinating complex and demanding conservation treatments on huge painted schemes that were often executed in an oil medium over plaster supports and in difficult or confined spaces.

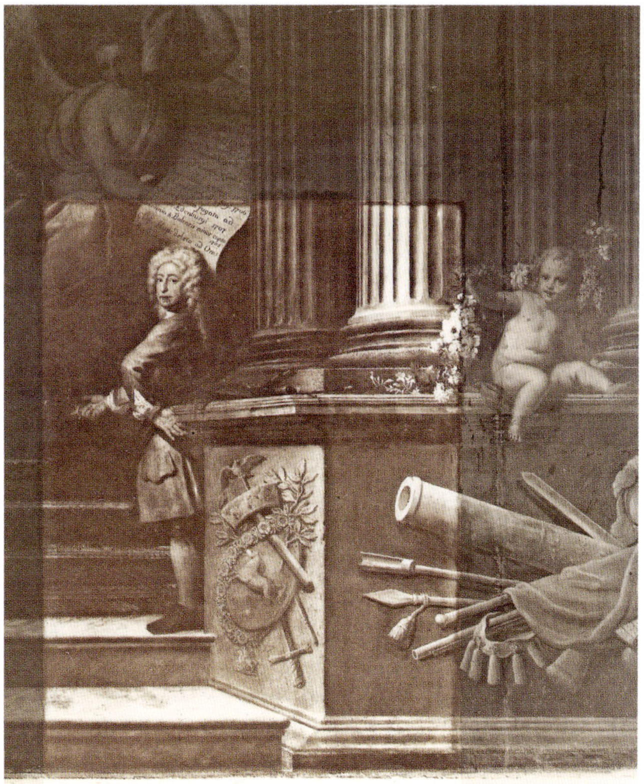

Fig. 9 In 1956 restorers from the Ministry of Works carried out an initial cleaning trial on the west wall of the Upper Hall.

The initial work in the Vestibule involved the removal of heavy deposits of dirt and grime from the surfaces and interstices of the walls, cornices and mouldings by the building firm J.G. Blyth & Co. In addition to this cleaning, areas of plaster were replaced and various figures restored, and some of the lettering on the lists of benefactors was partially restored by a signwriter. Some invasive interventions were also required, such as the detachment and reattachment of sections of original decoration that had been damaged as a result of severe beetle infestation of the vast oak timbers supporting the sloping painted ceilings of the north and south transepts. This work was largely completed by February 1958, and treatment then commenced on the ceiling of the Lower Hall. The ceiling was fully scaffolded, although the resulting lack of light and ventilation created difficult and at times hazardous working conditions throughout the course of the project (figs. 1 and 10).

At this point, Percival-Prescott's direction showed his determination to elevate the work from just another short-term response to the immediate conservation requirements of the paintings into a programme of detailed examination alongside a well-considered treatment methodology. He organized a series of interrelated investigations and interventions with a view to understanding not only how Thornhill had executed his remarkable paintings, but also how they had suffered since their completion.

A comprehensive survey consisting of 175 separate photographs was embarked upon, with all images taken at a fixed distance and in consistent conditions, to provide the first thorough record of the state of the paintings before, during and after cleaning. Percival-Prescott's innovative use of photography saw him also undertake macrophotography by adapting a camera as a low-powered microscope in order to examine Thornhill's original technique and assess further the nature of the deterioration of the paint layer, with the aim of designing the most appropriate treatments. As he described, 'These uses which were made of photography in the Greenwich restoration reflect some of the wider aspects of conservation work, in which the history of the painting and the study of the painter, his work and his intention, make a vital contribution to the successful treatment of the technical problems. The restorer's decisions in the critical stages of cleaning and the later replacement of missing parts are governed by artistic and historical considerations as much as by the technical and scientific aspects of his materials and their behaviour.'[14]

In addition, Percival-Prescott sought to procure the best materials and equipment. He explained:

Much of the equipment used in the restoration was specially designed to suit the conditions and the unusual scale of the work; the aim of using stable, non-darkening materials for the retouching, and varnishes which would darken to the minimum, was adhered to throughout the conservation. A suitable lighting for the correct matching of colours in the retouching was difficult to provide on the totally enclosed scaffold, and lighting units were designed, in which the correct colour balance was obtained by the mixture of fluorescent and tungsten light, and which enabled the light to be thrown on to the ceiling without interfering with the vision of the restorers.[15]

However, the condition of the Lower Hall ceiling posed significant technical challenges. Although Percival-Prescott noted that the original paint layer was in a 'remarkably good state', the severity of the main types of deterioration was considerable. Most problematic were the fifteen layers of often intractable darkened and opaque varnish coating the entire scheme: 'The darkening of these accumulated layers of varnish and repainting gave the painting an almost monochromatic appearance, and the original colour and vitality were much diminished if not entirely lost.'[16] Indeed, the photographic record taken at the time shows how compromised the paintings had become.

Then there was the extensive damage caused by earlier over-cleaning, which Percival-Prescott attributed to the use of caustic agents in 1733, when the paint had been unevenly 'skinned' and the finishing layers abraded. This damage led to repeated overpainting, in which not only the colour and texture but also the form and intention of the original were often lost. The dado panels on the walls of the Upper Hall suffered particularly badly in this respect.[17]

Percival-Prescott also noted how the paint layer had become increasingly translucent with age, exposing hitherto unnoticed pentimenti (visible traces of earlier painting). Flaking of the paint layer was highlighted as a serious issue, particularly on the south side of the ceiling and within the *Element of Air* (near the north-western corner, featuring the goddess Juno), caused by an early water-damage event. Percival-Prescott identified another form of deterioration as 'darkish freckles', which he linked to the presence of mould, particularly in the two western corners of the ceiling. Furthermore, he recorded that 'large areas had been filled in with picture putty, far beyond the actual extent of the damage, and had been repainted ... in a medium which formed an almost insoluble paint. The standard of the restoration was very crude and the whole area was later repainted in oil paint on top of the previous restoration.'[18]

The original plaster, however, was found to be in surprisingly good condition, with few cracks and no

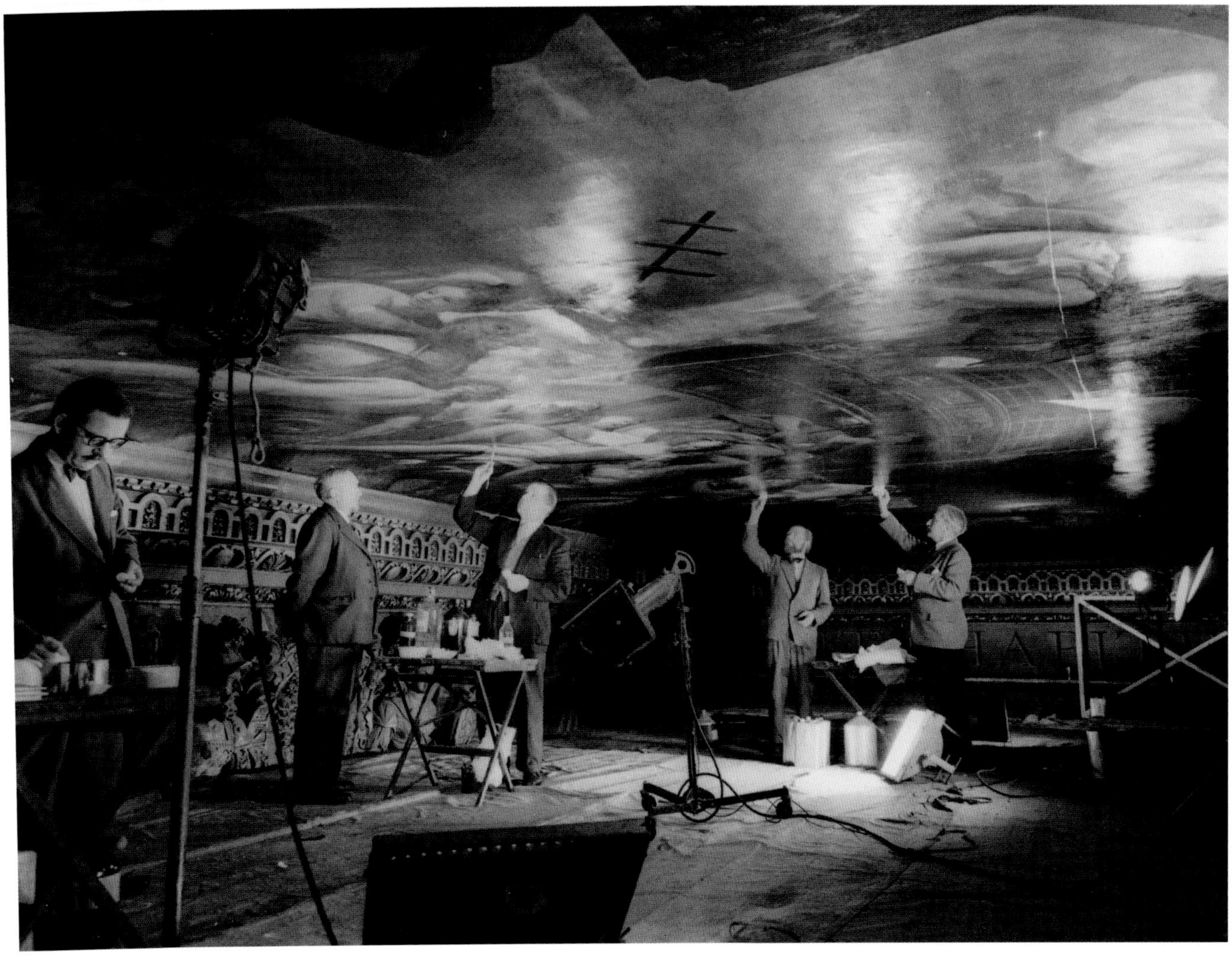

Fig. 10 A photograph of February 1958 shows work in progress on the Lower Hall ceiling by the Ministry of Works restorer/artists.

reported deterioration with the exception of the west wall, where movement of the wooden support had caused differential movement of the plaster, resulting in cracking – seemingly a historic and perpetual problem.

The main aim of the programme was, therefore, an extensive intervention to remove all non-original varnishes as far as possible, to undertake any essential reintegration of losses, and then to reapply a new varnish layer to 'protect' the painting in the long term. During the work, each restorer was made responsible for a strip of ceiling running the length of the Hall, and the team consulted together on the problems involved. The work was clearly extremely uncomfortable, owing to the solvent fumes and the difficult working positions required to access the ceiling. The multiple layers of darkened varnishes were removed in stages, using different solvents in response to the varying solubility of each layer. Percival-Prescott noted: 'It was found that the main features of the varnish complex were as follows – on top a layer of wax of varying thickness, then several layers of soft resin varnishes; below this a hard oil varnish and a coach varnish; then more soft resins, then a coat of size and finally another soft resin varnish on the surface of the paint.'[19] Localized reconstruction of various elements was also necessary, such as for the figure of Juno, which had sustained extensive damage.

Final varnishing was undertaken using either traditional dammar resin varnish or the ketone resin varnish AW2 dissolved in white spirit with a small addition of stand oil. This was thinly sprayed on to the surface, and synthetic wax was then applied in a very thin layer.[20]

Fundamental to Percival-Prescott's overall vision of the project was his goal of minimizing the need for further extensive treatment in the future. Crucial to this aim was his recognition of the vulnerability of the paint layer, the abrasion caused by repeated cleaning and the difficulty of removing the multiple varnish layers safely because of 'Thornhill's tendency, in the later stages of the painting …, to add varnish to his oil medium in ever-increasing quantities. These final layers of paint were sometimes little more than tinted glazes.'[21] Percival-Prescott's far-sighted methodology was therefore to reduce as much as possible the cyclical requirement for varnish removal and its reapplication during any subsequent conservation campaign; the paint layer could remain protected by the coating applied during the 1950s project and ideally would require only surface cleaning in the future.[22] In addition, even though some retouching was considered necessary, Percival-Prescott's intention from the outset was to undertake as little reintegration as possible, given that 'the pictorial intention of the painter was always the decisive factor in the extent and degree of inpainting'.[23] In this respect, his treatment philosophy of minimal intervention was highly innovative for the time (although this approach is sometimes only partially adhered to even today).

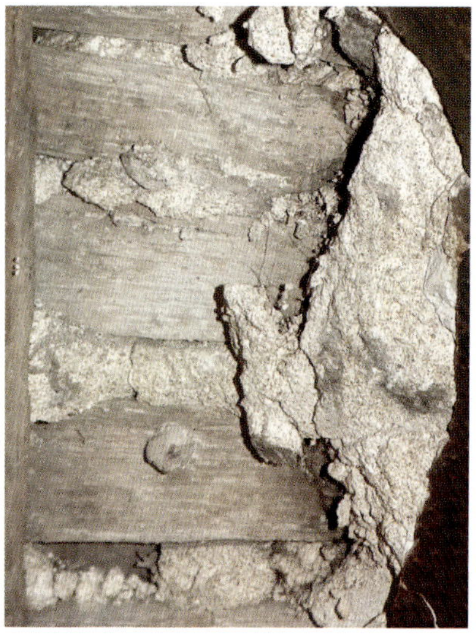

Fig. 11 A detail of the ceiling shows how it was originally constructed. Oak laths were attached to oak rafters by hand-made nails. The plaster (a mix of sand and lime, with added animal hair) was forced between the gaps of the laths and the surface smoothed with trowels.

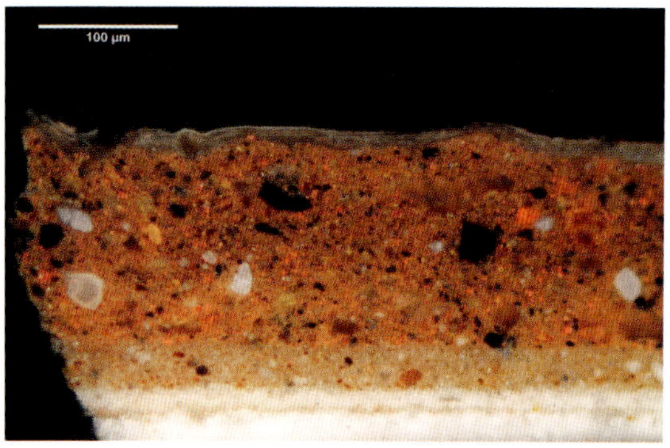

Fig. 12 A microscopic sample of the original painting, showing the paint layers when observed under magnification.

Ultimately, the project undertaken between 1957 and 1960 was a great achievement, and revealed the quality of the original painted scheme for the first time in many generations. Percival-Prescott also designed a special exhibition to celebrate the conservation programme. It was opened by HM Queen Elizabeth II in the Painted Hall in July 1960 and attracted more than 48,000 visitors over the course of twelve weeks.

Despite the success of the 1950s project, over the following decades a number of inspections were carried out, including by the Ministry of Works in 1977 and by English Heritage in 1999, when the gradual yellowing of the varnish coating, increasing deposits of dirt and grim, and localized water damage were noted. By 2012 concern was such that a review of the overall condition of the paintings was deemed necessary. The opportunity was therefore taken to carry out a series of targeted and interrelated investigations using all available documentation, especially that relating to the 1950s treatment, to establish the physical history of the paintings and the nature of past interventions.

Close examination of areas of the paintings in both the Upper and Lower Halls was undertaken using non-invasive diagnostic techniques in order to ascertain the nature and condition of the support, paint and plaster layers, and to clarify, if possible, the extent and type of materials added during previous restorations. These investigations revealed further information about the construction of the various schemes (figs. 13 and 14).[24]

An initial examination confirmed that the west wall of the Upper Hall and the ceilings of both the Upper and Lower Halls are composed of a lime, sand and hair plaster applied to a lath-and-timber-framed support

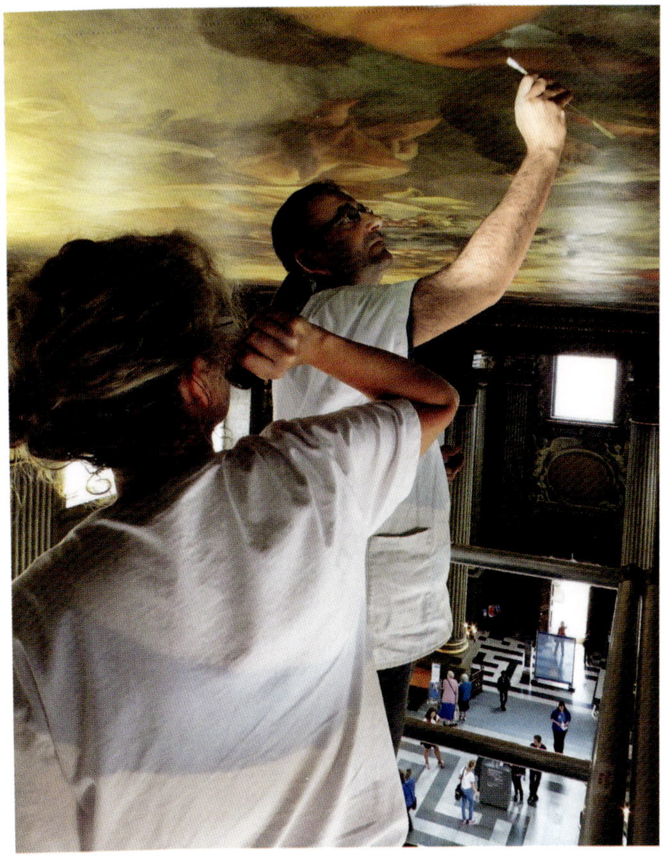

Fig. 13 A close surface examination and testing of materials formed an important part of the preliminary research process prior to the start of the conservation project.

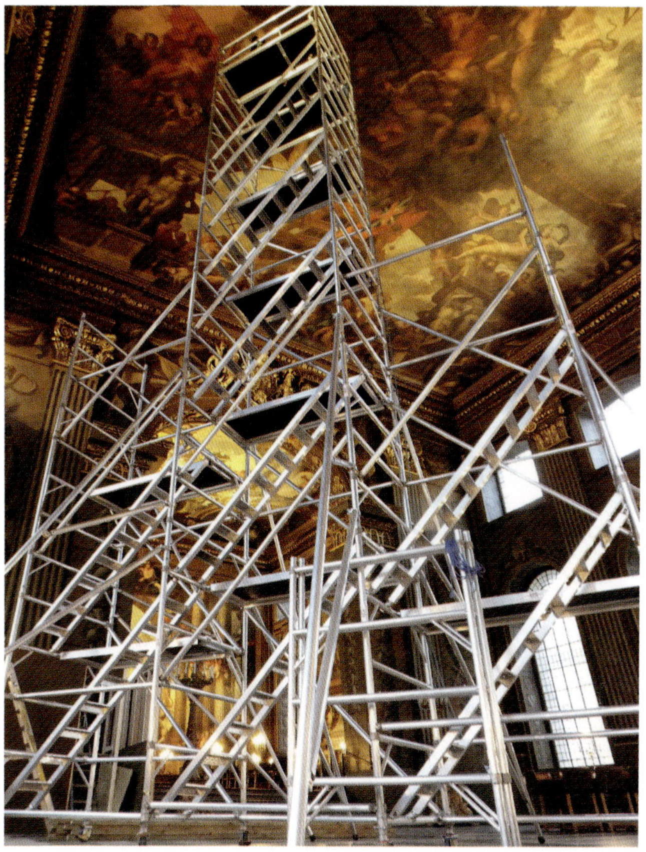

Fig. 14 A 44-foot-high (13.5 m) tower scaffold allowed unique access to the ceiling during the testing phase.

(fig. 11). It is recorded that this work was carried out from 1705 by Mr Henry Doogood (a member of a leading family of City of London plasterers and much favoured by Christopher Wren during his rebuilding of the City churches), who was instructed to prepare the plaster ceiling 'after the best manner fit for painting'.[25] Joseph Thompson (an employee of the Hospital) was later paid to 'paint three times in oyl and plain colour to prepare for Mr Thornhill's work'.[26] These coatings were applied to effectively seal and so reduce the porosity of the finely textured plaster surface, and also to introduce a mid-tone base colour for Thornhill to work upon. The artist and his team would therefore have entered the site with all surfaces plastered and prepared in readiness for the start of their work.

These historically documented preparatory methods were corroborated by a technical examination that used microscopy and instrumental analysis to determine the nature of Thornhill's painting technique (fig. 12). This revealed Thompson's preparatory processes, showing the initial sealant layer, a plain lead ground and then the buff-coloured ground layer above. A comparative analysis of Thornhill's near-contemporary scheme within the dome of St Paul's Cathedral showed a similar preparatory sequence of a sealant followed by two grounds.

However, Thornhill's method of transferring his designs on to the walls and ceilings remains unclear. For example, no evidence could be found of pouncing marks – a means of transferring a design by tamping charcoal dust through a pinpricked master drawing on to the plaster surface. Likewise, there are no incisions into the plaster or any indication of setting-out lines or other preparatory drawing.

A likely sequence for the layout of the overall design was fascinatingly alluded to by the diarist Dudley Ryder, who in August 1716 met Thornhill on the scaffolding at the start of his other great

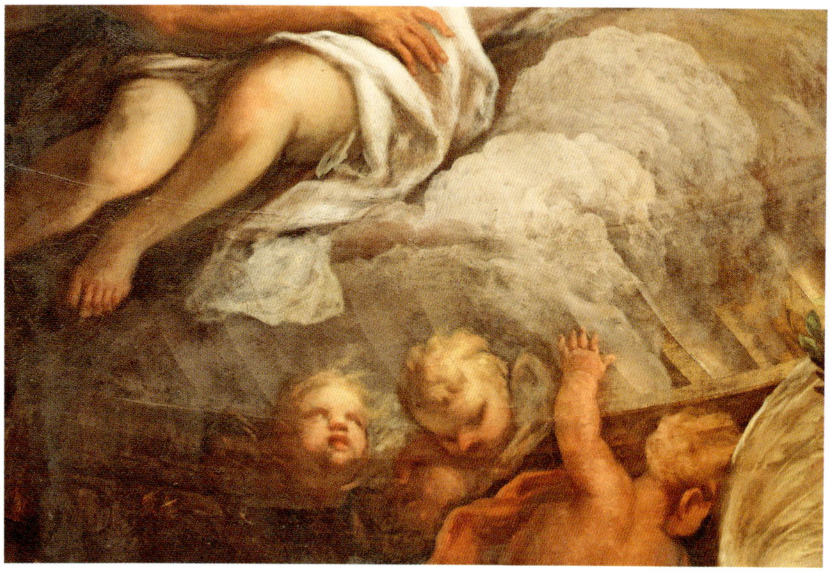

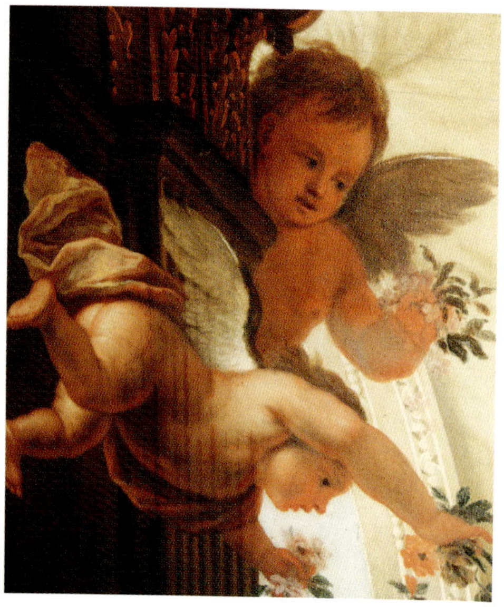

Fig. 15 These figures can clearly be seen to have been placed over the underlying architectural forms, and so suggest later additions within the sequence of Thornhill's build-up of the overall scheme.

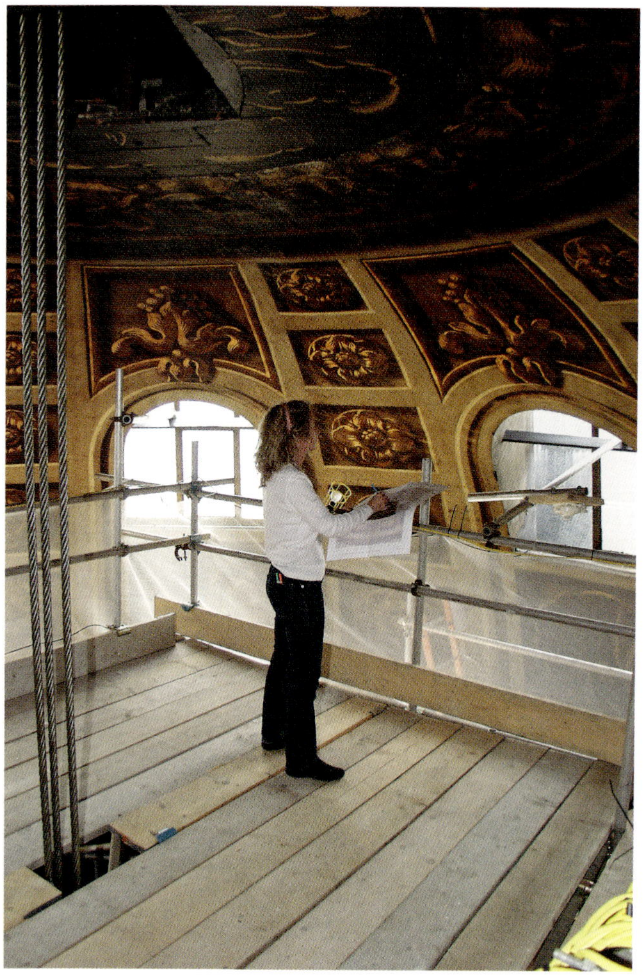

Fig. 16 Inside the cupola on the dome of St Paul's Cathedral, where the designs that Dudley Ryder commented upon when visiting Thornhill on site in 1716 can be seen.

work, in the dome of St Paul's: 'I made my bow to Mr Thornhill ... He told me this was a liberty which he did not usually allow to anybody, because if it was people would come in so great crowds that they would interrupt him in his study and painting.' Ryder goes on to record: 'All the architecture is already done, only the gilding and enriching the great part of it remains yet to be done, but then the history part is not begun yet.'[27] It is evident that exactly the same principle was applied at Greenwich, where the main fictive architectural forms were initially laid out to act as the principal framework for the later addition of the figurative and other decorative elements (figs. 15 and 17).

When Ryder ventured up into the cupola at the very top of the dome of St Paul's, he observed that it was 'painted chiefly with roses gilded within squares. It will be exceedingly rich. There are two or three more persons working at these figures but Mr Thornhill himself comes and overlooks them and directs them' (fig. 16).[28] This comment allows an insight into the nature of Thornhill's team – its size and the distribution of roles – as well as its management.

Different artists were employed by Thornhill to take responsibility for certain aspects of the design. Thornhill's chief assistant, Robert Brown (*fl.* 1707–1753), was much admired 'for his skill in

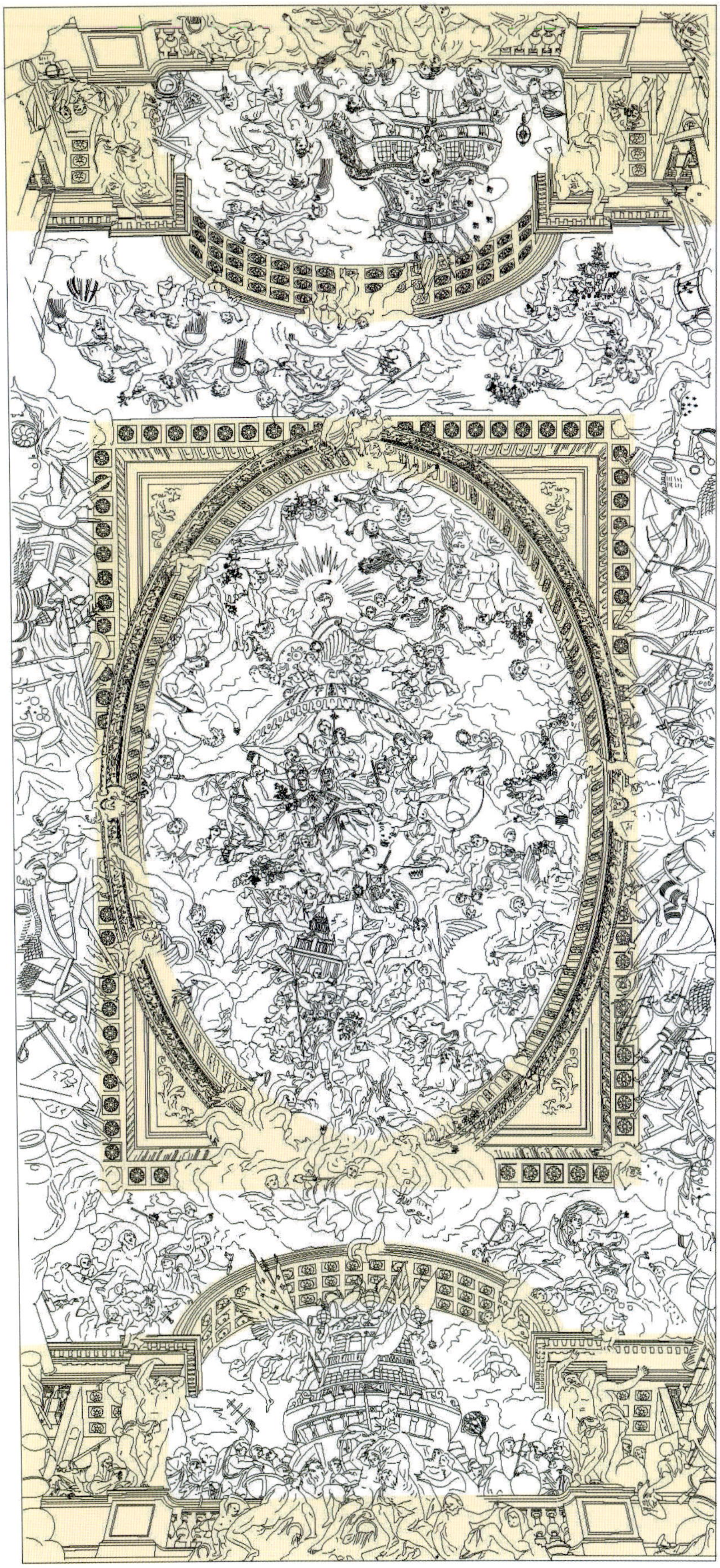

Fig. 17 The design required the architectural framework to be initially transcribed on to the ceiling – here emphasized in colour. Once this was established, the multitude of detail and figures could be added.

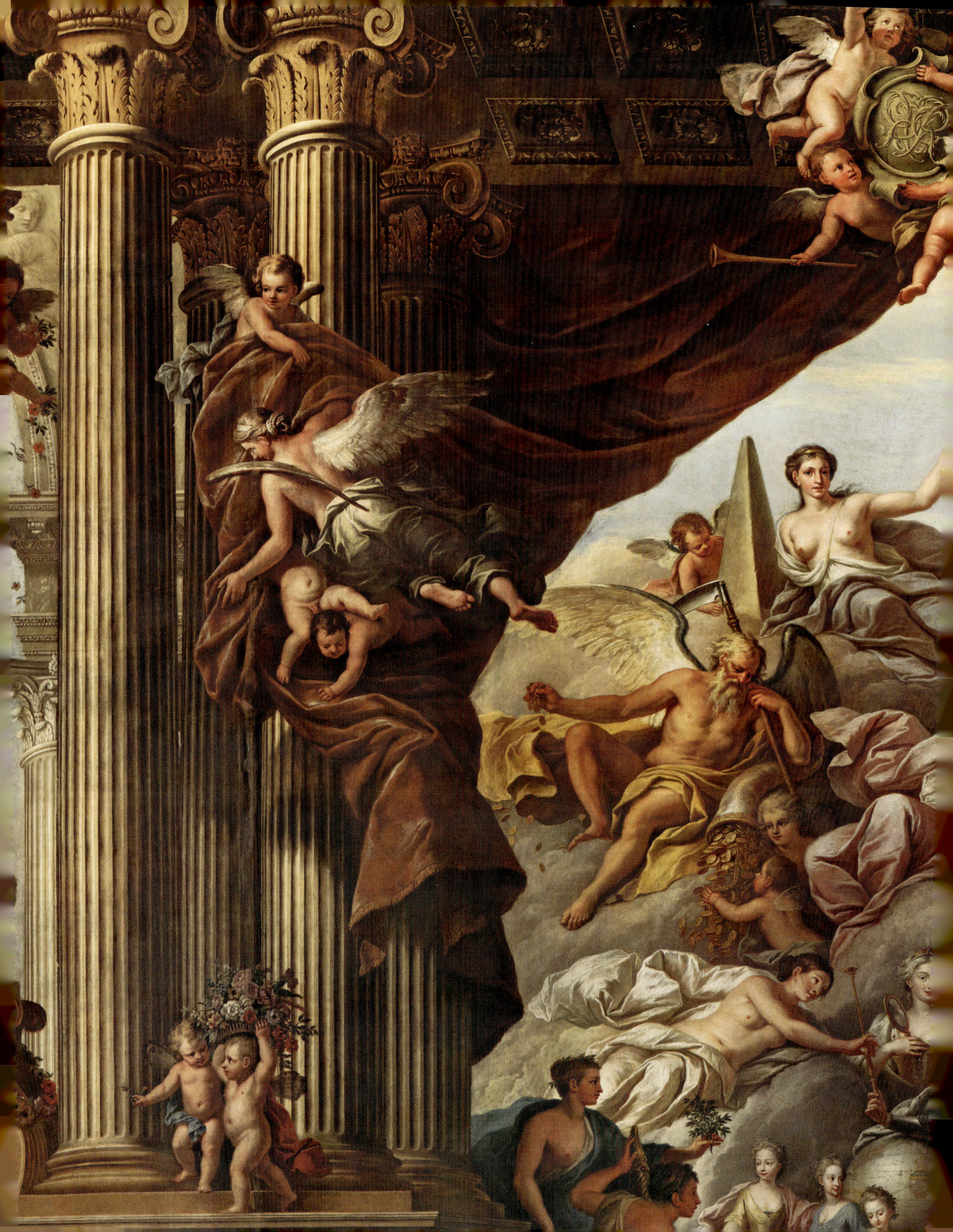

painting crimson drapery, apostles, and the stories out of the New Testament'.[29] His hand can perhaps be seen in the rendering of the great stage curtain that is pulled back by winged attendants and putti to reveal the royal family on the west wall of the Upper Hall (fig. 18). The magnificent still lifes of flowers that adorn much of the Upper Hall scheme are clearly by another hand, and may share stylistic similarities with the work of the French flower-painter Antoine Monnoyer (d. 1747), who had previously decorated the ceiling of the Chapel Royal at Versailles with swags of flowers, and was known to be in London between 1714 and 1729 (fig. 19). His more renowned father, Jean-Baptiste Monnoyer (d. 1699), from whom Antoine acquired much of his skill in portraying flowers, had similarly adorned the walls and ceiling of Montagu House in Bloomsbury (1675–79, now lost). Thornhill owned a flower still life by Monnoyer senior, and so the inclusion of Antoine in his team would seem an understandable choice.[30]

Thornhill was responsible for most of the allegorical figurative painting, although, interestingly, he did not execute the important group portrait of the royal family that dominates the west wall of the Upper Hall; it was painted by the artist Dietrich Ernst Andreae (*c.* 1680–1734; fig. 20). While he praised the Upper Hall scheme, Thornhill's son-in-law William Hogarth was prompted to note, 'Sir James Thornhill, in a too modest Compliance with the Connoisseurs of this Time, call'd In the Assistance of Mr Andrea, a Foreigner, famous for the justness of his Out line, to paint the Royal Family at the Upper End of Greenwich Hall, to the Beauties or Faults of which I have nothing to say.'[31]

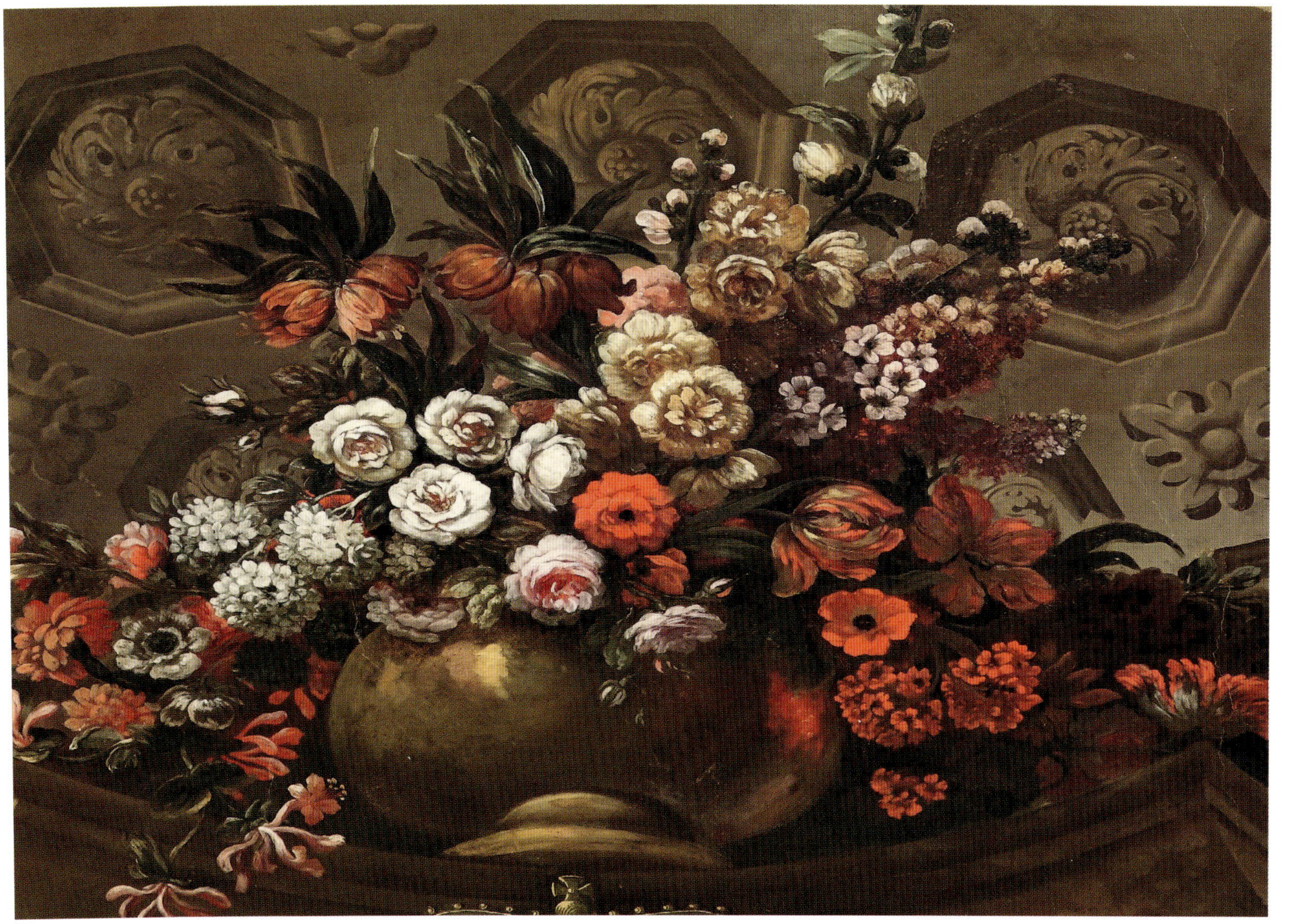

Fig. 18 (*opposite*) Thornhill's chief assistant, Robert Brown, was especially renowned for his skill in painting 'crimson drapery', as this fine example on the west wall of the Upper Hall demonstrates.

Fig. 19 (*above*) An example from the Upper Hall ceiling of one of a series of magnificent flower still lifes.

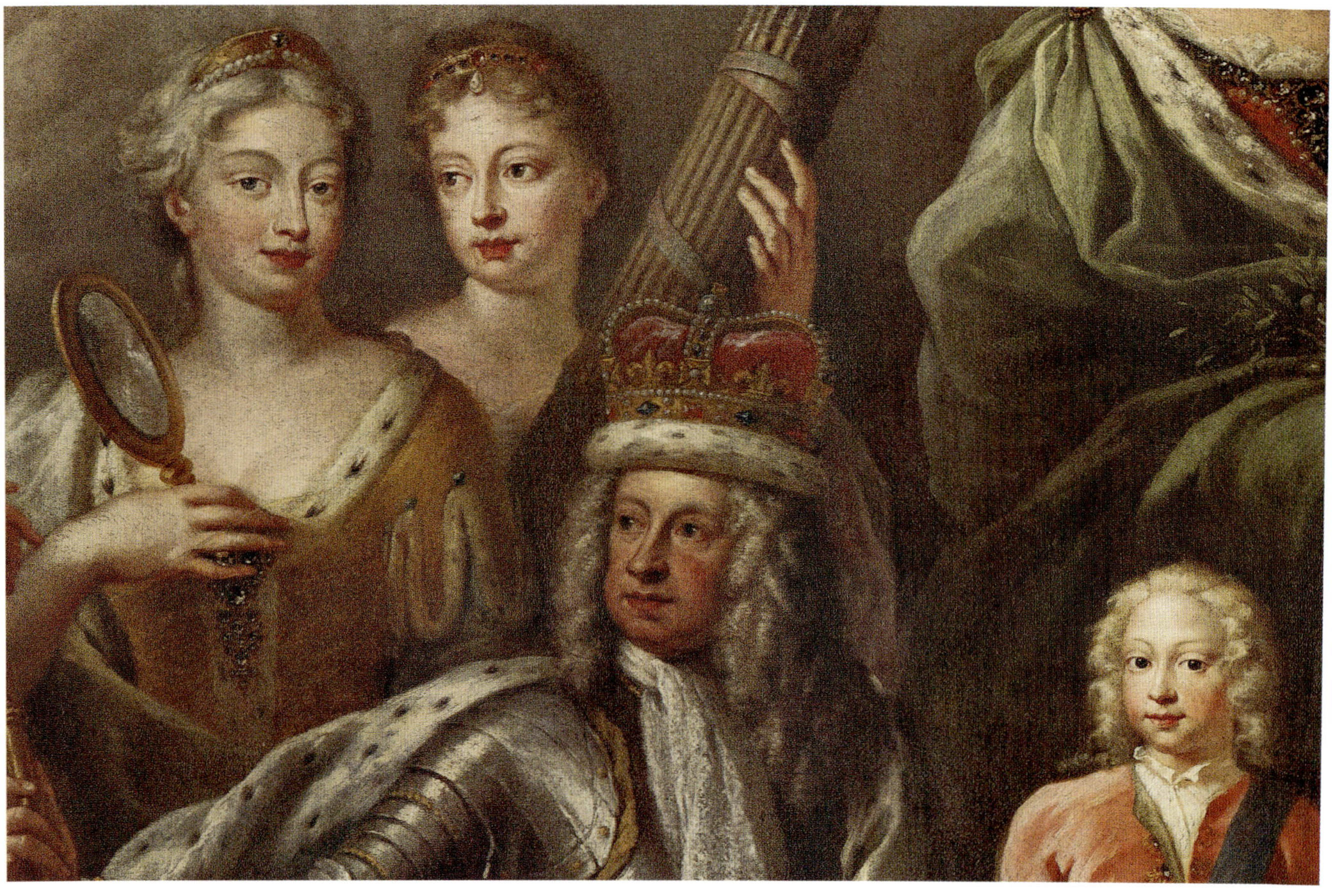

Fig. 20 The figure group of the Hanoverian royal family on the west wall of the Upper Hall was painted by Dietrich Ernst Andreae.

Thornhill's painting technique required the use of finely ground coloured pigment mixed with walnut oil (the painting medium), which was applied over a previously prepared plaster surface in varying numbers of layers and different thicknesses. As confirmed by Jane Davies, the pigments identified are typical for the period: lead white, bone black, ochres, red vermilion and ultramarine (figs. 23 and 24).[32] Thornhill said he had been paid 'only' £3 per square yard for the ceiling and £1 per square yard for the walls, rates that he was earnestly to dispute later in the project.[33] The most costly component of his palette must have been gold leaf, which was used to decorate the elaborate wooden cornice and the plaster and stone elements forming the capitals. Examination of these elements suggests that most of the original early eighteenth-century gilding has survived (fig. 21). The prominent carved figures on the proscenium arch and the relief sculpture on the soffit of the arch are an exception; they sustained a later regilding.

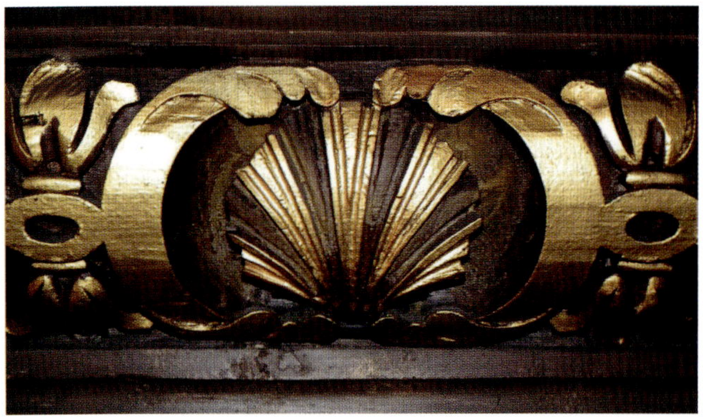

Fig 21 A detail from the cornice of the Lower Hall. This immaculately carved motif is made from wood, and recent research has shown that the gilding is entirely original.

Close examination of Thornhill's work reveals just how few corrections or alterations were made in the disposition and location of most of the figures and other features. This strongly suggests that almost every detail was planned precisely before the artist applied his designs to the ceilings and walls, and that any small compositional adjustments, or pentimenti, represent only tiny changes – for example, a finger or a toe shifted to a minute degree. Such minor adjustments at a relatively late stage in the painting process are perhaps more a reflection of Thornhill's tendency to fuss over his work than an indication of substantial changes to the primary composition (fig. 22). There is, however, one exception: part of a seated figure is faintly visible on the west wall of the Upper Hall, upon the steps where the royal family are positioned. This prominent figure was subsequently obliterated by the overpainting of the stone steps – a unique example of a significant late alteration to the overall design.

Perhaps the largest and most notable adjustment was the late decision to extend the area for painting on the Upper Hall west wall from a central zone flanked by windows to one that extended across the entire width of the elevation. Thornhill had already begun preparing designs for a narrower scheme fitting between the two windows. The rationale for expanding the design remains unclear, although the possible effects of *contre-jour* stemming from the two exposed windows might have been a deciding factor. In 1718, at Thornhill's request, the plasterer Robert Weatherill was paid £30 for 'closing the two windows on the west side of the Officers Hall for Mr Thornhill the painters work'.[34] The plaster used was described in the Hospital accounts as '202 yards of finishing done upon heart laths with the Hospital lime and sand'.[35] To this day, a clear distinction is apparent: one may notice two vertical cracks to the left and right of the main central area of plaster, and also observe the distinctly coarser quality of plaster used by Weatherill, compared to the much smoother central section applied by Doogood some thirteen years earlier.

Following the initial examination of the technique and condition of Thornhill's paintings, the report of April 2012 concluded that, although most areas were in a stable state, albeit very dirty, there was some deterioration on the ceiling of the Lower Hall – specifically, flaking of the paint layer and blanching of previously applied varnishes. In this context, 'blanching' refers to optical whitening of the surface, caused either by microfissures within the varnish layer or by delamination of the varnish from the paint

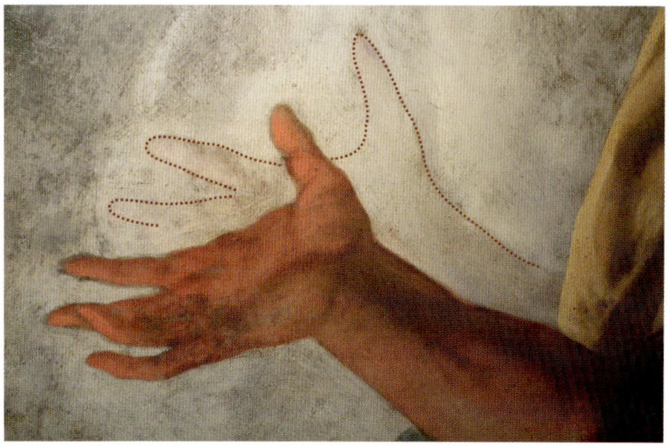

Fig. 22 Pentimenti made by Thornhill can be noted across the scheme. Invariably these adjustments are very small and barely perceptible when viewed from the ground.

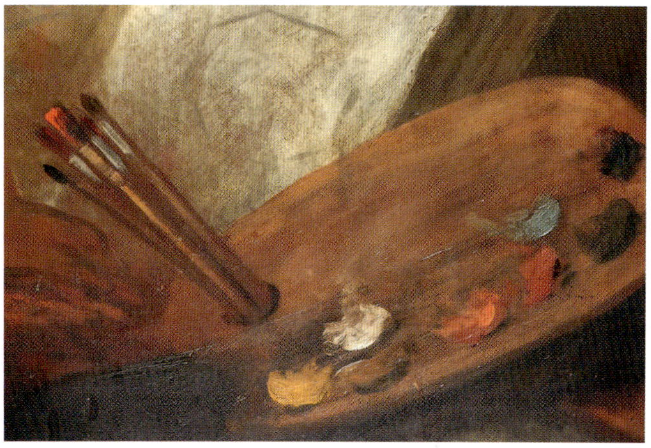

Fig. 23 A putto on the ceiling of the Upper Hall holds a palette that graphically describes the pigment range used by Thornhill and the nature of his palette and brushes.

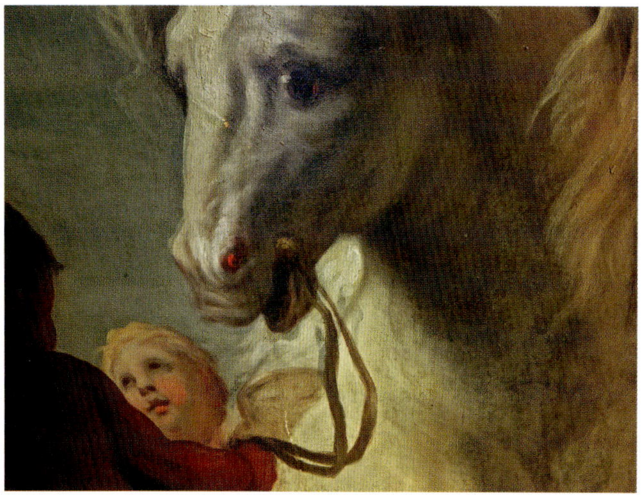

Fig 24 This image, taken from the Upper Hall ceiling, gives some idea of the colour range that Thornhill was able to achieve from his palette. Also to be noted is the thick impasto on the horse's forehead and the confident loose brushwork.

layer, both of which lead to light-scattering. There also appeared to be a link between these phenomena and high levels of light, specifically within the extensively glazed Lower Hall, but far less so in the darker Upper Hall.[36] However, all areas of the plaster were found to be in remarkable condition, in large part owing to the quality of the original plastering by Henry Doogood.

In tandem with the condition survey, treatment testing was undertaken to establish whether the appearance of the painted schemes could be improved by surface cleaning alone; this process would remove dirt and dust but leave the underlying varnish intact. However, such an intervention was approached with caution, as cleaning is in itself an irreversible intervention, and a primary aim was to ensure that a homogeneous level of cleaning was achieved using controllable methods that could be easily and safely applied over large areas. Various dry and aqueous methods and materials were tested, and it was found that very little contact with the surface was needed to remove a substantial amount of dirt and greatly improve the appearance of the paintings. The success of these cleaning trials was confirmed by analysis, which concluded that the materials used did not in any way solubilize or remove the varnish.

At the same time as the available options were explored and a methodology for the proposed treatment was developed, the desirability, or indeed necessity, of removing the final varnish layer applied during the 1950s restoration was carefully considered. Conservation conventions might argue that this was an opportunity to remove ageing varnish layers, an operation that could become increasingly risky over time, and then to reapply a modern material with known longevity that could improve the perceived appearance of the original scheme. Nevertheless, it was also clear that removing further varnish would expose the already overly treated paintings to yet another highly invasive and possibly damaging intervention. The harmful effects of solvent cleaning – specifically, swelling and softening of the paint medium, solvent diffusion and retention, and leaching (the extraction of soluble organic compounds from the paint layer) – are well documented.[37]

It was therefore concluded that full removal of the varnish layer applied during the 1950s was not merited, and that this project presented an opportunity to break the cycle of repeated and increasingly deleterious treatment. Testing also showed that surface cleaning would lead to an impressive improvement in the brightness and definition of the whole scheme. Removing the 1950s varnish would additionally have risked the erasure of an unquantifiable number of past retouchings, and would also have required the complete revarnishing of vast areas of painting – an extremely difficult intervention to execute uniformly and with the minimum of glare. Moreover, it was found that, after more than half a century, the 1950s varnish was still highly soluble and generally in good condition (apart from the localized areas of blanching in the Lower Hall) and its future deterioration could potentially be controlled by limiting levels of ultraviolet light through the installation of solar shading. The final presentation of the paintings post-treatment would also be significantly assisted by the planned introduction of a sophisticated modern gallery-standard lighting system.

This first phase of treatment, in the Upper Hall, was undertaken at the request of the Greenwich Foundation, and was funded primarily by the Heritage Lottery Fund (as it was then known). The project began in December 2012 and was completed by May 2013. The sequence of work involved an initial surface clean of the west wall and ceiling using soft brushes and light air extraction to gently remove dirt and dust deposits, followed by aqueous surface cleaning to remove more ingrained dirt.

The results were extremely satisfactory and vastly improved the appearance of the paintings, making them look far fresher and more vivid. The project also generated exciting new discoveries: for example, the wide range of tropical shells forming swags were specifically identifiable, and further research suggested that their design source may have been the important early eighteenth-century shell collection of Hans Sloane (fig. 26).

The situation in the Lower Hall and Vestibule was found to be far more complex. The 2012 condition survey established that the deterioration phenomena

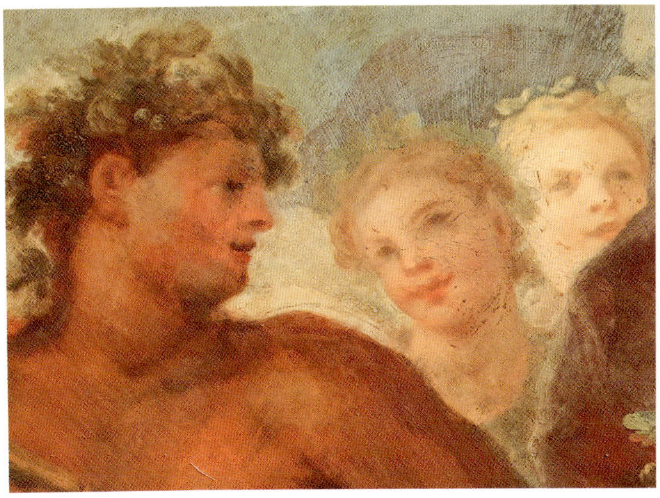

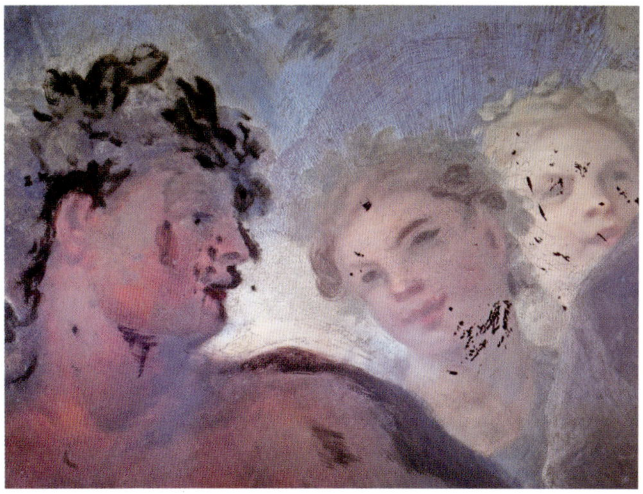

Fig. 25 Detailed imaging in ultraviolet light was an important tool to assess aspects of original technique and also evidence of past treatments.

affecting all areas of the paintings (microflaking and extensive blanching of later varnish layers) were severely compromising the appearance and aesthetic appreciation of the schemes. Further detailed examination and analysis were undertaken in 2015 and again in 2018, the aim of which was to understand more fully the nature of the later varnish layers and other non-original coatings used in previous restorations of the Lower Hall ceiling, and their relationship to the blanching phenomenon.[38] A limited number of minute samples were taken and examined using optical microscopy and instrumental analysis (FTIR-ATR). This established that the majority of the Lower Hall ceiling is covered in an upper layer of dammar resin varnish with an additional thin layer of beeswax (applied so as to reduce glare from the varnish), dating to the 1950s restoration, and that in certain areas – predominantly those of darker pigments – the dammar layer covers a deteriorated eighteenth-century diterpenoid resin varnish that is responsible for the blanching effect.

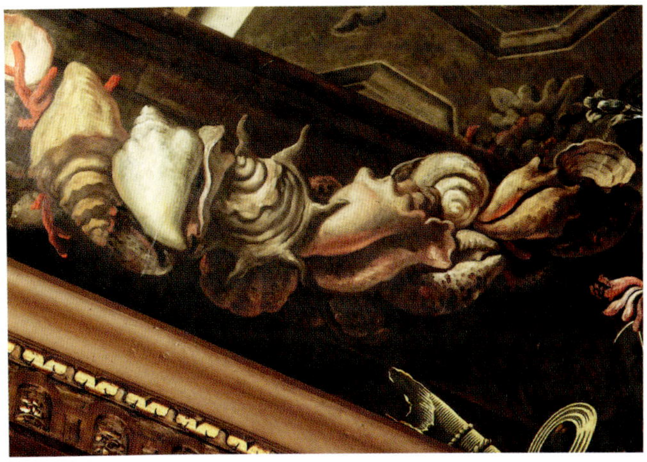

Fig. 26 A swag of shells, the individual species of which were easily identifiable after cleaning in 2012–13. Research indicated that they may have been copied from a significant 18th-century collection.

This was a significant finding, as the eighteenth-century varnish may be one of the various materials noted by Percival-Prescott during the 1950s restoration, most likely what he referred to as a 'tough oil varnish (like coach varnish), where the oil has become polymerised and cross-linked'. He also described it as 'extremely resistant to even the most active solvents, calling for prolonged application or brushing'.[39] The presence of this material and the difficulties involved in its removal may also explain why blanching occurred particularly in the darker passages of the scheme; this corresponds to the practice in the cleaning of varnished oil films whereby historic varnishes may be left in the darker areas of an aged painting but removed more extensively from lighter passages. Not only might the latter be more robust due to the presence of lead pigments, but also a more obvious visual effect would be achieved.[40] It would therefore appear that such selective cleaning was undertaken during the 1950s restoration. The whole scheme was then covered in the dammar varnish, which would have initially saturated and thus hidden the diterpenoid layer to a degree.

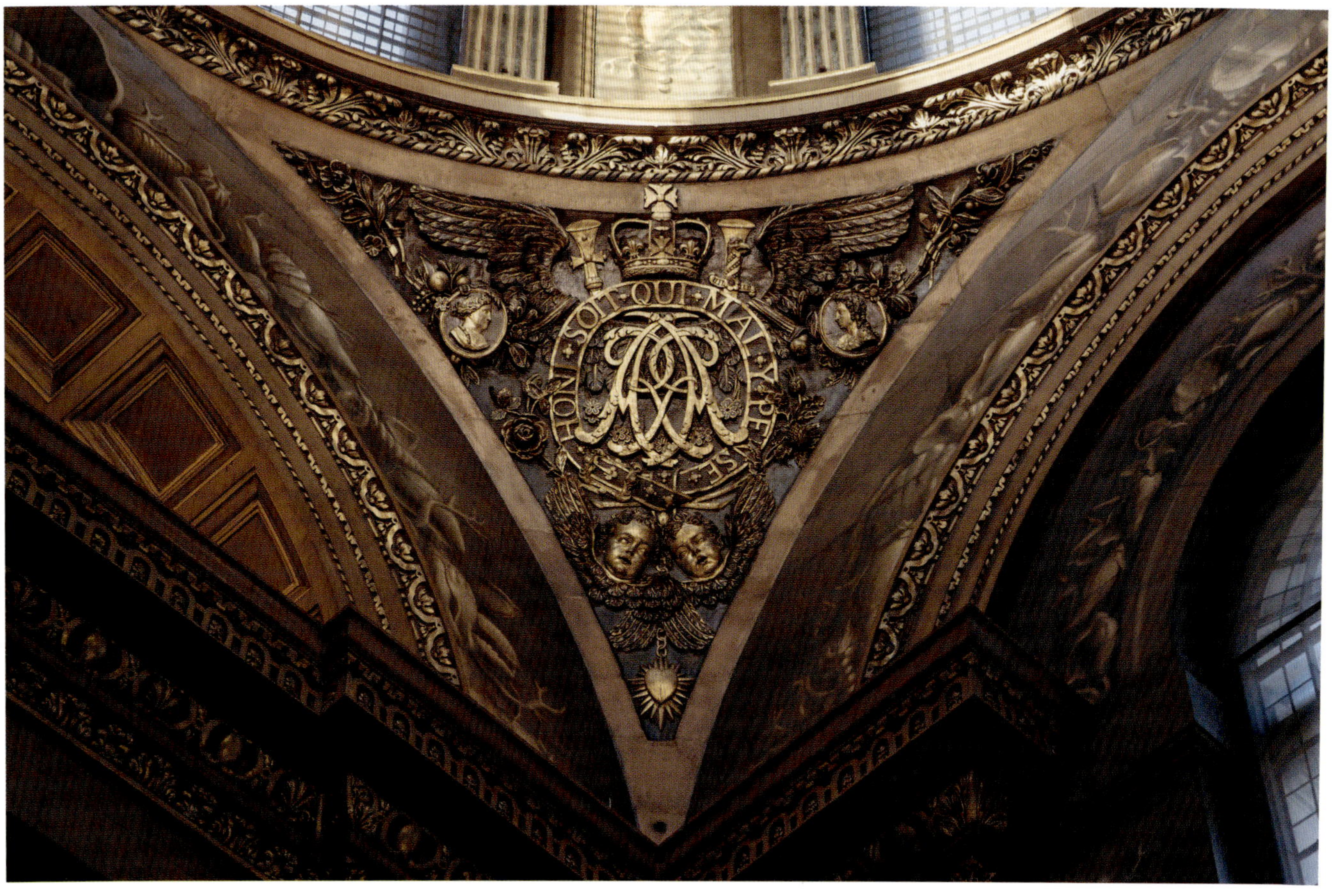

Fig. 27 The royal cipher of Queen Anne and Prince George, in one of the pendentives of the Vestibule dome. The Vestibule was the last area that Thornhill painted at Greenwich; he completed his task in 1726.

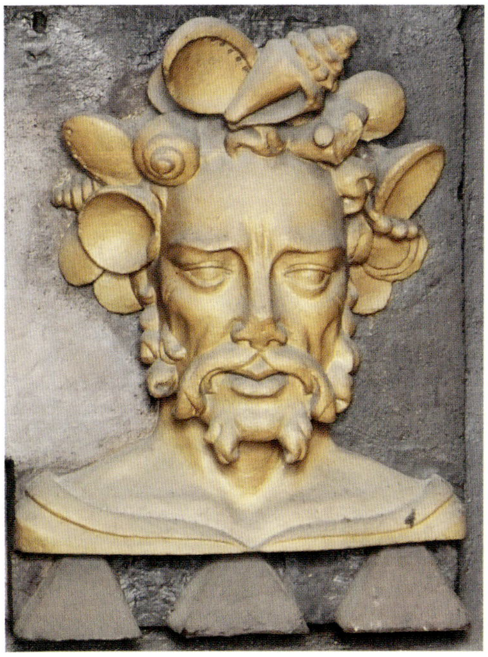

Fig. 28 The access afforded by the scaffold within the Vestibule allowed a unique view of much detail usually obscured by accumulated dust. Illustrated here is the very fine quality of Robert Jones's carving work.

However, the blanching perhaps became more visible as the dammar became more translucent over time.

After the initial further investigation and extensive planning and fundraising by the Greenwich Foundation, the second phase of conservation began in September 2016 (funded by the National Lottery Heritage Fund, with the generous addition of funds from charitable trusts and individuals). A preliminary phase of work completed the untreated surfaces of the Upper Hall remaining from 2013, but the project began in earnest in the Vestibule, where surface cleaning and repair of the gilded architectural mouldings were undertaken. It was a huge but ultimately successful endeavour, once again making it possible to appreciate the quality of the decoration (figs. 27 and 28).

The project then progressed into the Lower Hall, where work was initiated with a high-resolution photogrammetric recording of the ceiling taken from ground level, before the erection of scaffolding. This detailed survey utilized 438 individual images that,

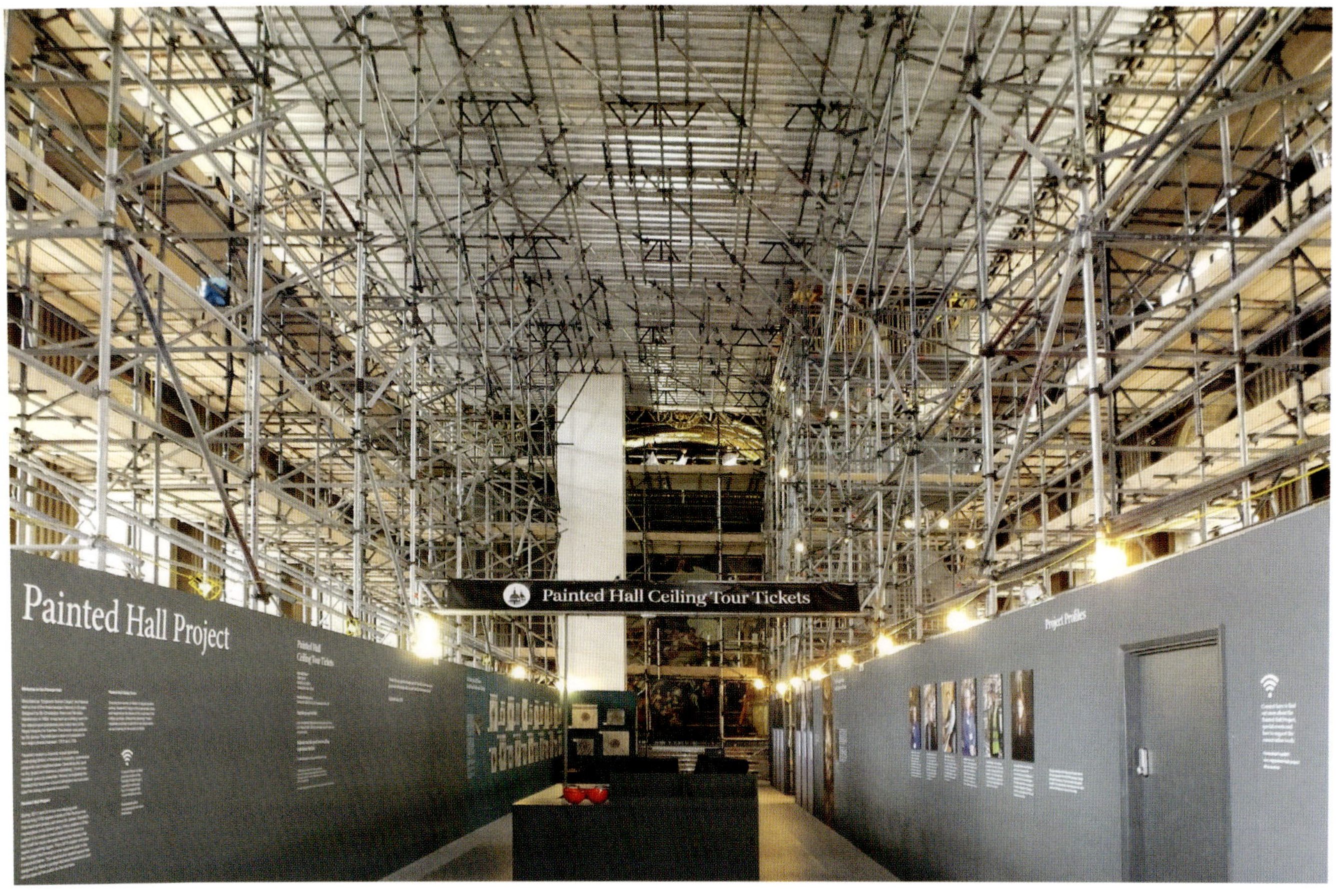

Fig. 29 The scaffold not only allowed the conservation of the paintings, but also gave visitors the chance to see the work in progress and to enjoy a unique close-up of the Lower Hall ceiling.

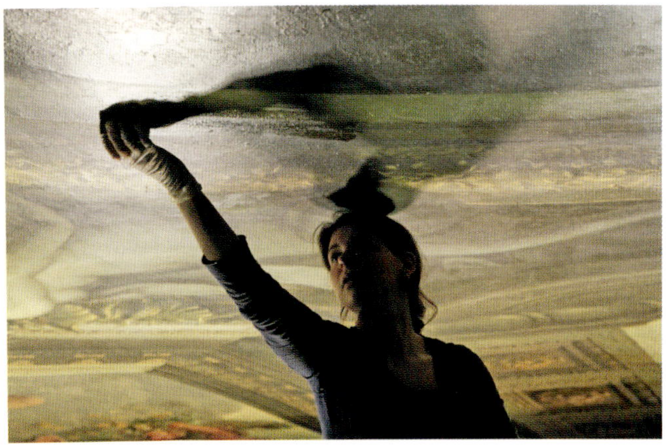

Fig. 30 After extensive testing, an effective, safe and repeatable process to surface-clean the paintings was developed.

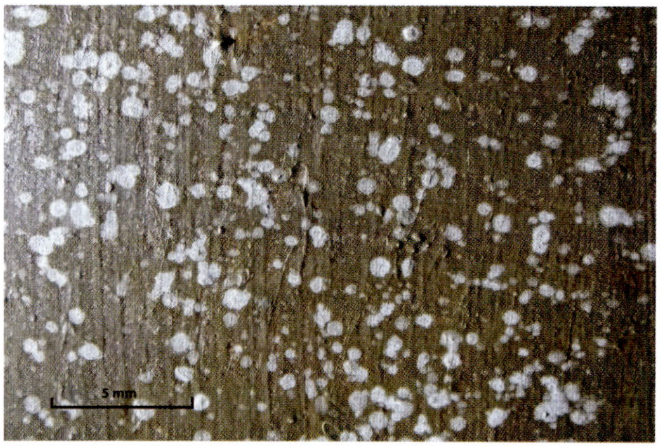

Fig. 31 A significant conservation and presentational issue, found across much of the Lower Hall ceiling, resulted from the formation of small white surface dots. The dots had formed as a consequence of the activation of lead soaps within the original ground layers.

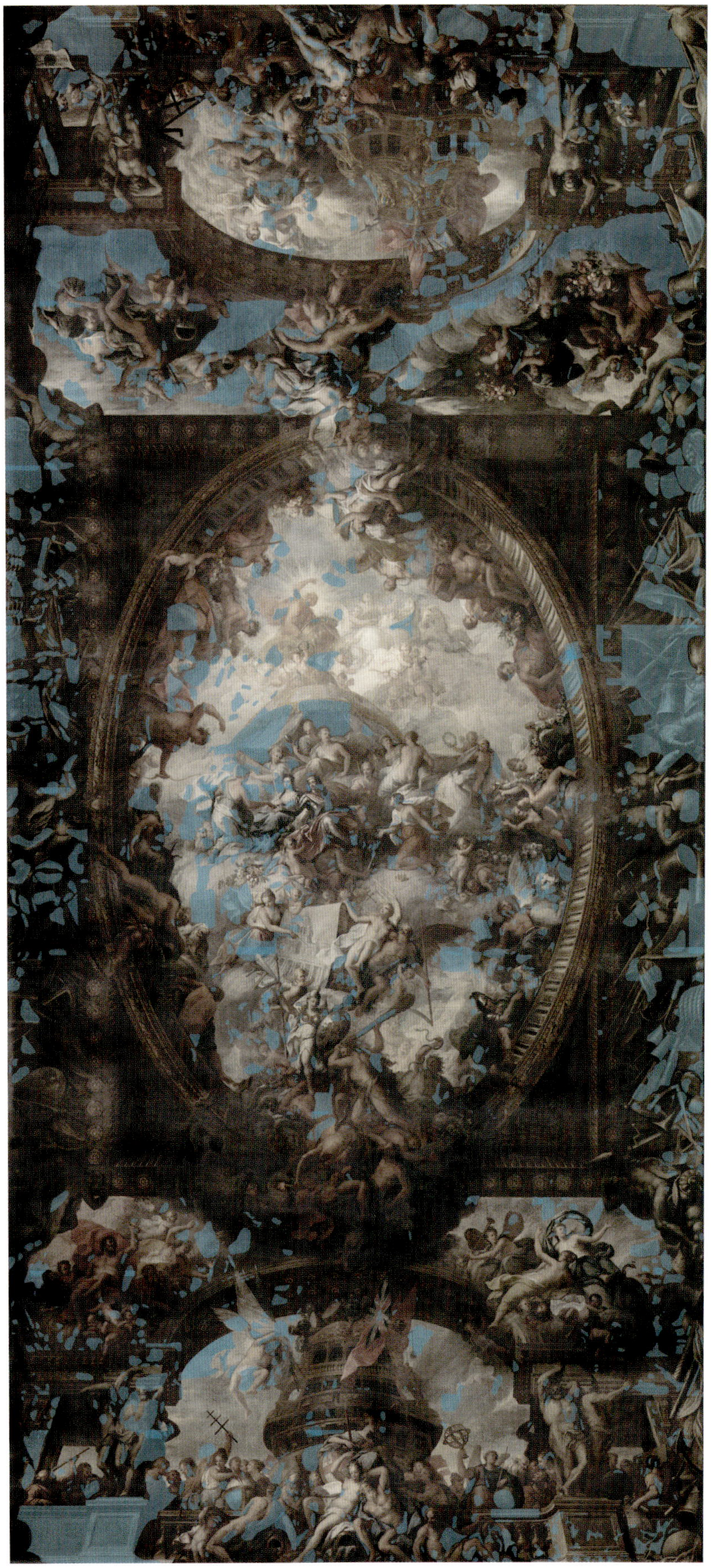

Fig. 32 The presence of lead soaps within the Lower Hall ceiling was mapped, showing a marked concentration along the south and north sides, closest to the windows. This suggested that light and thermal change were possible contributory factors.

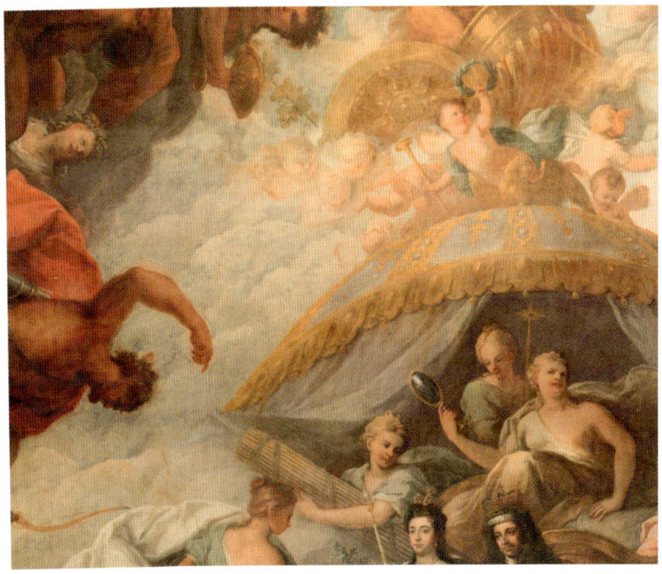

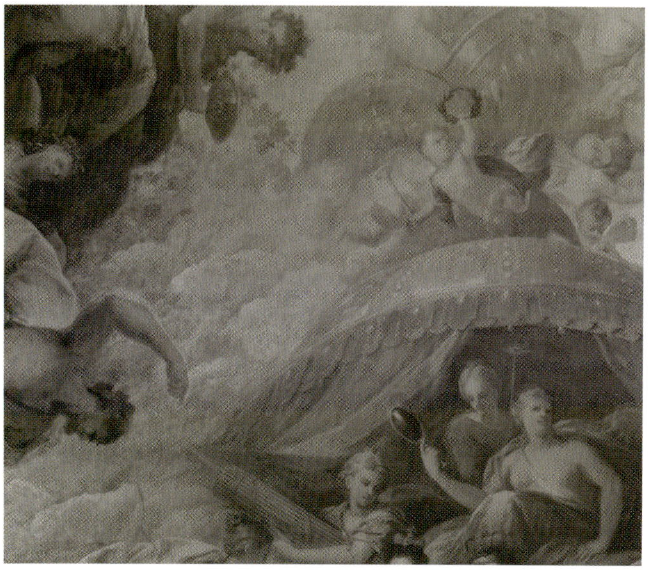

Fig. 33 A detail of the Lower Hall ceiling taken in normal light (left). The same scene photographed in infrared light serves as a non-invasive examination technique to allow observation of otherwise hidden phenomena, such as underdrawing, previous alterations and certain forms of deterioration.

when mosaiced together, created a highly informative surface record of the state of the ceiling before conservation. A specially designed platform scaffold was then installed throughout the Lower Hall that would allow an anticipated 100,000 visitors to observe the conservation process in action during the course of the project (fig. 29). Such access to the ceiling also allowed further detailed technical investigations of the painting to be carried out at close quarters, including high-resolution technical imaging using visible, infrared and ultraviolet light (figs. 25 and 33).

Treatment began in October 2017, and the methodology followed that undertaken in the Upper Hall – namely, leaving the 1950s varnish *in situ*, but focusing on improving the legibility of the scheme through overall surface cleaning. Extensive testing was again carried out, and it established that the embedded dirt and grime in the varnish layer could be quickly and safely removed using mild alkaline reagents. However, as in the case of the Upper Hall, the surface was water-sensitive, so it was vital to minimize the amount of moisture by using highly absorbent PVF sponges. The sponges retain a very small amount of water when they are wrung dry, and they allow for a mechanically gentle but highly effective cleaning action. In the hands of skilled conservators, this seemingly simply technique achieved a strikingly even and homogeneous cleaning level across the entire ceiling (fig. 30).

Even though Percival-Prescott's treatment methodology had been far-sighted, he could not have predicted the deterioration of the varnish since the 1950s project, causing areas of blanching that were contributing to an unsightly grey veil across a significant proportion of the ceiling. An additional blanching phenomenon, visible as small white dots, was distributed randomly over the ceiling's surface (fig. 31). Further analysis and examination confirmed that the dots were caused by lead soaps, which in cross-section appear as translucent beads embedded in the paint layer. Lead soaps may form when pigments such as lead white react with the oil binding medium in paint layers under certain environmental conditions. In this case, because the white efflorescences were distributed over large areas of the ceiling painting, it was concluded that their formation probably related to the lead-containing pigments found in the preparatory ground layers (fig. 32).[41] It was also clear that the soaps had been present in the paint layer for some time, as various areas showed attempts to conceal their presence with pigment – presumably applied during the 1950s restoration (fig. 34).

High magnification revealed that the soap agglomerates were expanding within the paint layer,

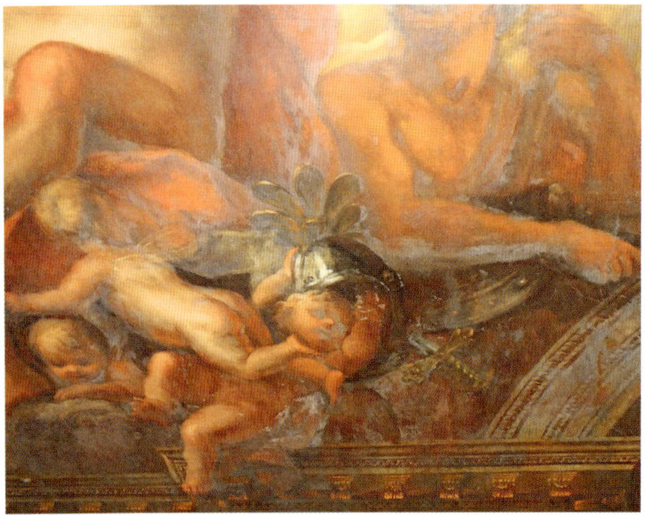

Fig. 34 An area of blanching before treatment shows how visually disruptive this form of deterioration had been to the ceiling scheme as a whole.

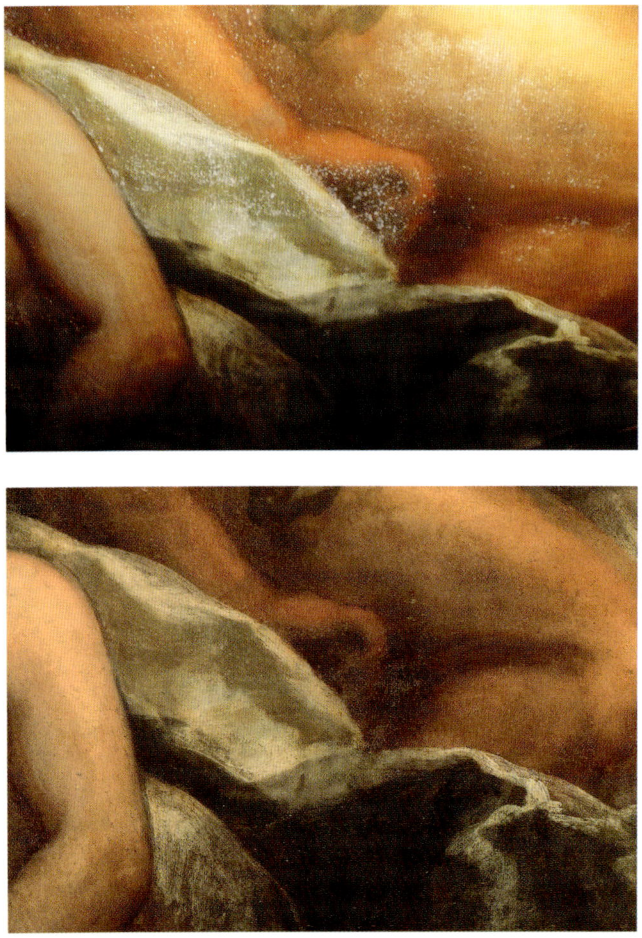

Fig. 35 An area of the Lower Hall ceiling shown before (top) and after treatment.

resulting in localized disruption of the varnish and the formation of 'dots' of white blanching. Although the exact mechanism is still the subject of research, the dots' formation in the presence of moisture and at high humidity has been frequently observed,[42] and indeed the environmental data for the Painted Hall, plotted over several years, showed periodic extreme environmental conditions with associated condensation events that could have impacted directly on the ceiling painting before the installation of a new heating system. The concentration of blanching along both the north and south sides of the ceiling may have been related to the proximity of large windows along each of these elevations.

Treatment was necessary to minimize the visual impact of these two types of blanching – the grey veil associated with the eighteenth-century diterpenoid varnish, and the white dots caused by the movement of the lead soaps present in the paint layer. In the case of the former, resolubilization using a mixture of alcohol (isopropanol) and white spirit passed over the area with a cotton-wool swab was found to be highly effective in redistributing the dammar varnish over areas of blanching, which in certain instances reduced the pale appearance of the diterpenoid varnish below. In localized areas where resolubilization had a limited effect, resaturation of the varnish was also achieved using the low-molecular-weight varnish Regalrez 1094.[43] This proved successful in improving the appearance of 'grey veil' by filling the microfissures in the early varnish layer and thereby reducing the light-scattering responsible for the blanching effect. Surface cleaning was very effective in reducing the deleterious visual effect of the lead-soap white dots by removing the overlying microfragments of disrupted varnish, but in localized areas some further colour reintegration was necessary using Gamblin Conservation Colors (fig. 35).[44]

Alongside the cleaning and resolubilization treatments, some remedial treatment of the painted surface of the Lower Hall was necessary, including flake-fixing to readhere localized areas of flaking paint and ground layers.[45] Further discrete reintegration was also required to reduce the visual impact of colour-altered old retouchings. The magnificent Doogood

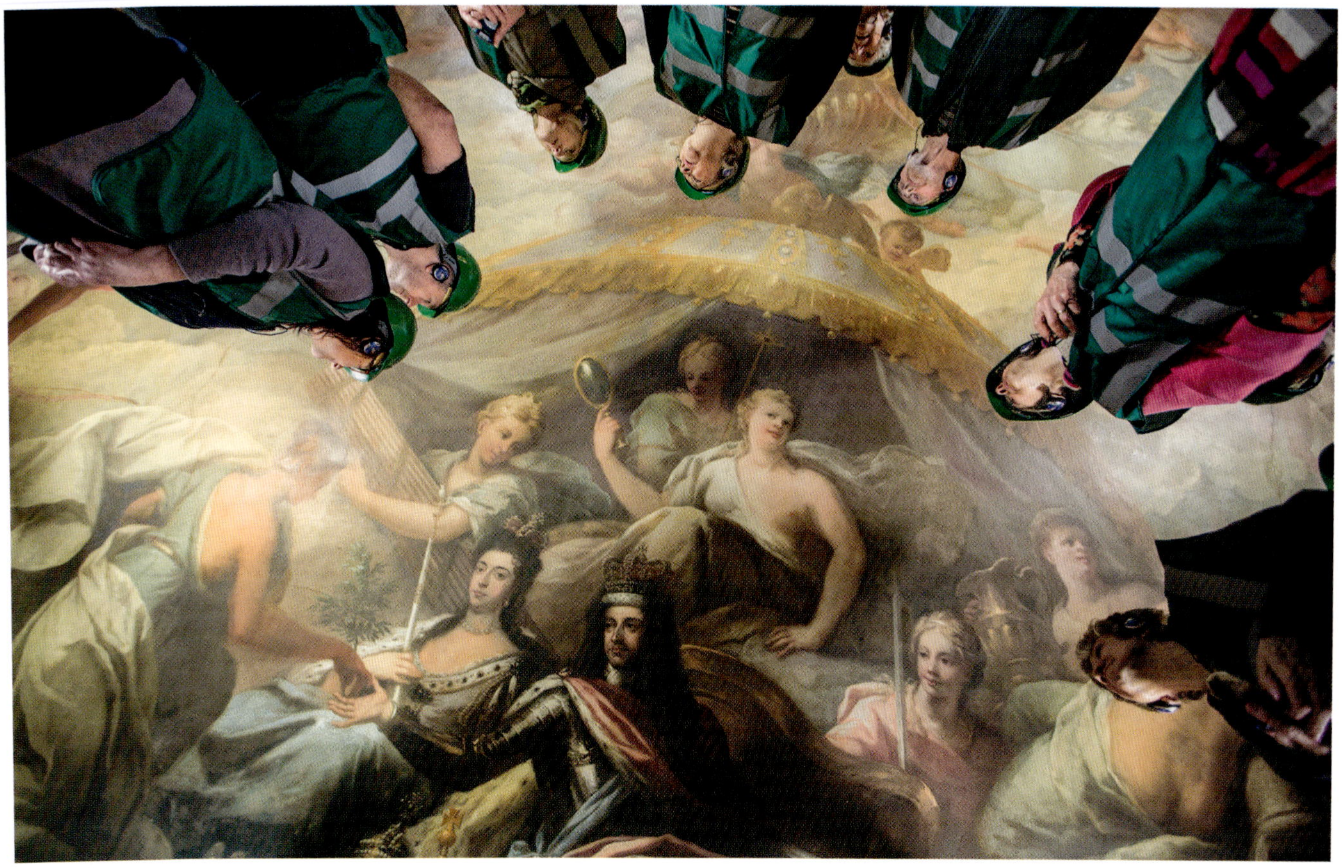

Fig. 36 Almost 100,000 visitors observed the conservation process in action and were able to appreciate at close quarters the team's success in revealing once again the true magnificence of Thornhill's scheme.

render was found to be in an almost flawless condition throughout, in terms of its adhesion and cohesion, and limited stabilization and repair were necessary in only a single localized area.

It is also important to note the treatment of all other significant areas of the Lower Hall apart from the ceiling scheme. First, surface cleaning once again revealed the quality of Robert Jones's magnificent carved stone elements and mouldings, many of which are lavishly gilded. In addition, the window soffits and other wall decoration, previously highly disfigured by blanching varnish, became once more clearly visible as a result of the painstaking and extensive treatment.

Although the short-term aim of the project was to ensure the stability of the paintings through remedial treatment, in the longer term the implementation of passive measures to control the environmental conditions will be essential to minimize or delay any future potential deterioration. In particular, the installation of solar shading has significantly reduced light levels, especially within the Lower Hall, which should drastically reduce further degradation of the varnish layers. Similarly, the new heating system will ensure that environmental conditions remain stable and will reduce further movement of the lead soaps; it will also minimize the incidence of other potential related deterioration phenomena. Finally, access routes into the Painted Hall have been changed to minimize the amount of dust and humidity entering the building, which will be monitored on a regular basis.

The final programme of treatment was completed in early 2019. Thanks to the immense care, skill and patience of the team[46] and all the specialists who have contributed to the project, the conservation of the Lower Hall decoration has once again revealed the magnificence of Sir James Thornhill's paintings; the Lower Hall joins with the Upper Hall and the Vestibule to complete his original vision for the Painted Hall (figs. 36 and 37).

1 Francisco de Goya, *Goya: A Life in Letters*, ed. Sarah Symmons, London (Pimlico) 2004, Letter 264, 7 February 1801, p. 264.
2 M. Kirby Talley, Jr, 'Miscreants and Hotentots: Restorers and Restoration Attitudes and Practices in Seventeenth- and Eighteenth-Century England', in *Studies in the History of Painting Restoration*, ed. Christine Sitwell and Sarah Staniforth, London (Archetype) 1998, p. 39.
3 Jane Davies, '"The negligence of men": Restoration Techniques and the Altered Appearance of Baroque Wall Paintings', in *All Manner of Murals: The History, Techniques and Conservation of Secular Wall Paintings*, ed. Robert Gowing and Robyn Pender, London (Archetype) 2007, p. 59.
4 As observed by Darren Clarke, Greenwich Foundation volunteer, 2017–18, during the 2018 project; pers. comm., 10 August 2018.
5 The National Archives, Kew (hereafter TNA), ADM 67/10, 22 May 1742.
6 TNA ADM 67/11, 1777.
7 'Proceedings in the Lords on the Duke of Richmond's Motions relating to an Enquiry into the Management of Greenwich Hospital', 1779, in *The Parliamentary History of England, from the Earliest Period to the Year 1803*, vol. 20, London 1814, p. 519.
8 *Ibid.*
9 Westby Percival-Prescott, 'The Hand of the Restorer', typescript of essay written for the exhibition catalogue *Idea and Illusion*, London, Royal Naval College, 1960, p. 4.
10 TNA ADM 67/10, December 1752.
11 TNA ADM 67/13, May 1797.
12 The restoration was undertaken by A.N. Stewart (Senior Artist, Ministry of Works), who was responsible for the project; Westby Percival-Prescott, who represented Stewart on site; and the following Ministry of Works restorer/artists: Henley Blake, John Meade, John Brangwyn and Maurice Keevil.
13 David Bomford, obituary of Westby Percival-Prescott, *The Independent*, 26 February 2005, www.independent.co.uk/news/obituaries/westby-percival-prescott-12858.html (accessed May 2019).
14 Percival-Prescott, 'Hand of the Restorer', p. 3.
15 *Ibid.*, p. 9.
16 *Ibid.*, p. 3.
17 Westby Percival-Prescott, 'The Restoration of the Painted Hall Greenwich, 1957–60', *Conference Proceedings of the IIC Meeting on the Conservation of Wall Paintings in the United Kingdom*, London, 25–26 March 1976, p. 8.
18 Percival-Prescott, 'Hand of the Restorer', p. 7.
19 *Ibid.*, p. 5.
20 Percival-Prescott, 'Restoration of the Painted Hall', p. 8.
21 *Ibid.*, p. 6.
22 Percival-Prescott, 'Hand of the Restorer', p. 5.
23 *Ibid.*, p. 7.
24 Paine and Stewart, 'The Old Royal Naval College, Greenwich: The Painted Hall. A Condition Survey of the Painted Scheme', unpublished report, April 2012.
25 TNA ADM 67/3, 12 July 1705.
26 TNA ADM 68/697, 'Measured Works in the Royal Hospital at Greenwich from July 1st 1718 to June the last 1719'.

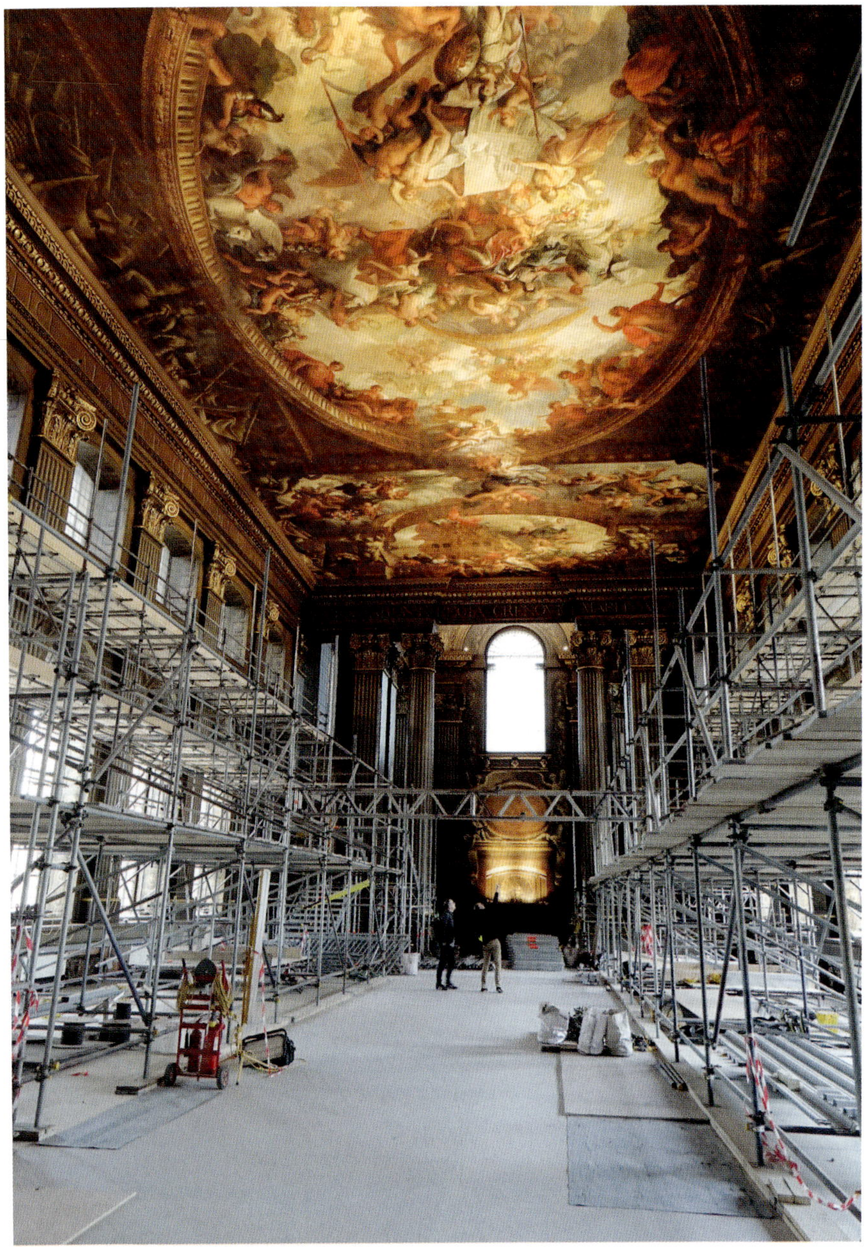

Fig. 37 The scaffolding starts to come down after more than two years' work, to reveal a scheme of history painting on such a grand scale that it was described by the art historian Edward Croft-Murray as 'one of the most complete realisations of Baroque scenography in an English interior'.

Thompson's work here relates to the Upper Hall ceiling, but the process had been the same for the Lower Hall ceiling.

27 Dudley Ryder, *The Diary of Dudley Ryder, 1715–1716*, ed. William Matthews, London (Methuen) 1939, p. 307.

28 *Ibid.*, p. 308.

29 George Vertue, 'Vertue Note Books: Volume II', *Volume of the Walpole Society* 20, 1931–32, p. 126.

30 It should be noted that Antonio Verrio, working at St George's Hall, Windsor Castle, similarly designated his flower still lifes to the flower specialist Antonio Montingo (*fl.* 1678–1690). Thornhill also owned a flower still-life painting by Montingo.

31 *St James's Evening Post*, 7–9 June 1737.

32 Jane Davies, 'Technical Analysis of Paint Samples Taken During Conservation of the Lower Hall Ceiling of the Painted Hall, ORNC', unpublished report, 2018, p. 3.

33 TNA ADM 68/699, Works, 1720–23.

34 TNA ADM 68/697, 'Measured Works in the Royal Hospital at Greenwich from July 1st 1718 to June the last 1719'.

35 *Ibid.*

36 Since December 2012, Tobit Curteis Associates has undertaken a comprehensive programme of environmental monitoring throughout the Painted Hall in order to understand the conditions affecting the paintings and to help design and implement the most effective environmental controls.

37 Alan Phenix and Richard Wolbers, 'Removal of Varnish: Organic Solvents as Cleaning Agents', in *The Conservation of Easel Paintings*, ed. Joyce Hill Stoner and Rebecca Rushfield, Abingdon (Routledge) 2012, pp. 524–54.

38 Both in-depth investigations were undertaken by Dr Charlotte Martin de Fonjaudran.

39 TNA HLG 126/296, untitled note by Westby Percival-Prescott, July 1958.

40 Phenix and Wolbers, 'Removal of Varnish', p. 526.

41 Results of analysis and examination made by Professor Klaas Jan van den Berg and Professor Aviva Burnstock in 2018.

42 J.J. Hermans, 'Metal Soaps in Oil Paint: Structure, Mechanisms and Dynamics', PhD thesis, Van 't Hoff Institute for Molecular Sciences (HIMS), University of Amsterdam, 2017, p. 12.

43 Regalrez is considered to be among the most stable low-molecular-weight resins available. See Michael von der Goltz *et al.*, 'Varnishing as Part of the Conservation Treatment of Easel Paintings', in *The Conservation of Easel Paintings*, ed. Joyce Hill Stoner and Rebecca Rushfield, Abingdon (Routledge) 2012, p. 644.

44 Made from Laropal A 81, mineral spirits and pigments.

45 Testing established that a solution of the acrylic dispersion Plextol B500 at 5% offered a controllable and effective material. This was injected behind flakes after pre-wetting with 1:1 water and Industrial Methylated Spirit (IMS).

46 The conservation team, overseen by Stephen Paine and Sophie Stewart, was led by Francesco Rosellini, with the assistance of Stefania D'Alba. They were joined during the course of the project by Valentina Gatto, Denise Invamoto, Eliza Doherty and Lucy Odlin.

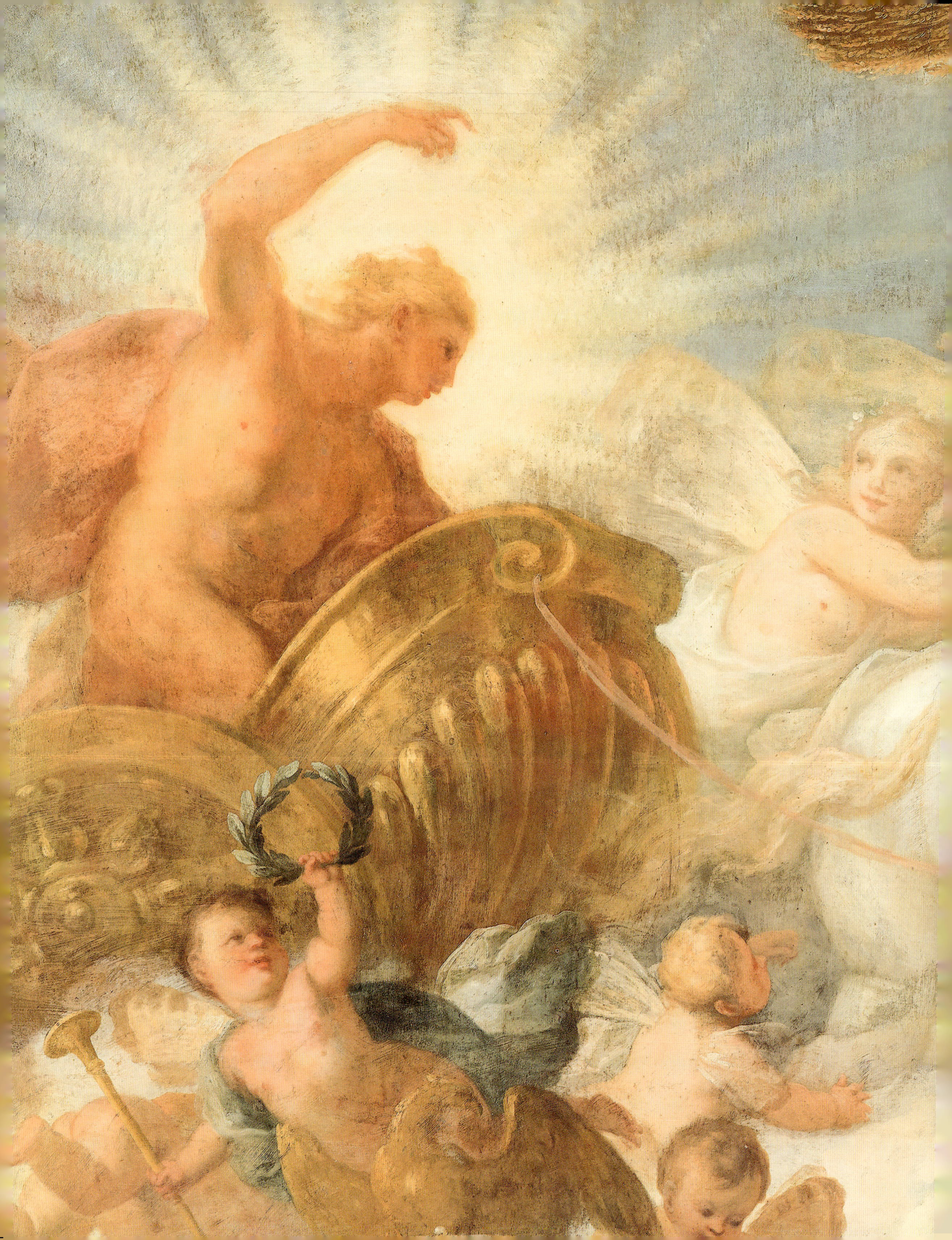

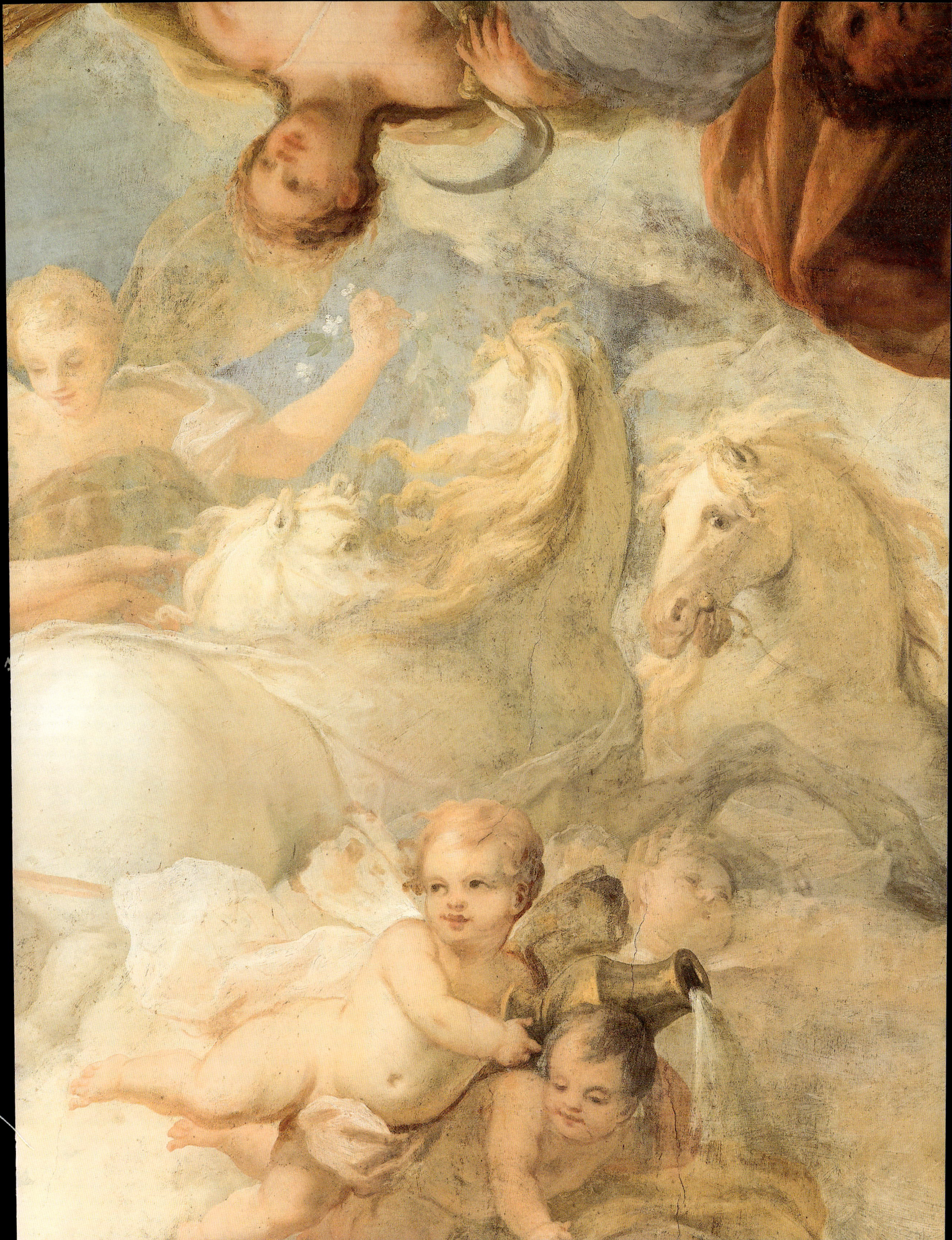

Lower Hall Ceiling

A Legendary Cast

1 William III
2 Mary II
3 Peace
4 Concord
5 Providence
6 Prudence
7 Temperance
8 Fortitude
9 Justice
10 Europe
11 Tyranny and Arbitrary Power (Louis XIV of France)
12 Spirit of Architecture
13 Truth
14 Time
15 Pallas Athene (Wisdom)
16 Hercules (Virtue)
17 Gorgon
18 Hydra
19 Pisces
20 Hyems (Winter – John Worley)
21 Aquarius
22 Capricorn
23 Sagittarius
24 Scorpio
25 Bacchus (Autumn)
26 Libra
27 Apollo
28 Virgo
29 Ceres (Summer)
30 Leo
31 Cancer
32 Flora (Spring)
33 Gemini
34 Taurus
35 Aries

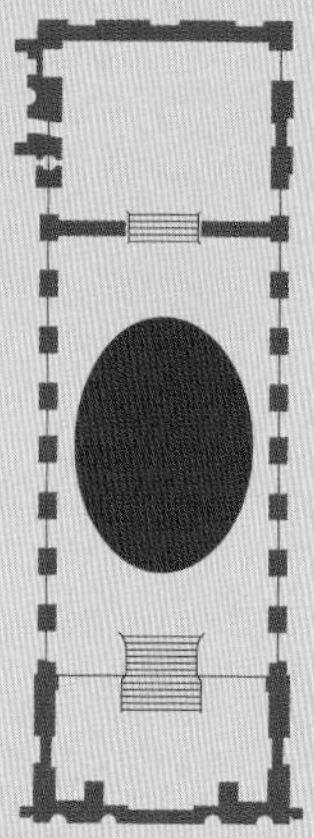

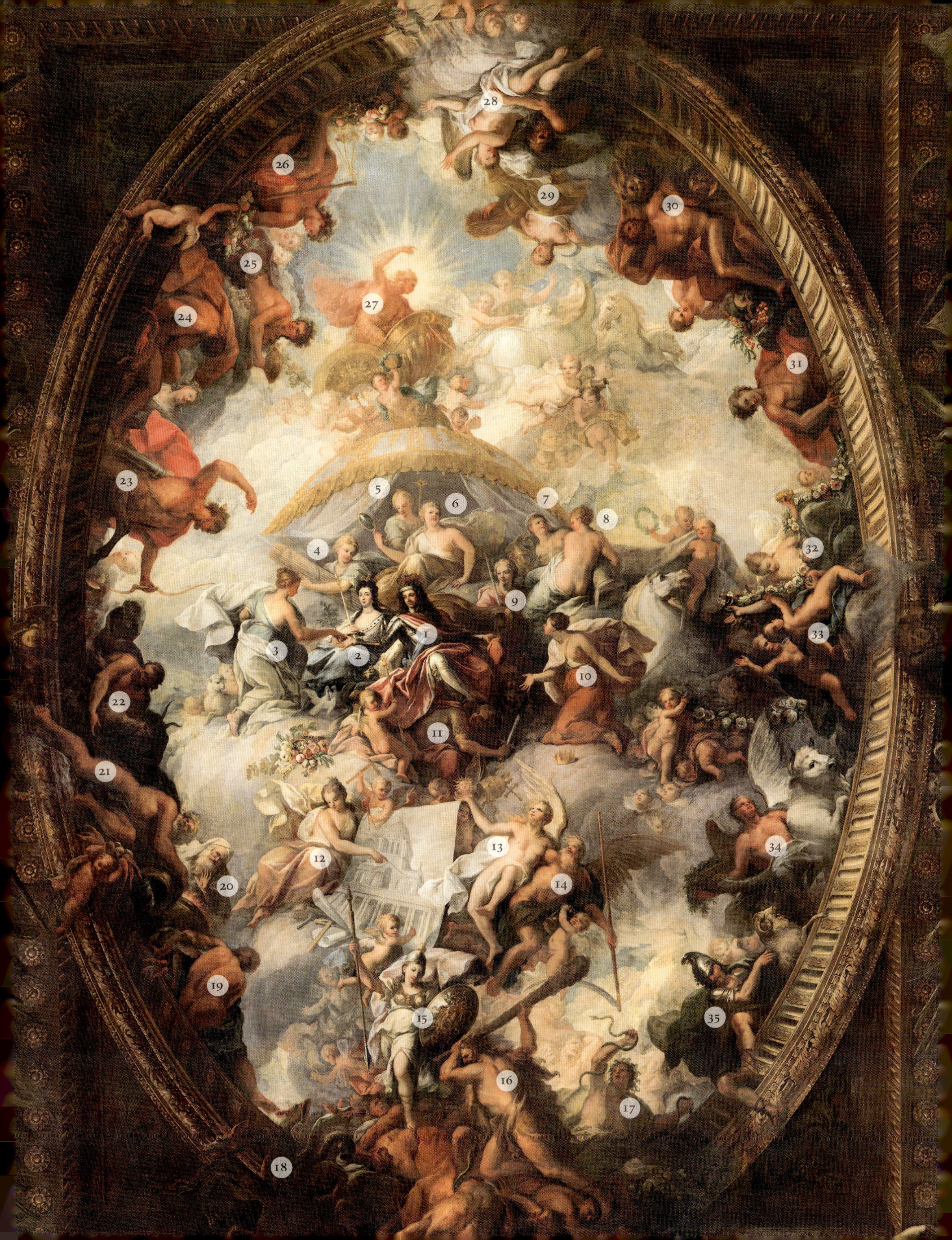
1
2
3
4
5
6
7
8
9
10
11
12
13
14
15
16
17
18
19
20
21
22
23
24
25
26
27
28
29
30
31
32
33
34
35

Lower Hall Ceiling

Science and Navigation

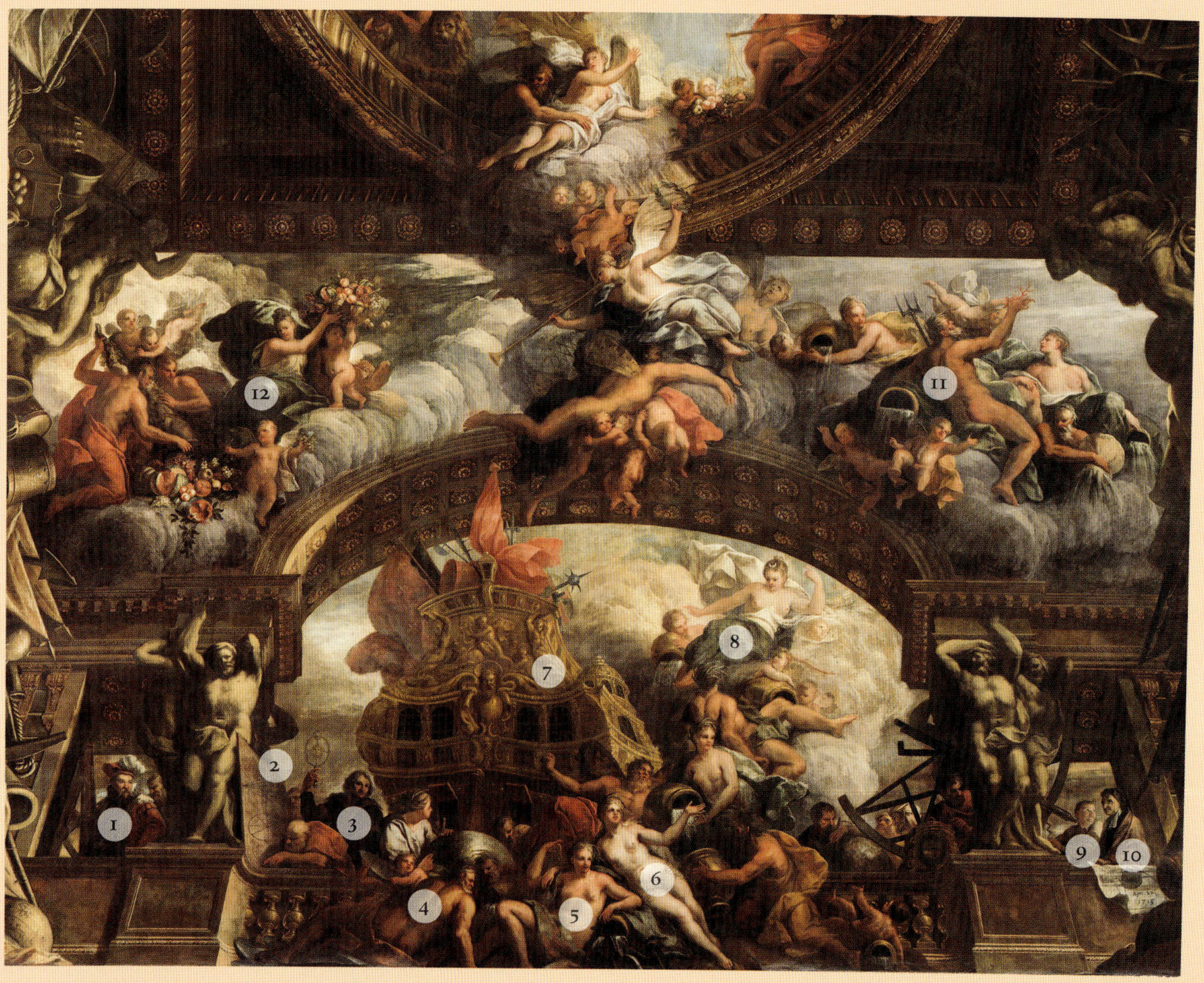

1 Tycho Brahe
2 Sir Isaac Newton's *Principia*
3 Copernicus
4 River Humber
5 River Severn
6 River Avon
7 Captured Spanish galleon
8 Diana
9 Thomas Weston
10 John Flamsteed
11 Neptune (Water)
12 Cybele (Earth)

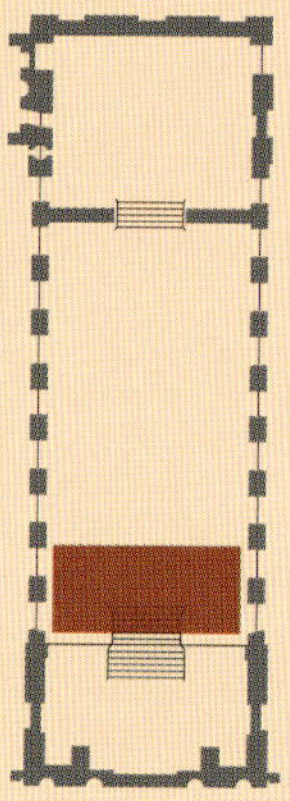

Lower Hall Ceiling

Britain's Naval Power

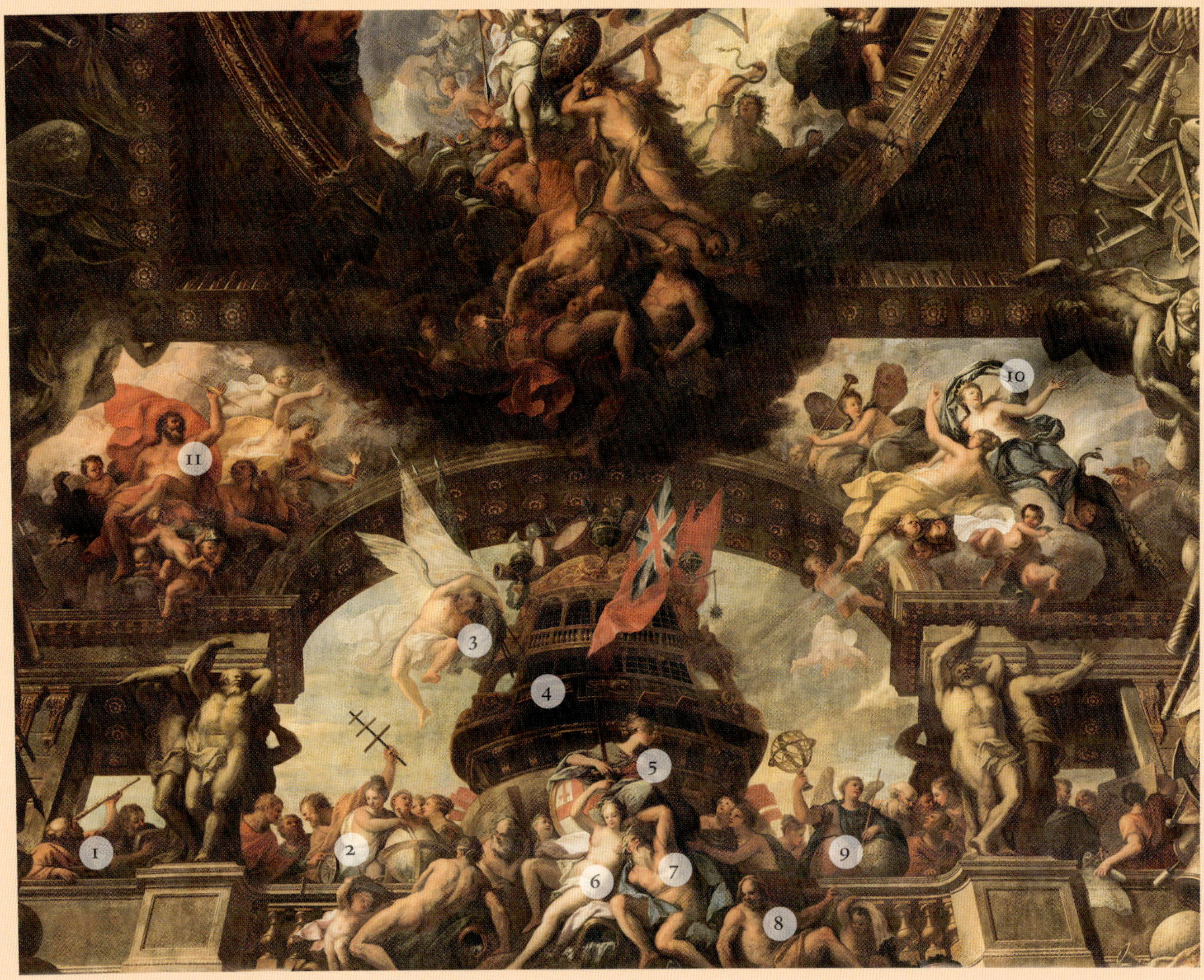

1 Galileo
2 Navigation
3 Victory
4 The *Blenheim*
5 City of London
6 River Isis
7 River Thames
8 River Tyne
9 Astronomy
10 Juno (Air)
11 Jupiter (Fire)

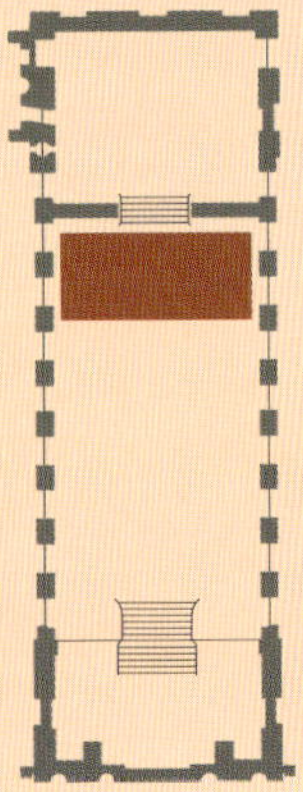

Upper Hall Ceiling

Among the Gods

1 Queen Anne
2 Prince George
3 Hercules (Virtue)
4 Liberality / Plenty
5 Victory
6 Concord
7 Piety
8 Neptune
9 Juno
10 Aeolus
11 Europe
12 America
13 Africa
14 Asia

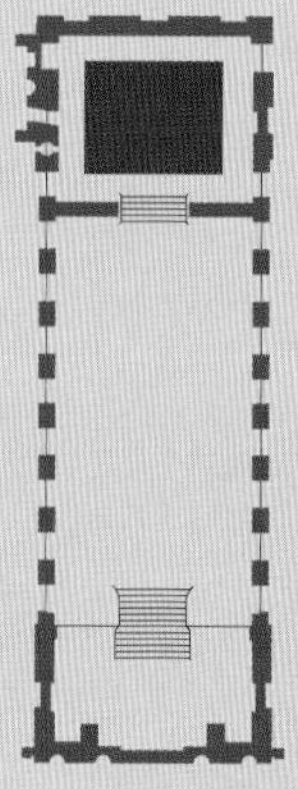

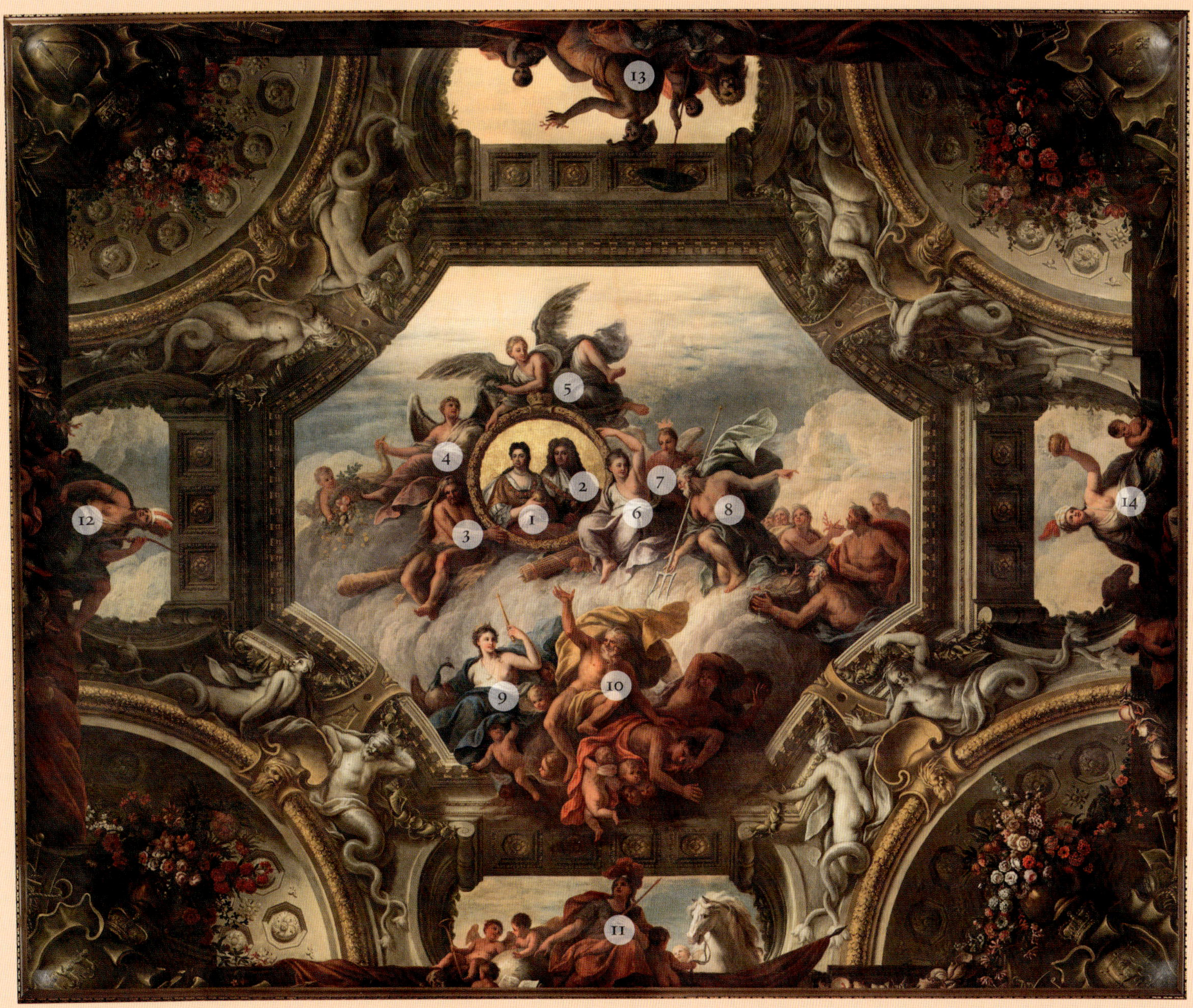

UPPER HALL CEILING

West Wall, Upper Hall

'A golden Progeny from Heav'n descends'

1 George I
2 Prince Frederick
3 Prince of Wales (later George II)
4 Sophia of Hanover (Cybele)
5 Sophia Dorothea of Prussia (Concord)
6 Princess Caroline (Prudence)
7 The grandchildren
8 Sir James Thornhill
9 Naval Victory
10 Justice (Astraea)
11 St Paul's Cathedral
12 Stability
13 Time (The Golden Age restored)
14 Providence
15 Peace
16 Plenty

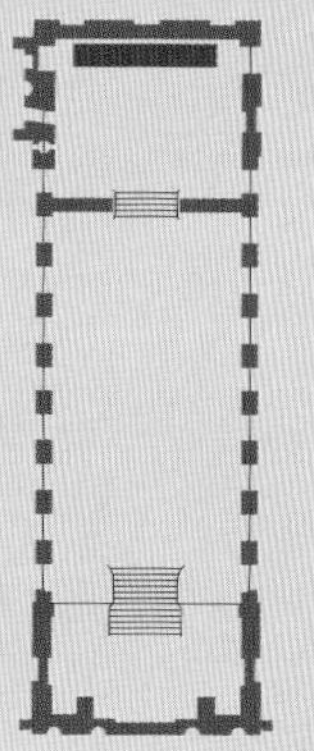

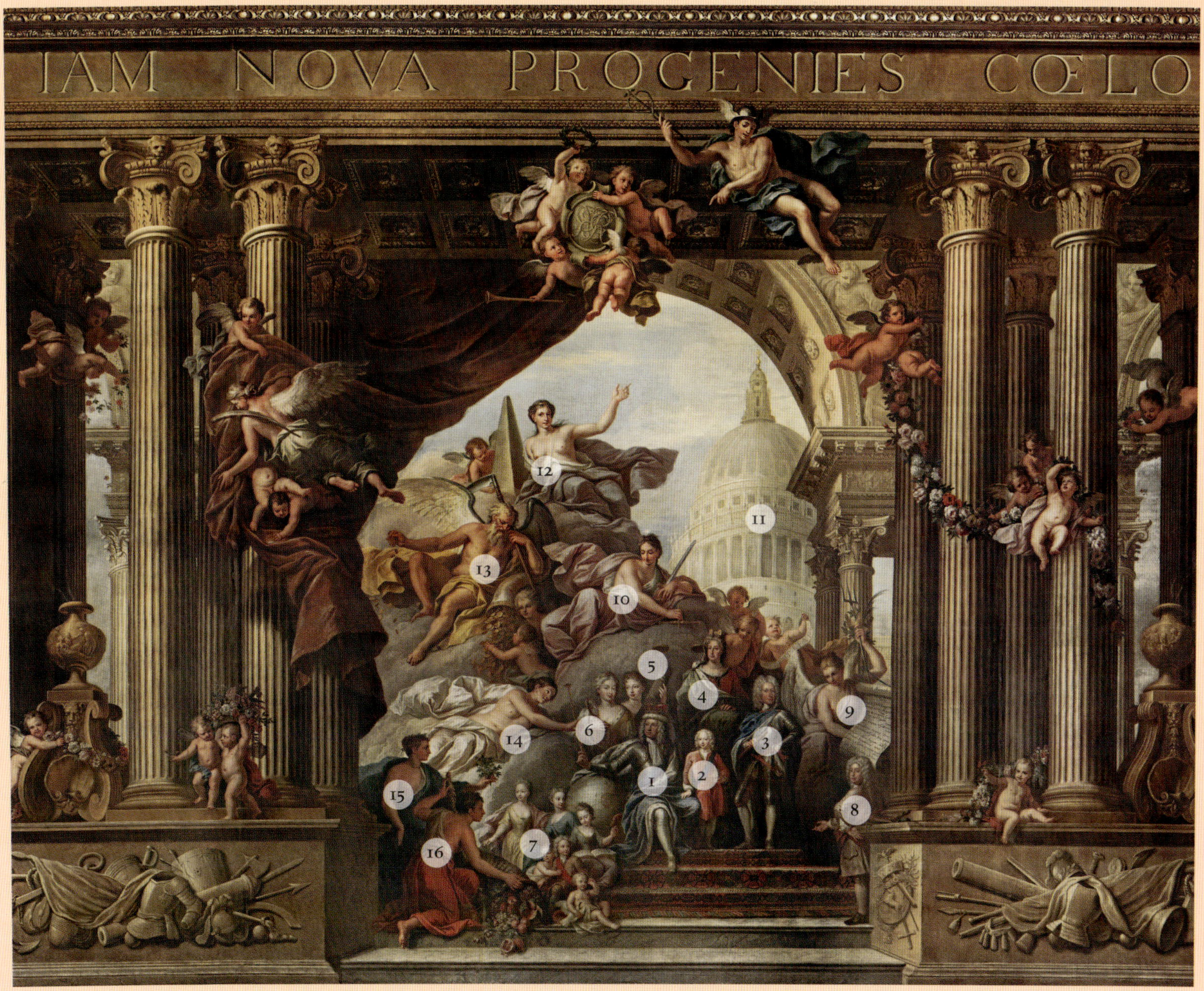

WEST WALL, UPPER HALL

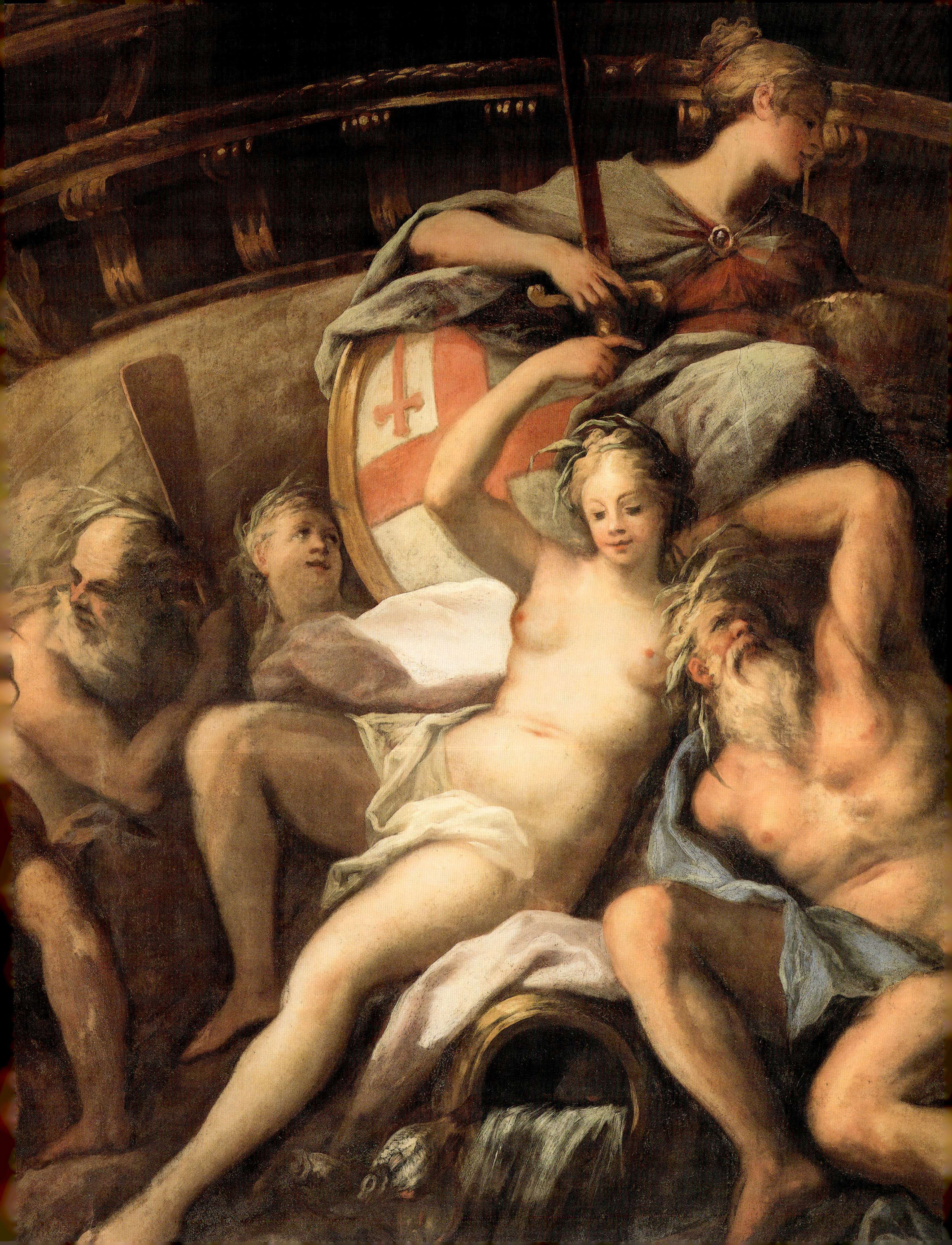

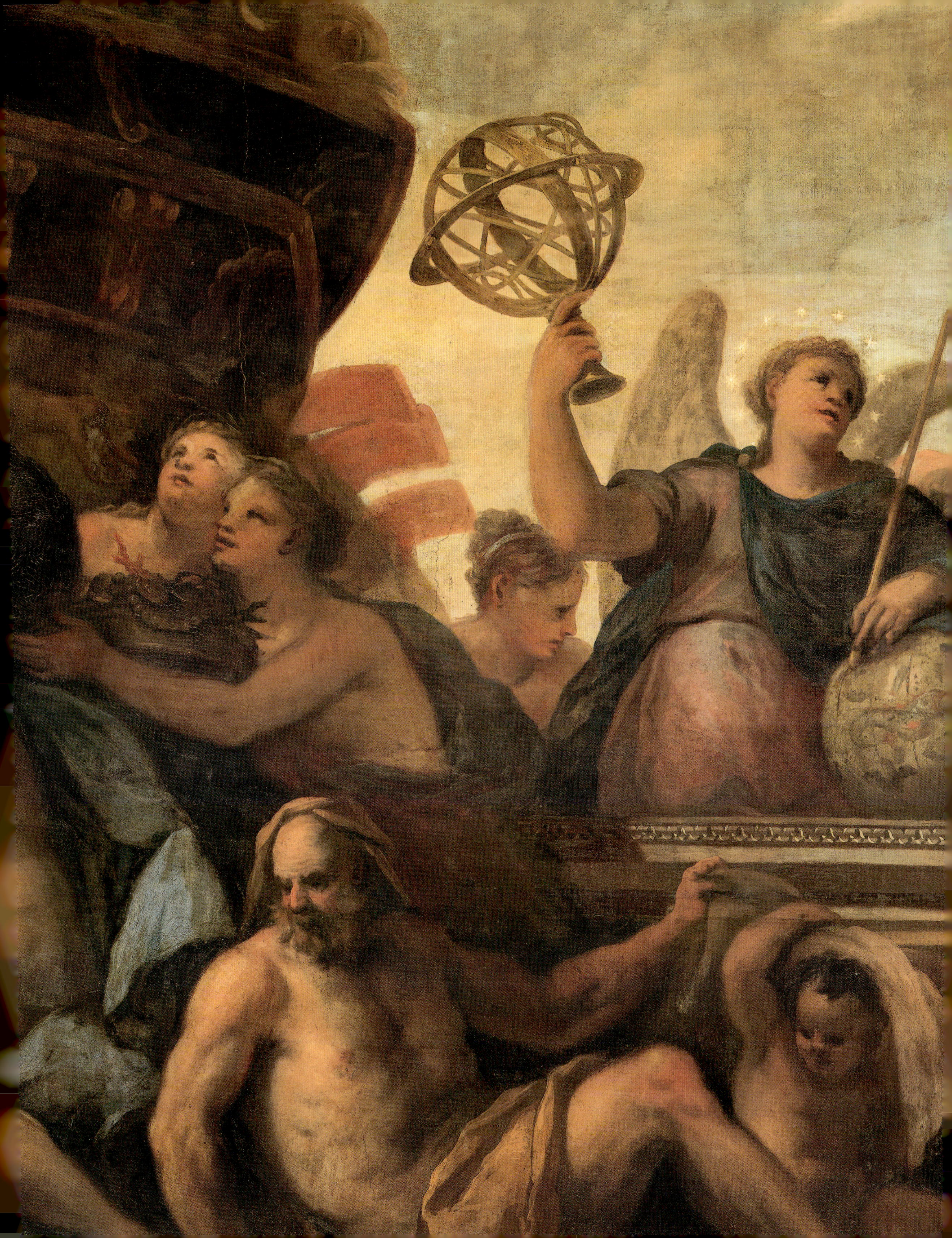

Further Reading

UNPUBLISHED WORKS

Richard Johns, 'James Thornhill and Decorative History Painting in England after 1688', PhD thesis, University of York, 2004

Paine and Stewart, 'The Old Royal Naval College, Greenwich: The Painted Hall. A Condition Survey of the Painted Scheme', unpublished report, April 2012

Tobit Curteis Associates, 'Environmental Survey and Monitoring of the Painted Hall Associated with the Conservation of the Wall Paintings: Preliminary Report', unpublished report, June 2013

PUBLISHED WORKS

Geoffrey Beard, *Decorative Plasterwork in Great Britain* [1975], Abingdon (Routledge) 2015

John Bold, *Greenwich: An Architectural History of the Royal Hospital for Seamen and the Queen's House*, New Haven, Conn., and London (Yale University Press) 2000

David Bomford, 'Three Days That Changed Conservation', in *The Picture So Far: 50 Years of Painting Conservation*, ed. Abigail Granville *et al.*, London (Archetype) 2017, pp. 1–8

H.M. Colvin (ed.), *The History of the King's Works*, vol. 5: 1660–1782, London (HMSO) 1976

Edward Croft-Murray, *Decorative Painting in England, 1537–1837*, vol. 1: *Early Tudor to Sir James Thornhill*, London (Country Life) 1962

Jane Davies, '"The negligence of men": Restoration Techniques and the Altered Appearance of Baroque Wall Paintings', in *All Manner of Murals: The History, Techniques and Conservation of Secular Wall Paintings*, ed. Robert Gowing and Robyn Pender, London (Archetype) 2007, pp. 59–78

'A Great and Noble Design': Sir James Thornhill's Painted Hall at Greenwich, exhib. cat. by Anya Matthews, London, Stephen Lawrence Gallery, University of Greenwich, September–October 2016

Nicholas Hawksmoor, *Remarks on the Founding and Carrying on the Buildings of the Royal Hospital at Greenwich*, London 1728

Richard Johns, '"Those wilder sorts of Painting": The Painted Interior in the Age of Antonio Verrio', in *A Companion to British Art: 1600 to the Present*, ed. Dana Arnold and David Peters Corbett, Chichester (Blackwell) 2013, pp. 79–104

Christopher C. Lloyd, *Greenwich: Palace, Hospital, College*, London (Officers' Mess) 1960

Anna Mason, 'Sir James Thornhill's Painted Hall in Greenwich Revealed', *London Art History Society Review 2018*, pp. 8–10

Pieter van der Merwe, *A Refuge for All: A Short History of Greenwich Hospital*, London (Greenwich Hospital) 2010

Christine Stevenson, *Medicine and Magnificence: British Hospital and Asylum Architecture, 1660–1815*, New Haven, Conn. (Yale University Press) 2000

Simon Thurley, 'Architecture and Diplomacy: Greenwich Palace under the Stuarts', *The Court Historian*, vol. 11, no. 2, December 2006, pp. 125–33

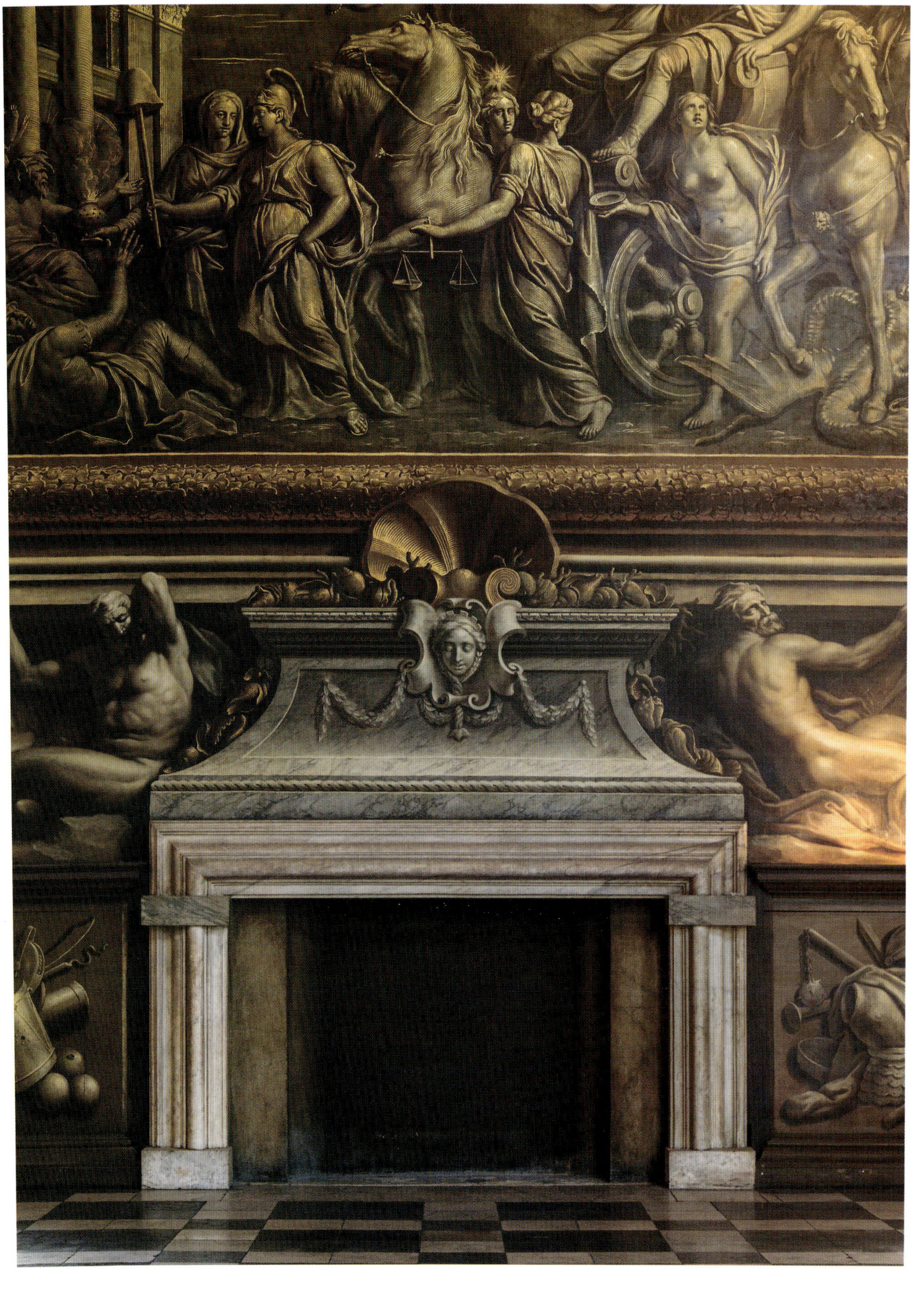

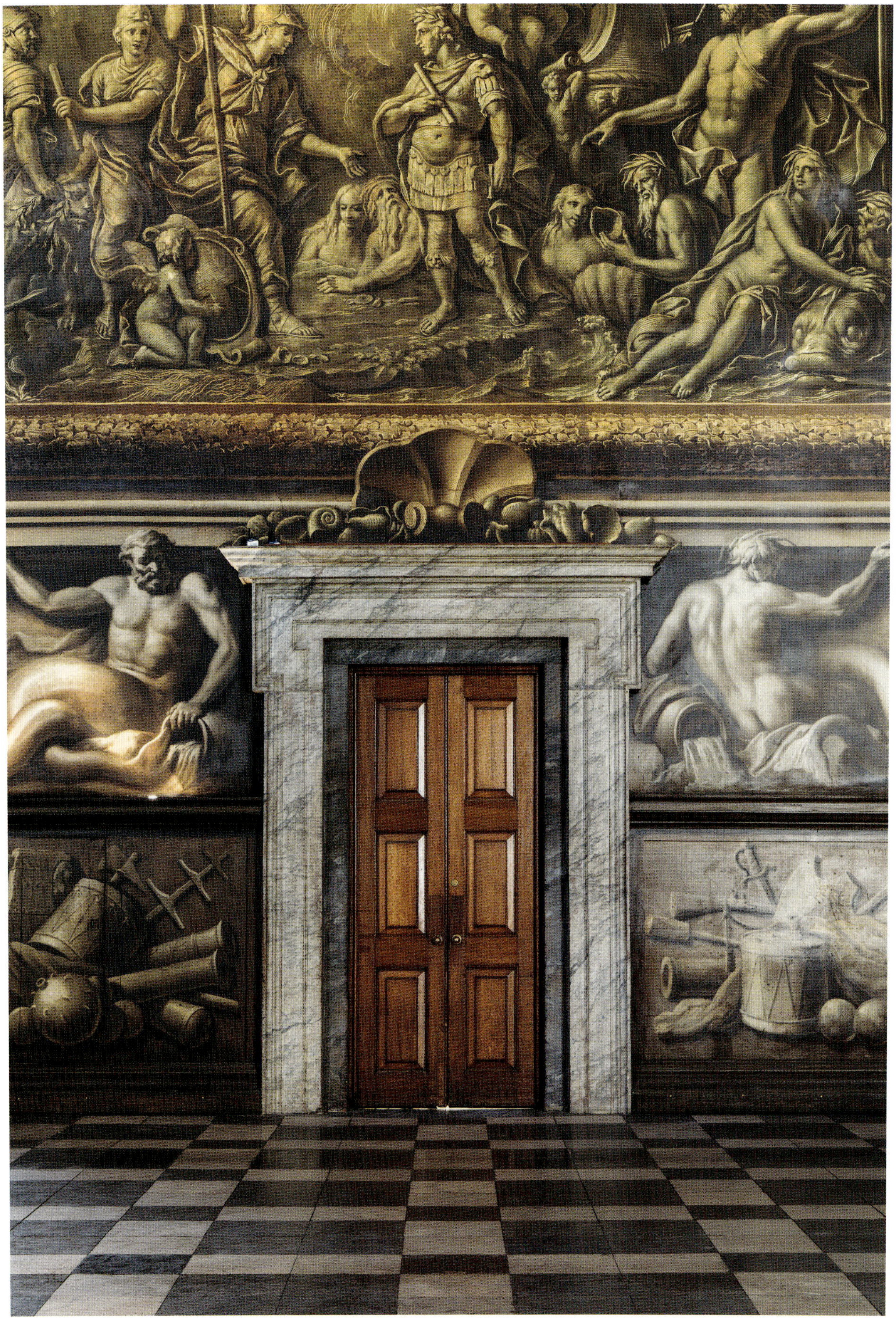

Acknowledgements

The Greenwich Foundation would like to thank the National Lottery Heritage Fund for supporting this publication as part of a major grant to the Painted Hall conservation project (2016–19). The Foundation is also grateful to the Paul Mellon Centre for Studies in British Art and the Charles Skey Charitable Trust for funding the project research curator and co-author of this book, Anya Lucas, and to Dr Ann Robey for her crucial role in collating and editing the various texts.

AUTHORS' ACKNOWLEDGEMENTS

Martin Ashley; Rupert Baker and the library staff at the Royal Society; Jeremy Barker; John Barnes; Dr Katy Barrett; Professor Klaas Jan van den Berg; Dr John Bold; Hugh Broughton; Dr Wolf Burchard; Professor Aviva Burnstock; Professor Sharon Cather; Andrew Clark; Louise Cooling; Valentina Costa; Jon Culverhouse; Tobit Curteis; Stefania D'Alba; Jane Davies; Professor Gary De Krey; Nathalie Debono; Eliza Doherty; Brett Dolman; Ray Faithfull; Dr Claire Gapper; Valentina Gatto; Eugenia Geddes da Filicaia; Professor Mark Hallett; Dr Lydia Hamlett; Dr Gordon Higgott; Denise Invamoto; Richard Ireland; Megan Kisters; Sarah Kmosena; Adam Knight; Dr Tamsin Lee-Woolfe; Emily Mann; Dr Charlotte Martin de Fonjaudran; Michael Morrison; Virginia Nouwen; Lucy Odlin; Teresa O'Flynn; Clara de la Peña McTigue; Dr Laurel Peterson; Jim Quenby; Robert Randall; Dr Christine Riding; Wendy Rose; Francesco Rosellini; Ashley Sands; Dr Jenny Saunt; Dr Rachel Sloan; Martin Stancliffe; Sarah Staniforth; Professor Christine Stevenson; Helen White

HERITAGE FUND

Author Biographies

DR RICHARD JOHNS is Senior Lecturer in the History of Art at the University of York and a former Curator of Art at the National Maritime Museum, London. He has published widely on British art from the seventeenth to the nineteenth century. He was a member of the advisory panel convened to advise on the conservation of the Painted Hall.

DR ANYA LUCAS is an art and architectural historian specializing in seventeenth- and eighteenth-century Britain. She wrote her PhD at the Courtauld Institute of Art (2015) on the livery halls of London and is co-author of Merrell's book on the subject, published in 2018. She has also written for *Country Life* magazine and *The Georgian Group Journal*, and contributed to the book *Court, Country, City: British Art and Architecture, 1660–1735* (2016). She most recently worked as Research Curator for the major conservation project at the Painted Hall.

STEPHEN PAINE studied history of art at University College London and subsequently obtained a diploma in conservation from the Courtauld Institute of Art/ Getty Conservation Institute. In 1992 he completed a Getty Conservation Institute post-diploma internship, leading to the award of a Courtauld Institute of Art Certificate of Advanced Practical Training in the Conservation of Wall Paintings. He has since worked as a private conservator, working on many significant wall paintings of all periods for a wide variety of clients in the UK.

WILLIAM PALIN is Conservation Director at the Greenwich Foundation for the Old Royal Naval College. From 2014 until its completion in 2019, he acted as Director of the Painted Hall conservation project, the largest open-access conservation project in Europe. He is an architectural historian and writer, working previously as Assistant Curator at Sir John Soane's Museum, London, and as Director of SAVE Britain's Heritage. He is a trustee of the Ancient Monuments Society and Chair of the Sheerness Dockyard Preservation Trust. He lives in London and Kent.

SOPHIE STEWART studied archaeology, anthropology and history of art at New Hall College, Cambridge, and then gained a diploma in conservation from the Courtauld Institute of Art/Getty Conservation Institute. In 1992 she completed a Getty Conservation Institute post-diploma internship, leading to the award of a Courtauld Institute of Art Certificate of Advanced Practical Training in the Conservation of Wall Paintings. She worked as a wall-painting conservator at English Heritage until 1999, since which time she has worked in private practice in partnership with Stephen Paine.

Picture Credits

KEY
l = left, r = right, c=centre, t = top, b = bottom

Eden Breitz / Alamy Stock Photo: 12–13; © Trustees of the British Museum: 27t, 55, 80l; The Burghley House Collection: 16, 56; CC0. Digital image courtesy of the Getty's Open Content Program: 48; CC0. Courtesy of HathiTrust: 50; CC0 1.0 via the National Gallery of Denmark, Copenhagen: 54t; CC BY 4.0 via Wellcome Collection: 22b, 79; © The Devonshire Collections, Chatsworth. Reproduced by permission of Chatsworth Settlement Trustees: 58; Historic England Archive: 106, 112t, 112br; © Historic Royal Palaces: 82t; EB7 F6137 715m, Houghton Library, Harvard University: 88b; © Illustrated London News Ltd / Mary Evans: 39; Jane Davies Conservation: 116b; Keystone Press / Alamy Stock Photo: 115; Raymond Kleboe / Picture Post / Getty Images: 112bl; © Paris – Musée de l'Armée, Dist. RMN-Grand Palais / Pascal Segrette: 22t; Courtesy National Gallery of Art, Washington: 20; © National Maritime Museum, Greenwich, London: 17t, 17b, 18t, 18b, 27b, 29, 32t, 60, 78t, 80r, 89b, 92, 93, 100; © National Portrait Gallery, London: 19b, 21b, 53, 85; The Old Royal Naval College, Greenwich: 76–77, 111, 113, 141; The Old Royal Naval College, Greenwich / Matthew Andrews: 6, 8tl, 8bl, 8r, 68; The Old Royal Naval College, Greenwich / Ardon Bar Hama: 78b; The Old Royal Naval College, Greenwich / James Brittain: back jacket / cover, 9, 10, 43, 44–45, 49, 74–75, 109; The Old Royal Naval College, Greenwich / Nikhilesh Haval: front jacket / cover, 31, 40, 41, 46–47, 69, 126t, 147, 148, 160; The Old Royal Naval College, Greenwich / Linda Nylind: 131; The Old Royal Naval College, Greenwich / William Palin: 11; The Old Royal Naval College, Greenwich / Sam Whittaker: endpapers, frontispiece, 4, 14, 52, 64–65, 66, 70–71, 72, 73, 84, 86, 90, 91, 97, 98–99, 103, 104–105, 108, 120, 122t, 134–35, 137, 138t, 139t, 143, 144–45; Paine and Stewart: 110, 116t, 117l, 117r, 118tl, 118tr, 118b, 119, 121, 122b, 123t, 123c, 123b, 125tl, 125tr, 125b, 126b, 127t, 127bl, 127br, 128, 129l, 129r, 130t, 130c, 130b, 132; © Martin Parr / Magnum Photos: 88t; Mo Peerbacus / Alamy Stock Photo: 34–35; The Picture Art Collection / Alamy Stock Photo: 82b; Plowman Craven: 94, 95; Private Collection / Bridgeman Images: 19t; Private Collection / Dave Penman / Moonfleet Photography: 30; Private Collection / Photo © Rafael Valls Gallery, London, UK / Bridgeman Images: 38t; Private Collection / The Stapleton Collection / Bridgeman Images: 89t; RIBA Collections: 36; Royal Astronomical Society / Science Photo Library: 87t; Royal Hospital Chelsea: 23; © The Royal Society: 21t, 28; © The Samuel Courtauld Trust, The Courtauld Gallery, London: 26; Simon Leach Design / David Sudlow Designers: 42, 136, 138b, 139b, 140, 142; © Sir John Soane's Museum, London: 24t, 24b, 25, 38b; Trinity College, Cambridge, UK / Bridgeman Images: 87b; © Victoria and Albert Museum, London: 57, 59, 81; Yale Center for British Art, Paul Mellon Collection: 32b, 54b

The publishers have made every effort to trace and contact copyright holders of the illustrations reproduced in this book; they will be happy to correct in subsequent editions any errors or omissions that are brought to their attention.

Index

Page numbers in *italic* refer to the illustrations.

First published 2019 by
Merrell Publishers, London
and New York

Merrell Publishers Limited
70 Cowcross Street
London EC1M 6EJ

merrellpublishers.com

in association with

Greenwich Foundation for the
Old Royal Naval College
2 Cutty Sark Gardens
London SE10 9LW

ornc.org

British Library Cataloguing in Publication Data. A catalogue record for this book is available from the British Library.

ISBN 978-1-8589-4679-5 (HARDBACK)
ISBN 978-1-8589-4680-1 (PAPERBACK)

Produced by Merrell Publishers Limited
Designed by Nicola Bailey
Project-managed by Claire Chandler
Picture research by Nick Wheldon
Proofread by Barbara Roby
Indexed by Hilary Bird

Printed and bound in China

FRONT JACKET / COVER
View from the Vestibule into the Lower Hall, with the proscenium arch and Upper Hall beyond.

BACK JACKET / COVER
The west wall of the Upper Hall.

ENDPAPERS (HARDBACK)
Detail from the centre of the Lower Hall ceiling.

FRONTISPIECE
Diana, goddess of the Moon, at the east end of the Lower Hall ceiling.

PAGE 4
George I takes a sceptre from Providence, on the west wall of the Upper Hall.

PAGES 64–65
A winged figure heralds the arrival of a captured Spanish galleon, at the east end of the Lower Hall ceiling.

PAGES 104–105
Aries and Taurus, among the representations of the signs of the zodiac on the Lower Hall ceiling.

PAGES 134–35
Apollo, the sun god, rides across the sky, casting light on William III and Mary II, on the Lower Hall ceiling.

PAGES 144–45
The City of London is held aloft by the rivers Isis (left) and Thames, at the west end of the Lower Hall ceiling.

PAGE 147
The fireplace on the north wall of the Upper Hall, with the arrival of George I above.

PAGE 148
The doorway in the south wall of the Upper Hall, with the arrival of William of Orange (William III) above.

OVERLEAF
View of the north-western corner of the Upper Hall.

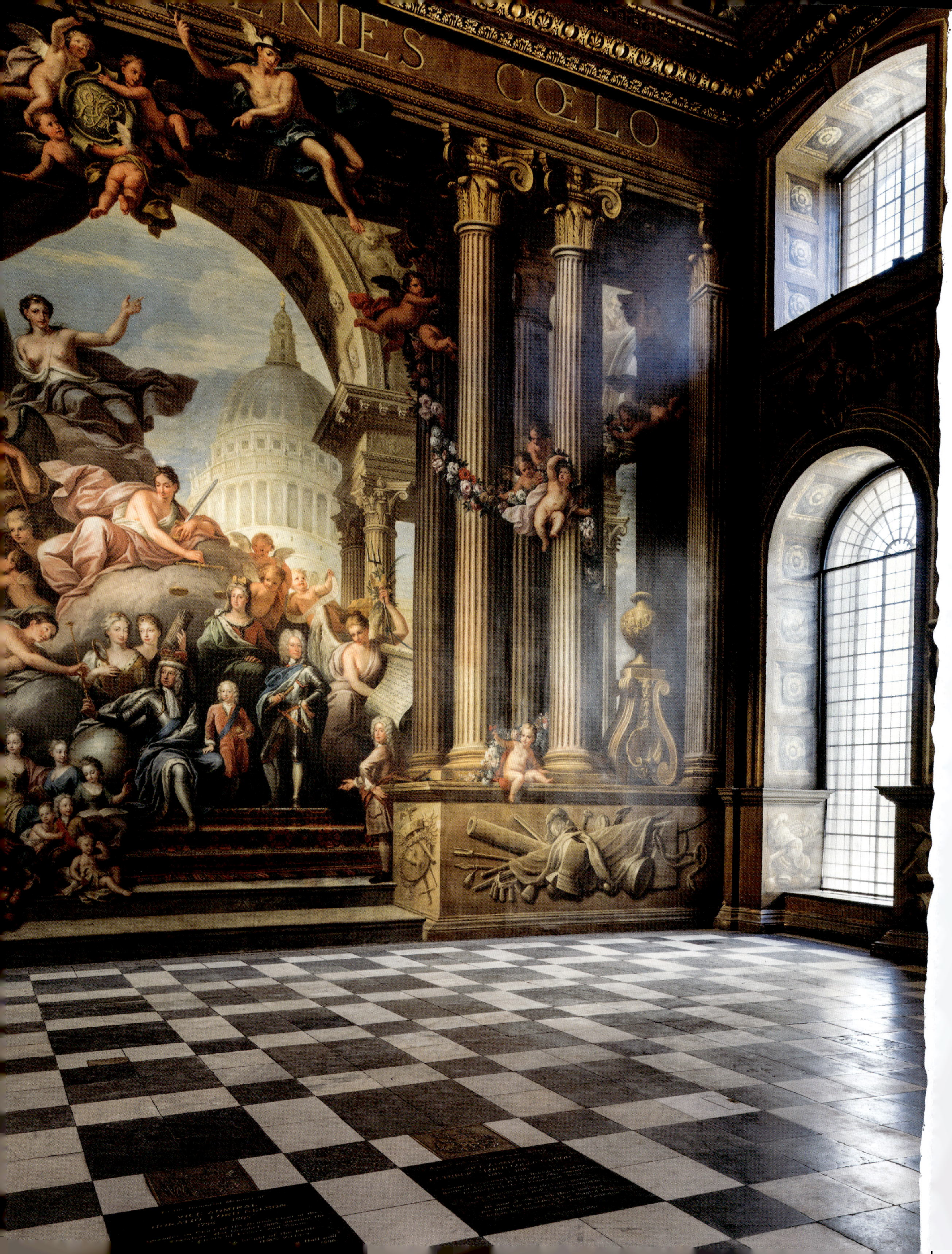
CŒLO

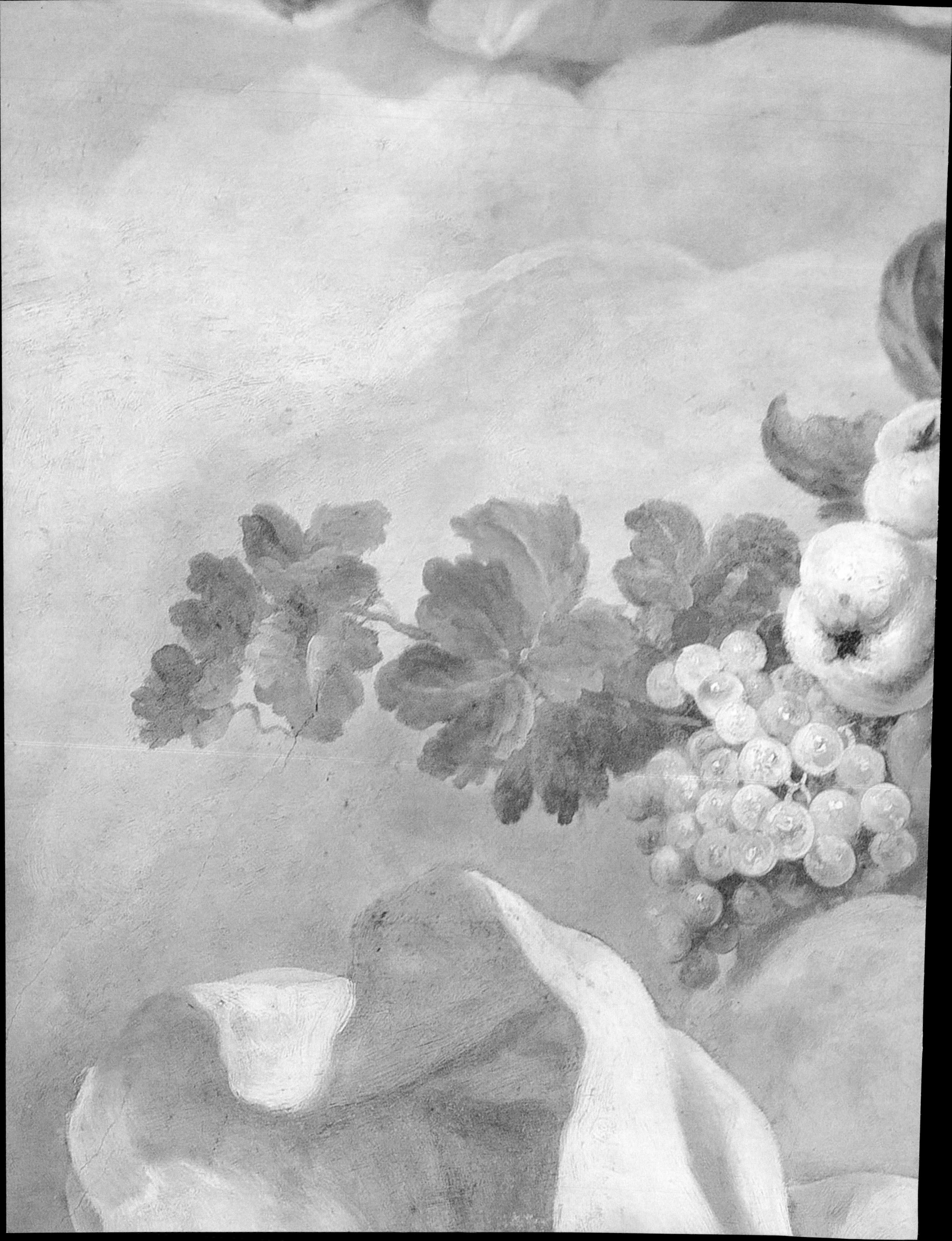